Bonita Bishop

Many bles your life " Carol / am.

FRONT LINE

A Daily Devotional Guide
for Christian Leaders

By

Carolyn Tennant, Ph.D.

MW01026465

Copyright © 2004
Carolyn Tennant
All rights reserved. No part of this book may be reproduced in any form,
except for the inclusion of brief quotations in a review, without permission in
writing from the author.

ISBN 0-9762461-0-4
Library of Congress Control Number 2004098000

Additional copies of this book are available by mail
for $17.95 plus shipping and handling.
For additional information contact:
Dr. Carolyn Tennant
16463 Grenoble Avenue
Lakeville, MN 55044
(612) 343-4749
Send e-mail inquiries to orderfrontline@aol.com

Printed in the U.S.A. by
Morris Publishing
3212 East Highway 30
Kearney, NE 68847
1-800-650-7888

Published by
North Central University Press
910 Elliot Avenue
Minneapolis, MN 55404
612-343-4200 or 1-800-289-6222

www.northcentral.edu

This book is lovingly dedicated
to
Rocky and Sherry Grams.
Rocky is the Director (President) of Instituto Biblico
Rio de la Plata, a college in Buenos Aires, Argentina, and
he is a leader who moves in the Spirit in ways that amaze me.
My very special friend Sherry was the first person
to read Front Line *in its entirety,*
and she offered a great deal of helpful advice and encouragement.
Thanks to both of you
for giving me a special environment "in the flow"
where I could finish this book!

Thanks also to Karen Farrington who did a great deal
of proofreading and editing on the early manuscript,
and to my husband who is more supportive and loving
than any woman could ever expect.
Thanks, Ray, for being my cheering squad par excellence.
Appreciation also goes to the NCU students throughout the years,
many of whom will recognize themselves in these pages. I love you!

Unless stated otherwise, the *Bible* quotations in this devotional guide are from
the New International Version (NIV),
Nashville: Holman Bible Publishers, 1986.

Foreword
By Dr. Gordon Anderson,
President, North Central University

God's Kingdom on earth, the church, is a front line church. It is on the move, and the gates of hell cannot stop its advance. It is a glorious church without spot or wrinkle, composed of people who are more than conquerors. Jesus said that His people would do mighty works, even greater than those that He Himself did. What a picture!

However, there is another side to this story. Hell does have gates, and victories only occur when there are conquests over serious problems. The *Bible* says there are powers and principalities and rulers of darkness who occupy high places of authority in a fallen world. The battle lines are drawn.

Front Line is a daily devotional for Christians in the fray, people who know that victories are not easy and cheap, people who have learned that victory celebrations come only after the battle. It is especially designed for leaders....pastors, lay leaders, and those in the marketplace who wish to live out their faith.

Through real-life stories, personal testimony, and biblical example, Dr. Carolyn Tennant lays out the strategy for victory on the Front Lines. Drawing on a lifetime of creative leadership, Carolyn is able to share the insights that only life at the front can provide. Her experiences as a teacher, preacher, administrator, writer, and conference speaker have given her the perceptiveness needed to help others along the way, and all this conveyed with wit, wisdom, and grace. This book is a treasure trove of help and encouragement for God's people, living life in victory on the front lines. I believe you will enjoy this first book published through our North Central University Press.

TABLE OF CONTENTS

JANUARY

FRONT LINE ASSIGNMENT

Read 2 Samuel 23:8-12.   *January 1*

It had been a difficult month. Changes were occurring, and people were feeling insecure about them. Nobody likes the shaking up that change always brings, and I, as the leader, was taking the brunt of it.

Sitting in a colleague's office, I was unloading my frustrations. I had to talk to somebody, and John was always insightful. He listened to me carefully and patiently that day. Then he said something that changed my life.

"You have a choice, you know." He looked at me with his chin up a bit and a challenge in his eyes. "If you don't like it in the front line, then get back in the ranks."

He was quiet then and let the full impact of the choice fall into my heart. I nodded, pressed my lips together, and gave a little sideways wave as I slipped from the room to be alone.

He was right, no doubt about that. It was the very essence of the whole situation. If I stayed with a front line assignment, I would most certainly get attacked. Not only that, the front line gets it first! I would be in the heat of the combat, taking the worst of the cannon balls and gun fire. Shrapnel would shred me. I'd be the adventurer in uncharted territory, the one taking the risk of treading on enemy mines before anyone else even knew they were there. I'd feel the responsibility for those coming behind me.

So then, what was my choice? I really didn't like the option of staring at someone else's shoulder blades. There wasn't enough adventure to that. I just wasn't the kind of person to play it safe and risk getting bored. Somehow—how did it happen anyway?—I knew I really liked to explore new expanse, be able to see out, gain the perspective of a panoramic view, and make choices.

This particular choice had been made, too. I knew I couldn't be satisfied with staying in the ranks, and so I stepped back into the fray.

RESILIENCY

Read Romans 15:1-6.   *January 2*

I had purchased a book on the history of the Wisconsin region where we were vacationing and found the reading fascinating, inspiring, and challenging. The area's history had produced stories of human courage, endurance, and ingenuity.

As I leisurely rambled through the pages of the book, I found myself alternately laughing, holding my breath in suspense, and shaking my head with incredulity. The truth that struck me most deeply was the endurance and resilience of those first pioneers. They held up under pressures and hardships that were amazing.

In 1864, on New Year's Day, one young man got lost in a blinding snowstorm after visiting his girlfriend on a northern island for Christmas. He went several days without food, sleep, or heat in his arduous fight for survival. Being extremely resourceful, he carried out this tedious work with valor.

At one point, he fell into the lake and got pulled under the ice. After a heroic struggle, he managed to resurface but couldn't get back onto the fragile ice. So, according to the account, "he stayed in the freezing water, using his ice-encased arms and hands as sledge-hammers to smash the thin ice and open a passage. He slowly moved forward, like an animated iceberg, half swimming, half crawling, by help of his elbows. This incredible struggle against the merciless elements continued for hours. Time after time he believed himself lost, but again and again he conquered, smashing, plunging, rolling, and swimming with the temperature at forty degrees below zero." [1]

This man's rescuers made the horrible mistake of plunging his limbs into kerosene, and he ended up with months of pain and the loss of his extremities before he could get to a doctor. Later, with the help of artificial limbs, he continued his business of drilling wells and reportedly had remarkable dexterity in handling the tools of his trade, never asking for favors because of his physical handicap (Holand 76).

As such stories were recounted in the book, one after the other, I considered the tremendous endurance that characterized those early settlers. They never gave up, lifting their chins and facing adversity with resolve.

And nowadays? We are apt to quit when the going gets a little tough. People bail out of jobs when circumstances become difficult or out of marriages when the relationship requires too much work. They tend to carry the same problems with them from place to place, never resolving issues or growing through the difficulties.

A little endurance, like those hearty pioneers, wouldn't hurt any of us. Let's toughen up and use our limbs as ice picks!

Work cited: Holand, H.R. Old Peninsula Days. Minocqua, WI: North Word Press, Inc., 1959.

LITTLE ITTY BITTY BABY PIRANHA

Read Romans 6:11-23.   *January 3*

Exhausted and frazzled at the end of a long workday, I dropped into my car and flipped on the radio. A little human interest story was being broadcast, and my distracted mind picked it up immediately.

A local pet store had received an order of fish The problem was that the shipment had arrived a day early and only about ten minutes before closing. The two employees knew that the fish needed to be unpacked and placed into aquariums immediately. Unfortunately, there were no aquariums ready. Water temperature needed to be just right and that couldn't happen in mere minutes.

The solution: place them into tanks already in use. They'd sort it all out in the morning, they said to themselves.

However, what were they to do with a pair of baby piranha which had come as part of the shipment? They saved them til the end and still had no solution. Technically, the piranha needed to be in their own tank since they munched other fish. But now it was already fifteen minutes past closing, and there were no empty tanks.

The employees studied the piranha carefully, decided they were so small that they were probably harmless, and dumped them into an occupied tank just for the night.

The next morning when the employees arrived at the store, they could only stare in horror. Those two little itty bitty piranha now had their own tank! They had eaten every single one of the other fish.

I was on the freeway by now and chuckled to myself. What a story! Then I sobered as a thought struck me forcibly.

What about the little itty bitty baby piranha in my own life? How often had I acted exactly the same way, reasoning that a small sin could stay in my life "just overnight"? How many times had I been too tired or too stressed to deal with a bad attitude or a wrong motive? In essence, I had just left it in my life until later.

Sin always brings death. Even what people consider "small sins" will eat up what's good in our lives.

I determined that day not to leave any little piranha in my life—not even overnight.

Now read 1 John 1: 5-10.

4

THE BATTLE FRONT

Often as leaders we find ourselves wrestling. We wrestle with problems. We scramble around the issues. We try to pin things down. We throw our weight behind what we want to see accomplished. Our goal is to win the match.

When we start wrestling with people, it can be quite a scene. Folks can take sides. They yell and scream for their favorite, boo and hiss for their antagonist. When people are of equal weight, it can be quite a match indeed.

Paul, however, reminds us that we do not wrestle against flesh and blood. When we are in the midst of a fight, the comment seems ludicrous. It's a person who is causing us the grief, that's for sure. He's not a Martian. She's not an elf. Certainly we must be wrestling with an individual...and a wild one at that.

So what was Paul saying? He stated that we were wrestling against principalities, powers, rulers of the darkness, and the spiritual hosts of wickedness in the heavenly places. This is quite an array indeed.

A leader must have double vision. He must look at a person who is causing spiritual grief and realize where the problem is actually originating. This allows us to love the individual, because the difficulty is not arising out of their own core as much as it is out of the gates of hell. We can all succumb to it unfortunately.

Why should we see this way? Because it allows us to pray properly. Verse 18 points out that we should be praying and making supplication at all seasons. It is important to pray for our own challenges, as well as to realize when our colleagues are in a spiritual battle. We are asked to intercede for them as well, paying attention to each other's needs. So often when we're in the battle, we can't see straight, and we need the prayers of others who can see the spiritual battle array more clearly.

Furthermore, we must keep on our armor. Any time we take

off a piece, we are opening ourselves to vulnerability, and our enemy the devil will find the soft spot to throw his poisonous spear. We must remember we are saved, have faith, keep sharing the gospel and stay at peace, maintain righteousness, and believe the Word. Let's not forget. We're in a battle, and leaders are right there in the fray.

OUR OWN GOALS
Read Proverbs 20:24.   *January 5*

Although goal-setting and planning are critical for our public leadership, there comes a time when God wants us to relinquish these activities as they involve our own personal goals.

Now before you disagree, follow my thought a little further. Indeed, I do believe in the importance of establishing personal goals. I have them, as well as an individual statement of mission. The latter has been reviewed and reworked regularly, and I find it to be a wonderful gauge regarding the priorities and commitments in my life.

So what was I referring to in the first sentence? Though these personal goals are written, always in the back of my mind is a higher commitment; that is to God Himself. The Lord's goals and plans supersede my own, and I am dedicated to those more than to my own.

This means that I am willing to scrap my own goals at a moment's notice. What I have written and thought through has been accomplished through prayer and seeking God. The product has, as much as possible, reflected my understanding of God's desires for my life. But still, the light has not yet been shed on every aspect, and therefore, as God opens up His plan for my life, additional insight is provided. I may have to add, delete, or revise what I first understood.

It is critical to hold loosely to our own personal goals and plans. If we grasp them too tightly, we may try to ramrod our own design against the very plans of God. Not a nice collision course! There is a lurking danger that we can get our own ambitions and our stubborn ways into the gears of what God is producing from our lives.

At one point in my life, as the Lord was dealing with me about these things, someone said to me, "Dr. Tennant, what are your goals for your life?" I looked down and thought to myself, "In a very real sense, I have none."

I went on to explain to this young lady that I had goals on paper—many hopes and dreams—but in the end, I knew God was in charge. And not only was that all right, but essential to my well-being. I didn't want to hold on so tightly to my own plans for myself that I could not easily or readily allow God to make some changes. In essence, God can do anything He wants, any way He wants, any time He wants. Have at it, Lord.

THE KNOTTED ROAD

Read Proverbs 3:5-6.   *January 6*

Analysis can be a very helpful process, but sometimes I overdo it and get myself into trouble. I think too much, ponder causes, plan strategies, and just run something into the ground. This tendency was playing itself out to the extreme one day while I was driving to a new destination where I had been scheduled to speak.

To get there, I needed to go through a large city with which I was unfamiliar. Usually, I read maps carefully, plan my course ahead of time, observe the signs, and it is all a snap. I even have a good sense of direction, and I'm definitely not too proud to stop and ask for assistance.

However, to say I got lost on that day would be an understatement. I was truly discomfited. One-way streets,

7

curves, overpasses, and few highway signs got me completely turned around in the city streets. Even asking directions didn't help.

My nerves tightened as 45 minutes disappeared, and still I had not found the highway I needed. Although I had given myself extra time for unforeseen emergencies, that buffer zone was dwindling rapidly.

In the distance I finally viewed a road sign. "At last!" I thought. "Now I can get this puzzle put together." As I got closer to the sign, I could scarcely believe the sight. I had somehow gotten on to the right highway, and I was even going the correct direction. Amazing!

Then the Spirit spoke quietly to my heart. He reminded me of the problem I had been pondering during the first hour of my drive. That problem defied solution. The more I tried to work it through and determine its causes, the more confusing it became. For months now, all my attempts at trying to fix the mess just made matters worse.

God prompted me to compare this with the road experience. Could I go back the way I just came? No, that was impossible. I didn't even know where I had been. I could never go over all those twists and turns in the road again, no matter how hard I tried. Nonetheless, I was now on the correct highway. How did that happen?

Suddenly I understood what God wanted to show me. I couldn't go back over the knotted road of this problem, either. There was no way I could figure it out. I couldn't backtrack and redo any of it. However, I WAS somehow on the correct path. What peace.

THE PLAN

In Christianity today, there is a tendency to be suspicious of planning and organization. A certain level of caution in these endeavors is probably healthy; however, a careful study of scripture reveals a God who is the best possible planner.

Sometimes His plans are only indicated by the context of the scripture reading. For example, consider how much thought must have gone into the complexity and inter-relationships of this world during its creation. As man has misused natural resources, he has discovered these inter-relationships, many of which he never understood or anticipated. There are so many details and discoveries which are still coming to light.

Often in the *Bible*, God's plans for certain human endeavors are clearly spelled out. Consider the narrative on how to build the tabernacle, which is complete and highly detailed (Exodus). Job descriptions are even included for the purpose of moving the tabernacle (Numbers 4) and also for the priests (Leviticus and Numbers). Clear instructions for an orderly progression of the people from Mt. Sinai are provided (Numbers 1 and 2). Explanation of offerings, of feasts and festivals, of numerous laws and directions of all kinds resound through the first books of the Old Testament.

God led Joshua with explicit directions and even had him look back and assess progress in Joshua 13. We could point to Nehemiah and the rebuilding of the temple in Jerusalem. So the list could go on as God reveals Himself to His people through plans, directions, and specific details. It all came to a climax, of course, in God's great plan of salvation, and even Revelation indicates that God already has a plan for the end of the age.

The greatest problems arise when we conceive our own designs and follow our own ways, for assuredly this can lead to doom. Biblical examples of this truth abound. There is the deceit of Ananias and Sapphira, the attempt to steady the Ark as David brings it back to Jerusalem, Joshua's pact with the Gibeonites, Samson's tragic choices, plus many more.

However, scripture also tells the story of numerous men and women who sought God for counsel and carefully obeyed whatever He directed. Consider Jehoshaphat's victory in the wilderness (II Chronicles 20), Joshua's defeat of Jericho, Joseph's interpretation of Pharaoh's dream and subsequent plans for the famine. Even when there seemed to be no way, God stepped in and provided all that was needed as He was trusted to do.

The reason for our planning should not be to strengthen our control or to go our own way. Might we seek the God-who-plans for His blueprints of the future. Then might we be willing to follow these plans in every respect as He chooses to reveal them to us.

LIMITED

Read Psalm 33:10-11.   *January 8*

God's greatest purposes will prevail. Of that, we can be certain. He has a plan that is much larger, more far-reaching, and far more encompassing than we can ever imagine.

We must remember that from our place in time and space, we can see and understand only very little. In truth, we forget how limited we are. We complain, murmur, and question God as if we knew as much as He does, saw as far as He can, and understood His greater purposes as clearly as He.

Job came to understand the limitations of his intellect when he questioned God. He, like us, found he did not have answers. Our human insight has a time-boundary. What we presently know is not enough to form judgments. We do not perceive the beginning from the end. Job told God (42:2-3), "I know that you can do all things; no plan of yours can be thwarted. You asked,

'Who is this that obscures my counsel without knowledge?' Surely I spoke of things I did not understand, things too wonderful for me to know."

God has greater purposes which are coming to fruition over time. It is through these larger purposes that we must view what happens to us now. There are so many questions we have regarding present-day events that seem unanswerable. Why do certain people die while others are miraculously rescued or healed? Why do some have to endure so much pain but others seem to have it so easy? I don't know.

But I do know that God's ultimate purposes will withstand the winds of time. We have a Sovereign God who is over all. I know that what God has planned will, without fail, come to pass. No one can thwart it. What God wants to do, He will accomplish.

Why does so much boil down to trust? Why can't we get answers? Why can't our own plans simply be blessed by God? Why, why, why? It's because we've got limits....and God doesn't!

PEOPLE!
Read Mark 6:30-33.   *January 9*

People. People everywhere. People lining up to see me. The phone kept ringing persistently. I checked after a meeting that had only lasted an hour, and sixteen voice mail messages had accumulated in just that short time. My e-mail is probably up to eighty, I thought wryly. Is this whole scene even real? And then there was that statement I have come to distrust: "Can I talk with you? It'll just take a minute." It never takes a minute.

It's all part of leadership, I know that. After all, if there weren't others looking our direction, whom would we be leading?

However, sometimes the demands become oppressive. I know the tricks of protecting my schedule and organizing my time. Even then, there are days when there simply isn't enough of

11

me to go around, even if I could clone myself three times over.

After several weeks of a particularly intense schedule, I happily left for vacation. The winter weather I had been struggling with had faded into sunshine in a warmer part of the world. We were in a closed environment with hundreds of people—on a ship. Young and old milled around everywhere.

My deck chair was as good as an observation tower. "I'm really enjoying this peace and quiet," I said to my husband, heaving a deep sigh. "It's wonderful."

"What are you saying?" he laughed. "There are conversations and laughter and kids squealing and music everywhere." He was right. There wasn't actually any quiet or calm, so what was I feeling?

Then came a sudden realization. It wasn't really people I was tired of. They were all around, and I still enjoyed watching them and being with them. No, what I was weary of was responding to them.

I imagine that Jesus also felt this way. In Mark 6 and other passages we see many people pressing around Him and His disciples—so many that Jesus often didn't even have time to eat. He too desired a quiet place and some rest, so He went off to a solitary place in a boat. Our desire for rest and space is something the Lord understands, and we need to get away at times, just as He did.

I smiled that day and turned off my "responder."

FINDING COMPASSION

Read Matthew 14:12-14
(and Mark 6:26-44 if you have time).   *January 10*

A closer study of yesterday's verses and context reveals even more truth. We see that His own personal grief was very likely part of the reason Jesus wanted to go to a solitary place.

John the Baptist was a relative of His and had accomplished the crucial tasks of preparing the way for the Messiah and baptizing Him. How sad it must have been for Jesus when he heard that John had been murdered, and what a horrible and gruesome death it had been! Surely the reality of this terrible event affected Jesus, grieving him deeply.

Jesus needed rest. However, He also needed to get away from people so He could reflect and work through His pain. It would have been understandable if He didn't want more demands placed upon Him—if He just didn't have any more to give out.

Expecting to come ashore in a solitary place, what must He have felt when He landed amidst a large crowd? Where did Jesus find the compassion He showed toward them? In the midst of His own pain and grief, how could He come to view them as "sheep without a shepherd" rather than a nuisance? Where did He discover the strength to teach them that day, to give out one more time?

Perhaps the answer can be found in Jesus' faith. He was connected to the Father, so He could receive God's viewpoint on life and appropriate the strength necessary to continue. He had faith that God would provide for Him.

It is amazing that as we choose to put aside ourselves, along with our own needs and desires, we find renewed strength flowing through us. When we step forward to serve others—to minister one more time—God gives new energy and life that enables us to complete the task.

Jesus dug deep in trusting God to meet His own personal needs. Even when He had the opportunity to tell the crowd to leave and go find food, He let compassion rule Him. How easy it would have been to send them all away so He could finally be alone. But He had seen God provide the strength to minister when He was hurting. It was time for faith again. If the Father could do that for Him, then surely God could meet the physical necessities of this crowd.

We first learn to appropriate the resources we need from the Father for ourselves. Then we can believe Him to work in mighty ways on behalf of other people.

DREAMERS OF DAY

Read II Kings 18:1-8.   *January 11*

What are you living for? What would you die for? If, at the end of your life, someone asked you if you had been successful, what would you say?

The other day I was thinking about such questions when a representative of an international directory interviewed me to determine if I was eligible for inclusion. Frankly, I found the interview amusing. It appealed to vanity and grated on me. One of the questions she asked was "To what do you attribute your great success?"

I laughed to myself. I couldn't help it. After reflecting for a moment and regaining my composure, I said to her. "You know, I'm not even sure that success, as you would probably define it, is even a concern of mine. I believe that helping other people, ministering to and serving them, is of far more value."

The interviewer cleared her throat and seemed to be searching for a response. I'm sure that most people she talked to would have felt wonderful that someone would consider them a "great success." Sadly, some people work their whole careers for those accomplishments which society would designate as indicators of success. In the end, however, what have they really attained? Was it worth enough to exchange their very lives for?

My personal statement of mission does not include the idea of success. Fame, riches, or position do not have to be a part of my life. Other goals are of far more value than that, especially character. Who I am has to be at the core of what I accomplish.

Judah's King Hezekiah was described as being successful

14

(verse 7) in whatever he undertook, but this was said of him because he followed the Lord and trusted Him. Hezekiah obeyed what God told him to do, and therefore he had a great impact on his society.

T.E. Lawrence (Lawrence of Arabia) wrote the following:

"All men dream, but not equally. Those who dream by night in the dusty recesses of their minds wake in the day to find that it was vanity: but the dreamers of day are dangerous men, for they may act their dream with open eyes to make it possible" (Introduction).

As Christians, let us dream for ourselves and others, for our institutions and our churches. But let us do it in the day, with the light of God shining full on it. Our goals and dreams must be in full view of God with His measures, priorities and values lighting them up. Let's be dreamers of the day!

Work cited: Lawrence, T. E. *The Seven Pillars of Wisdom: A Triumph.* Oxford: Oxford Press, 1926. From the suppressed introductory chapter first published in 1939.

WHICH WAY?

Read Proverbs 29:18.   *January 12*

So dream in His presence. Seek His face, and He may give you a revelation. For if the leader does not do this task, the people will not know where to go.

In the childhood story of *Alice's Adventures in Wonderland* by Lewis Carroll, Alice says, "Will you please tell me which way I ought to go from here?" And the Cheshire cat answers her, "That depends on where you want to get to" (51).

If that question is left to each individual in a group, then confusion and in-fighting will occur. Why? Because each person will choose his or her own direction. The group will not agree on which way to go, and there will be great disarray.

That is one of the main reasons that leadership exists. It helps

15

to provide coordination and motivation for the group. Input may be solicited, but the final decision lies with the leader and his team of counselors.

Proverbs 29:18 states, "Where there is no revelation, the people cast off restraint." Another version states, "Where there is no vision, the people perish"(NAS)...or "are out of control" (RSV).

You get the picture, I'm sure. Without this leadership task in place, the people have no restraint. They will go full speed with whatever "pet project" they like; they're not restrained by anything. Restraint, however, is crucial if the group is to work together for the good of the whole.

A dream or revelation must be from God. We need to seek Him until it is fully developed. It should be large enough, clear enough, and detailed enough to be understood and inspiring. It should not be insipid or unworthy or simply a catch phrase. And when one dream has been accomplished, another needs to take its place.

The leader's task is to find ways to articulate that prophetic vision, taking the dream from his own spirit and placing it into view so the people can grasp it, too. If they do not see the vision, the people will perish. Their work has no significance. So have you dreamed lately?

Work cited: Carroll, Lewis. *Alice in Wonderland.* 2nd edition. New York: W.W. Norton, 1992.

THE FRENCH MARATHON

Read I Corinthians 9:24-27 and Hebrews 12:1.   *January 13*

When I visited my brother in southern France, he described an unusual experience from his six-month sabbatical there. He was invited to participate in a marathon race across the French countryside. The course wound its way though the hills, past old country houses, and through some small villages.

16

Having run in many marathons in the states, Don anticipated a similar experience. It took him by great surprise and nearly ruined his running time when he came across the first cheering crowd along the route. It was amazing!

The onlookers had dressed in fanciful costumes, and they exuded an air of jubilant festivity. The celebration included an unusual number of cheering onlookers. Whole villages lined the route. Landowners packed out their country houses with family and friends. Music of all kinds, flowers, food, jugglers, and magicians highlighted the celebrations. People reached out to touch the runners and urge them forward.

When my brother described this remarkable experience, it reminded me of the verses in I Corinthians 9:24-27 and Hebrews 12:1. Indeed, as the latter verse indicates, we are surrounded by a great cloud of witnesses. They are watching us, cheering us on, urging us to keep running the race, encouraging us to go after the crown.

So often it seems as though nobody really knows or cares what we do. Why shouldn't we give up—or at least sit down for a time? Nobody is going to miss us anyway.

However, this image of the French marathon has come to my mind often in recent months. At those times, I can picture the crowds right now in heaven that are cheering us on. There are so many who have gone before. They view this race on earth as exceedingly important. And what a celebration it will be at the end, too! The rewards then will be worth the cost now.

"Lord, I want to keep on running!"

TWO PLUS GOD

Read I Samuel 14:1-15
(and 16-23 for a larger context).   *January 14*

While his father Saul sat pouting under a pomegranate tree with the remains of his troops, a mere 600 men, Jonathan and his armor bearer sneaked off for a stroll. What a different perspective Jonathan had. "Come, let's go over to the outpost of those uncircumcised fellows. Perhaps the Lord will act on our behalf. Nothing can hinder the Lord from saving, whether by many or by few" (verse 6).

These seeds of faith grew into complete trust as the two of them (only two!) displayed themselves to the enemy. It was as though they were dancing out into the spotlight in the center ring of the circus. The sign they had agreed upon beforehand was given, "Come up!"–and Jonathan's faith rose strong in his heart. "The Lord has given them into the hand of Israel."

What a brash and wild deed. They showed themselves to the enemy and then bore their taunts. Next, they marched straight to the outpost camp. What could they have been thinking? They were sure to get caught. And if the enemy troop discovered that this was the King's son, well, the results were unthinkable. They could have held him ransom until his father, Saul, surrendered. They might have murdered him and further demoralized the troops and Saul.

But Jonathan and his armor-bearer were young, dauntless and brave, so they climbed right up to the camp with faith instead of fear in their hearts. The two fought and killed about twenty men during the first attack in a mere half-acre territory.

Now for the good part. The Lord responded to their steps of faith and struck the whole enemy army with panic. The ground shook, Saul's lookouts saw the Philistines melting away, and the King immediately went into battle. The enemy soldiers were in total confusion. With this, the Israelite defectors finally got their

18

cowardly thinking straightened out and crawled from their hiding places. The simple conclusion: "So the Lord rescued Israel that day..." (verse 23).

All this started with two young men who decided to take some action and have faith in God. How many similarly hopeless situations I have witnessed in leadership. Since "two plus God is enough," it only takes several God-fearing people to accomplish the impossible. Have faith. Rise up! Act.

AFTER THE TALK

Read Isaiah 41:28-29.   *January 15*

Our move from beautiful Colorado to a flatter, much less scenic part of the country had been extremely difficult. Many trying events tested our spirits, and unhappiness pushed into our lives. My job kept me unbelievably busy, and I was more than tired—I was downright exhausted.

The four-hour drive I needed to make along the interstate that day became a perfect time to reflect. Grumpiness and frustration rose forcibly to the surface, and there I was, having one of those honest and forthright talks with God.

I have always been of the opinion that honesty with God is not only right but actually is essential. He knows it all anyway. He understands how we feel and what we think. Why try to hide anything from God? He knows how to handle our anger and pain. He understands us better than we even understand ourselves.

My tendency, however, is to try to get everything figured out and then to present it to God. I like to understand it, get my hands around it, and fit it into a charming, tidy package. Somehow, this never quite works. Even if I could fool myself into thinking I had it together this time, God would know better. In fact, I usually can't even get my attitude right without His help.

So that day I shared it all with God. I talked; I cried. I even ranted a little. God let me get every bit of it out. Finally, I sat there quietly and just drove; I had nothing more to say.

How good it felt to lay it all out on the altar-table in its totally messy form and then to be silent. What a perfect opportunity for God to get through to me and deal with it His way!

Sometimes we just need to pull everything out of ourselves and be quiet. Then after the silence, GOD....

THE FLAPPER

Read Isaiah 40:28-31.   *January 16*

During that silent portion of my drive, I began to realize that much of my frustration was of my own making. I was just too busy. I pushed myself to the edge in every way and didn't take much time for rest and reflection.

Suddenly, a small bird popped up from the right side of the highway. It was flying so low that it was directly in line with my windshield. The bird was flapping its little wings wildly, but its work wasn't too efficient. It certainly wasn't going very far very fast. In fact, I was afraid my car would hit it. In one of those crazy moments of mine, I even said aloud, "Hurry up, birdie, or you'll be smooshed!" I couldn't keep from laughing. The little bird was all right, but it was so scared that it ended up in the median, gasping. (I think I even saw its tongue hanging out of its beak. Well, maybe not.)

"That bird is you," spoke the still small Voice. Ooooh! I didn't want to hear that, but I knew it was true. I could really see myself, flapping my heart out but not getting very far.

As I was pondering this, I glanced up and saw a cliff. For this part of the country, which usually didn't even have a hill, it must have been a special, God-ordained cliff. The surrounding terrain was flat for miles!

Then I saw it. An eagle took off from that cliff and floated high up. It went so far, so fast—but its wings worked infrequently. That eagle was catching the wind, riding the currents. It was positively grand. It banked with such grace and beauty and caught the sunbeam. "And that is what I want you to become," that voice I knew said again to my heart.

I came to call that little sparrow "the flapper," and the Holy Spirit checked me often in the days ahead. Suddenly, I would see myself flapping through life. Then God graciously taught me how to ride the wind of His Spirit. I slowly began to understand the difference between the lifestyle of a flapper and that of an eagle. He taught me to take off from cliffs. It's so enjoyable, being an eagle!

YOU WANT THE CHOIR *WHERE*?
Read II Chronicles 20:20-30.   *January 17*

The events in this passage would be enough to see the size of a choir cut instantly in half, at the very least. It is not exactly the best recruiting tool for a choir director to have in the hip pocket.

Can't you just hear the choir members now? "What? The CHOIR on the front line? Who ever heard of such an idea? After all, the front line is always assigned to the bravest, largest, sturdiest, well-trained warriors...soldiers, you know! Surely it is no place for us puny singers. And you say the people were consulted, too? [verse 23]   I thought they were our friends. Maybe the anthem last week was a little weak, but it couldn't have been that bad!"

The choir director surely needed a few tips from a motivational seminar for this one. And once the choir did agree, what exactly would the singing sound like in such circumstances? A little weak and frightened maybe? How easy it is, though, to picture the songs taking hold in the spirits of the people, songs of faith and truth, hope and victory! Probably, it wasn't long before they were singing with gusto.

It is in worship where we can do spiritual warfare, preparing the way for the message from the Lord and for the other work that He wants to accomplish. When worship has gone well, it paves the way, opens hearts to God, and sets people free.

Even in the beginning of the praises with Jehoshaphat's army, God got busy setting up ambushes for the adversary. The enemies literally defeated themselves.

Imagine the amazement as first the choir, and then the rest of the army, came to the place overlooking the desert and found not one single enemy soldier left alive. They just stood there and stared in awe, never having to lift the sword or raise a battle cry. Booty and plunder were so abundant that there was more than they could haul off. Another praise assembly erupted spontaneously in the valley.

As they returned to Jerusalem, the people could have rushed off to their homes with new treasures. Instead, they went to the temple for more praise. Other nations noted these events and didn't dare to touch them.

Peace and praise reigned in the land, because Jehoshaphat knew how to lead. Think about it.

SIGNING UP

Read II Peter 2:19-22.   *January 18*

Paul and other apostles viewed themselves as the servants of Jesus Christ. What a profound and deeply meaningful commitment. Throughout the New Testament, this identification as a bondservant was used at the beginning of many of the epistles, almost as a badge of honor. Obviously, the apostles valued this title and the personal pledge it signified.

Being Christ's slave is a choice for each of us. We are not

forced, but rather choose, to be conscripted. Once this commitment is made, however, it has tremendous implications. For example, a bondservant is duty-bound for an endless period of time. This sort of long-term obligation is difficult to conceptualize, especially in a world where people believe that commitments are meant to be broken. There is a "bail-out" mentality that is popular today.

People tend to think in a give-up mode. "Well, if this is a bad job, I can just leave it and get a new one." Or "This marriage just doesn't seem to be working out, we should get a divorce." Or "This church is getting boring, let's find another one." Or "This friend is having so many problems, I think I'll just bow out gracefully; it's too much for me to handle."

Of course, when we enlist for Jesus Christ, opting out of His service is also a possibility. We continue to have free will. However, it is a miserable experience to give up on God. Scripture defines it as "a dog returning to its vomit" and "a sow that is washed going back to her wallowing in the mud."

When our duty to God seems particularly challenging, we may entertain the idea of giving up on it all. But leaving God seems to be a horrible thought. We think about what it would actually be like without Him, and that reality is far from pleasant. Imagine the void, the meaninglessness, the lack of life and love!

Sometimes what God is requiring of us while we are in His service seems so challenging, difficult, and uninviting that we don't wish to participate in it. However, the alternative doesn't seem like an alternative at all. Who wants to live without Him after really knowing Him? I have had people say to me, "I don't really have a choice."

Well, we do have a choice; we always do. It's just that we don't like the options. This dreadful quandary is probably a good one after all, because commitment to Jesus Christ is designed to be long-term. It's the best for us to be God's bondservant. Have you *really* signed up?

FREEDOM

Many people claim that they haven't chosen God because they don't want to lose their freedom. Satan gives an appearance of freedom to his minions. The enormous problem is that it is actually bondage. People who serve the devil end up as "slaves of depravity." It is really true that "a man is a slave to whatever has mastered him."

With this in mind, it is surely better to have a master like Jesus. Serving Him is not always easy, but His ways are good, right, just, and full of love.

In His closing talk with His disciples before He went to the cross, Jesus puts some of this into proper perspective. He explains in John 15 that although we may think we chose to serve Him, actually God called us first. Our perspective is one of servanthood, and Jesus could have left it at that. However, He chooses to take an additional step. He actually calls us "friends" instead of "servants."

Consider how wonderful it is to be called His friend. We wouldn't dare to think it for ourselves, since what we deserve is to be His slaves. In fact, we have to decide to do that first. He, however, can make the choice to move past that servant relationship and give us our freedom, making us His friends.

We are elevated to a different role entirely with this action. We are valued, enjoyed, and confided in. "I no longer call you servants, " Jesus said, "because a servant does not know his master's business. Instead, I have called you friends, for everything that I learned from my Father I have made known to you." Consider the great value of being counted a real friend of Jesus.

Do we act like it? Part of loving Him as a friend is to be in synch with Him, to do what He would like. We don't obey out of fear, because He is our master and we are His slaves, required to do what He says. Instead we obey because we love Him. What freedom! What a friend.

LEARNING TO OBEY

Read Hebrews 5:7-10.   *January 20*

I've observed it often: Human nature tends to rebel against rules and authority that do not come out of relationship. The only way to hold down that kind of rebellion is through fear, bondage, or coercive measures. These tactics may be covert, but the root of power is still present. Satan, in particular, knows how to maneuver well through this maze of power, control, and deception.

Obedience itself only works correctly when it arises out of an alliance of trust. Then we want to obey because we care about that other person, and we know he or she is committed to us and has our best interests at heart.

Even then, obedience is a learned behavior. We are provided with a gripping example in Hebrews 5. Here we are told that Jesus didn't really want to die and begged God to spare Him from this terrible trial. His entreaties were not light requests but rather were shared with "loud cries and tears."

We are told that Jesus made these pleas out of a submissive spirit. His reverence toward His Father and His love for Him made Jesus willing to obey. That, however, did not make the obedience any less difficult or costly.

God heard His Son's cries. Think of how this must have moved His Father's heart! Here was God's only begotten Son, in great pain and suffering because of what He was being required to do, and God chose to have Him go through with the cross anyway.

One might think that this was easy for Jesus since He was the Son of God. He was secure in this relationship and knew that God loved Him. Nonetheless, Scripture tells us that "although he was a son, he learned obedience from what he suffered." Obedience didn't come automatically; it had to be learned—even by Jesus. His suffering taught Him.

The suffering we face in our lives can teach us, too. Even as God's children, we still have to learn to obey. When God allows heartaches in our lives, we must stay secure in our relationship with Him, knowing that He loves us. Even when we don't understand the pain we are suffering, we can trust Him, and just like Jesus, we can choose to submit.

EFFECTIVE STYLE

Read John 13:21-26.   *January 21*

Much research has been done and countless articles written on various styles of management and leadership. Additionally, these styles have been analyzed as to their outcomes, utilizing many different variables and measures. Frankly, it gets a little dizzying and rather boring to me after a while.

So let's cut through all of this and look at the style of our model, Jesus Himself. What? Jesus with a leadership style? Of course! He was a very practical person, and I believe He thoughtfully considered just how He could be most effective in His leadership role.

First, Jesus carefully selected a dozen disciples, and these twelve became an inner band of friends. Throughout the gospels, there are numerous references to Jesus spending time with that group. He taught them, gave them additional explanations, and cared for them, often taking them away by themselves.

He was also personally acquainted with each one. Jesus understood the fact that Judas was a traitor, even before the Last Supper (John 6:70). He knew that Peter would deny Him (John 13:36-38). He understood Thomas with his doubts and fears (John

20:26-29).

There is much evidence of deep understanding and caring for every one of the disciples. He knew them well as individuals; He was quite aware of their strengths and weaknesses, their needs, their hopes and dreams. Jesus was committed to taking time with them and providing both input and support.

The result was that someone like John described himself as "the disciple whom Jesus loved." He was intimate enough with Jesus to ask for secrets to be shared. He was even "leaning back against Jesus." No one does these things with someone from whom he feels distanced or who is as cold as a mountain stream. Jesus obviously lived out His decision to call us friends rather than servants.

As Christian leaders, we should follow this wonderful role model. Jesus had a great deal to accomplish. After all, the establishment of the church rested on a few frail shoulders. However, Jesus didn't drive them to this task from a high and distant place. He wasn't a person to care simply in theory, but then be too busy for them, brushing them aside. Rather, He communicated, prayed, ate, and spent time with them. How loved, secure and valued they felt! Jesus knew that things have to get done through other people, and this happens most effectively out of friendship. In the end, consider what these twelve accomplished.

As a leader, do you demonstrate this same level of valuing and friendship with your team? Do you spend enough time with your close-in employees to let them know you are concerned about them and not just about how they perform? Do they know they are high on your priority list because you really do care for them as people? If not, why not?

FRITTERED FARTHINGS

The story of the prodigal son is one most know quite well. The youngster, of course, was crass enough to request his inheritance before his father had even died. The message was all too clear: He really didn't care about his relationship with his dad. All he really wanted was the money so he could go out and enjoy life.

The prodigal son frittered away his farthings. It appears that his desire to return home was caused less by missing his father than by missing the good life. In fact, his motivation seems to have been quite basic; he craved food. "How many of my father's hired men have food to spare, and here I am starving to death!" (John 15:17).

Nonetheless, he realized that he couldn't just go swooping in, expecting everything to be the same. He had spurned his father who he figured would be both hurt and wary of him. So he decided on a plan that might work. "I will set out and go back to my father and say to him: Father, I have sinned against heaven and against you. I am no longer worthy to be called your son; make me as one of your hired men" (John 15:18-19).

He expected to go back, not as a son, but in a master-servant context. Even that looked better to him than staying where he was. The miracle is that the father saw him "while he was still a long way off" and not only took him back as a son, but did it unreservedly. To the father, relationship had always been primary and remained unbroken.

Our focus on the other son is usually cursory, but this son likewise had multiple misunderstandings when it came to the relationship with his father. In verse 29 we have an interesting clue as to how the older son viewed all this. "All these years I've been *slaving* for you and never *disobeyed* your *orders*" (Italics added).

28

This young man also misunderstood his role as son. Basically, he viewed himself as a slave. From this vantage point, he had obeyed orders and done what his father had wanted him to do. However, he also had not appreciated what was available to him in a father-son relationship.

His father tried to bring this young man to a deeper understanding as well. He began with the kind words, "My son" (verse 31). The father gently reminded him of their father-son relationship and what it meant—always being together and sharing everything.

When will we learn? As Christians, God wants us in relationship with Him as His sons and daughters. This privilege is precious and should not be squandered, but rather is intended to be enjoyed and treasured. What a father we have!

ADOPTION

Read Romans 8:12-17.   *January 23*

God is so much into the Father-Son and Father-Daughter relationship that it is amazing. Consider for a minute: How could the mighty God of the universe actually choose to make us—His sinful, wayward, created ones—adopted children?

Why would God choose us? After all, children who are adopted are desired entirely by choice. Parents who adopt do so purposefully. They fill out paperwork, undergo interviews and reference checks. They must endure a waiting period, and they have to pay a price.

God did this sort of thing for us. He valued us so much that He was willing to wait for us and pay a great price. He purposefully set out after us, desiring to take us as His children. The Lord gives us all the rights and privileges of children who have access to a loving Father. What God desires, above all else, is to be in relationship with us. He wants children!

If, after this adoption process has taken place, the child does not act like a member of the family, then that is difficult for everybody. Perhaps he spurns the love of the father and mother by not communicating. Maybe he expects to work in exchange for his "keep." The new clothes purchased for him are left hanging in the closet while he mopes around in his out-of-date, worn ones. In short, he acts like a slave instead of an adopted child.

The concept of being a member of a family can be so foreign to some that it may not even be grasped. Some adopted children need to learn how to stop cowering because they were so abused and mistreated earlier. All they knew were hard work and harsh words. Protecting themselves physically, emotionally and psychologically can consume much time and energy.

What little material goods they have accrued, they may also protect, wanting to keep it close lest someone take that away, too. Even dirty rags are better than nothing.

Little by little, God tries to draw us out of such a mentality. He wants us to understand how profound the difference is between being a slave and being a child of God. We are so much His that we will even be full heirs. Relationship. A Father! How do you act with God?

ABBA

Read Romans 8:12-17.   *January 24*

Although no father here on earth is perfect, some people have had fathers who were so unloving or "invisible" that it is difficult to comprehend the concept of a caring heavenly Father. Just as orphans may spurn the true love of their adopted fathers, so might we shy away from God, fearful of punishment and potential cruelty or neglect.

Some people have experienced earthly fathers who were physically, sexually, or verbally abusive. Some were abandoned.

Others had dads who lived at home but were absent much of the time, non-communicative, non-interactive, and not giving much emotional support. These fathers may not have known how to express love and so were cold or indifferent. Some had fathers who were alcoholics or for other reasons needed to be taken care of instead of being care-takers themselves.

All such situations require a reworking of our concept of God as Father. We may be able to understand it intellectually, but not emotionally; so we are afraid to relate to God with our whole being, to trust Him, and to give Him our all.

If this is the case for you, I can personally assure you that God is capable of changing this area of your life. He is perfectly patient, gentle, and creative in His healing process. However, you must open yourself up to Him and let Him teach you and heal you. He can reach just as deep as the hurts you have.

As God reconstructs a better concept of father, there can come a wonderful freedom in relating to a God who desires to be intimate, caring, supportive, and truly loving. He is a Father who will never abandon us nor hurt us out of cruelty. He is there for us, and we are most dear to Him, the apple of His eye. How He values us just as we are, pouring out acceptance and unconditional love! These are truths, and it is only our false concept that keeps us from grasping them.

With time, we can come to understand that God does not want slaves who cower in fear of Him but rather children who relate with Him freely out of mutual respect and love. We can even call Him such an endearing term as "Abba"—Daddy.

Do you know Him like this? If not, open up and let Him begin the process of showing you exactly what it means.

DRIVEN

If love from our earthly families has been conditional or if we have not been secure in these relationships, certain personality traits are often exhibited. Many people spend a lifetime trying to win or earn love. This includes many leaders who consciously or subliminally deal with such issues. In fact, perhaps that's why they become leaders in the first place.

Many of us, as children, learned that achievement brought attention, acceptance, and love. If we did well, we were noticed and appreciated — or perhaps we only hoped we would be. For some, it never came, no matter how hard we tried.

Good self-image arises out of unconditional love, being certain that we are accepted no matter what we do. This sense of personal value elicits a security that allows us to relax and enjoy life. Action should be more a comfortable outgrowth of a full life than a drive that can never be satiated.

Drivenness is such an incredible fuel! There seems to be an endless supply that feeds our inner being, causing us to burn with a desire to produce, gain more, and find higher positions, greater earnings, and maximum fame. However, being driven is like an inner record that keeps playing, and we dance to the tune endlessly.

How do we break this inner record? How can we keep workaholism from consuming us? Drowning ourselves in our work may anesthetize our system for a while so we don't hurt quite as much or feel quite so deeply. However, sooner or later, we'll crash and have to face the truth: Ourselves.

This is why God so clearly states that we are not slaves. After all, a slave has to work hard to please his master. He has to generate more and more and is forced to go above and beyond his previous accomplishments. If he does not, he is afraid that his master will be angry and punish him.

On the other hand, work between father and son or daughter is carried out together for mutual benefit. There is enjoyment as the two work alongside one another. The son learns from the father, but the father usually does most of the work. And best of all, the son does not have to prove anything—he is already the son. He is completely accepted and loved as much as he ever could possibly be. ...And you?

SPIN-OFFS

Read I Corinthians 10:23-24.   *January 26*

Spin-offs. When we are leaders, there are always spin-offs from our own weaknesses and needs. It reminds me of the paint spin-art you can find at fairs. You know, the one where you can select the colors, then spin the disc, and the paint is thrown onto the paper, spinning off into other sections of the picture. Who we are likewise spins out, affecting those around us.

Certainly this is true with drivenness. Workaholism not only affects our personal selves, it has additional ramifications. Do we really consider these other spin-offs?

For example, what about our families? What are the consequences of not communicating with our spouse and children because we are too busy? What is being missed in the balance of life by not playing once in a while, enjoying each other, talking and sharing?

I remember a time when my husband made a challenging comment on a vacation trip we were on. It shook me up. One night he had put his hands on his waist and faced me down. "Look," he said, "you might as well have just stayed home and done your work!" He was upset.

So was I. "What do you mean?" I came back. "I didn't bring my briefcase or my laptop computer. I haven't picked up a single piece of paper to write nor have I once had my dictaphone in my hand. What are you talking about?"

"Oh, you're right on all counts," he said. "But you're still working. Your mind is on it. I can tell!"

He was right, and I knew it, even though I hated to admit it. I had been thinking about some bothersome things related to work. I took a deep breath, and we talked. I asked him to help me, because I was on a kind of merry-go-round. I had forgotten how to relax and have a good time.

Even with our employees and co-workers, our workaholism has its effects. For example, it may lead people to feel guilty if they don't put in the same long hours we do. We must be careful not to drive others because of our own "maxed-out" schedules, like when we expect an employee to stay late and complete a report simply because we didn't get it to her in time. Even salaried employees have their own plans and families and suppers to make. These can be affected as a leader drones on in an extended meeting that really could have been handled more succinctly.

When we are so busy, we might expect everyone else to make changes simply to meet our own needs, both personally and professionally. We are tempted to make subtle demands of those around us who have a servant-type nature. These people will get things done for us, wait on us according to our schedule, and bend to our whims, but that does not make it right.

Been involved in painting any "spin-off" pictures lately...?

PERFECTIONISM
Read John 13:31-38 and 21:15-17.   *January 27*

A trait that characterizes many leaders is perfectionism. If the work is not accomplished absolutely correctly, we may fear that we will be punished or rejected by a world which must have seen through us long ago. We are concerned that we may be despised...by others or by ourselves.

34

Peter's insistence that he will not deny Christ may be partially rooted in his zeal, but I think it is also a result of perfectionism. He really wanted—and needed—to do what was right. Out of this, he gained acceptance and love.

It seems that Jesus clearly understood the root of this need, and that is why He reinstated and restored Peter the way He did. Jesus explained that He loved Peter, not simply in a brotherly kind of human way. This sort of love could come and go like the tide of the sea. No, instead He loved Peter with the consistent, persistent, never-ending love of God.

This sort of love was not based on what Peter did or didn't do, but rather was truly unconditional. That's why Jesus loved Peter as much after he denied Him as before. Christ's love is not based upon our actions but out of His choice to love.

This should create a marvelous security in the lives of the recipients of this sort of love! Out of such acceptance, we can enjoy working, not to prove ourselves but because we want to.

Because of this, Jesus could say to Peter, "Feed my sheep." The Lord was saying this because He wanted Peter to serve, not out of fear, drivenness and perfectionism, and not to win love and acceptance either. Rather, Jesus wanted Peter to serve because he was secure in God's love and couldn't help but give it back.

Peter discovered that he did not have to be perfect, and he would still be accepted. What freedom! Do you accept yourself in the midst of your imperfections? Are you secure in His unconditional and steady love for you?

THE TIRADE

Read I Peter 5:1-6.   *January 28*

A tirade, that's what it was. He would simply let it fly, and woe to the person who happened to be in the way. Usually the pressures and frustration had simply mounted to the point that

35

they needed to be vented. Then the next error that merited a correction—even though it might be rather minute and inconsequential—became the target. It was no use arguing at that point. Either duck or take it. Then get out of there and handle it quickly because he'd keep harping on it until it was accomplished.

Some leaders are such perfectionists that not only do they deny their own imperfections, they can't accept mistakes in others either. This is especially true if it's a pet peeve or a special project that is at stake. Then they not only expect quality, but they demand the performance be flawless, precisely according to the way they see it.

Sometimes everything in their day has to be "just right" to the point of obsession. Certain items cannot be out of place or certain reports have to be in a particular spot at an exact time. The level of sound, the placement of a microphone, the turning off of a light, the number of rings of a telephone can send such people into a dither.

Usually colleagues do their best to handle these trivia. However, perfectionists really have no idea how other people view all this nor what it might actually take for their employees to address their whims. They might be startled to discover how they have cowed others into submission or how many projects have been interrupted simply to assure that their perfectionistic needs are being met.

As a leader, when is the last time you looked at yourself in this regard and paid attention to the demands you make? Have you really heard the edge in your voice or the impatience in your tone? Do you realize how clipped your speech may have become? Do you ever tend to lord it over others?

Executives can become so used to giving orders and having their every need met that they are clueless as to just how ingrained it has become. Power can—oh, so easily!—go to our heads.

Sensitivity to others is an important part of all good

relationships. Let's not allow power or our own ego and selfishness to keep us from being a caring, relationship-oriented leader. How fast we can fall into a "master" mentality, and what a tragedy, not only for the people who serve us but also for ourselves. Remember Jesus. He didn't choose "master-slave." Never!

A LOLLIPOP

Read Mark 10:13-16.   *January 29*

The man was working in his home office on a lovely summer evening. His little boy, Jeremy, wandered in and stood away from the desk, watching his father work. When the man finally glanced up from the report he was working on, Jeremy toddled over.

"Daddy!" the boy said, his blue eyes alight with excitement.

"What?" the man said rather distractedly.

"Can I just talk with you?" the boy begged.

"Can you wait for a while?" the father asked. He was already looking back at his paperwork. "Daddy has a lot of work to do."

The boy hung his head, his blue eyes flat now. He started toward the door. Something checked the man, and he thought about his son. There were only 365 days while the boy was three, and half of those were already gone. What was really most important?

"Oh, come here, Jeremy!" his dad set down his pen and held out his arms.

Jeremy's face became alive again, and he came running back to his father. He raised his little arms up, and his dad scooped the lad into his lap. The man smiled and looked into his son's happy face. Was that his own image that was reflected in the boy's eyes?

"What did you want, Jeremy?"

"Oh, I have a surprise," he giggled.

"Well, I thought maybe you would tell me about a new toy

you saw today when you and mom went shopping."

"No!" Jeremy said emphatically. "I don't want anything at all. See, mommy just gave me this lollipop, and I haven't even licked it yet. It's for you!" Happily, the boy yanked off the wrapper and stuffed the candy into his father's mouth.

"Thanks," his father mumbled around the lollipop, a deep huskiness cracking in his voice. "But you didn't have to give me all your candy!"

"Oh, I love you!" Jeremy said, throwing his arms around his dad's neck.

In order to be genuine, a relationship has to be mutual. I think we, too, can touch God's heart as we give unselfishly to Him. After all, He is so good to take time for us whenever we need it or want it!

It has been said that the amount of time that we spend with someone indicates the worth we ascribe to that individual. With this in mind, there are probably people whom we do not value as much as we should. A great deal can be accomplished when leaders extend even a little attention on someone else. How we all need to share with each other. Probably in the end, we'll be getting much more than we give.

Want my lollipop? I haven't licked it.

IF THE SPIRIT WERE TO LEAVE
Read Zechariah 4:1-6.   *January 30*

If the Holy Spirit were to be removed from the earth today, I wonder how much of what we label as "God's work" would continue. How many churches would still have their doors open? Which church programs would still be operating? How many sermons would be preached from the pulpits next Sunday? Which Sunday School lessons would be taught? What would we still be trying to accomplish on our own? It's a sobering thought.

In Zechariah 4:6, the Lord said to Zerubbabel, "Not by might, nor by power, but by my Spirit, says the Lord Almighty." God desires to accomplish His works by His own Spirit.

Many times we exert much energy in trying to make something happen. We get an idea and then set about trying to bring it into reality. We strain, extending ourselves and working very hard. If there could just be more time or resources or influence, we think there would be greater results. How frustrating it can be to toil and then not see much effect.

The answer is not in gaining more power to force what is desired, however. Neither is it found in strength or position. Instead God wants us to look to Him. He alone is Almighty.

As we focus our hearts upon God, we come to see that what He purposes in His Spirit to do will certainly be accomplished. He has the means to do it. Whatever we try to do though will not be enough by itself. No matter how spectacular it might seem, work done without God is meaningless and not maximally effective.

Let us allow the Spirit to accomplish His work and stop frustrating ourselves by attempting to do the Lord's work on our own. In essence, God's real work stops when the Holy Spirit is not doing it! Everything else is a sham.

GOD'S WORK OR OURS?

Read Luke 4:40-44   *January 31*

Are we doing God's work or our own? If our own work is a good work, then it doesn't seem that there should be a distinction. If it doesn't involve a sinful action or motivation, then won't God be pleased? It should be enough that our work is done for the church or the poor. Surely God will be happy with it then. This reasoning is faulty, however.

The difficulty arises from the fact that God wants us to do what He desires. Instead, we often do something and then ask

Him to bless it. If we do what He wants, however, He will bless it automatically. We are making a mistake when we choose our own works by our own plans and then expect God to bring results out of them. Just because something is a good work or is not directly sinful does not mean that it is specifically what God desires to accomplish. It may not be His best choice.

This is particularly important when it comes to the church calendar. We may add events or programs that are pleasant, but are they God's desires? Are these how He wants us to expend our energy? Will they bring about maximum results in the Lord's work? Will people get saved or grow in the knowledge of Him? Will the events be effective from God's point of view? Is the timing correct? Has God gone before us to prepare the way?

These are critical questions if we are to be Christians who are doing God's work, not just our own. Otherwise we labor so hard and get tired out for nothing. We are busy doing good things, but not God's things. This difference is profound. It is the reason we sometimes feel burned out.

"Oh, God, I need to do things Your way! Help me to stop wasting my energy and time on what is not Your desire or plan."

FEBRUARY

THE LORD OF THE WORK

Read II Samuel 7:5-16.   *February 1*

David was eager to build a house for God, but the problem was that God didn't have this in mind. He enjoyed David and desired to spend time with him. The Lord wanted to build David's house instead.

The Lord of the work must always come before the work of the Lord. As we think through the implications of this statement, the concept takes on profound dimensions.

Sometimes we get so involved doing works for God that we miss God Himself. We can attend a church event, but not regard the Lord while we are there. We can have fellowship with other people, but not relate with God. We can go through the motions of a church service and not touch the Lord or allow Him to minister to us. It is also easy to worship in such a way that it is dictated by habit and not by our hearts.

At times, I find that there is a kind of veil or wall between God and me. As I sit in a church service, it seems as though God wants to remove that and come close. But I am afraid. I worry that I may cry or that I might be embarrassed. I may not want to hear what God has to say to me if I let Him get too close.

We have a tendency to hide ourselves from God, skirting those face-to-face confrontations that could be life-changing. Because of this drift away from the Lord, it is really easier to stay involved in "God's work"—doing things "for" Him—while all along He just wants us to sit down and be with Him. We stay busy with good deeds so we don't have to lay our hearts out on

41

the altar and allow God to touch our lives.

Let us not become so busy with the work of God that we miss taking time for the Lord Himself. We desperately need to spend time *with* God, not just doing things *for* Him. The Lord of the work should take priority over the work of the Lord. If this does not happen, the work will be impotent.

TEA BAGS

Read Exodus 14:5-14 (and through the
end of the chapter if you have the time).   *February 2*

A leader is like a tea bag. His true strength comes out under hot water. Want to know what you're made of on the inside? Then exert pressure and heat on the outside, and you'll discover what comes out into the open.

Often we do not know how strong we really are until a crisis occurs. Suddenly, we find an inner strength from God that arises, along with wisdom, peace, and faith. God is there, giving us what we need to lead the people.

When the Israelites were fleeing from Egypt, they became terrified as they saw the Egyptians marching after them. Crying out in fear, they actually wanted to go back to their slavery. However, Moses had the inner fortitude to stand firm and tell them not to be afraid. He promised the people that God would deliver them.

What a brave promise that was. Danger was imminent, but the leader did not give up. Instead, he became stronger. Where did he discover the inner fortitude to stand up to them all and make these courageous and almost silly promises? Where did he find the faith? How could he come up with a statement such as "The Lord will fight for you; you need only to be still"? This is not logical.

Often, leaders have to stand by themselves against incredible odds. They don't have all the answers and, just like Moses, they could never even guess what God might do. After all, whoever heard of extending a staff and seeing a major river part? Even today, God is still coming to the rescue and accomplishing what we cannot even begin to imagine.

As a leader, what approach are you going to take? When the going gets tough, will you simply give up? That option seems both logical and necessary at times. However, it does not take into consideration who God is. We forget about His power, His creativity, and His ability to perform the impossible in the face of unbelievable odds.

As we trust in God, He will provide us with all that we need. However, it is critical that we arise and take a stand. In the end, what we need will be there in the midst of the pressure. God will perform a miracle, and the people will place their trust in Him and in their leader (verse 31).

HOME ALONE
Read Galatians 1:6-10, I Corinthians 1:10-11
and II Corinthians 13:1-10.   *February 3*

When a church is without a pastor for a time or a business is without a leader, the results are often interesting to observe. Sometimes the dynamics of such a situation resemble those of children at home for a few days without their parents. Without direction, disorganization can easily reign. Cooperation may be reduced, with each person going his own way. Little is accomplished, and vision and goals are easily lost.

Children alone eat whatever they want. Meals are not likely to be balanced. Vegetables may get eliminated, and ice cream and candy bars can rule the day. Time may be squandered, spent in watching TV and videos rather than studying or doing chores.

In adult life, the same kind of sweet-tooth mentality may crop up in sermons, agendas for meetings, discipline, and goal-setting. Wasted time can bring a whole organization grinding to a halt or a slow crawl. Wild ideas can abound, some of which may collapse or even bring bedlam to the entire group. People who shouldn't be in charge of anything may be allowed to slip into the leadership slots while chaos reigns. It might not even be noticed for a while where the locus of control has actually shifted.

This scenario can easily become the next sequel to "Home Alone." Siblings can get in tiffs, with fights and rivalries developing. Standards and established rules of order get twisted around. The enemy may still be staved off, but the house can be a disaster by the time a parent finally returns.

Some good examples of the "Home Alone" situation turned up repeatedly in Paul's epistles. When he left a church, error and lack of discipline were apt to creep in, and then he had to exert leadership all over again. It was time for correction and order to be reestablished. Sometimes it's just not easy being a leader!

CHARACTER

Read II Chronicles 16:7-9. (Read all of chapters 15 and 16 for important context)   *February 4*

Since leadership is often lonely and isolated, it is a particularly dangerous place to serve. A leader can easily become deceived because there are few people who will provide a reality check. After all, who wants to risk confronting their supervisor? It is quite easy for leaders to hide, simply shrugging off any confrontations they do receive. Hypocrisy can develop easily when the secret self becomes different from the public self.

I once heard it said that "character is what you are when no one is looking." Although we may be able to conceal it for a long time, ultimately our true characters will come out for all to see. In crises, we often discover what we are really made of because we are so severely tested. Sometimes it surprises us what we discover, both for good and for ill.

What do we really believe and how deep does it go? What comprises our actual priorities? How much do we really trust the Lord? As we endure a crisis, we find answers which we never knew before.

When the heat is on, other people observe our true characteristics. We uncover what is inside us as we decide whether or not we will make ethical choices, do what is right no matter what the cost, and obey God completely.

Asa has always fascinated me. His first years as king were excellent. He took some tough stands for 35 long years, and then circumstances changed. Somehow, in secret during those years, Asa's trust in God diminished. When we find him in crisis with King Baasha, his colors unfurl. Instead of trusting in God, he looks to another king.

In II Chronicles 16:9, we note a marvelous verse. Think about what it is really saying. "For the eyes of the Lord range throughout the earth to strengthen those whose hearts are fully committed to him." God Himself is looking around, searching throughout the entire world. He is trying to find that person of character who in secret has set his heart completely on the Lord. For such people, when the times get rough, the true nature of their characters will be revealed...for the good.

What about you? What are you made of deep down inside in those hidden places? Are you ready for that answer to be made public?

A LONG OBEDIENCE

Read II Chronicles 15:1-2.   *February 5*

A number of years ago, Eugene Peterson published a book with the great title, *A Long Obedience in the Same Direction*. That phrase has greatly strengthened me throughout my ministry.

It's no news: Leaders are often tempted to quit. The number who actually do seems quite large sometimes. They start out with a burst of zeal and enthusiasm, but mid-course this begins to wane. They get tired, worn out, disillusioned. The newness wears off, and the plodding is interminable.

The crux of the matter is often reduced to obedience. Will you or won't you? Each day you have to decide. As the days mount up and the years are stacked, the journey seems so long.

However, when once a leader has set his face toward God, he simply needs to keep moving in the same direction, over and over again. It reminds me of the description of Gideon and his three hundred men in their fight against the Midianites. In Judges 8:4, they are described as "exhausted yet keeping up the pursuit."

In yesterday's verses, we saw Asa involved in many good actions and reforms. We also discovered how Asa ended by not looking to God. Indeed, during the thirty-ninth year of his reign, Asa had a disease in his feet, and scripture informs us that "though his disease was severe, even in his illness, he did not seek help from the Lord, but only from the physicians" (II Chronicles 16:12).

Before this, Asa was warned in 15:1-2 through a prophet. "The Lord is with you when you are with him. If you seek Him, He will be found by you, but if you forsake him, he will forsake you."

So come now. Will you stay with God, continuing to look to Him and trust Him? Will you keep seeking Him, or will you forsake Him? This decision in the middle of the journey is critical. Keep on choosing that long obedience, headed in the same direction.

Work cited: Peterson, Eugene H. *A Long Obedience in the Same Direction: Discipleship in an Instant Society.* Downers Grove, IL: InterVarsity Press, 2000.

MID-WAY

Mid-way through anything is a dangerous point. If it's a project, just the initial enthusiasm and creative flow alone can carry us half-way. Then reality sets in, and the work becomes more difficult and plodding. The real mark of a leader is shown at this tedious mid-point.

Paul realized this truth, also. In these verses, he states that even though he has gained a great deal, it is still not all that can be obtained. He describes himself as continuing to press on, seeking to take hold of absolutely everything that God has in store for him.

Lately, I have noted that defectors are abounding in leadership circles, particularly during mid-life. Although this problem is complex and there are undoubtedly a variety of causes, I think a lot of people just wear out. What a tragedy this is!

Many people start off well, but then they don't perform like they felt they should. Success, as they define it, has eluded them. They have lost sight of the meaning of their work, and they have expended a great deal of effort for what they consider to be a meager return. Where was their shining day?...the applause of the crowd?...the great example they had hoped to be? Plain, normal, tired, unnoticed.....is this all there is to life?

Paul, however, stirs us to forget what lies behind. We are to put aside our mistakes and failures, our disappointments and unfulfilled dreams. We also are asked to place behind us our successes and accomplishments, because even these aren't enough for tomorrow.

Then, we are to press on, moving forward and reaching toward whatever God has for us in the future. We are not to stop trying. Rather, we are to keep going on with consistency, refreshing ourselves in the Lord, and finding renewed strength and creativity for each new day.

Remember, we are aiming toward heaven. A prize awaits us

there if we finish the race (I Corinthians 9:24-27). Let's keep straining to finish the course and at the same time to win. Press on, and don't give up now!

WORKED VERY HARD

Read Romans 16:1-3, 6, 12.   *February 7*

Paul's personal list of greetings is quite extensive in Romans 16, and each person who is mentioned seems to have made a contribution to the work of the Lord.

In this chapter, four women are noted for "working hard": Mary (verse 6), Tryphena and Tryphosa (verse 12), and Persis (verse 12). This is quite a compliment, for Paul valued work that was accomplished "in the Lord," work that was done under the Lord's guidance and direction.

Also in this chapter, Paul complimented Phoebe for being "a great help to many people, including me" (verse 2), and Priscilla and Aquilla were noteworthy as Paul's "fellow workers" who even risked their lives for him (verse 3).

Paul greatly appreciated people who were "sold out" to the cause of Christ, just as he was. He valued those who had their commitments straight. These are the kind of people who someday will "win the prize." They have exerted extra effort, strained forward, pressed in. They have looked toward heaven and gone after that which will last into eternity.

Often, people who are busy in the work of the Lord are misunderstood. Others wonder why they don't lounge around, watch TV a little more, make room for recreation, and learn to waste a little time. Don't get me wrong; I believe in balance. However, when we're talking about God's work, how can we really do much lounging about? It's like letting up in the race, sitting down by the sidelines, and becoming a spectator.

No, personally, I'd rather keep running. I prefer to spend my time on something that will be eternal. I'd rather have the "prize" of seeing people won to the Lord and opportunities to minister into the hearts and lives of believers. How much more rewarding it is to spend a half an hour in prayer than to watch some insipid sit-com.

Let's continue working hard, pouring out all we've got. The stakes are really high...all the more reason to keep our eyes on the prize and be sold out believers!

WORRY

Read Philippians 4:4-9.   *February 8*

Leadership has something that is never missing: Things we could worry about! It seems that leaders get more than their fair share. They are the ones who hear everyone's complaints. Often sandwiched in the middle from those above and below them—whether it's board members, supervisors, workers, children or department heads—leaders hear everything.

What do we do with all this, anyway? Many times, we are the ones who are looked to for a solution, so we have to think about it. Furthermore, the concerns are often serious ones which we cannot neglect. How can we not worry about these things?

Philippians 4 gives us a door that opens up some answers to this question. First of all, we are commanded (twice!) to rejoice. This is a powerful tool, for as we focus on the Lord in every single circumstance, we are reminded of His might and power, His love for us and these other people, and His sovereign control over everything. The Lord is nearby and not far away. As we look to Him, God provides wisdom and begins to work in the midst of the difficulties. We are not meant to mope around downcast and downhearted, but rather we are asked to rejoice in the Lord.

Secondly, we are told not to get anxious about anything but rather to turn every single concern over to the Lord in prayer. By talking things over with God, a great burden can be lifted. He invites us to present our requests to Him and to thank Him for His care and future answers.

As we act in these ways, the peace of God will warm us and will calm our troubled minds. It's peace we don't entirely understand because the situation is still difficult. However, as we allow His serenity to permeate our lives, He guards our hearts and our minds, our emotions and our thinking. We can concentrate on what is positive and the awesome "God of peace" will stave off the worry.

Frankly, anything else is sin. When we continue to worry, we are actually saying that we don't trust God, that He doesn't care, that He is not in control. So stop worrying and look to the Lord. Just do it!

ATROPHY OR A TROPHY?
Read II Timothy 4:1-8. *February 9*

Atrophy is a natural law unless exertion is made to counteract it. Skills and talents, disciplines and learning we had once gained will all deteriorate without use.

We are told to "be prepared in season and out of season," ready for whatever God has for us. Preaching and teaching, correction and encouragement are all to be at the surface of our lives and readily available for our immediate use. We are to keep our heads on straight and to endure whatever difficulties might arise in our lives, continuing to discharge our duties in ministry and leadership. Though this may be a costly sacrifice, these moves keep us from atrophying.

Because Paul had experienced these things and had not given up in the fight, he knew that he had successfully finished the race. With complete assurance, he could say that he had kept the faith. Even when he hadn't felt like it, he had continued on anyway.

When tempted to give up, he had pressed on instead. When the pressure seemed too great and collapse appeared to be inevitable, he chose to keep running.

Think about the joy of Paul as he made the triumphant comment that he had kept the faith. He knew he was a winner, as opposed to someone who had defected, quitting in the middle of the battle. Paul had his eyes on that trophy. He could picture that "crown of righteousness" which the Lord would award him in heaven.

Sometimes we do not place such a reward clearly enough in our minds. We lose focus on the prize. Perhaps we feel it is prideful to think about this or maybe we simply have a weak picture of heaven. However, I believe God would encourage us to keep our eyes on that trophy—to run hard to win it. Without this goal in our minds, it is far too cozy to sit down on the job. Which will it be? Atrophy or a trophy?

KNOWING GOD'S WILL

Read Psalm 40:7-8.   *February 10*

One of the most difficult tasks of life is trying to decipher what God is doing with us. It's so hard to see the whole picture. Every so often, when we do get a glimpse of the future, our hearts leap, and we want to see more of that picture. However, we might well ask why we want to know the will of God anyway. Just to know it, or to do it.

Knowing God's will for their lives is a topic that consumes a good portion of the thinking of the college-age students with whom I work. They stew and fret, wanting to know what God has in mind regarding their future. I remind them that if they actually did discover His total plan for their lives, they likely wouldn't be able to handle it. They'd see the plan as far too difficult and run away from it as quickly as possible. At this early stage in their lives, they can't yet conceive of how God is going to prepare them so they will some day be ready for it all.

Or perhaps they wouldn't believe God's total plan because presently, in the midst of their inadequacies, they can't begin to picture themselves doing this. They haven't yet seen how God can use them in the midst of their weaknesses. Furthermore, there are too many pieces missing in the puzzle, and it is almost impossible to figure how God will bring this all to pass.

Even if we did see what God has in store for us, the temptation might be to raise up the vision in our own power or strength. We might not rely on God and allow Him to do the work.

God prefers for us to wait on Him, trusting in Him day by day. His will for our lives today is for us to serve Him, obey Him, know Him, wait in His presence, and become what He wants us to be. This is enough for now. When we do it, everything else will fall into place.

DOING GOD'S WILL

Read I Thessalonians 5:16-18.   *February 11*

One time when I was preaching a message in our chapel, I began by announcing to the university students that I could tell each and every one of them, unequivocally, what God's will was for their lives. I waited for the inevitable chuckle to ripple through the audience. Then I grinned.

"Well, I know what you're thinking," I laughed. "You're thinking that Dr. T. has really flipped this time. She's not omniscient! She's not God! If I come up to her, she can't possibly tell me, 'God's will for your life is to go to the mission field in Africa' and 'You over there are to be an evangelist' and 'God wants you to be a youth pastor.' But that's not what I said," I went on. "Turn to I Thessalonians 5:16-18."

52

In these verses, Paul clearly delineated God's plan for us today. "Rejoice always," he begins. This is not easy. When trials, difficulties, and suffering come, it is not natural to be joyful.

However, there is a difference between joy and happiness. Happiness is based on circumstances, but joy is based on a trust in the almighty, sovereign God. We know He will help us get through the hard times. Ultimately, positive changes can result in our growth and development, such as perseverance, proven character, and hope. We find our foundation stands, and we don't have to wimp out.

"Pray without ceasing," Paul goes on to say. This does not mean to spend all day on our knees, but rather to develop a lifestyle of being open to God, abiding in Him and developing a listening heart.

"In everything give thanks," Paul finally directs. We are to have good attitudes, not grumbling and grumping, complaining or murmuring. Paul explains that God wants us to be thankful for what we have. "This is the will of God for you in Christ Jesus," he states.

As we rejoice and trust in God, we develop a strength to do what God wants of us. We will hear His still, small voice directing us as we pray without ceasing. And our sweet spirits and good attitudes will put us in a position to be used. God's will in our lives will arise automatically out of these things. We just can't miss it if we follow the directions.

PERCEPTION OR DECEPTION
Read II Corinthians 4:2.   *February 12*

"Perception is the ultimate reality." So goes a familiar marketing maxim. Well, when it comes to sales and products, this is probably the case. The perception of value can seal a sale, and once purchased, the perception of quality can heighten the satisfaction level of the buyer.

When we consider a leader, however, perception is not enough. Some leaders don't believe this. They work hard on their image, polishing it to perfection. They are concerned with their clothes, their smooth manner, their demeanor, their voice tone and level, their smile and composure. With great control, they are self-contained and careful in their communication.

Sadly, perception of a leader can crack as easily as it can with a product. If a buyer purchases a product based on a false perception, then this will be discovered upon use. The product will not be soft enough, strong enough, efficient enough, beautiful enough. A dissatisfied buyer will not re-purchase the product, and word may spread to friends and relatives. Likewise, a leader who bases everything on perceived image will find the same reaction from disillusioned followers.

It is also difficult to place trust in such a leader. After all, what are they really like? Are they actually as "together" as their image portrays? What's truly going on behind that polished exterior? Are they that perfect? Don't they ever feel anything, cry, or lose it? Are they real?

Why spend so much time and energy trying to be something we are not? Ultimately, the facade will crack; the false front will fall; the uncostumed actor will stand alone.

People do not like to be deceived. When the truth finally comes out, anger against the deceiver is likely. Just be yourself. Aren't you all right that way?

LIVING AND ACTIVE

Read Hebrews 4:12-13.   *February 13*

Not only is it possible to deceive others, but we ourselves can even be deceived. We can rationalize away our sin, justify it, or minimize it. We can even be unaware of our sin, covering it over by the complexities of our thinking and our emotions.

Here is a main reason why we must keep reading the Word of God. Rather than being a dead book, the *Bible* is living and active. As we read and consider God's Word, the Lord takes it and thrusts it into our hearts. It cuts two directions, going to the depths where nothing else can penetrate.

Whereas words from other people may help us, their effect is less pervasive and not as long-lasting. God's Word goes so deep that the very thoughts and attitudes of the heart are judged. We may think we're acting a certain way, but a well-timed scripture can convict us that we are not, that we have actually deceived ourselves. Or perhaps we think our motives are pure, but God's Word points out that they are not as unselfish as we had originally thought. Or we may be deceived into thinking that our wrong attitudes are really justified under the circumstances, but a certain scripture verse shows us that this simply is not true.

The *Bible* pierces to the kernel in the center of it all. Suddenly, we understand what sin in our soulish nature has negatively affected our spiritual lives. The most minor distinctions of our inner lives are laid bare.

After all, God sees and knows it all anyway. There's no fooling Him. That's a major truth about deception. As much as we don't want to face up to the reality of our sin, some day we're going to have to do it. God will uncover everything, and our lives will be open. What was done in secret will be shouted from the housetops. Deception will no longer be possible.

So why not let God do His work now? Let the Word speak deep into your life.

VALIDATION

Read John 5:31-47.   *February 14*

Not all people will believe the truth, not even if it is right before them in living color. Jesus had an interesting problem. How could He help others to understand that He was really the Son of God? It couldn't be simply because certain people said so. Jesus knew that human testimony was fickle, often incomplete in its understanding and articulation, and therefore not to be relied upon. Because of this, Jesus did not accept praise from man (verse 41).

Think about how often we not only accept but even desire the praise of men. It can become a validation to us that we are doing well. It can even seem like a stamp of approval for our work and our very selves, authenticating our existence.

Jesus, however, had a different insight on this, one from which leaders could glean much insight. "I have testimony weightier than that of John," He said. "For the very work that the Father has given me to finish and which I am doing, testifies that the Father has sent me" (verse 36).

Although it was nice that John the Baptist understood Jesus to be the Son of God, Jesus didn't count on this for proof of His deity. True, John the Baptist's testimony was one that many people wanted to hear. John had prepared the way for the Savior, preaching repentance and baptizing people. Undoubtedly He was sensitive to spiritual things, and so His testimony regarding the Messiah was certainly a valuable one.

Jesus, however, minimized even this human testimony. Jesus explained that if people wanted an even weightier proof, then they should look at His work. He was doing what God wanted Him to do. It was the purpose of His life to finish that work. If His work was studied, people would understand that the Father had sent Him.

Jesus was more concerned with the praise of God than the praise of men. He did what the Father desired of Him so that God would be happy with His work. It did not matter whether people liked what Jesus did or not. What counted was what God thought.

And you? Do you delight in the praise of men and adjust

what you choose to do according to what will please certain people? If so, then when men do not praise you, it will be tempting to become discouraged and give up the work.

We need to know what God wants us to accomplish and focus upon this on a consistent basis. In the final count, it is His praise—and His alone—that will matter. Listen to what He is saying to you. Finish that work.

THE HUMAN LAWNMOWER
Read Daniel 4.   *February 15*

One of the greatest dangers of leadership is in the power we wield. The more we use it, the easier it is to take it for granted.

We can become blind to the effort that others expend in order to accomplish our needs or whims. A leader can give an assignment to someone else, and the next day the report appears on the desk. The cost of getting it there is of little concern.

We can also get used to people agreeing with us. Perhaps we have those who will dare to contradict us, but even they have learned when to back off. How many times have I heard employees in various settings say, "Oh, well, he's the boss. Just do what he says."

It's true that someone has to make the final decision and not everyone will like it, but this maxim can also be an excuse for us to get our way. Subtly we can use our power for selfish reasons, manipulating and controlling in such smooth ways that it is barely even noticeable.

So if we're in charge, who will stop our misuse of power? Nebuchadnezzar discovered that God had an answer to this question. King Nebuchadnezzar had "become great and strong," and his dominion extended "to the distant parts of the earth" (verse 22). What a powerful man.

He knew it, too. One day, as he was surveying his domain,

57

he said, "Is not this the great Babylon I have built as the royal residence, by my mighty power and for the glory of my majesty?" (verse 30). The power had gone to his head, and his egocentric use of it was not pleasing to God. The Lord decided to remove his royal authority then and there.

The great king "flipped out," as we might say in the vernacular. He became a human lawnmower, eating grass like the cattle. His royal coiffure looked more like eagles' feathers, and his nails became like claws. Where was that manicurist? Not a pretty sight, this king.

When we wield power with abandon for personal gain and glory, it is abominable in the sight of God. After all, He is the one who has the power and glory. We should never act as though these attributes belong to us.

Let us beware of the subtleties that can lead us into a misuse of power, or we, too, might just discover what it is like to mow the lawn...with our teeth!

FRUIT

Read Matthew 7:15-20.   *February 16*

I always find our apple trees interesting to observe. Those wee little apples of the spring keep expanding until they are fully grown and deliciously sweet "honey goldens."

Jesus said, "By their fruit you will know them" (verse 16). He was talking about being able to distinguish false prophets from the true ones. We might be fooled by a disguise if a wolf comes to us in sheep's clothing. However, the fruit test never fails.

After all, no one can tape fruit on to a tree. I suppose a person could try, but it would have to be quite spectacular tape to hold the fruit on to that branch for any length of time. Sooner or later, the weight of the fake fruit would get the better of the deception—or the fruit would rot.

Delicious fruit can only be produced from vigorous sap flowing through a sound tree. As a matter of fact, a good fruit tree can't help but yield fruit. With little visible effort, it will naturally produce. Growing fruit is what the tree is all about.

No matter how hard it tries, furthermore, fruit cannot grow out of a thornbush, a thistle, or a dead tree. If the tree is bad, it simply will not bear fruit.

The fruit of the Spirit is listed in Galatians 5:23 and is singular in number (*fruit* of the Spirit) because it all comes together out of the Holy Spirit. We cannot be satisfied that we have one fruit, but not something else. If we are living in the Spirit, it will all come in its entirety. This fruit includes love, joy, peace, patience, kindness, goodness, faithfulness, gentleness, and self-control. If these are missing in someone's life, beware! They should be expanding, becoming like wonderfully delicious "honey golden" apples.

In contrast, the acts of the sinful nature are enumerated right above this list in Galatians 5:19-21. They are sexual immorality, impurity and debauchery, idolatry and witchcraft, hatred, discord, jealousy, fits of rage, selfish ambition, dissensions, factions and envy, drunkenness, orgies and the like.

Besides listing some gross and obvious sins, there are many in this list which have to do with the breaking up and tearing apart of positive connections between people. In fact, the majority of the sins in this list are concerned with relationships and deeply affect other people. Whoever is involved in such activities is in great danger.

Let us beware of such a person, for by their fruit we can know them. A thornbush with fruit attached by tape is still a thornbush!

HEAD TO HEAD

Read Psalm 37:7-17.   *February 17*

Sooner or later in life, we will come face to face with a wolf in sheep's clothing, someone who has deceitfully tried to tape on fruit. I remember vividly having had to work with such a colleague. This person could smile on the outside and appear to be so kind, yet turn around and stab you in the back. He cunningly subverted whatever he could. Since he was both slick and smooth, it all took a while to be noticed. In the meantime, he had spread many lies and created much upheaval and destruction.

While I was in the midst of this study of human nature, I finally came to the place where I recognized his use of power. Simply put, he had to have it. He would do anything to get it: manipulation, conniving, subtle power plays, and brute force. Confronted with such a compulsion for power, who can stand up in the face of it?

That, in fact, is the problem. If the victim comes back with a show of force, such a power-hungry individual as we are discussing simply has to exhibit more. Soon both individuals are going at it head to head, each person trying to outdo the other one. The situation continues to escalate. The formerly innocent person becomes ensnared in the power game and gets trapped in the ultimate explosion that is bound to take place.

Psalm 37 gives us clear directions on what to do in such a case: Don't get entangled in power plays. We are told not to get angry or to fret because this "leads only to evil." The tactics of the enemy are not to be absorbed into our lifestyles.

Rather, as we wait and trust in God, He will handle the situation. "For evil men will be cut off," the Psalm promises. "A little while and the wicked will be no more." This is what happened to the person I mentioned earlier. He made a mistake, showed his true colors, and was gone in 24 hours.

The wicked may plot against the righteous, gnash their teeth at them, and draw the sword to stab them in the back. However, God's power is above theirs. Jesus knew this to be true when He overcame Satan, not by playing into his power games, but by humbly dying. Ultimately, God will ensure that the righteous and the meek will inherit the land. The Lord will see to it that the power of the wicked is broken. Don't go head to head; it leads only to destruction.

DOMINANCE

Read I Samuel 18:1-16.   *February 18*

The need to dominate is a driving force. It can hound us into great sin. Various examples are given throughout scripture of persons with just such a deep-seated need.

Saul allowed his drive for domination to have free rein and thereby suffered serious consequences. He sought to be totally in charge, on top, in control. He desired all of the praise and wanted to be thought of as more distinguished in every way than any other person.

The word "dominant" is derived from the Latin word *dominus* which means lord or god. Indeed, Saul wanted people to consider him in just such a way. As Christians, we may not want to admit this secret desire because it seems so blatantly appalling. However, at the core of power, control, and dominance is the desire to be a demi-god. We might couch it in many ways; however, we must all face this tendency in ourselves so it can be rooted out.

Saul didn't do that. When David won a huge victory over the Philistines, for example, Saul was galled instead of being happy. Why? Because people sang a little ditty that shared the news, "Saul has slain his thousands, and David his tens of thousands." Saul should have been pleased that he was mentioned — and even mentioned first — in this refrain. Instead, he was upset that he was not ascendant in the number attributed to him.

Then he grew jealous. He threw a temper tantrum and became infuriated. He allowed rivalry to rule his attitude towards David...all because he wanted to be on top.

Furthermore, he tried to pin David to the wall with his spear.

61

Why do that? To show that he was in charge. To control. To dominate. Although it isn't accomplished with an actual spear, people today still attempt to pin others to the wall in order to demonstrate their superiority. They gloat over "winning that one."

Saul himself became obsessed by the thought of David and also afraid of him. Saul didn't want to lose his power or his popularity, and so he held on to it so tightly that it resulted in an evil spirit coming "forcefully upon Saul." Not confronting this need for controlling circumstances as well as other people can result in dreadful consequences.

Leaders, beware! We, too, might begin our leadership by hiding behind the baggage (I Samuel 10:20-24), but end up consumed with maintaining dominance. It's not a pretty journey.

I'M WRONG

Read Proverbs 28:13.   *February 19*

My parents had a funny saying that they would sometimes use during a spat: "I may not always be right, but I'm never wrong."

How difficult it can be simply to admit that we are wrong. Our rationalizing abilities come into play. We may think, "Well, if only this hadn't happened, then I wouldn't have behaved like that." Or "If that person hadn't driven me to it by what he said, we wouldn't have this situation." We all hate to come to grips with just flat-out being wrong! It hurts our pride.

It's all right to make a mistake, you know.   Do you know? Leaders are often such perfectionists that they honestly don't know this, not deep down. To make a mistake is a terrible thing in their eyes. To them, it may even affect their continued ability to lead. After all, how can people trust a leader who makes mistakes?

Quite well, I might say! Leaders do not have to be perfect. The only perfect person who ever walked this earth was Jesus

Christ. We are all entitled to make errors in judgment, let our flaws show through, be at fault.

Not only will this be inevitable, but we ought to be secure enough to admit it. How pitiful it is to watch the gyrations of a leader as he tries to squirm out of an error. He can misuse his power and blame someone else. He can dig in his heels and insist that he did the correct thing all along. He may deny that the mistake ever happened or make it appear that everything was planned this way all along. Or he can stay close-mouthed and look strong, pretending that everything is fine and hoping that sooner or later everyone will forget.

None of these methods for dealing with error is healthy. Each one actually induces distrust among followers. They say, "If he's not telling the truth about this mistake, I wonder what else he is covering up?" So what's so bad about apologizing?

Spending time with God and confessing our sins before Him helps in this ability to be honest regarding our faults. We find that He loves us and accepts us anyway. This makes us secure enough to be able to come out of ourselves and admit, "Yes, I was wrong." Do it the next chance you get! That'll probably be soon....

FILE RAILS

Read Proverbs 19:11 and 17:22.   *February 20*

The file cabinet arrived without rails, and the width of the large file cabinet mandated hanging files. The maintenance department told me that they would find some rails to fit and get them installed.

Throughout the college year I stuffed the files in, finding it difficult to locate what I needed with the weight of the files falling over on each other. As the year came to a close, I was chatting with a colleague who supervised the maintenance department and mentioned that I wished they could get those rails installed after all these months.

The next day my secretary came to me and said that the head of maintenance had called. He had apologized for the missing rails and said he had thought they had been installed long ago. I raised an eyebrow and pulled out a file drawer. Was it possible?

I looked into the drawer, and there, right before my eyes, were the hanging file rails all installed beautifully. I had been frustrated with that file cabinet all year long, and the rails had been there all along!

I was embarrassed, of course. How could I have missed this? Why hadn't I noticed them? Had they been installed while I had been on a business trip? That must have been the case, I concluded. The thought ran through my mind that I could blame them for not telling me they had completed the work. However, it was also possible that they had told me and with my busy schedule, it simply hadn't lodged in my consciousness. What should my reaction be?

Well, I started to laugh! I called the head of maintenance and told him that the rails were indeed in the filing cabinet. I made fun of myself. I also called his supervisor and told her what had happened so she wouldn't think he had actually neglected the task.

We would all do well to be as kind as the maintenance man was. Also, we should continually try to have a sense of humor when it comes to ourselves. We do not need to be perfect, and, as a matter of fact, we can do some downright silly things. We need to laugh more and take ourselves more lightly. It's a giant step toward mental health!

CORRECTION

Read Proverbs 10:17 and 12:1.   *February 21*

Correction. What a difficult topic! It always reminds me of

the red pen on my returned English compositions.

Leadership, however, demands that we correct others. If we have a desire for quality, the ability to communicate correction becomes essential. Some leaders do it harshly and judgmentally. Unfortunately, this approach only induces resentment on the part of those who are corrected. They feel diminished and demotivated.

Many leaders, on the other hand, have learned to correct with savvy. They make suggestions that are happily accepted. The relationships they have built are solid, and the workers know they are valued and trusted. Therefore, correction does not come as a blow to their self-worth. Leader and worker can join together in solving a problem or in finding ways for employees to learn new skills so they can grow in needed areas. This approach can be most positive.

Often, leaders resist correcting people because they think this will mean using the first method described. They let others deliver their bad news for them. Or they talk about their employees behind their backs and get frustrated, not ever dealing directly with them about the problem, even in a performance review.

As we gain skills in correcting others, we as leaders also need to become more open to correction ourselves. These proverbs indicate that if we ignore correction, we can lead others astray. We continue making the same mistakes and model them to others who in turn follow our examples.

It is essential that we are personally open to correction, demonstrating how to weigh it and learn from it. We should invite input for change and not be defensive when it is given. Once an employee has enough courage to make suggestions to us, we shouldn't try to persuade them that we are correct. Nor should we insinuate that they are really the ones who need to change... or that they just need to adjust to us and get used to it. Actually, how we handle their suggestions will teach them much about how they should handle ours.

Have you developed a non-defensive attitude that promotes growth, communication, sharing of ideas, and mutual correction? Let us learn both to give and receive it with grace.

THE MARKSMAN

Read Isaiah 48:3-7.   *February 22*

I once heard a story of a man who was traveling in the rural West. In one town he saw targets all over, on trees and telephone poles and other such spots. Every single one of them had a bullet hole shot smack through the center.

Amazed, this man started asking around about who shot all the bullseyes. Finally, he was introduced to the man. "I'm so glad to meet you," he said. "You're an incredible shot! How did you get to be so good?"

The marksman smiled a sideways grin and said, "Oh, it's nothin', really. I just shoot first and then draw the bullseye around where I shot."

This occurs in leadership; I've seen it! As a matter of fact, if goals aren't publicly stated, then it's very easy to pull off this sham. No matter what the results, the leader can simply act as if he had aimed for them from the start. That way, he can pose as a competent and successful leader. He just sees what happens and then moves the target to match it.

God, however, does not draw the target later. In Isaiah 48, God states that He proclaims ahead of time what will happen. This way, it is clear that He alone deserves the credit and praise rather than some idol or person. God is in charge. The Lord actually puts up the target first, then shoots. He speaks forth His plan through the prophets, and then He brings it to pass.

No matter how much people may try to connive in order to stop God's prophetic word, He can act suddenly and bring it into reality. Sooner or later, His plan will transpire without fail. If there's a painful promise—like Isaiah's prophecy that the Jews would be taken captive by Babylon—we may stiffen our necks and try to stop it. But it will happen nonetheless.

If, on the other hand, the prophetic word is something we wish for, we may wait impatiently, wondering if it will ever occur. But we don't have to move the target. Just wait. There'll be a bullseye every time.

A STIFF NECK

Read Proverbs 29:1.   *February 23*

My experience gives evidence that God will attempt to deal with people regarding their faults and sin. I have known pastors who have fallen who had been clearly warned about the roots of their problems, years before they fell into disgrace. However, they did not choose to listen. They stiffened their necks, raised their chins, looked to the side, and would not repent and change.

Once, for several weeks, I literally had a stiff neck which was both painful and annoying. I prayed about this, rubbed in analgesic balm, took aspirin, and still it persisted. One night as I was praying, I began to pray about stiff-necked people. The Lord laid on my heart to intercede for a particular situation.

Over the next days I learned so much as I prayed for these people and experienced that stiff neck. I couldn't move easily, so I found that I walked as if I had on blinders, not looking much in various directions. My view was thereby limited. A low-grade headache nagged persistently, and there was little sense of freedom or joy. I didn't want to budge, and every move became calculated.

People who refuse to change after being rebuked, indeed act as if they are stiff-necked. They are not willing to turn. They will not look in the new direction that God has for them.

What will God do with those who are stiff-necked and do not want to listen? He will simply remove them. Proverbs even warns that they "will suddenly be destroyed—without remedy." There will be no way back. Someone can't say then, "Ok! OK! I'll change now! I see you mean it!" There will be no redress then.

If we do not give in to God's will and plan, it may be too late. God sees our stubbornness. He watches us as we do things our way and move the targets around to orchestrate everything exactly the way we desire. However, in the end, He will simply do what He wants: Bullseye! And our stiff necks may be snapped.

So remember, don't fight God. He is in charge anyway. Stubborn streaks are not popular with Him. Flex up! Do it the Lord's way.

SOVEREIGNTY

Read Isaiah 28:14-21.   *February 24*

Several weeks ago, my husband and I were in a terrible hailstorm. The hail was as large as baseballs, the biggest I have ever seen. We were inside a museum with several stories of glass windows which were being pelted by the horrible storm. Our car was dented in many places across the hood and top. All over town, car and house windows were bashed in. The damage was significant to crops and anything at all that had been left outside.

Whatever is outside of God's protection is likewise open to destruction. Our own scheming will get us nowhere. There is no place of safety except in taking the Lord as our refuge.

Indeed, God is over all. His reign is higher than every other reign. His kingdom is above all other domains. He is the One who is really in charge. Only by trusting in Jesus Christ can we truly be safe.

Personally, we may plot and scheme, but it will come to naught. We may cover every angle and think we cannot be touched, but we will be. We may be able to get by for a time with fronts and lies to our co-workers and employees, but ultimately, these can be ripped away. As Isaiah 28:17 states, "Hail will sweep away your refuge, the lie."

If we are stubborn and try to push through our own plans, it does not necessarily mean that what we desire will come to pass. As leaders, we may have become accustomed to getting our own way. We may know how to control and plot to make things happen. We may even have the power to get our wishes accomplished. However, in the end, we are not in charge.

What? Isn't that what leadership is all about—being in charge? Yes, but only because God has allowed it. He is the One with the ultimate authority. God alone is Sovereign! Isaiah and the other prophets call Him by this descriptor often. Just watch for this term in the scriptures, and you may well be surprised at just how often it comes up.

We have a Sovereign God who is ultimately in control of everything. Thinking otherwise is foolish. We shouldn't trust in ourselves or in anybody or anything else...but only in God. He will do what He wants. He can bring about the impossible. He alone is our Sovereign Lord.

POWERLESSNESS

Read Isaiah 42:1-3. *February 25*

Powerlessness is not a good feeling. How hard it is to watch some brash upstart sidle up to our supervisor and wheedle his way into favor. It doesn't seem right when someone else gets all the resources, and we can't seem to get much...but then we get penalized for not producing as well. It's tough when we need to fix a problem but the psychological or political dimensions of the situation leave us powerless to do so. It is not a comfortable state of affairs to have to watch while injustice prevails, without being able to do anything about it.

Actually, we shouldn't forget that it is not necessarily our place to right every wrong. Isaiah's prophecy regarding Jesus in today's verses indicates that it is His task to "bring justice to the nations."

We might get tired and feel defeated by trying to set things straight. But Isaiah stated that Jesus would bring forth justice "in faithfulness." We are even told that He would "not falter or be discouraged till he establishes justice on earth."

What good news this is! We cannot, nor are we expected to, make everything right. We can be salt and light. We can attempt to have an effect. We can speak out against what is wrong and try to influence events. In the end, however, the establishment of justice will only be accomplished by Jesus Christ.

We should wait patiently and not seek for a rod so we can beat people into submission. It is not God's plan to force justice into every situation at this time. If we try, our misuse of power will bring forth further sin.

We need to feel comfortable in our own powerlessness... knowing that God both has and deserves all the power, realizing that in the end He will definitely prevail. Take heart, and be of good courage. Trust in God!

A FUTURE

Read Jeremiah 29:11.   *February 26*

When we give ourselves up to a Sovereign Lord, we may feel as if we were reeling into a pit. How can we go somewhere if we don't have any control over our destinies? How can we accomplish anything if we don't have the power to make things happen? We feel as if we were throwing happiness and fulfillment to the wind. Why not just climb into a coffin and pull the top down over us?

Certainly it is a terrifying thing to place our whole lives into the hands of someone else, especially if the someone else is our God who is unseen. Perhaps we are not convinced that He actually has our best interests in mind. Does He care? Is He utilitarian? Will He use our lives without regard for our good? Could it be that He will sacrifice us? How painful will this be? What might He require of us?

I am convinced, however, that if sacrifice and pain should be asked of us, we can come through it better than we started...if we trust in the Lord. I didn't say "JUST trust in the Lord," as if this were a light and easy task. Sometimes it is extremely difficult and gripping! But a deep-seated and profound trust in a mighty, Sovereign God can become a strong foundation in our lives.

We can come to know He really loves us and others as well. We can begin to see His power at work. In Jeremiah 29:11, God said, "For I know the plans I have for you—plans to prosper you and not to harm you, plans to give you hope and a future."

Our Sovereign God has put together plans for us that we can barely imagine. We don't see the whole picture and probably couldn't understand it even if we did. But His plans are for our good. We will change and become more like Him. Our sin will fall away, and we will be lighter, better, more free and whole. God has never had a design to hurt us. Rather, when we see the plan all laid out someday, we will be able to understand that our hope and trust were not in vain. We will perceive that all along we have been laying up treasure for an incredible future.

HOPE

Read Romans 5:3-5.   *February 27*

No one likes to be tossed about on a raging sea when the storm is lashing out. We don't enjoy suffering. How helpless we feel!

Scripture, however, is informing on this subject. "We also rejoice in our sufferings," Romans 5:3 states. We do? How can we rejoice? Notice, this verse did not say that we are happy in our sufferings, but it does explain that a deep-seated joy can arise.

As we trust God through such times and hang in there, our sufferings produce perseverance. We can become more patient as we endure trials. Although we feel as though we might buckle under, we don't, because we are growing in our knowledge of God and of ourselves. Out of this ability to persist arise substantive character traits. We discover what we're like inside because we are tested, and what we are really made of is revealed. Our characters prove themselves to others, ourselves, and God.

Through trials, we learn to rely on God and His strength. We find that He is there for us and will be that solid rock through the storm. This knowledge brings hope. It's not just hope as in "I hope so" or "Maybe it will happen—do you suppose?" This word for hope means surety, a firm substance in which we can trust, a "light at the end of the tunnel," if you will. And we believe we will come out on the other side.

This kind of hope is most precious. You might wonder, "Do you mean to say that what I get at the end of all that suffering is something as simple as hope?" Correct. And it's worth it, too! At the end of it all, though we may be powerless and everything may be out of control, we have hope in a God we can trust completely.

Remember the song that goes "On Christ the Solid Rock I Stand"? Sing it. Right now. Go ahead.

OVERFLOWING

Read Romans 15:13.   *February 28*

When a leader loses hope, the effects reverberate through the system. It is amazing to see how rapidly hopelessness can spread through an organization or group. Usually accompanied by lethargy, cynicism, and confusion, the feeling of hopelessness can bring everything to a screeching halt. Perhaps that is why our enemy the devil tries to sow despair wherever he can.

Staying hopeful is not necessarily an easy task for a leader—especially when the circumstances cry out against it. Logic can speak loudly and clearly: Give up! You're going to lose it all in the end, anyway. This is impossible; it will never happen.

In the midst of such foreboding realities, the God of hope can enter the scene. He will fill the leader with all joy and peace. While others around him are falling apart, the leader who trusts in God will discover that deep sense of joy which is contagious. Instead of exhibiting nervous tension and hyper activity, such a leader can demonstrate a deep serenity. These, too, can permeate an organization. Soon such traits overflow, bringing hope.

I recall eating at a lovely boat restaurant in Toulouse, France, and finishing that delicious meal with an exotic dessert called "Ile Flottante." Translated "Floating Island," this wonderful light meringue floated in a pool of creme anglaise and was drizzled with caramel. I have sometimes linked this name, "Ile Flottante," with leadership in the isolation and loneliness that can occur. We can feel like a "floating island," letting circumstances move us where they will and allowing them to mandate our thinking.

Rather, we are to position ourselves firmly. We can trust in a God who understands us. Therefore, our lives can overflow with joy and peace as we exhibit, for all to see, the great hope that is possible in God.

AMBITION

Read I Thessalonians 4:11-12.   *Leap Year*

Ambition: What's yours? Search your heart right now, and answer that question before reading on.

Perhaps that was a difficult task, because our real ambitions are sometimes buried in our subconscious or mixed up with our motives. It's the areas we get disappointed about when we don't achieve them. Then we discover how much we really wanted that promotion, that title, that acknowledgment, that award or honor, that house, that particular achievement by our children, that fame.

What is your ambition down in your hidden self? I talked to someone the other day whose friend was disappointed that he had just missed being named a "Torchbearer" for his company. "Why wouldn't God let me have that honor?" he had asked.

However, God is not nearly as wrapped up in our ambitions as we are. We often become "invested" in areas that God views to be not nearly so important. This makes Paul's comment in Romans 15:20 even more amazing. "It has always been my ambition to preach the gospel where Christ was not known, so that I would not be building on someone else's foundation."

This is a wonderfully unselfish ambition, set on accomplishing something for the kingdom of God rather than for personal gain of any kind. Might our own ambitions be considered in this light. It is not wrong to have ambitions, but the question is whether or not they are centered upon ourselves or upon God and other people.

Another passage provides perspective to this concept. It says in I Thessalonians 4:11-12, "Make it your ambition to lead a quiet life, to mind your own business and to work with your hands, just as we told you, so that your daily life may win the respect of outsiders and so that you will not be dependent on anybody."

Personal honor may bring acclaim, but it also brings jealousy and competition. Winning respect from others is much more valuable than receiving a temporary honor. A person's lifestyle is ultimately more valuable than a momentary achievement. The quiet, internal, character-building traits win more respect over the long haul than the external "fluff."

So I ask you gain. What is your ambition? Perhaps more importantly, what would you like it to be?

MARCH

WHAT IS MAN?

Read Psalm 19:1-4.   *March 1*

March 1 finds most northerners extremely tired of winter. Nothing about the dreary season appears lovely in any way. Forget the Christmas wonderland; it's over. No more ice skating, sledding, snowmen, or ice fishing. The joy of it all has disappeared, and people yearn for flowers and sunshine. Folks get grumpy, wondering if any signs of life will ever arrive and fearing that they may be watching the July 4th fireworks from their snowmobiles.

This first day of March, however, was stunning. Hoarfrost had covered everything for miles. The usual dull trip to work wound through a world of unusual glory. Every tree and its branches, even the tiny twigs, were covered with frost and looked like lace. The pine trees, the bushes, even the straggly weeds were resplendent with a glittering beauty. The world was transformed!

In reflection, I realized that all this design had been there before—the intricate lacework of the trees and every little detail. I hadn't been able to see it, however. It took the frost to highlight the wonderful complexity.

Why is it so easy for us to miss the beauty of the world around us? God has indeed set His glory above the heavens, but we need to look up. The world He created is so large—the moon and the stars, the ocean and the wind—that it is hard to imagine He could care for man so much. We feel so insignificant.

75

That day on my resplendent road I pondered these sights and realized how God pays attention to detail. It just has to be highlighted with frost once in a while. We need to see it all and not just pass by. God cares about so many particulars, and we are inclined to miss them.

It is often our own fault if life becomes boring and dull. As we sigh about the routine of our "every days," we need to look afresh at the splendor of a winter morning and the wonder of God's work in our world. And yes, spring will arrive.... "How majestic is Your name!"

DIRT DESSERT

Read Romans 1:18-20. *March 2*

The recipe was intriguing. It included oreo cookies on the top and bottom, with a creamy pudding mixture in between. The oreo cookies made it look for all the world as though you were digging into a bowl of dirt.

The illusion was even more perfect when I got dozens of little flower pots, tied ribbons around them, and pushed silk flowers down into the "dirt dessert." It was fun, and all the guests enjoyed the little ruse.

It's not funny, though, when you realize that many people actually have dirt for dessert when it comes to morality. They enjoy sin and find it a treat.

Scripture tells us that God's wrath is being revealed against all godlessness and wickedness of men. This is a most serious warning. It's not popular to speak out against sin in our present society because too many people like it. They don't want to be told that they can't have dessert!

Unfortunately, their wickedness actually suppresses the truth. God is trying to reveal Himself to them, but they don't want to see it. Even in nature, God's flowers, rain, sky and all of creation speak out that there is a God. Instead, people choose the fake silk flowers "growing" in a pot of dirt dessert.

Romans 1:19 states that "what may be known about God is plain to them, because God has made it plain to them." It obviously took an eternal power greater than ourselves to create the world. A divine nature that is higher than our own must have conceived this place. It's so obvious, but people still don't want to face it, even when it's right before their eyes.

The result of this continued "squelching" of the truth is that people actually lose the wisdom, understanding, and insight that God has given them in the first place. They almost become "dumb" (or "dum" as a group of junior high students once spelled the word). They are unable to perceive what is right or wrong anymore and are incapable of understanding the truth that is so evident. They wind up selecting dirt dessert. Bon appetit!

THWARTED PLANS

Read Psalm 33:6-22.   *March 3*

Planning is a good activity—but only when we pursue it through prayer and then subject the results to the will of God. Down through the centuries, this truth has been repeatedly validated. Psalm 33 explores the differences between the purposes and plans of man and those of the Lord.

We must remember that Almighty God sees the big picture. Psalm 33:13-15 points out that He looks down from heaven and sees all of mankind, watching them and considering everything they do. He understands their motives and ideas because He formed the heart of each one. Nothing can be hidden from Him.

From man's incomplete vantage point, a leader's position can appear perfectly safe and uncontested. A king may survey his vast army and equipment and feel quite invincible. This is false security, however. As verses 16-17 explain, no one should trust in his own strength. Though a leader may feel that all is well by relying on holdings, attendance records, investments, or stock, in the end all these things can fail.

Planning must be submitted to God. "The Lord foils the plans of the nations; he thwarts the purposes of the peoples" (verse 10). Even though leaders may lay out the best plans and generate the most creative ideas, God can baffle them instantaneously. The Lord understands the secret purposes behind each move a leader makes, and in a moment, this strategizing can be set awry.

The ideal is to plan, create, and think with the Lord. "But the plans of the Lord stand firm forever, the purposes of his heart through all generations" (verse 11). Man's purposes can be selfish, evil, self-aggrandizing. Our motives for power, wealth, and fame may exist, even though they are hidden by rationalization or lack of self-understanding.

God, however, knows our hearts even better than we do. His purposes and plans are pure and based upon the total view. They are lodged in a heart of love for all mankind, and there is no doubt that His plans and purposes will remain firm forever. That is why we need to search for God's design and fit our plans into His. Only then can we have the confidence we need to lead.

LEADING THE WAY

Read Mark 10:32-45.   *March 4*

Jesus was resolute about going up to Jerusalem. He knew exactly what would happen there, and still He walked on. How could He march right into a situation that was a powder keg? He told His disciples that He would be betrayed and then condemned to death by the Jews. The Gentiles would mock Him, flog Him, and finally kill Him. Why didn't He run from this?

Not only did Jesus not give in to these forebodings; verse 32 tells us that He was "leading the way." What a picture this is! He

78

didn't just go along with the flow; He led it. The cup He was to drink and the cross He was to bear would demand everything, both for the Leader and ultimately for His disciples.

How do you respond when you are called upon to lead directly into painful circumstances? Do you shrink back from situations that could be costly to you personally, even though you know it's the correct way to go? When hard decisions need to be made, do you move ahead with resolution?

How tempting it is for any of us simply to wait and see. It is easier to stand still and let the mob carry us along. We let fate have its way rather than lead the way ourselves. Although this tendency is understandable, the difference between this and true leadership is profound.

The Mark passage tells us (verse 32) that there were two reactions to Jesus' clear leadership. The general populace was afraid. They didn't understand any of it. The heaviness of it loomed over their lives. They sensed that something important was going on, but they weren't sure exactly what.

The disciples were astonished, not understanding the action that Jesus was taking. His leadership was moving them in a direction they had not yet gone.

Jesus had taken His leadership team aside and explained everything to them step by step. He no sooner completed this briefing than James and John showed that they didn't understand any of it. Here was Jesus deeply and profoundly choosing servanthood. James and John, however, wanted precisely the opposite.

How lonely leadership can be at times. Yet how important it is to lead—even if it means you have to set your face toward Jerusalem.

CONTROL

Human beings like to be in control. We want to control our circumstances, be in charge of the outcomes. We also desire to control other people, trying to make everything work out the way we think it would be best. This temptation and our subsequent giving in to it happens to all of us at various times, and we are blind if we do not see it.

Part of the problem is that we may not always be aware of what is occurring. Control can be subtly rationalized. We may feel that the outcomes we desire are really God's will, even if others don't see it. Then we may feel justified in manipulating them, reasoning that it is, after all, what the Lord desires.

However, Jesus did not control and manipulate people. He let them do what they wanted. Surely it was in their best interests to acknowledge that He was the Son of God, but He didn't pound it into them or keep trying to persuade them. He allowed them to make up their own minds.

Often we feel like we have to jump in there and "help God out." Sometimes we force others, plan and plot. This is a particularly dangerous trait for leaders. Before we realize it, we can become conniving, controlling individuals, subtly forcing others to do whatever we desire. Sometimes we do this with a look, a well-planned moment of silence, bringing something up several times, the tone of our voices. People capitulate, but not necessarily with freedom.

God's way is to let people decide freely. He lets us select Himself or Satan. We are free to choose, free to sin, and free to reap the consequences of sin. He allows us to go our own way or to follow Him. He is not there hounding us, pressuring us, or needling us. His sweet Holy Spirit will speak quietly, but the choice is ours.

Let's be more careful as leaders to notice our misuse of power,

80

control and manipulation. We must ascribe all power to God, allowing Him to deal with circumstances and other people to bring about what He desires, when He wants it. Let's not try to play God.

JUST MAKE IT HAPPEN!

Read Genesis 16:1-4, 11-15.   *March 6*

When God speaks to our hearts about a thing He wishes to accomplish, we can make a fatal error at this very juncture. We can begin to own the outcome. As we speculate and "buy into it," the dream takes on increasing proportions. We can picture what it will be like, and the thought of it becomes gripping.

Soon we have woven our selves into the picture. Here, our ego can take over. We like what we envision and want to see it come to pass. When our selfish nature and our personal motives get enmeshed in the vision, then there's the likelihood that we will meddle. That's right...meddle. We get in the way, allow our fleshly nature to get involved with what God wants to accomplish, and taint His work with our own thoughts. We get ourselves mixed up in the Lord's work and...what is sad...we barely even realize it.

When we think something is God's will, then it is tempting to utilize our influence, power, and authority to force it into existence. Before we know it, we are trying to control people and events to make the dream become a reality. If we are familiar with leadership and wielding our delegated power, this misuse may not even feel wrong. We are so into the flow of making things happen, we don't discern that we are using power improperly.

This is a terrible trap for a leader. Ultimately, it is akin to a person who is working for us choosing to take on more power than he or she has been given, usurping authority and grasping at control. This is serious when we see it in another person. Anyone who is power hungry and into building a "kingdom" of his own is frightening. But we, too, can do this when it comes to the things of God.

If we choose such a controlling spirit, Ishmaels can be produced. After all, isn't it up to us to do something about this finally and bring this dream to fruition? Can't we just move in there and talk some sense into people and get it to happen? Surely they can see that this is God's plan. We don't want them to miss it.

However, as we try to force matters on "God's behalf," the results can be devastating. Something is soon produced all right, but it's a hairy Ishmael, a pugnacious young man, and not the true child of promise.

Wait! Don't raise your level of power and control...even on behalf of God.

POWER — GOD'S WAY

Read Acts 1:8.   *March 7*

Power is never meant to be resident in us. When it is, misuse of power is more than possible, it is probable. When we take up power and wield it ourselves, the results can be devastating. Our selfish ambitions, ego-centricity, personal desires and motives can all taint our use of power.

Rather than residing in us as a permanent fixture, power is meant to flow through us from God. He is the one to whom we ascribe all power. That means that the Lord is the One in whom every bit of power resides. The source of it and the choice of when and how to use it should be left entirely in the hands of the Sovereign Lord.

God has the wisdom to know what to do with power. He never makes a mistake in its use. He does not utilize it to control us, but rather exerts it for our good.. He sets us free, He leaves us free, and He wields His power to keep us free.

God uses His power to break the bondage of the enemy. He exerts His force against Satan, and it is for this purpose alone that He gives us His power. It flows through us to do the Lord's work on the earth.

By the presence of the Holy Spirit in our lives, God Himself provides the power to witness effectively throughout the world (Acts 1:8), to share the testimony of Jesus being raised from the dead (Acts 4:33). It is through God's power that the sick are healed and demons are cast out.

When we try to use our own power in our own way, it actually blocks the power of God from working through us and accomplishing His work. For this reason, God states that His "power is made perfect in weakness" (II Corinthians 12:18). When we give up, when we don't know what to do, when we feel the lack of might and power personally, then it is the time–not to vie for more power for ourselves–but rather to let God's power be at work in us and through us. Let go of any power struggles, and let God do it.

A SPECIAL MOMENT IN TIME

Read Esther 4:18. (Read Esther
chapters 4-7 if you want context.).   *March 8*

Esther was definitely in the perfect place at exactly the right time. Some would say that it was merely due to her beauty queen image and a few good breaks. Perhaps. But Mordecai had other ideas. "And who knows but that you have come to royal position for such a time as this?" he asks (Esther 4:18).

Often, what looks like normal but lucky circumstances are really indicators of the Lord at work. Could He not have orchestrated this whole situation for Esther so she could be in a position to change events? It was her *kairos* moment—God's

83

special time for her.

Besides being beautiful, what was Esther really like? What was inside her? This was her opportunity. The matter had to be decided and made evident. Would she risk her own life for the chance of saving her own people? Would the King have her killed for her impudence? Even is she were allowed to speak, would it make any difference whatsoever? Fasting and prayer become most serious at such times.

Esther was sensitive to timing. Even at the first banquet, she did not share her mind but rather requested a second time with the king. God Himself perhaps intervened that night when the King could not sleep. The reading of the official records would be boring enough to be the equivalent of counting sheep.

However, the King heard what was necessary. He was reminded of the assistance and loyalty of Mordecai. The tables were turning, and all it took from there was a word from his queen that night. Esther had indeed come to the court for "such a time as this."

Such circumstances can happen today. We might wonder why we end up in a certain place in a particular position. Perhaps it's for our work, but it may also be for these special moments in time. Pivotal events can occur when we least expect them, and we must be ready internally or we will miss our place in them.

Be alert, prepared, and ready to hear from God. Be strong for immediate action in that special *kairos* moment God has prepared for you.

THE END OF THE GAME

Read II Timothy 3:1-14.   *March 9*

"Most anyone can start a game," the coach said, "but you want to be sure to put in the best players at the end when the game is tied."

In these last days, those who are alive will have to face increasingly difficult situations. During the past decade more people have been won to the Lord than in all of history before it, and Satan is not pleased. Our enemy is out to defeat us, and the battle is intense. We're the ones who have been chosen to play in the game during the last minutes, while the heat is on.

No one ever said it was going to be easy. The stress and strain is incredible. The opposing team has saved some of the best and most cunning plays for the end. Everyone is tired, and it is difficult even to be aware of what's happening. Keep your head. Continue moving. Give it all you've got.

This is the picture of what should be occurring. However, the team, as I observe it, seems to be different than this much of the time. Fatigued, lethargic, dragging, they are lagging behind in the crucial hour. What are they doing? Couldn't they see that coming? Come on! Think! Watch! Heads up! There, that's better. You can do it.

Doesn't it excite you that you have been selected for this last great effort? Who's going to win? If you weren't meant to have a part, you wouldn't have been selected to be out there anyway. You were one of those that the coach believed in, so don't disappoint Him.

Just like with Esther, it may only be one move that can turn the winning point. It can be one basket, one field goal, one less stroke with the golf club, one more point in tennis. The buzzer is going to sound any time now so, as the old Latin phrase goes, *carpe diem.* Seize the day! Latch on to the moment with all vim and vigor, and take hold of whatever opportunity presents itself.

It's certainly challenging, but isn't it fun to play the last string? There'll be a victory march soon.

EVEN IF NOT

Read Job 2:6-10 and 13:15.

As we have been considering Queen Esther, we noted her heroism in a moment of crisis. She took a risk to go before the king uninvited, knowing full well that it could mean her death. However, she was determined to do what she could, trusting God for the outcome no matter what that might be. "And if I perish, I perish," she stated with a quiet resolve (Esther 5:16).

In similar straits and with like reasoning, Shadrach, Meshach and Abednego faced the fiery furnace and what appeared to be certain death. "If we are thrown into the blazing furnace," they announced, "the God we serve is able to save us from it, and he will rescue us from your hand, O King. But even if he does not, we want you to know, O King, that we will not serve your gods or worship the image of gold you have set up" (Daniel 3:17-18).

It takes a great deal of fortitude, trust, and faith in the Lord to serve Him, no matter what happens. Esther had decided to throw in her lot with her people, the Jews, and to do what seemed right, even if it meant her death. Likewise, Shadrach, Meshach, and Abednego had chosen to follow God. With great faith, they were determined to trust Him for their deliverance, but their faith in God was not dependent upon how the Lord chose to act.

Job, too, was resolute about serving God. When trouble came along, coupled with great pain and personal loss, Job's wife encouraged him to give up on God. (She was not a particularly wonderful support person!) Still, Job chose to believe in the Lord, even if he did not understand what was happening to him. It is tough when God does not come through for us, as we had hoped. Where is the Lord when He chooses not to deliver us?

This is a decisive point for every leader. Our response at a crisis moment is absolutely critical. Will our belief and trust in God be based upon circumstances? Will it be changed if God does not accomplish what we think He should on our behalf? These are important and gut-wrenching questions which get down to the depth of our commitment.

Job, in the midst of his confusion, was still able to make the profound statement, "Though He slay me, yet will I hope in Him" (Job 13:15). Our very life is placed in God's hands at such a moment of decision, and we decide if we will let Him do absolutely anything or if we will place limitations on our "total commitment."

What a test! However, there is something powerfully freeing in the decision when we come to it. Take our houses and our goods, our families, our money, our jobs, our ministries, our reputations, our health and even our very lives....yet will we serve Him. How deep....How profound....And you?

IN ITS TIME

Read Ecclesiastes 3:1-11. *March 11*

Time: the commodity which has frustrating limits! There is never enough of it (unless something painful is not resolved and then there is too much of it). Normally, there are far too many demands and not enough time to accomplish them. This stress is especially frustrating for active, take-charge, get-it-done type of people. Leaders have multiple demands that usually appear impossible to meet.

We have to understand that there is a season for everything. Each activity has a time, and we probably create our own stress by placing activities into our lives that are out of their times. We need to keep pace — not with others' expectations and demands on us–but with the duties God gives us to do. That is enough work all by itself. Why add more?

Living in a place where there are seasons is a delight to me. In the last months the snow settled in, and there were some evenings by the fireplace with a mug of hot chocolate. Spring buds will come soon and turn into a reminder that life always springs from death. Then the lushness of green and the fruit and flowers of summer will arrive. And finally back to fall–my favorite–where everything turns crispy, colorful, and crunchy underfoot.

So go our own lives, for there are times in our relationship with God or in our careers or ministry when each of these seasons is felt. We don't always understand or like each moment in time, but it will pass. Something different and new will flow in to take its place. New life will come after a winter of pain. Time of dying out to self will arrive because the old has to be blown away to make room for the new. Times of growth will occur along with moments of reaping the harvest.

Be patient, my friend, for there is a time for everything under heaven. Wait and see and never give up. "God has made everything beautiful in its time" (Ecclesiastes 3:11).

THE BURDEN

Read Nehemiah 2:1-9.
(Read Nehemiah 1 for more context.)   *March 12*

When the Lord intends to use a leader in an unusual way, He often begins by burdening that person's heart. Such was the case with Nehemiah, for his reaction to the news from Jerusalem was not particularly reasonable. True, the city wall was in ruins, and this was dangerous because of the lack of protection and also dishonorable because no one seemed to care about it.

As sad as this was, Nehemiah would not need to be affected personally. He was in Babylon, being held captive, but he had a very "cushy" job as cupbearer to the king. That was a real position of trust. The cupbearer had to be certain that the king's wine was not poisoned and that it would be properly pleasing. He had no immediate plans to go back to Jerusalem, so why get so upset at this news?

"When I heard these things [about the wall]," Nehemiah said, "I sat down and wept. For some days I mourned and fasted and prayed before the God of heaven" (Nehemiah 1:4). Why did he have such a strong reaction?

I have observed this in other leaders who receive a God-given burden. It is almost as it they receive the Lord's pain, His heart for the matter. They can hardly eat or sleep for the heaviness of it.

Nehemiah prayed about this situation day and might. He was moved by the sins of the people and confessed them before God. He understood God's decision regarding captivity because of the unfaithfulness of the people, but he asked the Lord to work out a miracle so he could speak to the King about Jerusalem.

Everything was against him. Why should the King let him leave his service to go back to Jerusalem and repair it? We're talking about enemy territory for this King so why should he risk having it refortified?

But Nehemiah had prayed and fasted. As fearful as he was about the King's reaction, he boldly stated his concerns, praying all the while. Not only did the King allow him to leave, but he provided a contingency force as a guard along with resources from the royal forest.

A leader can be mightily used to accomplish what God desires, even against impossible odds. This begins with a burden from God. It moves ahead through prayer and fasting. And, in the end, God can execute the "impossible."

JUDICIOUS CAUTION

Read Nehemiah 2:11-12.
(Read on through chapter 3 if you have the time)   *March 13*

When Nehemiah arrived in Jerusalem, the weight of his burden could have caused him to forge ahead immediately with the task at hand. Instead, he observed quietly for three days. This is a wise move on the part of a leader. It allows time to grasp a situation, ask questions, gain needed information, and accurately assess the project.

Even then, he continued his evaluation strategy in secret. He chose a few men and set out at night to survey the walls. He didn't want many people knowing about this yet, not until God directed and he was ready to move. "I had not told anyone what my God had put in my heart to do for Jerusalem," he stated (Nehemiah 2:12). Nehemiah had not wanted to talk until he understood what they were going to face.

I admire this caution and planning in Nehemiah's strategy. Those who are loose-tongued about their ideas and plans should exercise restraint lest they talk about what they will find impossible to produce later. That can be embarrassing to the leader, but also defeating and demoralizing to the group, causing the loss of trust in the leader and his word.

Obviously, Nehemiah was a strong motivator. When he did finally announce his plans, the people were with him The various priests, leaders, and rulers of the different districts took up their part of the work. With everyone doing a portion and setting their efforts to a particular section, what seemed to be impossible in the beginning actually became realistic.

Nehemiah was wise enough to know that he could not accomplish this giant task on his own with just a few personal workers. He needed the support and assistance of everyone. He was able to delegate the work, assign clearly defined tasks, and be certain everything was coordinated.

Even in spiritual matters, to build up the walls around a situation in the spiritual realm, many must be encouraged to pray and intercede, to repair their part of the breach, to fight for their portion of the territory to be built up again.

God give us more leaders like Nehemiah.

THE INEVITABLE OPPOSITION

Read Nehemiah 2:10, 19-20 and 4:1-3.
(Read on until Nehemiah 4:23 if you have the chance.)   *March 14*

When people are moving out for God, opposition is inevitable. The Lord's enemies are not pleased. Those who are against it will try everything they can to stop the work from proceeding. They get angry. They mock and ridicule the people of God. They try to make what is good look like it is bad such as when they accused Nehemiah of rebelling against the king.

Through all of this, Nehemiah continued as he had started: looking to God. He could confidently make the claim that "the God of heaven will give us success" (2:20).

When intimidation, smirks, and threats do not successfully stop the work, the ire of the enemy rises even higher. "When Sanballat heard that we were rebuilding the wall, he became angry and was greatly incensed" (4:1). The derision level was stepped up. How effective this can be. People hate to be made fun of and will often shrink away from mere insult.

When the affront is disregarded, however, and the work of the Lord is not deterred, then all-out warfare is the next level. Nehemiah and the people responded with prayer and set out a plan to warn each other in case of attack. The trumpeter was prepared to sound the alarm. Guards were posted in exposed niches as lookouts, and everyone was armed.

Besides this kind of preparation and alertness, Nehemiah encouraged the people. "After I look things over," he said, "I stood up and said to the nobles, the officials and the rest of the people, 'Don't be afraid of them. Remember the Lord, who is great and awesome, and fight for your brothers, your sons and your daughters, your wives and your homes"(4:14). Everyone stayed in their clothes, kept their weapons on at all times, and continued to work.

Often Satan will forge such tactics against the work of God.

He is good at producing skirmishes on the sidelines, frightening us and demoralizing the troops. What Satan wants is for the work to stop. But if we keep our eyes on God and trust in Him, properly alert and prepared, we can keep focused on what the Lord has told us to do. Rather than get sidetracked, we must keep doing what God has called us to accomplish. Then, like Nehemiah, we will ultimately see the work completed.

THE MONEY SCENE

Read Nehemiah 5:6-11.
(Read the whole chapter for context).   *March 15*

Many complained that other Jews were taking monetary advantage of them. It had become so bad that they had to mortgage their fields, borrow money to pay their taxes, and even sell their children into slavery in order to meet their payments.

This made Nehemiah very angry, but instead of simply lashing out, he thought first. "When I heard their outcry and their charges, I was very angry," said Nehemiah. "I pondered them in my mind and then accused the nobles and officials" Nehemiah 5:6). Nehemiah was not reactionary, but neither was he frail in his response. He told it like it was, and when he finished, "they kept quiet, because they could find nothing to say" (Nehemiah 5:8).

Even then, he just went on, pushing the point home. "So I continued," he said simply. "What you are doing is not right. Shouldn't you walk in the fear of our God to avoid the reproach of our Gentile enemies?" (Nehemiah 5:9). He confronted them head on. He wanted to make them think about their witness and the issues that were larger than their petty selfishness.

We also see in this chapter that Nehemiah himself was generous. He and his men lent money and grain. Not only that, but he didn't even take what was due him as the governor and did all his official entertaining on his own budget.

He pointed to former governors who took money in taxes from the people. Furthermore, he said, "the assistants also lorded it over the people. But out of reverence for God I did not act like that."

I admire Nehemiah's leadership. Not in it for power or money, he was committed to justice. In our day and age, he would not take an exorbitant salary, even if it might be justifiable, nor would he misuse his expense account. Perhaps, he would not even have an expense account. He heard from God and courageously did what God placed on his heart, even if it was not popular. He was more free to do this, because he was not tied to his professional perks.

Today we need more persons of perfect integrity who will resist all temptation to "pad" their own personal coffers. Even choices that will promote personal prestige such as car telephones, types of company vehicle purchased, and places chosen for business entertainment need to be weighed carefully in light of expense. People could look at Nehemiah and not find fault when it came to such areas. He was careful and astute in such decision-making, which allowed him to correct others in this area when it was needed. Let it be so for all of us.

PLEASING GOD

Read Nehemiah 6:9-13 and 8:1-10.
(For a broader context read chapters 6-8)   *March 16*

The last leaf of this series unfolds with great spiritual insight coming from Nehemiah. He was so in tune with God, that he could sense a trap. God provided Nehemiah with great wisdom and understanding when a sticky situation arose. "I realized that God had not sent him," Nehemiah said, but that he had prophesied against me because Tobiah and Sanballat had hired him. He had been hired to intimidate me so that I would commit a sin by doing this, and then they would give a bad name to discredit me" (6:12-13).

Often we get into the middle of strain and stress, only to be so tired that we can't think straight, resulting in a big mistake. But Nehemiah sought God at this point and prayed, "Now strengthen my hands" (6:9). God did, and the work was completed.

Good people were appointed to the positions of leadership, and Hananiah was commander of the citadel "because he was a man of integrity and feared God more than most men do" (7:2). God continued to lead Nehemiah in assembling the people (7:9) and in having Ezra the scribe read the Book of the Law (8:1). There was rejoicing and praise as the people lifted their hands in response and shouted, "Amen!" Then they literally fell on their faces before God (8:6) and wept as they were convicted by the reading of the Word (8:9).

Nehemiah turned the people to their God during his reign. He made the great statement, "Do not grieve, for the joy of the Lord is your strength" (8:10). He was a living example of this truth since, throughout his leadership, he did not let circumstances defeat him. Looking to God and trusting in Him, Nehemiah allowed the Lord to do profound things for him and through him. God provided Nehemiah with wisdom, insight, strength, patience, absolutely everything that was needed to lead successfully.

As we finish the chapters of the story of Nehemiah, we see a time of revival in Jerusalem. Reforms are made, and everything is affected because God is in charge. Nehemiah's spiritual sensitivity has been the impetus for restoring Jerusalem in every way.

"Remember me with favor, O my God," says Nehemiah in the last verse of the book. This leader obviously had placed the task of pleasing God above all else. What a model for us today. For what do you want to be remembered? Will it happen?

FRESH FISH

A story came out from the days when the British invaded Scotland, intent upon subduing this rugged people. The British were arrogant because of their huge forces and thought they could overcome anything by sheer numbers.

A single Scottish castle was selected, and the British forces simply camped outside, believing the Scottish garrison would ultimately be starved out. They sent a message to the Scots with the demand for immediate, unconditional surrender. The answer was thrown out over the wall: a nice, flapping, salt water fish, still dripping with water. The castle had a subterranean passage which was linked to the sea, providing an unending supply of fresh food.

I have often observed Satan's tactics in relation to this story. Basically, he thinks to "starve us out." He tries to buffet us with derision, problems, stress, and pressure. Sometimes, this all gets so overwhelming that a person truly wonders if he can make it. Perhaps he will have to give up.

However, God always provides a stream with fresh fish. It's in Him. This is why it is so important to stay united to the Lord, attached to the vine.

Proverbs 8:34 states, "Blessed is the man who listens to me, watching daily at my doors, waiting at my doorway." Listening to God is not a nice option for a leader. It is life! Without it, he'll get starved out. Without it, he'll get discouraged and surrender to the enemy. Without it, he'll make wrong choices and thereby lead others astray.

It is imperative that we come to the doors and enter into God's presence, not just once in a while but every single day. We need to wait right there by the doorway throughout the hours, listening for Him to call our name and give us directions.

Through such a process, God will provide at all times—even

in the midst of siege, even during stress and pressure. It will be on-going and never failing, and in the end, we will be triumphant.

LISTEN

Read I Samuel 3:10. *March 18*

On the wall of my office is a print by the French painter Jacques Bastien-LePage. The original, which hangs in the Metropolitan Museum of Art in New York City, captures my attention whenever I visit that wonderful place.

Here is a peasant girl standing by a tree in the European-style backyard garden of their village cottage. She is staring off in the distance as if listening intently. Behind her are three angels, one of whom is in full armor with his own sword strapped to his side and also with one across his hands which he is offering to her. She had obviously been working with the making of thread on a frame, but the little stool on which she had been sitting was tipped over in her hurry to get up and hear from God. At least that's how I have always interpreted this painting of Joan of Arc.

Although mystery has shrouded her real life, one thing is sure. Joan accomplished a mighty deed for France, and she believed in her divine appointment to lead out the troops and sway the battle against England, restoring the French monarchy. Her nation was saved because of her courage, and she was willing to die at the stake rather than to renounce her belief that she had heard from God. Even Mark Twain became so enamored by her heroism and deep beliefs that he spent nearly ten years of his life researching her in the archives of England and France and writing her biography. (Yes, I did indeed say Mark Twain!)

The bottom line is that the world needs more courageous people who do what they feel the Lord has directed them to do. We are desperate for people who will drop their work, get up, and listen. Even from the most unlikely places — such as a teenage girl

96

like Joan—God can raise up a warrior who can lead out demoralized and defeated troops. A young Samuel can be awakened to take a warning to the priest Eli. The youth David can defeat Goliath. Whenever there is somebody, almost anybody, who will listen and obey, God can do great things.

So listen. It doesn't matter who you are!

Work cited: Twain, Mark. *Joan of Arc.* Fort Collin, CO: Ignatius Press, 1989.

WHO SAID THAT?

Read John 10:1-16. *March 19*

It can be difficult to decipher the source of our thoughts. Is that thought of God? ...of my own flesh? ...or of Satan and evil?

The other day I picked up the telephone and heard a familiar voice. She started talking without identifying herself, secure in the fact that I would know who it was. I knew that voice, and yet I couldn't place it. My mind sifted through church, the university, my friends, relatives, people I had met in my different speaking tours—but to no avail. Finally, she said something which allowed me to get out of my quandary. I laughed to myself and continued the conversation with assurance.

The same phenomenon can occur when it comes to our ideas and impressions. Who is this anyway? Sooner of later, as we listen, something will reveal it for what it is.

In order to aid in this process, I once did a useful exercise. I took several pieces of paper and drew three columns. At the top of one I wrote GOD; at the tope of the second column I wrote SELF/FLESH; and for the third I put down SATAN. Then I studied the scriptures to find descriptors for each. It took me a while, and I kept adding to the list for weeks. But in the end, I began to see a pattern.

Under Satan, for example, I put "steal, death, destroy, kill, deception" and so forth. For God I had words like "truth, life, light, love, peace." For self and man I had "selfish, self-aggrandizing, power-hungry, self-promoting, ego-centric." As circumstances arose, I could sort out the probable source much more quickly. If I just waited and played the situations out in my mind to consider the consequences—the fruit likely to come from it—soon it became even more obvious.

"Hello. Who is this?"

GOODBYE

Read John 13:3-17.
(For a full context read John 13-17)   *March 20*

If you knew that tomorrow was going to be your last day here on earth, and you could put together a speech for your co-workers, what would you say? What would be foremost on your mind, throbbing on your heart, the last reminders that you care passionately for and want others to follow?

These chapters in the gospel of John unfold the way Jesus handled just such a situation. First, He reminds his disciples of the importance of a servant lifestyle by washing their feet. He does this for everyone, even the one He knows will betray Him and the one He predicts will deny Him. He works hard at comforting His disciples and encouraging them, talking to them about the work of the Holy Spirit.

A theme that runs throughout this gripping last speech, however, is that of love and unity. "A new command I give you: Love one another. As I have loved you, so you must love one another. By this all men will know that you are my disciples, if you love one another" (13:34-35).

Jesus encourages the disciples to stay close to Him, as attached as vine and branches. "May they be brought to complete unity to let the world know that you sent me," He prays in 17:23. Jesus yearns to have the Father and Himself and us all unified in each other, working together as one.

As leaders, this should be our heart throb. If it was so important to Jesus that He would take time to plead for it in His last speech, it ought to be important to us as well. Sometimes where I work we quote a little saying that we fight to keep unity. It's true. It's hard work and sometimes we "go at it" to get out what's bothering us. However, in the end, we know we must stay united, even if we have to agree to disagree. Love and unity must ultimately prevail.

Could it be that as Christians we are not winning the world as effectively as we should because they cannot see enough examples of true love and unity at work? God help us to lead out in this area and be models of this critical theme at work and in our daily lives.

NOT MANY OF YOU

Read James 3:1-18.   *March 21*

"Not many of you should presume to be teachers, my brothers, because you know that we who teach will be judged more strictly"(verse 1). This is a powerful warning, especially to leaders who tend to be naturally verbose and generally confident of their own ideas and words.

It is probably presumption, though, to assume that we have anything worthwhile to share with anyone else. We must be aware of such arrogance. It all can bore people, be inappropriate, or even be incorrect, thereby leading others astray. We can be affected negatively, too. Later we will be judged for what we have taught, and we will be held responsible. It will be even stricter judgment than for those we taught, and so we need to be particularly careful.

As leaders, we do teach almost as a matter of course. Others watch us and learn. We teach what we believe by what we do and don't do. All our decisions teach values and priorities. People listen to our words, but they also drink of our spirits.

Words are also extremely powerful. They are able to heal, encourage, and lift people up to loftier purposes. We can minister through words in the power of the Holy Spirit. However, words can also be used to bring confusion, fear, anger, division, and strife, and we have the option to choose.

If a leader is wise and understanding, then he should evidence this and teach through his very lifestyle. The deeds he chooses should come from wisdom and not from "bitter envy and selfish ambition" (verse 14). The latter brings "disorder and every evil practice" (verse 16) into a group or organization. If a leader is subtly motivated by competition, unforgiveness, and a desire to be "tops," then the leader can infuse deep problems into the rest of the group.

James describes the good kind of leader and teacher as one who has a wisdom from heaven. This wisdom "is first of all pure, then peaceloving, considerate, submissive, full of mercy and good fruit, impartial and sincere. Peacemakers who sow in peace raise a harvest of righteousness," he states in James 3:17-18. This type of leader touches hearts and changes groups—for the better!

STAND UP

Read Jeremiah 1:7-19.   *March 22*

When God calls a leader, there are certain directives which are a part of that call. With Jeremiah, God was most definitive.

"You must go to everyone I send you to and say whatever I command you," the Lord directed (verse 7). With this, Jeremiah was on divine assignment. He was not to sort out or design for himself how he would accomplish a task—whom he would see or what he would say. When God told him to go to a certain person, he was to obey, whether that individual was great or small, rich or poor, in a position of power or not.

This is not easy to do at times, especially with the rest of the statement in mind. Jeremiah was to speak whatever God told him. If the person was in a powerful place of influence or was famous, then this might be a particularly tough assignment, especially if the message was not an appealing one.

At times God asks us to do something we don't readily want to do. We are to confront somebody or present a strong perspective on a situation at hand. We are sometimes frightened to do it. What will they think of us? How will they respond?

But God says to do it, and we really should obey. "Do not be afraid of them," He says, "for I am with you and will rescue you" (verse 8). God says He will put His words in our mouths, and we can trust that when we open them, His words will flow out. Then God promises to be "watching to see that my word is fulfilled" (verse 12). God not only gives us the words, but also follows through on what He warns or states so explicitly through us.

Finally, there are times God needs us to do this sort of work not only with an individual, but perhaps even with a group. We are to take a stand and speak up. "Get yourself ready!" the Lord says to prepare Jeremiah. "Stand up and say to them whatever I command you" (verse 17). God asks us to be firm and strong in certain issues and at particular times. We are not to sit down to deliver the message, but we are to take our place confidently and speak out before them all.

Our assurance at such times? God will be with us. Don't be afraid!

GROUP THINK

Read Ezekiel 13:1-17.   *March 23*

In today's verses, we see the danger of "group think." These false prophets were sharing "out of their own imaginations."

Some would give out a plausible idea, but it was out of their fleshly thoughts and not from God. Others would publicly concur, saying it sounded good, and then embellish it a bit. Because they agreed together, perhaps they actually felt they had the viewpoint of God.

The Lord, however, thought differently. "Woe to the foolish prophets who follow their own spirit and have seen nothing.... Their visions are false and their divinations a lie" (verses 3 and 6). The female prophets also joined in the lies, giving out good news to the people by telling them what they wanted to hear.

Although there are numerous examples in the scriptures of false prophets who did not wish to upset the kings and leaders, there are also many examples of true prophets who spoke up. People like Jeremiah and Ezekiel state what God desired them to say, declaring the truth at all times. They did not allow concerns for their own safety or reputations to make them hesitate.

Today we continue to need people who will be firm and proclaim what must be said. We must have those who will confront sin and graft, who will give warnings when necessary. Where is the courage of the clarion call for God's way in our society today? Where is the person who will stand up for what is right, no matter what the cost is personally?

Even though others may be saying nice things, this should not sway us if we know God sees it differently. There is still a difference between right and wrong, truth and lies, morality and sin, ethical practices and unethical ones. Who will speak up if we do not?

It is certainly difficult to be the only one who is the bearer of bad news. We would rather join in with the group. We can perhaps even rationalize that so many can't be wrong. But they can. And we are to take our cue from God and from Him alone. Are you brave enough to do and say what's right, even if you're the only one?

IT STANDS OUT

Read Judges 16:15-20.   *March 24*

What about you stands out to others? When people meet you for the first time, what makes an initial impact and seems to "go before you"? The answer depends upon your priorities in life, what you deem most important.

Some people, for example, see their physical appearance as primary. They may spend hours in exercise and training to gain a perfect physique. They may shop for hours to get just the right look for every situation. Hair and cosmetics can take much primping time. Jewelry and accessories may easily become exorbitant expenditures.

I am not talking here about whether people are beautiful or not, but about whether appearance becomes a matter of extreme personal priority. They might be the type who has to move just right so as to be noticed or to swagger in order to appear in control. Just the right look is critical for every situation. My husband and I call them peacocks.

Samson was probably just such a person. His character was lacking, and his brawn was prime. He loved his physical feats and was fond of the women. Little else regarding him stands out, for he was not spiritually inclined on a regular basis nor did he make a strong moral or ethical impact in his role as a judge.

Different areas seem to be primary in other personalities. For some, their emotions seem overpowering. They are hyper and nervous, perhaps, or unhappy and distressed. They may be angry or hurt, and these types of emotions are sensed almost immediately when meeting the person.

For still other people, their intellect is primary. They like everyone to know that they are bright, educated, and knowledgeable. They have to make people aware that they have the answer or understand the topic at hand.

There is nothing wrong with being in shape, having feelings, or being intelligent, of course. What matters is which of these takes on primary importance. For example, when a problem is presented to you, do you fight over it, get depressed about it, or try to find the answer first before you even pray about it? God desires for the Spirit to be supreme in us. When He has the supremacy in our lives, people notice it.

Some people are so in touch with God that their spiritual self is the most outstanding thing about them. People sense the Holy Spirit in their lives almost immediately. God is so alive in them, that this is what others notice first.

What has supremacy in your life?

FOUR CONTEMPORARIES

Read I Samuel 2:12-26; Judges 15:15-16.   *March 25*

Individuals make such different choices. Some choose to follow God whole-heartedly and stand up for what is right, even making correction in ungodly social trends. Others choose to go their own ways, and they sin greatly before God and man.

It is engaging to explore the differences in four contemporaries: Samson, Hophni and Phinehas, and Samuel. They all seemed to have good family foundations. After all, an angel came to Manoah and his wife (Judges 13) to share with them about the birth and upbringing of Samson. Hophni and Phinehas were "PKs," born into a priest's home. Hannah, of course, birthed the special baby, Samuel (I Samuel 1). Upbringing does not appear to account for the variations in these four young men.

Samson was all brawn without much brain or spiritual sensitivity. He did not seem to think much about the consequences of his actions. Although he delivered Israel from the hands of the Philistines, he did it through brute strength and finally at the cost of his own life.

Hophni and Phinehas were wicked men. Though they had

104

access to learning and training, their education did little for them. They did not handle the sacrifices as they had learned to do. Both of them were crass, rude, and insensitive. Sinning openly, they had no respect for their father, Eli, let alone God Himself. In the end, they, too, died in ignominy (I Samuel 4:10-11).

Samuel, on the other hand, made entirely different choices. He heard God, and even as a boy, God used him to rebuke Eli regarding his two sons (I Samuel 3:10-12). Samuel was sensitive to the Lord and was recognized early as a prophet. Scripture tells us that God "revealed himself to Samuel through his word" (3:21). Samuel, of course, was used in powerful ways to impact all Israel through his relationship and correction of Saul and later through his anointing of David.

Samuel allowed his learning under Eli to bring him closer to God. He let his spirituality be the prime strength about him, the first thing people "met" in him.

The choice is each of ours. Will the Spirit be the dominant factor, like it was in Samuel, or will it be something else entirely? Same upbringing, same society, different choices.

JUNIOR PARTNER?

Read Ephesians 1:17-23.   *March 26*

Partners. Does that describe you and God? Are you working together, consulting with Him and striving toward the same goal? This concept is fine, as long as it is clear that God is the one who is giving the directions. He, and He alone, is the one who should be making the decisions.

The problem is that as take-charge leader types, it is easy to slip into a pattern in our relationship with God. Before we know it, He has been relegated to a junior partner. We prefer to work things out for ourselves. We may even delegate areas that we don't wish to handle to the Lord, while we continue to hold on to everything we think we are able to manage. God may not even receive much attention.

This is a sad state of affairs and most rude. It is akin to treating the owner like he is a part-time window washer. We do not bother to consult a window-washer. We might ask for him to spruce things up and help us out a bit, but his place is obvious. It's outside the realm of decision-making.

Even elevating God to senior partner status is not the answer. We are not equal to God, though at times we might act like it. We should not be deciding what to do and then asking God what He thinks. Rather, the Lord is fully in charge.

This truth is evident in today's verses from Ephesians. God is "far above all rule and authority, power and dominion, and every title that can be given..." (verse 21). This makes Jesus the one and only CEO, and we had better not forget it.

Jesus Christ is appointed to be head over everything for the church. As His children, we are to take orders from only Him. Direction, coordination, thought and wisdom are all from the One in charge. If we try to take over any of these responsibilities, we will make for ourselves a two-headed monster.

Difficult as it is sometimes for a leader to be a follower, we had better learn it when it comes to God and His position over us. We work with him and share in His plans for mankind, but He is most certainly not a junior partner!

BUT YOU

Read II Timothy 4:1-5.   *March 27*

With challenges, difficulties, and problems on every side, what's a leader to do? Some view leadership as a large office where power is at your fingertips and ease is readily available. For many, it is the ultimate gain to be at the top.

However, leadership in reality is a lot of problem-solving, the making of difficult and often unpopular decisions, and the receiving of bad news. When "fire alarms" are pulled by employees who need to indicate the existence of a problem, the leader has to decide how to put out the fire. He also has to do it in the quickest and most efficient way possible.

That is why Paul advises Timothy about such crisis situations. He tells the young man that when everything is going from bad to worse, that is the very time to stay calm. "But you," he says in verse 5, "keep your head in all situations, endure hardship, do the work of an evangelist, discharge all the duties of your ministry."

This is superb advice. Everyone else may be running around, trying to decide what to do in a demanding situation. The leader, however, cannot afford to "lose his head" in the midst of the crisis. He must stay calm, acting quickly and communicating clearly. Everyone else may be falling apart, but the leader cannot afford this luxury. He is needed to "keep his head in all situations."

These verses also say that in crisis, the leader must simply endure hardship. Yes, the stress of the situation may be not only difficult but well nigh impossible. Still, stand firm and bear up under the crisis, no matter how troublesome it is.

If a leader keeps his head and patiently endures, he is a great witness. We can keep doing what God has called us to do, and others will be encouraged by the normal work. Calm can invade an entire group as others observe you serenely doing what needs to be accomplished, staying composed and steady. Keep discharging your duties, and God will use your model–simple as it might be–to bring peace into a situation. Just keep your head!

OUTSIDE MY FRONT DOOR
Read Isaiah 57:14-15.   *March 28*

My three-month stay in Argentina had been a dream that was five years in the making. Besides some writing goals, I wanted to find myself again. I don't actually know where I left "me." Perhaps it was on one of my numerous weekend preaching trips—I can't remember just where—Arkansas, or Texas, or Ohio, or California maybe. Or perhaps something had just gotten away from me back home in Minneapolis. I only remember that there had been more, and something was missing.

Then there was the fact that God had said, "Go away and listen." I had felt that He wanted to prepare me for something new. What, I couldn't say. But in order to be ready for what He had next, I needed to pray, fast, think, relax, sleep even—all those things that can so easily feel squeezed (not squeezed out, really, just squeezed) in the midst of a busy life.

Why Argentina? The waves of revival that have swept over Argentina for decades drew me in. I desired to be a part of it. Seeing the fervency of the churches and joining in the worship, hearing scores of testimonies of God's greatness, all of these were wonderful.

Nonetheless, in the midst of all of this, do you know what impressed me the most? It was the students at the Instituto Biblico Rio de la Plata. That was the Bible School where I stayed, in a little white cottage-style house with a green door. The campus is a haven, developed from the mansion and grounds once owned by one of Hitler's attachés. They have built dorms, married student housing, a chapel, a cafeteria.

But I would wake up at 6 a.m. and hear someone praying in one of the classrooms. Starting at 9 p.m. various of the classrooms would be full with the sounds of groups in rousing prayer. When I walked along the paths, the students would greet me warmly in the Latin way of a kiss on both cheeks. They came to talks I gave on the prophetic, on intercessory prayer, on Christianity and the arts....and stayed to weep and pray. In the chapel services the worship was wonderful, and God's presence was palpable. I was at Thursday evening services that lasted until 2 a.m. When I wandered over to the chapel to pray, students would be kneeling up at the altar or pacing in prayer. They would sometimes sit on the floor by my feet and cry. Their hunger for God was amazing.

I came to Argentina to seek revival. I found it outside my front door. Have you looked there lately?

THE CITY OF DARKNESS

Read John 3:19-21.   *March 29*

Buenos Aires, Argentina is a world-class city. Full of European-style architecture built by the many immigrants who came here, the city boasts great walking streets for shopping, classy restaurants, and a wonderful theater district. An obelisk stands at the city center, and when lit, the monument can be seen for miles. The French architecture, the plazas and the broad avenues, the statues in the parks...it's all really lovely.

There's just one habit that seems very strange. The roads aren't well lit. Even when street lights are available, often they are not turned on. The situation is further exacerbated by the fact that the Argentines generally do not use their car headlights. No, not even in the dead of night.

Cultural differences always fascinate me. So what is this deal with the darkness, I wondered?

One night as we drove along a main road that was especially dark, people were running across the street right in front of the cars. "Don't people get hit?" I asked my Argentine friend.

"Well, yes, as a matter of fact they do," she said. "Especially in this area."

"So why don't they turn on the lights?" I asked.

"Hhhhmmm. Good question," she mused.

John said that there was a "verdict." The judged slammed down his gavel and said, "The truth is.....these people love the darkness rather than the light." Why? "Because their deeds were evil."

109

People don't want to expose their evil deeds. They would rather hide them in the dark. After all, it is painful to see the evil. When the light shines on it, its true ugliness is revealed. It looks old, twisted, sick, rusted.

What is interesting about Argentina is that the people love living in the dark in other ways as well. Their houses do not have nearly the amount of light as in the U.S. Big shutters close down on the windows, protecting but also closing in and isolating. The people eat at 9 p.m. or later. Many restaurants are open into the early morning, and it is not unusual for society to be on the move well into 3 a.m. Even as it gets dusk in the park in the winter, one can see the picnickers hanging out in the dark.

Is there a spiritual connection here? Probably! I believe that such trends may very well say the most about the spiritual state of affairs in a society. With the economics crashing in Argentina, frustration has led to a lot more crime. There is a great deal of robbery, car theft, kidnaping...and the favorite time is at night. The church has to be a bright light in Argentina. Thankfully it is, but this is a great job spiritually.

FULL OF LIGHT
Read Matthew 5: 14-16.   *March 30*

In a country like Argentina that seems to be a "night owl," it is amazing to see the light involved in the churches. They certainly do not hide their lamps under a bushel.

I am staying at Instituto Biblico Rio de la Plata this winter (summer for us in the U.S.), and I have noticed something interesting. The Bible college students do not watch videos or TV in their spare time. They don't run off to see the latest movie, and they don't waste hours on computers and with technological games.

What do they do for entertainment, then? Why, they get

together and go out witnessing. The first time I saw this, I could hardly believe it. Here it was on Friday afternoon, about the time that college students usually throw off the robes of academia and head for some fun and relaxation.

"Hey, where are you headed?" I asked a group of happy students. "This looks like quite a gathering!"

"Oh, we're excited," said one of them. "We're doing what we like best. We're going out to talk to people about Jesus."

Besides these sorts of impromptu witnessing ventures, organized evangelism teams help with new church plants. They visit door to door, pray for people, and pass out information on the churches. Some teams go to where there are special needs, to the hospitals, mental wards, prisons, orphanages, old peoples' homes. They organize children's crusades, play music for teen groups, teach Sunday School, and preach. The opportunities in their churches are nearly endless.

That's why on Monday mornings they take their chapel time and give testimonies. Of course they have some exciting stories. They have gotten out there, and God blesses them. There are accounts of healings, and people who have come to the Lord. No wonder it's so much fun. Putting your light on a lamp stand certainly spreads it abroad. And when this happens, God does the work.

TO SAMARIA

Read Acts 1:7-9.   *March 31*

Every country I have ever been to has another people group that they despise. In the "United" States we make fun of other states. In seems like it is inherent in man to try to raise himself up by putting someone else down.

This was true in Jesus' day as well. If someone wanted to go north from Jerusalem to Galilee, they had to go through or around

Samaria. Most Jews went around. They hated Samaria. It meant that they had to put an extra hundred miles or more on the their sandal treads, but to them it was worth it.

Jesus was doing something nearly unthinkable by going through Samaria. Not only that but he stopped to talk to a woman at a well, one who had lots of problems and little reputation. When he told the parable of the good Samaritan, it was a person from that "low-down" country who did the right thing and bound up the wounds of the man who had fallen among thieves.

Jesus was always busting up stereotypes. He had compassion on all kinds of people. So he was being very specific when He chose the words to the great commission. It was apparently the last statement He made to His disciples before the ascension. "You will be my witnesses in Jerusalem and in all Judea and Samaria, and to the ends of the earth" (verse 8).

Sending out missionaries is not enough. We have to be willing to reach the people right around us. In essence He was saying to His disciples that He wanted them to start precisely where they were. There were hungry people right around them. Then they could expand to the territory immediately surrounding Jerusalem, namely Judea.

But Samaria? Could they be hearing correctly? Absolutely. In fact, as a friend of mine once said in a sermon on this topic, "We will never reach the ends of the earth if we get stuck on Samaria." We can't go out and love others effectively and skip right over the personal hang-ups about our own Samaria.

God intends for us to set aside our prejudices and fears. He demands that we value everyone and have a heart to set them all free. All of them.

APRIL

BOGUS OR GENUINE?

Read Acts 8:9-25.   *April 1*

The genuine article is always more beautiful than the replica. Place a real star sapphire next to a faux stone, and the difference is immediately discernible. Set a famous painting by a reproduction or print, and the variations in colors, shades, and details are readily evident.

Sometimes, however, people can be fooled by the fake. This is especially true if the real item or demonstration is not available for comparison. Then the observer might be unaware of the differences and settle for what is false.

Such was the case with Simon the sorcerer. People followed him because he performed many signs and wonders. We are told in Matthew 24:23-25, that this will also happen at the end of the age. Many false miracles will be performed, and even the saints are in danger of being deceived.

We must learn to sort out the real from the fake, the true from the false, the bogus from the genuine. It is not enough to decide that we will not believe any signs and wonders so that we are not in danger of being deceived. In doing so, we will then throw out the genuine along with the fake. We will not recognize the true work of God when we see it.

God worked His miracles through people such as Philip, a true believer. The real work of God was valuable and not to be purchased by anyone like Simon who wanted it for show.

Genuine people of God cannot be bought and sold. They hear from the Lord and are not manipulated by others to "perform their act." Resisting all temptations to any bogus, they would rather do nothing than to be involved in something that is not authentic.

THERMOMETER OR THERMOSTAT?

Read Revelations 3:14-16.   *April 2*

Which are you: A thermometer or a thermostat? The question goes to the core of who you are.

A thermometer reacts to its environment, simply registering whatever occurs around it. If people are grumpy, moody, and irritable, the thermometer-type person will reflect this. Should others display bad attitudes or frustrations, the thermometer takes them on as his own. The thermometer person will go along with what others think rather than to risk standing alone with his own viewpoint.

These sorts of reactions happen with the spiritual also. For example, if God moves in a mighty way, then the thermometer will warm up accordingly. He will join others at the altar and perhaps have a temporary change of heart. However, this can be short-lived. As the church community becomes more cold and lethargic, he will become that way also.

A thermostat, on the other hand, sets the tone for the entire environment. It regulates rather than merely responding. When others are in a poor mood, this individual can remain cheerful. When others are hyper and stressed, he can still be calm and at peace in the Lord. If some of his friends gossip, he doesn't participate and instead seeks to move the situation toward resolution, love, forgiveness, forbearance.

A thermostat-type person has determined to stay on fire spiritually. He will remain hot when others are lukewarm. Though the trend may be toward a lackadaisical perspective toward the things of God, the thermostat will set his own temperature and stay enthusiastic, motivated, and alive in Christ.

114

A hot drink will become lukewarm with time if left to itself. This seems to be what happened to the church referred to in today's scripture verses. It was a thermometer church, and it registered what was around it. They were soundly rebuked for this.

However, if you decide to do so, you can be as on fire as you choose to be and set yourself to stay there. You will then positively affect others. If you're on fire, even the thermometer will register higher. Which are you again?

BITTER OR BETTER?

Read Acts 16:16-34.   *April 3*

Paul had a reason to be bitter. All he had done was set this slave girl free by casting an evil spirit out of her. The result was a mob scene against Paul and his friend Silas.

Then, as if that weren't awful enough, the magistrates had Paul and Silas stripped and severely flogged. As a final insult, they were thrown into prison.

Imagine yourself in chains, like Paul and Silas, aching all over and bleeding. You had just been humiliated publicly. You were simply trying to serve God and now here was your reward: a dark, musty, prison cell. It would certainly be enough to make any person afraid and angry at God for allowing this to happen.

However, scripture tells us that the scene was different. Instead of getting depressed and grumbling, we find Paul and Silas at midnight sitting in their chains and "praying and singing hymns to God" (verse 25). Think of that! They used this opportunity to praise God and witness. Scripture tells us that "the other prisoners were listening to them."

You can be sure that those fellow prisoners would have overheard them if they had been complaining and murmuring instead. What kind of a witness would that have been? Who needs to listen to that? The prisoners would simply have had more of their own personal self-talk. But praise and prayers, no that was different. They hadn't heard anything like that in difficult circumstances before.

How do you respond to trial and tribulation? What do you do when hard times come your way? One of my friends once preached a sermon entitled "Bitter or Better." That's the bottom-line choice, really. You have an opportunity to become either bitter or better.

Paul and Silas chose to get better. I'm certain that it was no easier for them to stay positive than it would be for us. However, they decided not to become jaded and hopeless, and then God did a wonderful work inside of them. Their faith welled up and their trust in almighty God showed through. Ultimately, God performed a miracle and opened the prison doors, after which a whole family was wondrously saved.

Bitter or better. Which will it be? The question is important for you...and for those who watch your life.

BUILDING

Read I Corinthians 3:10-11.   *April 4*

The process of building a huge new structure has always amazed me. As the foundation is laid, the dimensions of the building become more apparent. That foundation needs to be carefully established so it will hold the weight of the building and provide correctly aligned measurements. As such, the importance of the foundation is inestimable.

This fact needs to be considered when setting the foundation for a new program. If a leader moves too quickly and doesn't lay a firm base, the program can easily collapse or be built askew. The wise leader will consider every detail of the foundation very carefully.

As Christians, we must acknowledge that God is the foundation of the church, and, I believe, He should be the foundation of whatever else is built through our lives. Some leaders try to make themselves the foundation. However, no person will ever be strong enough to hold the weight or straight enough to set the direction perfectly. Sooner or later, an individual will collapse under the load. I've seen it happen, and the results are pure rubble. It is not a pretty sight.

Furthermore, "each one should be careful how he builds" (I Corinthians 3:10). If each person builds with whatever materials he chooses in any style he wants, the result will be ugly. God will share the blueprint of the church with the leader, and people are to join together to produce a beautiful, coordinated structure. God will work through them to build what He desires.

Psalm 127:1 states, "Unless the Lord builds the house, the builders labor in vain." God has the wisdom, insight, blueprint, strength, technical expertise, overview, and experience to be an effectual builder. Simply put, we do not. Why labor without His resources? It will come to nothing but a hideous, uncoordinated, unstable mess.

You have one of those? Let it collapse, and then go back to the foundation. Do it right this time. God, indeed, is the master builder.

FORM OR FUNCTION?

Read Matthew 16:18 and 28:16-20.   *April 5*

Originally, one would assume, there was a purpose to each program or structure that was designed. Somebody had a reason that it should be built—a *raison d'etre*, if you will.

After a time, the structure that was originally formed for a purpose may lose its meaning. Perhaps the purpose no longer exists. Maybe the needs have changed. Some people may have forgotten its initial reason for being. The structure becomes lifeless and void.

It is lamentable when no one recognizes this. A great deal of energy, time, and resources may continue to be poured into structures and forms which no longer have a purpose. They have become an end in themselves, and no one remembers any longer why we continue to have them. It's habit, tradition. It's "just what we do around here."

Every so often, we should evaluate all forms to see if they continue to be effective. Are they still accomplishing what they were originally intended to produce? Are there changes that need to be made so that the programs can better serve their stated purposes in this time and in these circumstances? No form or structure should become sacred for itself.

It would be interesting, I think, to carry out this re-evaluation every five years. Then hold a type of "funeral service" to officially dispense of all old, meaningless forms. We are afraid to do this because people have become too attached to these programs. However, if this practice happened regularly, everyone would get used to tombstones and might not take it so personally.

Even the purposes or functions should be habitually re-evaluated. Are the needs for which this was designed still present? Are there new needs that are not even being addressed? Form should always follow function and not the other way around.

Perhaps this is why Jesus said that He would build His church. He didn't tell us to build it. Rather, He gave us instructions regarding function: to go and make disciples of all nations. The Lord will continue to show us His viewpoint for how to build and what to do in this generation in order to effectually accomplish the purposes He has given us.

Let us not be so busy maintaining old structures and forms, that we miss His plan for today.

WHAT DO YOU THINK?
Read Matthew 17:25, 18:12, and 21:28.   *April 6*

Questions. Jesus asked a lot of them. Questions make people think. They have to work things through, draw conclusions, and face the truth squarely.

With lots of specialized training in questioning techniques and thinking skills, I have come to treasure the formulating process of a good question. A well-considered question can draw people up short. When they stop long enough, then the Holy Spirit can do His work.

Perhaps one of the most important tasks of a strong leader is being able to ask the right question. Why? Where will that lead? What other options are there? What made you decide on that solution? What do you think will happen next? How is that different from what you're doing presently? What might have caused her to respond in that way? Next time what would you do differently? What led you to draw that conclusion? Why do you think that's how he feels? What did you notice about the dynamics of that meeting? What is causing you to hesitate? Which one is most important? What do you think that situation will be like tomorrow? What have been some of the effects of your decision?

These kinds of questions let us discover what is going on inside the people who are working with us. It assists them to gain processes that will help them be better leaders, decision-makers, and problem-solvers. By hearing the questions we ask, they learn to consider those same sorts of questions when later situations warrant it. This helps them to be better thinkers, not make so many mistakes, consider all the angles, and devise better options.

Too often as leaders we take an inordinate amount of time expounding our own thoughts. We give answers for which no one has even asked questions. Jesus took time to open people up, find out what was inside them, and make them think. It's good for us, too. We all need curiosity and freshness of thought.

NOT RECOGNIZING THE TIME

Read Luke 19:28-44.   *April 7*

Jesus' Triumphal Entry into Jerusalem is reminiscent of the huge triumphal processions that were typical of Rome at this time. As the Roman Empire would conquer lands as far away and varied as Africa, Britain, the Holy Land, and Gaul, great parades would be held when the military returned home. The soldiers were dressed to the hilt, their beautiful horses groomed and bedecked. They carried their captives in wagons to be viewed by everyone. Their spoils were also put on display, along with various kinds of exotic animals. Huge crowds lined the streets for these parades. Nobody wanted to miss it.

The entry of Jesus into His holy city is so directly opposite of this. Here is the true King coming into His city....on a donkey. A little colt at that, so Jesus' legs would have dragged on the ground. No beautiful banners here, only some hastily removed palm branches. No lovely fabrics...no wild colors....no musicians. The people are getting a little too excited in their praise, and the Pharisees tell Jesus to rebuke His disciples. He says, "I tell you, if they keep quiet, the stones will cry out." Even the cold stones knew the wonder of what was occurring!

What is sad is that the Jews had been waiting for a long time for their Messiah. When He finally came, they did not recognize Him. On the day He should have been hailed as their King, He came in on a donkey and was rebuked. They missed it.

Jesus prophesies the future of Jerusalem and ends it by saying, "....you did not recognize the time of God's coming to you." What an indictment. God help us now. When He comes to us, do we recognize Him? Do we understand the times? Do we know what He is up to in this day and age....or will we miss Him again?

REACTIVE OR PROACTIVE?

Read I Peter 1:13-16.   *April 8*

Some people are scattershot leaders. When they get nervous or uptight in a crisis, they pull out their shotguns and start firing away. Although their frustrations are due to other causes, their anger bubbles over, demanding to be released, and whoever is standing nearby may get hit.

Likewise, scattershot leaders attempt to solve any problems that crop up by using the same approaches. They try this and that, hoping something will hit the cause and the problem will be handled. Are you laughing? You've seen it, haven't you? Under pressure you're even tempted to do it, aren't you?

Reactive leaders are hard to work around. They even tend to scattershot at targets. Their goals are not particularly purposeful, and they try to hit whatever target pops up on the horizon. If someone shares about a current crisis or enthusiastically communicates a deep-felt need, that becomes the new target.

In all aspects, reactive leaders are not nearly so effective as those who are proactive. Verse 13 states, "Therefore, prepare your minds for action, be self-controlled."

We need to think. As we pray and stay calm, we can maintain an intentionality of action that produces self-control. Preparing in advance how we can respond rather than react in various situations will help us be proactive. God Himself will give us peace at the core of our being, provide us with wisdom, and help us to be strong and full of faith in the midst of pressure. We can look to God and then do what needs to be done with purpose.

God calls us out to be holy in all we do, even in the midst of stress, crisis, and pressure. Are you a reactive, scattershot leader who tends to unload your round? Or are you a calm, proactive leader who thinks, prays, and then acts with godly intentionality?

WHILE I MOVE ALONG SLOWLY

Read Genesis 33:12-15. *April 9*

I'm a change agent; it's part of my innate make-up. Innovation is exciting to me, and I enjoy watching the processes of change so I can be better at directing it in the future.

With any change process, there are early adopters who share enthusiasm at the early stages. They are vibrant people who have lots of good ideas and will provide input to improve the plans for the project. They catch the vision rapidly and are flexible, able to make the needed adjustments with ease. Personally, I like these kind of people.

The middle adopters require more patience. It is wise to plan how these people might be brought along in their understanding of the project. Communication must be thorough and anticipatory of their negative responses. Questions must have answers. Implementation of the change must come in palatable pieces so that the plan is accepted and "bought." How critical it is to take the time to build ownership!

The late adopters, well, now there's an interesting group. Leaders are usually the visionaries, the thinkers and creators, the doers, the change agents. They tend to get out-of-sorts and impatient with the slow movers. By the time the last group of adopters has arrived on the scene in their thinking, the leaders have often gotten bored and moved off in another direction to a new project. The slow adopters can therefore go for years without touching base with a leader in the change process.

In these verses today, we see Jacob with great sensitivity toward the slow-moving, the weak, and the tender. I really enjoy the challenge of this verse, because Jacob did not desire to drive them, not even for one day. He did not choose to be irritable or hard on them, but rather to utilize a decelerated pace on their behalf. Not only that, but Jacob moved along slowly right next to them.

As a leader, let us be sensitive to the pace that people set around us and not be a hard driver. It is unfitting.

NEW THINGS

Read Isaiah 42:9 and 48:6 & 7.   *April 10*

God is into things that are new and fresh. He makes men new. He gave a new covenant, and someday He will reveal a new heaven and earth. The Lord likes new wineskins and new wine. His mercies are new every morning, and He has times when He brings forth new things.

We are never quite sure when these new things will occur. We could never have guessed them; they were hidden away and then suddenly revealed. They might be new events in the world where walls between nations come crashing down overnight or powers and countries fall in a day. They might be changes in our own lives: a turn in career or a new place of ministry or even a whole new calling.

I have always enjoyed it when I have been searching with one purpose in mind and God has a spiritual serendipity in store for me. Suddenly, a new insight comes into focus in His Word or something breaks or changes inside of me. What a wonder!

Surely God desires us to be open to development, change, and growth. It is sad for an individual to become hard and stagnant. We were meant to keep learning, becoming more like Jesus, and discovering new truths.

God Himself is alive. His Word is full of fresh insight and life-changing applications. The Lord gave us so many options and possibilities, a multitude of places to explore and people to meet, such beautiful things to create and to enjoy in His creation.

I love to travel and meet different types of people, see unfamiliar places, and observe other cultures. My life is richer for it. I also enjoy reading because exploring certain literature and drama opens up so many new vistas. Learning a new skill, another language, or a craft is always such fun. Music and art are rich, architectural lines are gorgeous, and textile texture and color can be incredibly wonderful. New ideas gleaned from discussion with people can be life changing. There are museums to explore, a new route to take to work, sports to try, places to wander into, parks to walk through, and restaurants to try with new foods and recipes. There are zoos where God's creativity and zest are so evident.

Bored lately? Why? Perhaps it's a day for new things. Open up and let God take you by the hand.

ZEAL

Read Romans 12:11.   *April 11*

The Lord desires us to be on fire spiritually, demonstrating a zest for the things of God. We cannot wait around, expecting God to "zap us" with this. It is an attitude we have to choose.

If someone else were asked to rate your spiritual fervor and zeal on a scale of 1 (low) to 10 (high), what would she say? Are you excited about the Lord? Do you have a fresh testimony? Did you learn a new fact about God because He revealed more of Himself to you this week? Could you share a new insight you recently received from the Bible? Are you excited about God and your Christian life?

Leaders who can honestly say "yes" to each of these questions are very interesting to be around. Others want to spend time with them, to share in their discoveries.

It's fun to be a "shaker and mover." That's what leaders do well. Someone hands them a spoon, and they stir the pot. The ingredients get shifted around, eliminating burnt food and scalding. Someone has to stir!

Change for change sake is not what I'm advocating, either. But purposeful moving and a little mixing and shaking can be just the thing to bring back meaning into peoples' lives. We have to get out of our comfort zones, too!

A few years ago when I preached a particular message, I remember taking a step that was really big for me. As I was speaking, I felt the Spirit moving me in a different direction than what I had prepared. So I took a risk and threw away my notes—crumpling them right in front of a few hundred people. That stirred the troops. It stirred me, too. It certainly hit my uncomfortability zone! But the altars were packed afterwards and the service lasted for over five hours as people were moved on by God.

We have to be willing to let our zeal show through. Sometimes people seem almost ashamed of their enthusiasm and excitement, hiding it all under a mask of sophistication and control. If you're going to be good at being a "mover and shaker" in peoples' lives, you've got to be willing to be shaken up a bit yourself.

Risk-taking can be frightening, but also powerful. Step out into what God is asking of you. Come on, be adventurous!

THE BETRAYAL

Read Matthew 26:45-56.   *April 12*

Sooner or later every leader will probably experience betrayal by a subordinate or co-worker. This experience can grip us and wound us terribly.

It is especially difficult for a leader who likes people, trusts them, invests time in them, and wants to see their growth and well-being. Surely it is not expecting too much to receive basic loyalty and support in return.

I can still recall the pain I felt when two people who worked for me breached this trust. I had always tried to be a team builder and to make each member of the group feel valued and appreciated. I had invested in their lives.

Therefore, it was a shock to find out that behind my back they were pulling off all sorts of shenanigans. They were gossiping, spreading rumors, criticizing, and basically generating disunity, strife and confusion. Some derision and laughter could be thrown in for the mix, not to mention that they didn't pick up their share of the work load.

Let's be honest. I put up a good front, but I felt betrayed. How could they do that after I had tried to be kind? How could they treat their other team members so badly? My husband and I went on a long automobile drive across the country on the day after I discovered the severity of the problem. I had a lot of time to ponder the duplicity and feel it, too. There was no way I could cover up the pain with activity since I had miles of riding to sit quietly and think.

It was time well spent in the end. I realized that Jesus had experienced the same pain when Judas betrayed Him. Actually, it was probably worse. Judas was responsible for His death! Furthermore, think about how Jesus had cared for His disciples, how much He had loved them. Even this perfect example of servant-leadership could be double-crossed. It was comforting somehow.

I pondered how to respond to the situation and what to do when I returned to the office. Then I found Matthew 26:50. He called Judas "friend" right during the betrayal. Ooohh! Difficult as it was, I knew what I had to do, what my attitude must be. The rest would come later.

CROWD PRESSURE

Read John 19:1-16. *April 13*

Pilate was in a true leadership predicament. Personally, he did not think that Jesus was guilty. There was no basis for a charge against Him, and Pilate had told the Jews that.

126

The crowd pressured him, however. The Jewish officials were shouting, angry and agitated. They wanted Jesus dead, that was clear.

There was something about Jesus that bothered Pilate. He wasn't like other prisoners. He didn't try to defend Himself, and He was strangely calm and peaceful in the midst of this angry mob. These attributes disturbed Pilate greatly. Jesus demonstrated a great deal of equilibrium, even when His very life was at stake.

What caused Pilate to go against his best instincts? Why did he finally turn Jesus over to the mob to be crucified? He could have stood his ground and done what he thought was right.

Leadership does bring us to crisis crossroads where decisions are momentous. We can choose at such a time to hold to what is right or, like Pilate, we can give in to political pressure.

The Jews knew what would worry Pilate. He feared that rumors would get back to Caesar that Pilate was not loyal in his duties. The Jews were calculating when they kept shouting, "If you let this man go, you are no friend of Caesar. Anyone who claims to be a king opposes Caesar."

Pilate disliked such an interpretation of this event, but rumors can be dangerous weapons. He couldn't risk this one if he valued his career. Finally, Pilate capitulated and handed Jesus over to the Jews.

Washing his hands did not mean that Pilate could actually exonerate himself of this choice. He caved in to crowd pressure and made a decision against his better judgement. We, likewise, should beware when people and factions are pressuring us. During these times, we desperately need the God-given fortitude to stand strong for what is right.

"Lord, provide us with the strength to dispense justice and to make correct decisions—even when they are not popular. Might we be willing to pay a price personally, if need be, in order to do what is right."

LET US DRAW NEAR

Because of the fact that Jesus Christ died for us, we have the confidence to enter into the presence of God. Though He is holy and hates sin, our sin is wondrously and graciously covered by the blood of Jesus shed on the cross for us. What a wonder! We should never lose sight of this miracle, for by it we are redeemed and can come into the very presence of God.

Many, however, are still afraid to enter in. They can go for weeks and months without drawing near to God. Even worship and prayer can become forms that we simply perform without connecting to God Himself.

Often people feel unworthy to come to God, and this sense of unworthiness makes them reserved. They might feel they have not been good enough or worked hard enough. They are ashamed of sin in their lives. However, the problem is not in our sin but in our not accepting the totality and completeness of what Jesus has already accomplished.

God invites us to draw near with a sincere heart. We can be honest and "real" before Him. The Lord knows us anyway. He is aware of those problems and sins with which we are grappling and understands our temptations and weaknesses.

It is not necessary to figure out everything and pull it all together before going into the presence of God. Many people delay entering in to God's presence because they think they should get all their problems in order first. They'd like to get it all wrapped up and tied with a bow nice and tidy-like.

God, on the other hand, says to come with a sincere heart and share all that's on our hearts. It might be messy, but He insists that we should have the confidence to draw near. Then in His presence, He sheds His light on what needs to be fixed and changed. At the same time, His Holy Spirit comforts us and comes along side to help us. We are forgiven and changed. He provides wisdom without upbraiding us and shows us His love.

Why would we ever try to get it together by ourselves and not come to Him for this help? We will fail if we try independently to take care of our sin; we need God for that. We should never let our sin keep us away from God where our only hope lies.

Oh, my friends, if you have accepted Jesus as your Savior, dare to draw near. He invites you to do so, no matter what is happening with you right now.

TRANSPARENT FLAWS

Read I John 1:8-10 and 2:1-2.   *April 15*

Hide. Blend in. Cover up. Keep it together. Look good at all costs. Don't let them know it hurts. Maintain the image. How much energy it takes to sustain camouflaged perfection! If we feel that we have to present a certain front to others, then we have to cover over anything that we perceive as less than adequate.

This is akin to stuffing things in a closet till it can barely hold another item. When we're doing this, we know that sooner or later we'll crack open that closet door, and everything will come crashing down and pouring out.

Indeed, camouflaging our faults doesn't mean that we get rid of them. We just squeeze them in the closet so visitors can't see it behind the closed door. They can admire our clean house, but we know what's really inside.

When a person takes the step to reveal his flaws, then something important happens. Showing it all out in the open means that it doesn't get stuffed away anywhere. Transparency is truly refreshing.

Watch children for a while, noticing their honesty and straightforward communication, and we can see how far adults have strayed from real transparency. We have lost spontaneity, genuineness, and truthfulness about feelings, and it's hard to retrieve these as adults. We're afraid to open up the closet door for fear of the pent up anger and frustrations that might come gushing forth.

How much better it is to move through these risks and chance being real. It enables us to come in touch with our real selves, and perhaps that's just as important as getting enough rest and keeping our lives balanced.

To assist me in this, I like to go to a special restaurant which has a rather scrubby parking attendant who in many ways is quite ragged around the edges. For a while, all he would do is grunt at me. He was wounded, and his heart was protecting itself. But now Howard is so honest with me and our communication is flourishing. I need to be with "real people" outside the professional atmosphere.

In order to do this, my husband eats breakfast on his day off at a local, down-home restaurant. They know he's a pastor, and they share their hearts. He's talked to a lady whose sister was dying, a policeman dealing with a divorce, and a struggling waitress. Flaws, feelings, and all, they shared a lot. Don't camouflage!

SURPRISE!

Read Exodus 32:1-9 and 15-21.   *April 16*

Surprises. Leaders usually detest them. It's not the surprises of fun and parties we're discussing here. It's the surprises of crises and bad news. I'm not fond of someone being allowed to sneak up on me from the back. I trust others to see to it that such unexpected maneuvers do not happen. I get startled and out-of-sorts, and it tends to bring out a reaction in me—which reminds me of a story.

My husband and I enjoy tenting where the scenery merits it. There's something about that crisp night air with the smell of pine and the sound of a bubbling brook. But there was one surprise episode which occurred in our tenting experience that we will never forget.

We awoke after our first night camping near Niagara Fall and found the contents of the trash bag we had left outside our tent strewn all over our campsite. We cleaned up, muttering at the raccoons which we assumed had munched down a feast at our expense.

The next night I was awakened from a deep sleep by my husband pounding on the sides of the tent. He threw back the tent flap and then froze. Sinking back into his sleeping bag, he whispered with intensity, "Oooh, noooo!"

"What's wrong?" I whispered back. I was wide awake by this time but saw his eyes wide in the moonlight that streamed through the tent door and understood the unmistakable warning: "Shhsh!"

I waited quietly in expectancy and at last we heard the movement of animals. "What is it?" I whispered with curiosity, mingled with fear.

"Skunks!" he replied. "Not raccoons, but striped pussy cats!" The little family had been frightened when Ray beat on the tent and had run for protection—under our new car!

Thankfully and providentially, they did not let off their rank odor. But I never think of surprises without considering those skunks. You just don't want to launch a surprise attack on anybody who can be a little stinky, you know.

Moses was not a "happy camper" when he came down off Mt. Sinai after a wonderful meeting with God, only to find the people had created an idol and were running wild. This surprise did not put him in a good mood, to say the least.

When Moses saw the revelry, "his anger burned." He threw down the tablets of the ten commandments and broke them on the ground. Then "he took the calf they had made and burned it in the fire. Then ground it to powder, scattered it on the water, and made the Israelites drink it" (verse 20). There's a natural place for leaders to display righteous anger and throw a stink!

ANTIGONISH

Read Matthew 24:30-33.
(Read all of chapter 24 for context)   *April 17*

Our second tenting surprise occurred during a wonderful camping trip in Nova Scotia. We had arrived late one evening into the town of Antigonish and had quickly pitched our tent in the dark, crawled into our sleeping bags, and fallen fast asleep.

As morning broke in our new surroundings, we both awoke with a start, staring at each other. What was that odd sound? It seemed familiar, but we had never heard anything quite like it either. Poking our heads out through the tent door, we discovered that the campground was beginning to stir with numerous people in kilts and full Scottish regalia. They began warming up their dance steps and getting out their fifes and drums. We had unexpectedly happened upon the region's Scottish Highland games!

As for the sound, it turned out to be a whole regiment of bagpipes practicing at the fairgrounds clear across town. The eerie sound of all those pipes together carried for miles. I could see why it might strike terror as it warned of the approach of a Scottish army in the historical past. It seemed fearsome, foreboding, and intimidating.

In Scotland, the surprise would come with the warning, not the attack. The bagpipes were designed to hit a clear note of alarm and approaching doom.

God is doing this with the human race. He has played the bagpipes. He has warned that He will return. He has talked about judgment. Hell, death, and fire have been described. Who would be naive enough not to prepare at the sound of those bagpipes? Yet, the world does not heed the warning, and they will be surprised because they have not.

In verses 32-33, Jesus warned, "Now learn this lesson from the fig tree: As soon as its twigs get tender and its leaves come out, you know that summer is near. Even so, when you see all these things, you know that it is near, right at the door."

Just as we have learned to observe tell-tale signs of early trouble in our people, our budget, and our work, so we need to heed the bagpipes and watch the fig tree for the warning signals of the end of the age. Wake up and look around you.

THE WIENER DOG BALLOON

Read Jeremiah 18:1-16.   *April 18*

He took that balloon and began blowing, holding it tightly in some places and coaxing it into shapes. By not allowing the air into a certain section, it forced out another part and with only a few twists and turns, he set the wiener dog-shaped balloon on my desk with a grin.

Suddenly, I realized how that process was akin to the one God had been using in my life. I could see it in the lives of many others as well. God eliminates something or doesn't allow a certain area to expand. How difficult that is because it doesn't feel at all natural. It is so constricting, uncomfortable, and troublesome. Then, poof! Before we know it, another whole area has popped into existence.

When it seems that life is not allowing us to expand or grow in an area that we feel is important, what is our response? Do we moan and groan, yearning and pining for it? Do we kick and thrash around, trying to get it? Perhaps it's professional development opportunities, travel experiences, speaking engagements, a better social life, or a close friend that we desire. Sometimes we want these things so much that I wonder if they are even an idol to us. Since they don't seem bad in and of themselves, why wouldn't God give them to us?

But perhaps He is simply keeping that section from expanding so we can pop out and come alive in a whole new area.

133

Maybe He wants to get closer to us and allow more of our excitement, growth, and satisfaction to be found in Him.

Although the shaping of our lives is not an easy task, God takes great delight in it. He is the master potter forming the clay into a vessel of honor. Pressure in certain places is not comfortable, but it allows a whole new shape to emerge. Let's remember that it is entirely up to the creator—the potter or the balloon man if you will—to decide what He wants to make. We need to stop complaining about the shaping process, and let God create His work.

TODAY WAS A BLAST

Read II Corinthians 1:8-11.   *April 19*

This never happens to me. I never win anything, and I rarely just "happen" to be in the right place at the right time.

However, today was different. They were planning to blow up the old Metropolitan Center Stadium at 9 a.m. Since it was Christmas vacation at the university, I was driving in to work later than usual. I knew my typical path would take me by the targeted building that day, but what would be the odds that I would be driving by at exactly the right moment? Not likely. There were too many variables to juggle, including the unknown variable of traffic—lots and lots of it that day!

That's why when I passed right by the building at exactly 9 a.m., I was in shock. I pulled over to the side of the road, and there wasn't even a single highway abutment to spoil my view. I had a perfect vantage point as the blast occurred.

My four-wheel drive vehicle shook in the winter wind as hundreds of pounds of dynamite exploded. The enormous structure with its four huge main beams collapsed, still leaving two outside walls that would need to be knocked down later. However, the majority of the building was now a heap of rubble as smoke surged out of the collapsed debris in a gigantic cloud. I wondered if the windows of my vehicle would break, and the shock waves could be felt for minutes afterwards. What an experience!

It's the way I feel now and then. Ready to implode. The pressure builds and threatens my very survival, or so it seems. Leadership brings with it days, weeks, and even months of unusual stress and pressure, strings of crises and emergencies, loads of disappointments. The tension mounts, the pain numbs, and the hits are felt.

Paul knew this pressure and tension also, describing it in his second letter to the Corinthians. But through it, he also knew God's deliverance. "We're under great pressure," Paul said, "far beyond our ability to endure, so that we despaired even of life. Indeed, in our hearts, we felt the sentence of death. But this happened that we might not rely on ourselves, but on God, who raises the dead."

Feeling stress and pressure? Ready to implode? Rely on the Lord, my friend!

FINISHED WORK

Read John 5:36 and 19:28-30.   *April 20*

What a wonderful feeling it is to complete a large project. Months or even years may have been invested in a particular task, but one day at long last that book is finally in print or that production goal has been met or that breakthrough on an invention or research project has finally come.

Leaders, however, are often so action-oriented that they let the moment of triumph go by almost without notice. I once heard of a person who worked hard at restoring antique cars. He spent all his spare moments on a special model-T Ford, but the very day he finished it, he sold it. He didn't even drive it, and he barely looked it over. He did not take the time to note the finished product, and he did not fully comprehend the fact that his work was completed.

Not so with our Savior. In John 5: 36 we read that the Father had given Him a particular work to accomplish. Jesus not only understood what that work entailed, but He was fully aware that He was accomplishing it. In fact, Jesus said that this very work provided a testimony that God had sent Him. In the end, He could emphatically conclude on the Cross, "It is finished."

As I look at my work, I think that sometimes I am far too action-oriented. I am driven, getting busy with certain tasks and not feeling satisfied unless I'm active. Could it be that I work at tasks that actually are not even mine to accomplish? If that's true, then I probably leave undone a number of jobs that God would like me to finish. I thereby miss the testimony to Jesus that these works could have brought.

Let us determine what God has set our hands to do, and then at the end we can identify what has been accomplished. Following this procedure is much different than the drivenness of personal goal-orientation. At the end of our lives, God wants us to be satisfied in having accomplished what He had in mind. Then, and only then, can we say, "It is finished."

Thankfully for us, Jesus completed that work He was sent to do by the Father. He died for our sins, and on the Cross He could say with a vast depth of meaning, "It is finished."

ON THE ROAD

Read Luke 24:13-35.   *April 21*

Jesus is dead. All the disciples' hopes have been dashed. As Cleopas and his friend are walking from Jerusalem to the town of Emmaus, they discuss the almost surreal events of the day. The women had gone to the tomb early in the morning and reported seeing an angel and then Jesus Himself. It didn't seem possible; it just didn't make sense.

As Cleopas and his fellow traveler share these things, Jesus Himself comes up and starts walking with them, but they do not recognize Him. Jesus asks what they are talking about (as if He didn't know), and Cleopas' answer is rather humorous. He says, "Are you only a visitor to Jerusalem and do not know the things that have happened there in these days." Haven't you watched TV or read the newspapers, man?

Here they are, incredulous that Jesus doesn't know what is going on...but in reality they are the ones who don't realize what has happened. So Jesus opens up the scriptures to them and explains the prophecies and how He fulfilled them. Still they don't recognize Him.

As they come to Emmaus, Jesus acts as if He will go further, but they beg Him to stay with them. They "urged Him strongly." If they had not done this, Jesus probably would have continued on His way. Then they would not have known who He was, and we would not even have this story. It wasn't until they broke bread together that their eyes were opened, and they recognized Him.

In our lives, we often don't understand what is really happening. God can come alongside and we don't even know it. We walk down the paths of our lives, laden down with our troubles, our heads hanging and our hearts heavy. Still there is Jesus walking right with us. Step by step He is going along.

As our hearts are stirred in life and the Lord's presence seems to be with us, we need to beg Him not to leave. We should "urge Him strongly" to stay with us. When the Holy Spirit visits our services, we should not move along in our programs and plans, but rather stop and listen. We should set everything down and break bread with our Savior. How our mourning will be turned to joy!

WAGES

Wages: an assessment of the value of our work. Often this assessment has been done accurately, but sometimes it has not. What we are paid can be higher or lower than what we deserve. A six digit figure, for example, does not necessarily equate with what a person accomplishes, while a lower figure does not mean that in God's eyes, this individual isn't doing something extremely important.

In heaven, "many who are first will be last, and many who are last will be first" (Matthew 19:30). Some of us may be surprised at what this actually means in the scope of heavenly events. God has a way of setting everything right side up again. It will be interesting to discover His perspective of our lives.

Perhaps our assessment of value and wages blinds us to the wages of sin also. Romans 6:23 states clearly that the "wages of sin is death." How many people will ultimately reap wages for sin? This will be an accurate assessment by God Himself of what sin is worth.

As I deal with people every day, I have become convinced that most people no longer understand the concept of sin. Actually, it's a word that is little-used, one to which people seem to take offense. Nonetheless, sin exists. Old-fashioned evil with a capital "S" is still rampant.

We try to excuse people for their sin today—because they have "deficiencies" or have been "victimized" or otherwise were "not responsible for their actions." In our politically correct age, we might even be "error challenged." But try as we might to rationalize it all away, sin still exists in the human race. It's still just as horrible and black as it ever was, and its results continue to be just as devastating. Like it or not, the wages of sin are death.

Whenever we sin, something within us dies. We were not made to sin so it hurts us every single time. We reap pain and less than God's best. The Lord doesn't tell us not to sin just to make life difficult for us, but because each incidence of sin negatively impacts us. Always there are consequences to adultery, extortion, lies, cheating on income tax, and being arrogant and prideful. Every single time we get paid our wage—our just due—inside of ourselves. We might "get away with it" when it comes to others, but we will never get away from it inside of ourselves. There's always a price to pay.

Thankfully, Jesus came to cover this for eternity. How amazing!

CONSEQUENCES

Read Romans 2:8-9. *April 23*

"I have no right to deprive you of the consequences of your actions," I told the student. "If I do that, you will not learn or grow through this. If there are no consequences, if there is no pain at all, it will only make it easier for you to sin next time. God places consequences in our lives so that the memory of the pain will keep us from doing this hurtful thing to ourselves over and over again—just like you've been doing."

The young man scowled at me. He wanted to have no negative results of his actions. "If God forgave me, why can't you?" he said. I explained how I did forgive him, but that there still would be consequences. Those were two entirely different things.

As leaders, we cannot be so soft that we never confront in love or mete out results and consequences as they become necessary. If we don't do this, justice gets turned upside down, and sin is allowed to prevail. No, this cannot be!

However, neither are we to provide consequences out of judgment, anger, or frustration. Consequences are to be present only to bring people around to what is right, to really see the negative state of their sin so they will want to get rid of it. The consequences should be deep enough to root out the evil and bring a good change in a person's life.

I remember once having to inform a young lady that she would be dismissed from the college because of her ongoing promiscuous lifestyle. She was very upset with me when she heard this news. I tried to explain how much I cared about her and wanted to see her choose actions which were better for her. Though I tried to show her love in the midst of redemptive discipline, she stomped off in anger and went to live with her boyfriend.

Several years later she came back to the university, and when she saw me in the hallway, she threw her arms around me. "I just had to find you!" she said. "When I had to leave the school I was so angry because I wanted to continue in my sin. If you hadn't talked to me straight and warned me, I would still be doing all that today. But I kept thinking about what you said, and one day I left that guy and went back home to Mom and Dad. I got my life straightened out. You kept me from hell!"

Yes, consequences and loving confrontation can wake people up. As leaders, we have to care enough about people to do it. Even when it is uncomfortable for us.

PAINFUL DISCIPLINE

Read Hebrews 12:4-13.   *April 24*

A good earthly father provides discipline. Its purpose is to root out of our lives whatever is not good. It helps us grow up knowing right from wrong and assists us in exerting proper self-restraint.

People tend to respect those in authority who exercise some discipline in the ranks. Though employees might not like it at the time, they ultimately appreciate being challenged to greater things. Leaders who allow sloppy practices such as ongoing tardiness, long breaks, too much chit-chat, and slovenly clothes or grumpy attitudes will find the situation continually deteriorating.

Employees who find discipline to be consistent and fair will bear up well under it. They are quicker to develop a sense of pride in the quality of their work.

For these reasons, God rebukes us. He loves us, and He wants us to grow as His sons and daughters. As such, He will discipline us. If He refrains, it can seem that He doesn't really care. How could He just let us do things that will hurt us and not say a word?

How well do we mete out discipline? Even more importantly, how well do we take it? When hard times come, do we moan and cry or do we endure the hardship, allowing ourselves to grow through it? It's true that "no discipline seems pleasant at the time, but painful" (verse 11a). It's not easy to get our hands slapped. If we had changed earlier, heeded the warning before, exerted more self-discipline, we probably wouldn't even have needed that pain. As it is, now the pain is necessary to pull out the root of the problem and change us.

"Later on," verse 11b states, "it [discipline] produces a harvest of righteousness and peace for those who have been trained by it." What a wonderful end result! This should motivate us as leaders both to mete it out as needed and to accept discipline gracefully.

MERCY OR JUDGMENT?

Read Isaiah 30:1-3, 18-19.   *April 25*

Is the Lord a God of mercy or of judgment? It was an important question for me to rectify when I was involved in handing out discipline. How much mercy should be given and how much judgment? In what proportion? What's too hard? Too soft?

Often, I would see God in His role of being merciful as it is evident throughout the scriptures and wonder if I was being too exacting or demanding. At other times, I would view God in His role as judge and then ask if I was being too soft and not sharing with people enough about the serious ramifications of their sinful ways.

One day, it occurred to me that I was viewing God almost as if He were a schizophrenic, someone who chose mercy at one time, but then had this whole other side that He switched to. Since I knew that God was most certainly not schizophrenic, I wondered what I could learn here.

Suddenly I realized that God was all of both and that the truth lay in this very fact. He was all-merciful and yet He passed out judgment. He wanted to see people who were sinning to be confronted with the seriousness of their ways so they would stop. But in the midst of it all, He sent His Savior to help us.

This picture of God is so clear in the book of Isaiah. The prophet goes on for pages about the consequences that will soon come upon the Jews, but also upon other nations as well. He writes graphically about judgment and is full of woe, doom, warnings, and vivid descriptors of his people as obstinate, rebellious, faithless, and blind to the truth.

On the other hand, Isaiah has more insight into the Messiah, the hope of God's mercy, than perhaps any other prophet, He sees the truth of a God who is so extremely merciful that He sends His Son as a suffering servant.

In reality, God is a combination of both mercy and judgment. He cannot tolerate sin, and any perspective of a wimpy God who doesn't care whether we sin or not is simply wrong. God cares all right. Sin is really serious. But in the midst of it all, our merciful Father sent His Son to visit this earth and pay the price, thereby turning the rightful wrath of God away from us and onto Himself.

Mercy or judgment? It's not an "either-or" but a "both-and"!

AN ATTITUDE

Read Ephesians 4:20-27.   *April 26*

Self-discipline can keep us from needing external discipline, and one of the greatest areas where this should be applied is in our attitudes.

Negative attitudes can seep into our lives for a variety of reasons. Whether related to gender or racial concerns, looks or intelligence, family or our jobs, there are challenges to maintaining a good attitude.

In one of these areas, I once faced a real difficulty to my peace of mind. I was completely snubbed to the point where the person was downright rude. It was as if I didn't exist in a situation where I had contributed a great deal.

As I got into the car and drove home afterwards, I could feel the anger raging inside of me. "After all, I am a person, too," I thought to myself. "Doesn't he understand what he did?"

Suddenly, it hit me. No, he actually might not have understood. After all, he wasn't used to dealing much with people in my category. Perhaps, in some very real ways, people like me really didn't exist! Would he change? Not likely. Would I meet this type of person again? Undoubtedly.

Finally it struck me that I could spend the rest of my life getting angry repeatedly about such things, or I could decide right then not to let it upset me. I had a paradigm shift! I was, after all, in charge of my own emotions and my reactions to situations, even if I might not be able to keep negative things from happening.

My equilibrium over the years has felt great. I'm not just stuffing my anger and frustrations. Rather, I feel safe and secure in who I am and in what God has called me to be. This attitude has served me well over the years and opened many doors of opportunity. It has also provided me with a lot of time and energy to do positive things rather than waste it on a bad attitude.

If you're hurt and seething over some unfairness in your life, you can let it go right now. That's why the scripture says not to allow the sun to go down on your anger. Hand it over, won't you? It'll be worth it.

WAS THAT BENEFICIAL?
Read Ephesians 4:29 and 5:1-7.   *April 27*

When we have a poor attitude, it rankles our spirits. Anger, frustration, and bitterness vie for full control, allowing for little else to share the space.

Along with a nasty attitude comes bad talk, which is unwholesome. What's inside will ultimately come out. Grumbling, gossip, slander, and lies take over. Coarse jesting or dirty jokes behind doors will finally slip out.

As a listener, what will our response be? I once knew someone who told jokes with sexual innuendo that I found offensive. When I did not laugh, that person shook his finger in my face and said, "Who do you think you are, not to laugh at a simple joke? You act holier-than-thou!" In spite of such pressure, I knew it was my choice what I wanted to participate in. I even walked out of the room at times, it got so bad. Later, that person was discovered to have a moral problem. We should not feel socially pressured to join in with a person to ease his conscience.

As leaders, it is important for us to deal with what's on the inside in our attitudes and lifestyles. If not, negative results will occur in our speech and communication sooner or later, poisoning those who work with us.

Ephesians 4:29 states we should let only such words as are edifying come out of our mouths—something that "is helpful for building others up according to their needs." This will benefit them instead of tempting them to sin along with us.

Instead of enticing others sexually through dirty jokes, instead of encouraging elitism and pride through racial or gender humor, instead of encouraging judgmental talk by sharing our bitterness with others—scriptures ask us to let no unwholesome word whatsoever come out of our mouths. If it is not beneficial and edifying, it is not even to be said.

God help us to be leaders who practice this admonition.

SABBATH REST

Read Exodus 31:12-17.   *April 28*

Being is more important than doing. Leaders can cognitively comprehend this statement, but often are unable to understand it emotionally. We are far too action-oriented and our self-image is often interwoven with our performance. Since it is more difficult to measure internal growth, a leader's drive for progress and results is focused upon what is observably attained through action.

God understands this. That's why He insisted that we rest for a day every week. The Jewish Sabbath began on Friday evening at sun-down, starting with a night of rest. The concept of a "day" like this is that God works through the night while we rest, and we wake up to join Him in what He has already initiated. Instead of this model, we work hard first, and then rest, falling into bed exhausted and nervous. Rather than a lifestyle of WORK, rest, WORK, rest---God wants REST, work, REST, work.

Unfortunately, the concept of a Sabbath has become obscured in our society. It used to be that stores closed on Sunday, but now Sunday is nearly like every other day. People are called in to work, and we often join in, almost without a thought.

This is dangerous, however, for it feeds our working, doing, accomplishing mentality. And this can become most voracious, always demanding more and never being satisfied. Our merry-go-round lifestyles don't stop, and we become exhausted. I hear people crying out to God because they are so tired, but they should first try following God's command to rest. Even God Himself chose to rest on the seventh day in His creation schema.

God's emphasis on rest is important for our well-being. Without it, we become so busy with well-doing that we obscure our internal selves. We don't perceive what is happening in us; self-awareness is limited and often inaccurate. We don't pay attention to growth in the most important part of our being. It's out of the abundance of our hearts that the mouth speaks, and it's out of internal nature that we act. Give it a rest.

THE SABBATH

Read Exodus 34:21.   *April 29*

We had dreamed of this trip to Scotland for a long time, and one of our desires was to spend a Sunday on the northwestern island of Harris and Lewis in the Hebrides. This was where the famous revival had occurred in the 1950's with Duncan Campbell, and the stories that I had read about this remarkable move of God drew us. Our kind host, knowing my interest in the revival, had gone to the local library and collected a pile of island revival material that waited for me when we arrived. My husband laughed, joking that he would talk with me again when we got on the ferry on Monday. I did read and write like any happy scholar.

What was most stunning, though, was that on Harris and Lewis basically the entire island keeps the Sabbath. We had never seen anything like this before. Everything was closed. Yes, everything. No gas stations were open. No convenience stores. No restaurants except two in the tourist hotels. No ferries were running. As we made our way to church on Sunday morning, people weren't working in their yards; they were streaming to the churches. Those in the small town church obviously knew we were visitors, but so many talked to us and welcomed us to their luncheon.

We had gassed up our car on Saturday so we could take a

146

drive around the island after church on Sunday. The pile of revival material had included brochures, little booklets, and even a tape of Duncan Campbell himself with testimonies from the revival. So on our Sunday afternoon drive, I inserted the tape into the car's recorder. It so happened that as we would listen to a story, we often were coming into that very village. "There it is!" I exclaimed. "That's the very church where God moved. Wow! I can hardly believe it!"

What hurt, though, was my realization about how far we have come from keeping the Sabbath. We get so tired out. We run around and are constantly busy, including Sundays. People hardly have time for church or for each other. We wonder why we are so weary all of the time. How often are we breaking the Sabbath anyway?

I AM

Read Exodus 3:14.   *April 30*

To be or not to be, that is the question. At least it was the question for Hamlet. Of course, he was looking at the question of whether to live. For us, however, the question is whether we will "be" or "do."

Would you feel OK about yourself if you never accomplished another single thing? Our self-talk regarding this question reveals how much doing is inherent in our sense of self-image. Somehow we feel like we have to do more. We can't just stop, can we?

However, what would happen if God didn't use you for anything else at all? Would that be all right with you? Sometimes a particular instrument or tone is needed only once in a concerto. What if you've already been used for what God intended, and there will be nothing else? Or what if the one reason for which you were created doesn't occur until you're 80? We need to feel—truly feel—that this is all right.

147

Anna's most important contribution came as the old lady who saw the baby Jesus and prophesied over Him. Rahab accomplished one large feat for which she became famous—just one. But this one action brought her into the Jewish nation, and this brought her a famous son, Boaz, who ended up in the lineage of David and thus the Messiah.

What makes our lives important? It may be one single, simple act. Just one. Just once. And so what else counts? Us!

This is why God chose to name Himself as the great I AM rather than the great I DO! Who He is definitely is more important than what He does. Do you treat Him this way, or do you expect Him to perform for you, accomplish things on your behalf, execute great deeds?

Get to know the I AM so you can be like Him. Rest, my friend, and discover who you are. It's definitely important.

MAY

PROMOTION

Read Psalm 75:6-7.   *May 1*

Our fragile sense of self secretly yearns for praise, appreciation, and attention. Oops! That sounds prideful; I didn't really mean that. Or did I? Let's face the truth.

We all enjoy being noticed for something. We like to be known as profound rather than shallow, spiritual instead of fleshly, intelligent rather than slow. How delightful it is to be honored for our accomplishments, looks, hard work, or creativity. We carefully protect our characters and reputations, for these are important to advancement or self-image.

When these become driving forces in our lives, however, there is real danger. We may try to manipulate events and how our lives appear to others, hoping for promotion or exaltation.

Psalm 75:6-7 states, "No one from the east or the west or from the desert can exalt a man. But it is God who judges: He brings one down, he exalts another."

We are not to be looking here and there, trying to find supporters. People can spend a great deal of time trying to build up a network of friends who will be helpful to them at a particular time. Some are hungry for the secret scoop, wanting to be a part of the inside circle.

One of the great pieces of literature is C.S. Lewis' graduation address called "The Inner Circle." He says the drive to make it into the inner group is inherent in all of us and can lead to detrimental results. In his book *That Hideous Strength* he plays out this theme to its extreme. The story gives reason to pause.

God makes it clear that true promotion does not really come from people in high places or those in the right spots. God Himself is the one who judges and who determines what will happen. Even if a person manipulates his own way into a position, God can take him down. As secure as a man might feel for finally reaching his desired place, as much as he might think that his supporters are all safely lined up, in the end, God can remove him in an instant.

The good news for non-manipulators is that God can just as easily exalt a person. Think of Joseph, Moses, and David. Then let's look to God instead of our own devices.

Works Cited: Lewis, C.S. "The Inner Ring," Memorial Lecture, King's College, University of London. London, 1944.
Lewis, C.S. *That Hideous Strength.* New York: Scribner, 1996.

THE EYE OF THE STORM

Read Mark 4:35-41.   *May 2*

The car I was driving would provide little protection against a tornado. I knew that much. But what was I to do? Which way was I to go?

When I had left the business luncheon and headed off to the other side of town for another meeting, there wasn't any warning at all of what was about to occur. Although the sky was dark and threatening and it was beginning to rain, this gave me no real cause for alarm.

There were touchdowns by four different tornados that afternoon. If I turned around, there was one in that direction, according to the reports on the radio. In fact, they seemed to be trekking in almost any direction I considered.

Shaken and unable to decide on a different course of action, I simply kept driving on the freeway. About half a mile away from me, a funnel cloud touched down and ran parallel to my car, ripping and tearing through the suburban homes and businesses that lined the freeway.

I hope I never have to repeat the experiences of that day. At various times, the circumstances of life seem just as confusing, terrifying, and destructive. Their driving forces have ripped up foundations and wreaked havoc. What took years to build has been destroyed in quick order, and it appears to be almost impossible to rebuild ever again, so devastating is the damage.

In the same way, the enemy has come to steal, kill, and destroy. What we need to remember is this: God has miraculously provided the eye of the storm. In this calm place in the middle of the havoc, God dwells, and we can reside there in peace and safety if we choose.

Should we step out from the eye of the storm to check on what is happening, however, we will be greatly endangered. We can be hit by a cow or a roof. Debris can knock us senseless, and we can be injured or swept away.

God greatly desires for us to remain in the place of safety that He has designed for us. In the midst of the difficulties and stresses of life, He Himself is our peace. Be still. Stay close to God, and do not be afraid. He is there!

KEEP THOSE HANDS UP!

Read Exodus 17:8-16.   *May 3*

So what if a leader walks out? ...Gives up? ...Quits either in reality or in attitude? What difference does it make? A great deal.

The story in Exodus that relates the defeat of the Amalekites is helpful in understanding this dynamic. Moses, as the leader, had to keep his hands upraised as the battle raged. When he put his arms down, the battle turned against the Israelites. However, as long as his hands were raised, they were winning.

When the battle gets long, and the leader becomes weary, it

seems not only logical but also needful to give up the fight. After all, people can't keep their arms lifted up for huge periods of times. Aching, cramped, painful, their arms will finally get tired and drop down.

"Who knows? Who cares?" the leader might ask. If I give up quietly and slither out the door, probably no one will even take notice. I'll find something else to do, somewhere else to go. I just can't take it any longer.

However, the responses of the leader to the challenges before the group are totally significant. No leader can skirt around this fact, much as he or she might like to do so. If the leader can't stand up in the fray, then everyone becomes weakened. He needs to be strong in the midst of the pressure and continue looking to the throne of God.

From the spiritual vantage point, as the leader shows confidence in God, the Lord moves in and responds to this faith. The leader's courage is caught by the people, and they are willing to persevere. They gain strength as they observe their leader's endurance, patience, and hope.

When the hands are just too tired to keep up any longer, every leader needs an Aaron and a Hur beside him. Share the concerns and the load, allowing these faithful cohorts to come in close to hold up your hands.

I've had people who have supported me so visibly, that as they've prayed for me, they've literally held up my arms. I know that they have chosen to stand with me. What a blessing this can be! Together, we will certainly win.

THE COURAGE OF OUR CONVICTIONS

Read Exodus 32:21-25.   *May 4*

General George Marshall, Army Chief of Staff during World War II, was once asked what he sought in potential leaders. "Courage," he said, "because all else depends on that" (U.S. Air Force, coreval).

Courage is indeed essential in difficult situations. Leaders must be strong in the fight, and they must also stand up for what they believe without hedging.

How disconcerting it can be to watch a wishy-washy leader who can't make up his mind. He makes a decision, but then a small group puts pressure there, so he changes his mind and says something else. He moves with the flow and takes the path of least resistance.

This presents a problem because the leader's word cannot be trusted, and it is difficult to determine where he even stands. People fear that this decision or statement is only for today and cannot be relied upon tomorrow.

We need leaders who have convictions and the true courage of those convictions. What they say, they mean. They will stand by what they believe when the going gets tough. They are able to make decisions, live with any fallout from those choices, and just get on with life.

In today's *Bible* verses, we see Aaron hedging, going with the flow and taking the easy way out to please the people. The results were disastrous. "Moses saw that the people were running wild," Exodus 32:25 states, "and that Aaron had let them get out of control and so become a laughingstock to their enemies."

So Moses takes his stand and begins to sort it out. The Levites join him, but then they are given a difficult task to accomplish—all because they had the courage of their convictions! In the end, however, order is restored, and Moses is again leading the people in the direction they should go.

Let me ask you two questions and request that you not pass them off too easily. 1) What are your convictions? 2) Are you standing for them?

Work Cited: *U.S. Air Force Core Values*. 72 CS Web Services, 13 Sept. 2004. U.S. Air Force. 25 Sept. 2004. <http://137.240.249.5/coreval/proread.htm>.

WHERE DID ALL THE LEADERS GO?

Read Judges 21:25.   *May 5*

Leadership is essential. As we saw yesterday, when Aaron was left in charge during the time that Moses was on the mountain, he virtually abdicated his delegated leadership role.

Later he complained to Moses, "You know how prone these people are to evil. They said to me, 'Make us gods who will go before us'" (Exodus 32:22-23). Well, so what? Just because the people are disposed toward evil doesn't mean that Aaron had to give in to it. He simply buckled under and told them to give him their jewelry. "Then they gave the gold, and I threw it into the fire, and out came this calf!" Sure, come on. Poof! A golden calf just emerges out of that fire all by itself.

We need to see that as leaders, we are responsible to stand for what is right. If we don't, the people will take over and run amuck. Everything will be disorganized and out of order. Sin can run rampant.

The last line of the book of Judges is a profound one. "In those days Israel had no king; everyone did as he saw fit" (verse 25). Can you imagine the results of this philosophy? If each person does just as he or she pleases, then chaos will ensue. People all have their own ideas, and these don't usually mesh. One wants to go a certain way and another person desires a different direction. Who is to decide which is correct? A leader, of course. But without a leader, the whole process gets bogged down as each person pulls against the other.

154

Today in our society, we are in desperate need of leaders who will take a stand on issues, who will speak out against sin, and who will provide direction. We don't need any more so-called leaders who want to please everyone and so waffle on everything. In essence, these aren't leaders at all.

It is time to arise and be counted, to be consistent and strong, to step forward and say what we think. In short, it is time to lead!

WE'RE IN TROUBLE NOW!

Read Exodus 5:19 and 6:1-12.   *May 6*

In trouble. That's what they were. "The Israelite foreman realized they were in trouble," Exodus 5:19 states, "when they were told, 'You are not to reduce the number of bricks required of you for each day.'" They were provided with less resources but were expected to produce the same amount.

We can try to work people harder, but there comes a time when the adversity becomes too much. Even though we attempt to make do with an exceedingly low budget for a period, after a while the limitations take their toll. Our people can combine jobs and take up the slack of workers who have been laid off, but they can manage this only for a time. Sooner or later, production lags. Without enough resources, the expectations are simply impossible.

When the situation is tough, where do the fingers point? To the leaders, of course. And Moses and Aaron were not immune to blame. It must have been quite disconcerting for them because they had barely started their assigned task to negotiate the release of the Israelites. The two of them felt helpless. They couldn't provide straw or persuade Pharaoh to lighten the load. In fact, the more they tried to accomplish their duties, the worse the situation was likely to become.

God reminded Moses that He was in charge. The Lord gave him many promises. So often, God provides to the leader both a vision and the faith needed for it. However, the people don't want to hear it. "They did not listen to him because of their discouragement and cruel bondage" (Exodus 6:9).

This can be disheartening for a leader and place him in a lonely position. It is difficult when there is no way out. If the leader follows God, the circumstances may get even worse before they get better. When things are already bad, the people will become discouraged, get angry, complain.

When this happens, will you stand? Will you follow God no matter what? Can you have faith for the ultimate victory celebration?

THE SPRING BOUQUET
Read Ephesians 2:10.   *May 7*

A January blizzard was raging outside. I was so thankful to have the night at home. My husband was involved in a meeting at the church, but I didn't have to be there this time. I had just banked the fire in the fireplace and started into a book when the doorbell rang. Who could it be on a night like this?

With a sigh, I uncurled myself and hurried up the stairs. A lady with a distraught expression peered through the storm swirls. "I'm so sorry to bother you," the stranger apologized. Her voice was shaking, and her eyes were filling with tears. "My car broke down several blocks from here."

"Come in!" I insisted. "It's too cold for you to be standing outside." She explained that she needed a phone but hadn't wanted to bother anyone so she had started walking. Why she had finally chosen our house to approach for help...well, she wasn't quite sure.

I smiled and took a deep breath. These things always take time. I knew my cozy evening of relaxation had just evaporated. It's not necessary to detail the next several hours. Suffice it to say that I had to go out into the blizzard after all, but then there was also some meaningful conversation. I arrived home about the time my husband returned from his meeting. That was that.

In May when the flowers were nudging through, I decided to host a spring luncheon for my friends. I enjoy hospitality so I had great fun planning my guest list, the theme, the menu, and the table setting. Everything was perfect except that in my imagination, I could see a big basket of fresh cut, mixed flowers on my table. I am of a practical bent, however, so the expenditure seemed a little extravagant to me. Besides, I thought about our missions offering goals and decided against the flowers.

The day of the luncheon dawned full of warmth and sunshine. The birds were chirping in the woods behind our house, and the smell of spring wafted in on the breeze. The guests were to arrive at 11 a.m., so I was surprised when the doorbell rang about 10 a.m. It was the florist. Guess what? The lady in the blizzard had sent a belated thank-you, a basket full of mixed spring flowers that exactly matched my fancy! I still smile when I think about it. The Lord has His ways of "paying us back." Cost now....joy later.

LET US DRAW NEAR
Read Hebrews 10:19-22.   *May 8*

Because of the fact that Jesus Christ died for us, we have the confidence to enter into the presence of God. Though He is holy and hates sin, our sin is wondrously and graciously covered by the blood of Jesus shed on the cross for us. What a wonder! We should never lose sight of this miracle, for by it we are redeemed and can come into the very presence of God.

Many, however, are still afraid to enter in. They can go for weeks and months without drawing near to God. Even worship and prayer can become forms that we simply perform without connecting to God Himself.

Often people feel unworthy to come to God, and this sense of unworthiness makes them reserved. They might feel they have not been good enough or worked hard enough. They are ashamed of sin in their lives. However, the problem is not in our sin but in our not accepting the totality and completeness of what Jesus has already accomplished.

God invites us to draw near with a sincere heart. We can be honest and real before Him. The Lord knows us anyway. He is aware of those problems and sins with which we are grappling and understands our temptations and weaknesses.

It is not necessary to figure out everything and pull it all together before going into the presence of God. Many people delay entering in to God because they think they should get all their problems in order first. They'd like to get it all wrapped up and tied with a bow nice and tidy-like.

God, on the other hand, says to come with a sincere heart and share all that's on our hearts. It might be messy, but He insists that we should have the confidence to draw near. Then in His presence, He sheds His light on what needs to be fixed and changed. At the same time, His Holy Spirit comforts us and comes along side to help us. We are forgiven and changed. He provides wisdom without upbraiding and shows us His love.

Why would we ever try to get it together by ourselves and not come to Him for this help? We will fail if we try independently to take care of our sin; we need God for that! We should never let our sin keep us away from God where our only hope lies.

Oh, my friend, if you have accepted Jesus as your Savior, dare to draw near. He invites you to do so, no matter what is happening with you right now.

MY FATHER THE CEO

Read Revelation 4.   *May 9*

Coming into the presence of a holy, mighty God can be a rather frightening thought. He is so powerful, omniscient and perfect. How could He relate to little old me with all of my weaknesses, inadequacies and sin? Still, He asks us to draw near.

As I was thinking about this one day, a wonderful analogy came to my mind. It is as if you are a child of a famous dad. Imagine this father as being the CEO of an enormous conglomerate. He is wealthy, powerful, and in charge of many things.

One day, you—his two-year-old son—visits his office. It is on the top floor of his 80-story office building, and it takes up the entire floor. This place is plush! It is richly furbished and complete with a spacious conference room, a bank of secretaries and computers, a private shower, everything that one could imagine.

This man is obviously busy—and protected. His administrative assistant will allow no one by without an appointment, and that list is always full. Every phone call is carefully screened, and no one gets in by simply walking past her. Except you, his son.

You have never seen this office before, and you are in awe of everything. You are a little frightened, but you really want to see your dad and so you run toward the door your mom points toward. You run right past the administrative assistant and stand on tiptoe to open the door.

As you peek into the huge office, you see your dad working at his executive desk. He looks up somewhat sternly to begin with, but when he sees it is you, a smile lights up his face. He gets up and comes around the desk, holding out his arms to you. You, of course, run into them for this is your "Abba, Father." You have a special relationship with him.

Yes, it's true. Dare to draw near. Those arms are open and waiting for you. Yes, you!

GET A GRIP!
Read Hebrews 10:23 and Romans 8:18-25.   *May 10*

Relativism and tolerance are the tunes to which our society dances. They provide for an eclectic approach to our value system and beliefs. They allow for opposites to be mutually embraced and for lackluster standards which shift with the tides. Although it is not popular today, there are, nonetheless, moral absolutes. Likewise, there is sin, and there is even a heaven and hell.

How can I be so sure? Because I know the One who embodies the Truth. Furthermore, this Jesus has promised that someday we who have believed in Him will be with Him for eternity. This is a great hope, and it is my sincere belief that we should get a firmer grip on this wonderful truth.

Even though right now we may be groaning and life may be difficult, we know that someday we will have the redemption of our bodies. The adoption process as God's sons and daughters will come to fruition, and we will be able to stay with Him where He is. Heaven is a real place.

What is difficult now is that heaven seems so far away and vague. It is hard to maintain a firm assurance and a strong hope in a place we have never seen. If we had seen it, though, then it would be ours, and there would be no need for hope.

We are encouraged, therefore, to get a grip on this hope. We have something wonderful coming up in the future if we do not lose heart and give up. Even though it is not a popular thing in this day and age to have strong beliefs, we must hold on to God unswervingly, not allowing others to jeer us or embarrass us into compromise or even silence. The Truth is as real and alive today as ever, and others will not be able to know that or find Him if we capitulate for the sake of popularity. Although we do not have to be Bible-thumpers, we can be bold and strong in sharing the reality of a living Savior.

Come now. "Let us hold unswervingly to the hope we profess, for he who promised is faithful"(Hebrews 10:23). Don't be wishy-washy, even in the midst of a world awash in a state of flux.

WITH ETERNITY IN VIEW
Read Romans 8:17-28.   *May 11*

The suffering of this world seems so senseless at times. Why do we have to put up with it? Why can't we just have it over with? It's not that simple though. Romans 8:17 states that we are "heirs of God and co-heirs with Christ, if indeed we share in his sufferings in order that we may also share in his glory."

Heaven comes with the package of suffering on this earth. Jesus suffered, and we can expect it, too. We will share with Jesus as heirs, but we must also share with Him in His suffering. We will be a part of Jesus' victory and glory, but here on earth there will be pain first.

It is costly to share the good news with a world that does not want to hear it. Pastors and missionaries may give up high salaries in order to serve in needy places where God calls us to minister. Organizational budgets can also be tight. People problems can emerge. Times can be hard in so many respects; we live in a fallen world.

However, Paul saw all of this with eternity in view. "I consider that our present sufferings are not worth comparing with the glory that will be revealed to us," he said in Romans 8:18.

If we do not keep heaven in mind, then our present sufferings will be overwhelming and will probably appear meaningless. God's great purposes in and through us will get lost in our every day lives. From heaven's vantage point, however, it will be worth it all to be involved in God's eternal plan. We will see people in heaven who were saved and changed, and then we will rejoice.

With eternity in view, we find strength to go on from day to day. We can stand firmer in our beliefs, not give up so easily, keep working and trusting, build our faith even more. Though we are weary, we will keep running the race because the prize at the end is worth it. Heaven will be glorious! How could we give up here on earth and in the process lose treasure in heaven?

God will take all things we face now and somehow work them out for good if we just keep loving and trusting Him (verse 28). Anything that besets us, no matter how difficult, will not separate us from God's great love which we will see in new ways some day in heaven. Keep eternity in view—all of the time.

SPUR ON ONE ANOTHER

Read Hebrews 10:34-35.   *May 12*

We need each other, especially in these difficult days. When it becomes challenging to stand up for our beliefs, we need others who will stand by us, pray for us, and encourage us in the fight.

Scripture exhorts us not to give up meeting together. If we do, we become weakened. The Body of Christ is meant to stay bonded together so they can share each other's burdens, bounce off concerns, discuss Christ-like approaches to problems, and pray for each other.

Have you been encouraging to someone else recently? When is the last time you wrote a positive note to another Christian, telling her how much she means to you or how much you appreciate him and his contribution to your life? When have you patted someone on the back for a job well done? I have always tried to make it a habit to tell a person when I compliment them "behind their back" to someone else. Why shouldn't they know what I say about them?

Have you encouraged someone else to do a good deed recently? These verses today tell us to "consider love and good deeds." A spur does something special to move one to action. How can you do that effectively, moving both yourself and others toward considerate, compassionate, and caring actions?

Could you turn a negative conversation into a positive one? Could you share an idea that would bring you and a friend together to accomplish a kind deed? Could you do a better job of reinforcing the "love and good deeds" that are taking place around you so that more of such behavior is likely to occur? So often we take these things for granted, barely noticing or saying thank you, even when they are directed toward us.

Sometimes I don't think we realize the importance of a simple action. Just today one young man opened the door for me and then turned around and went back my direction. He had taken some extra steps simply to open the door. Another came up and told me I looked especially nice today. Yet another young lady dropped by and said, "Could I just give you a hug? I thought you might need one." Another left an encouraging little message on my voice mail. All this in one day!

Are you an encourager? Do you spur on more positive action in those around you and join in the good deeds yourself? Try three in the next twenty-four hours.

EXAMPLES

Read Hebrews 12:1-3.   *May 13*

The lives of many Christians who have gone before us ring out as reminders of what it is like to be sold out to God. These watch from heaven and cheer us on. Their lives still challenge us and are examples that spur us on to live for God.

Whenever I get to feeling sorry for myself and am tempted to slow down or even give up, I pick up a biography of a famous Christian. These have had a powerful impact on my life.

My favorite is *A Chance To Die*, the story of the great missionary to India, Amy Carmichael. This wonderful book was written by Elizabeth Elliot, the widow the Jim Elliot who was martyred by the Auca Indians. This fact lends another level of meaning to this powerful biography of the woman who gave her whole life to save children in India. Running an orphanage by faith is not an easy matter, but Amy Carmichael demonstrated great love and complete obedience to God.

Then I think of the biographies and stories of Gladys Aylward (China), Mark and Huldah Buntain (India), Lillian Trasher (Egypt), Adoniram Judson (Burma), and Hudson Taylor (China). I think of the faith of C.T. Studd and the prayer life of Rees Howells and David Brainerd. I consider the lives of a Moody, a Spurgeon, the Wesleys, a C.H. Mason, a Tozer, a William Seymour, and Count Zizendorf.

I have met only several of these people, but the lives of all of them have greatly impacted mine and encouraged me to greater dedication to God. Although they were ordinary in every basic respect, they were extraordinary in their commitment to the Lord. What a challenge they present! All of them were determined to lay down their lives for God. They allowed Him to do with them anything at all He chose.

Jesus, also, was willing to lay down His life for us. God did not make Him obey. He chose to give of Himself because He wanted to see us saved, to be in heaven someday with Him. Satan didn't make Jesus die on that cross, forcing our Savior under his control. The Lord chose to lay His life down.

Satan doesn't have a hold on our lives either. We also have a choice. Will we follow the Lord at all costs or won't we? Will we be completely devoted, becoming a part of what God wants to accomplish on this earth, or will we choose otherwise? The decision is up to each one of us. Just keep in mind, if we choose to commit, we will have joy in heaven. There will be people who are saved because we were faithful. What glory! What a day that will be.

Work cited: Elliot, Elizabeth. *A Chance to Die*. Grand Rapids, MI: Fleming Revell, 1987.

WHAT'S REAL?

Read II Kings 6:8-23.   *May 14*

Which world is real: Heaven or Earth? Sometimes we get so tied down to the mundane that we aren't even aware of spiritual realities. Nonetheless, the spiritual forces exist and are at work.

Elisha's servant at first saw only with his earthly eyes. He was afraid, for a strong enemy army with horses and chariots had surrounded the city during the night. They were after Elisha, the man who was so spiritually astute that he was foiling the plans of the enemy because he heard from God. No wonder Elisha's servant was frightened. I am not surprised by the consternation he shows when he exclaims to Elisha, "'Oh, lord, what shall we do?'" (verse 15).

"'Don't be afraid," the prophet answered. "Those who are with us are more than those who are with them'" (verse 16).

Imagine how this answer must have initially frustrated the servant. Couldn't Elisha tell that this was a serious situation? The king of Israel was not present with his troops, so who was "with us"? Perhaps the prophet had lost his wits this time.

But then Elisha prayed and asked God to open the servant's spiritual eyes so he could see the realities of that realm. Suddenly, everything looked different. The servant "looked and saw the hills full of horses and chariots of fire all around Elisha" (verse 17).

Indeed, Elisha trusted his security and safety to God. He knew that the Lord would be his defense, and God was truly there for him! The enemy army was struck with blindness and became confused. They were led right into the hand of their very enemy, the king of Israel, in a sudden switch.

We need to become more aware of the realities of the spiritual realm. God is still alive and at work today. He is a powerful and ever-present help in times of trouble. In the spiritual realm, the battles are raging. We just need to ask to have our eyes opened more regularly to these realities.

I believe that God wants us to be aware so we can pray and intercede. As II Corinthians 10:3-4 states, "For though we live in the world, we do not wage war as the world does. The weapons we fight with are not the weapons of the world. On the contrary, they have divine power to demolish strongholds."

Let us take the sword of the Spirit, which if the word of God, and do battle, not in the earthly realm against flesh, but in the spiritual realm where reality exists.

VIRTUAL REALITY

Read I Corinthians 13:8-12.   *May 15*

After attending several seminars on "virtual reality" and having the opportunity to experience it for myself, I am amazed at its technological possibilities. Like all media and technology, it has the potential for being used for the good of society, but it may also be used for negative purposes. It all depends on who gets hold of it and whether or not they decide to exploit it. Where will those with the capability of advancing the technology stand in their moral and ethical perspectives?

Many times, Christians wait until a neutral area had been taken over by evil and then they preach against it. Isn't it also our responsibility to be salt, affecting everything for good and claiming it for God? We need to become more proactive in these matters as Christians.

Although many computer items are labeled "virtual

reality,"(VR), they are not really VR in the true sense of the word. Virtual reality is a way for humans to visualize, manipulate, and interact with computers and extremely complex data. Presently, virtual reality requires a headset which puts one into an environment which is computer designed to appear as real.

A person can actually manipulate items in a VR environment, and it seems like reality. This can be used for the medical field, in space, in architecture, and in scientific exploration of our world. The possibilities are both numerous and exciting.

One of the discussions, however, is whether people will be confused regarding what is actually real. Some have experienced a certain amount of disturbance from being moved out of virtual reality into actual reality.

It is amusing, in a way, that mankind is trying so hard to simulate reality. So far it is not quite the same since it is lacking certain detail, plus the weight of objects as well as the placement of sound are still being worked out to make VR more lifelike. Some are giving their whole lives to discovery and development in this field.

In the same way, earth is but a virtual reality of the reality of the spiritual realm. Here on earth, we see in shadows. "Now we see but a poor reflection as in a mirror," I Corinthians 13:12 states, but "then we shall see face to face."

Someday we will actually be able to understand, and what is now imperfect, incomplete, and not quite understood will come into perfect focus in the reality of heaven.

HEAVENLY MINDED

Read Isaiah 61:1-3.   *May 16*

Most have probably heard the saying that we can be "so heavenly minded that we're no earthly good." That sounds reasonable, but experience doesn't ring true with it, somehow.

Have you ever seen such a person in real life?

The individual I've met who was most heavenly minded was actually of great earthly good! He breathed prayers all the time. In the middle of a sentence, he might stop and say a few words to God. This man was very much aware of the Lord and His presence. At the same time, he probably did more to alleviate human suffering than any other person I have known personally. He built hospitals, developed feeding programs, and cared for the needs of thousands of people. Huge numbers came to know God through him. He lived out the Lord's care for the multitudes in India. That was Mark Buntain.

Indeed, people who know God and who are "heavenly minded" seem acutely aware of others. Those who have touched the heart of God are moved to compassion, love, care, and good deeds. They share the wonderful story of a Savior with a lost, hurting, and dying world.

This was precisely Jesus' calling. He preached good news to the poor and bound up the broken places in their lives. He brought people out of the clutches of Satan and set them free. Brimming with comfort, He poured out of Himself to touch the hearts of those who were in grief and mourning. Jesus cared. If we are truly heavenly minded, we too will have this same care for people.

The truth is, we are usually too earthly-minded to be of any heavenly good. We get wrapped up in our own cares and needs and do not seek the heart of God. Now that ought to concern us.

We desperately need to have a heavenly perspective of justice, right and wrong, sin and judgement, forgiveness and grace. Our viewpoint of people must become more like God's. We need to learn His love, care and concern for the human race. How else can we comprehend a God who gave up His only Son to save us?

I guarantee it. The more heavenly minded you become, the more earthly minded you will also become!

UNITY

Read Ephesians 4:1-7. *May 17*

The commitment to unity must start at the top. If the leader doesn't care about it, then unity is difficult both to develop and to maintain.

In Ephesians 4:3, Paul insists that we "make every effort to keep the unity of the Spirit through the bond of peace." This does not mean that everyone always has to agree. In fact, that would be insipid and bring less than quality results. No leader is wise to place a group of "yes-men" around him. Strength comes from different perspectives and views, even confrontation and challenge when they are needed.

However, none of these should disrupt unity. We can still remain friends, loyal to each other and respectful, even in the midst of disagreements. Ephesians 4:2 explains how this can happen. The verse suggests that it is in the attitude. If we stay "completely humble and gentle" (verse 2), then sharing our varying viewpoints will be done in a loving way that maintains the unity. We don't communicate our views out of arrogance or slash away at another person's ideas without consideration of his person-hood. Rather, we submit our ideas out of humility, carefully presenting what we think.

This verse also tells us to "be patient." We can let disparate thoughts be aired without feeling attacked or taking it personally. We are patient as people work through ideas in their minds. While they are in the process of forming their opinions and committing, we can wait and permit them space to process.

Finally, we should be "bearing with one another in love" (verse 2). Wherever there is divergence, we can respect this and allow the other person to have his or her own opinion. Our love for each other is all-encompassing, bringing us to the place where we can still be friends and work together, even when we see things distinctively.

Psalm 133:1 says, "How good and pleasant it is when brothers live together in unity! It is like precious oil poured on the beard, running down on the beard..." When we have a primary commitment to unity, the depth of our love, respect, and trust for each other is profound. It's the smoothness of oil right in the midst of disagreements. We know the solidity of relationship, even when we don't see eye to eye. We respect individuality within our deep dedication to each other in community.

THE SHRINKING OASIS

Read James 3:13-18.   *May 18*

One of the most engrossing lectures I have ever heard was presented in a community education program on the topic of oases in the Saharan Desert. An oasis is a fascinating place! Having been used for centuries by Bedouin caravans, the inhabitants of the oases have set their entire culture in perfect balance to ration that precious commodity, water.

There are 300,000-500,000 palm trees in a typical oasis. This may sound lush and permanent, but I learned that oases can dry up. Many actually do. The members of the community must plant new trees and plants constantly in order to maintain the water cycle. They have to fight against the encroaching sand literally on a daily basis, just like we do with sin. If they don't all work together to get the sand out of the water beds and out of the oasis, in a short period of time the oasis will shrink. Soon dried up leaves and sand will be blowing through the old buildings. As the greenery shrinks, the water level drops, finally sinking below reach. The community must abandon its place, giving way to the shifting sands and inexorable heat.

The community shares its water supply through irrigation ditches which wind their way through each plot. Land is sold and purchased in terms of the *cadusas* of water needed to support that land. This means that as the water flows through the irrigation system, it can stay a certain amount of time at each plot. Then the gates must be raised, allowing the water to continue on to the next plot.

For any community member who is stingy enough to keep the water too long on his land, there is a judicial court setting. Selfishly holding back the water is a serious crime, and it has ramifications for the entire community which will shrink without its share of water.

Anyone who is out for selfish ambition in any context affects others. When people want more for themselves and do not value community, the results can be tragic.

In certain oases near the Mediterranean, some have purchased land and built big hotels to attract tourists. However, one tourist, in just one day, uses twenty times the amount of water that a local person uses in one month. This is threatening the very survival of the oasis community. Self-centeredness and grasping for unfair shares can destroy a whole community anywhere.

So now, as a leader, will you let this sort of thing happen within your context? Will you perhaps even participate? Are there rationalizations that help you bear with such injustices? Do you call it by other names? God help us!

THE BODY

Read Ephesians 4:14-16.   *May 19*

The concept of the "body of Christ" is a marvelous and yet challenging one. "Marvelous" because it speaks of the oneness we are to have in Christ, of the fact that we are not alone, and of the need for many different types of people to work together. "Challenging" because often we want just the opposite of these things: independence, individualism, going our own way, and working only with people who are like us. The American idealization of the individual does not make this any less challenging, either.

Sometimes I will hear one Christian say to another, "It is really no business of yours what I do. What difference does it make to you if I sin or not? I can do whatever I want to do!"

Well, from a non-Christian vantage point, perhaps that has more meaning, but in the Christian context, it is simply not true. As a body, when one part of the body lets in an infection, it can spread like gangrene. Or when one part of the body is hurt, the rest of the body certainly knows it. Break your ankle, for example, and see how many other parts of your body have to compensate.

Any Christian who lets the infection of sin into his or her life will weaken the rest of the body. We are not independent beings, unaffected by each other. What you do affects me, and what I choose affects you–either for good or for ill.

When a particular part of the body tries to run around independently, it is hideous. Ever see a little finger marching around on its own? Of course not! It would be a surrealistic nightmare actually to encounter such a thing. But Christians who try to live the Christian life independently are just as much of an aberration.

The head, Jesus Christ, has miraculously planned for all people to be connected. Furthermore, as we listen to Him and obey Him, we will all function together smoothly. If we don't pay attention to Him, there is palsy. I wonder what Christ's body actually looks like here on earth?

PARTS OF THE BODY

Read I Corinthians 12:12-30.   *May 20*

Everybody is worth something. That's a simple statement, but profoundly true.

We forget it sometimes, though. We are tempted to see

someone's lesser contribution and not value them as much as the person making the huge contribution.

However, these verses in I Corinthians 12 show us that each part of the body is important and ought to be valued. In fact, there's a divine plan to equalize everything. Weak parts are indispensable, and less honorable parts we treat in special ways. We are meant to acknowledge and value our interconnectedness.

Sometimes I have viewed it as a picture puzzle. A puzzle may have thousands of pieces and each one may be put in its place, forming a beautiful and even complicated picture. However, the beauty is greatly diminished if even one puzzle piece is lost. There is a hole that mars the entire picture. In the same way, we greatly need each part and should value every one.

We must even have other people to help us discover ourselves, to find out what is inside of us. Someone once said, "It's too bad that the only way to be a good sport is that you have to lose."

Our relationships with other people helps us understand what we're made of. We discover our level of patience, our ability to forgive, how well we can love, and just how selfish we truly are. Even the simplest person has something to teach us, and God helps us as leaders not to forget it. Our arrogance can so easily get in the way!

God, in His wisdom, spreads out the gifts of the Spirit so that we must rely on each other. He places us in different positions where we are dependent upon each one if we are to be complete. Our functions may be different, but some day we will see the value God has placed upon each part.

Therefore, let us be diligent to preserve peace and unity. Let us not be derisive, opinionated, selfish, and proud. As we look to the head, Jesus Christ, we will all work together to accomplish the task God has given us to do. Personally as well, we can learn from and be ministered to by all kinds of people. What value there is in the Body of Christ!

LIGAMENTS

When certain parts of the Body of Christ grow and other parts do not, we have a strange conundrum. Your lack of growth in the Christian life affects me because you cannot function so well, and vice versa. God intends for us to become mature and to be fully grown in stature and strength.

Some people grow in certain parts of their lives, but not in others. Some train their bodies, but not their minds. Others are strong intellectually, but stunted emotionally. Whenever any person decides to stop his or her growth spiritually, then that immaturity affects the rest of the Body. People who are not strong spiritually get whipped around. They hardly know what they think and can be swayed by any spiritual fad or even deceived.

That's why we need each other so much. Others are meant to speak the truth to us so we will not fall into error. We are meant to confront our friends in love and help each other out. This way we will all grow. There is no room for stark individualism, arrogance, and independence in the things of God. It is humbling to admit, but we desperately need other people.

Sometimes we are so blind to ourselves. We have places hidden inside that we can't see. As we open up and share with others, we become vulnerable, but we also build a trust level. The other person begins to feel comfortable in discussing those personal areas to which we are blind. As a result, there is greater self-awareness, more self-understanding. When we speak the truth like this, we will all grow together into Jesus Christ, the Head of the Body.

Can you imagine what our bodies would be like if there were no ligaments holding together our bone structure? The ligaments and cartilage are what keep our bones from rubbing against each other and wearing each other out. It creates a support system which makes the entire body function. We are connected integrally, attached to others in the Body of Christ. Only when we act like it will we grow into what God intends for us to be.

Leaders often act "above" this concept and stay in isolation from other people. However, ultimately this stunts the growth of the leaders and of those who follow them as well. Let's be a part, the way God intended for us to be. It's His plan after all.

CONTENTION

Read Romans 16:17-20.   *May 22*

In every organization, it seems, there is someone who specializes in causing division, dissension, and disruptions. These contentious people appear to find some joy in creating disturbances and watching others squirm.

Sometimes their true spirits are wrapped in deception. They appear to be intellectuals, only seeking "truth" or setting crooked things straight. At times, they are adept at what I call "hit and run," getting matters stirred up someplace and then stepping away while the commotion continues. Some seem to be religious contenders for the "true faith" and defenders of what is right.

However, in whatever guise the situation is concealed, the end results are dissensions and strife. In Romans 16:17-18, Paul warns the Corinthians to "watch out for those who cause divisions."

"Keep away from them!" he clearly commands. "For such people are not serving our Lord Christ, but their own appetites. By smooth talk and flattery they deceive the minds of naive people" (verses 17-18).

Again in Titus 3:9-11, Paul cautions Titus to avoid "foolish controversies and genealogies and arguments and quarrels about the law, because they are unprofitable and useless." He goes on to say that such a person should be warned once, then a second time, and after that they should have nothing to do with him.

"You may be sure," says Paul, "that such a man is warped and sinful; he is self-condemned."

Although these are strong words, we would do well to pay attention to them. About two-thirds of the deeds of the sinful nature listed in Galatians 5:19-21 revolve around relationships. Consider words like "discord, selfish ambition, dissensions and factions" and the clear warning that "those who live like this will not inherit the kingdom of God."

That is serious, but it is why we should beware of people such as these, heeding Paul's warning to have nothing to do with them. Their contentious spirits will breed trouble and discontent every time, and the results in a group can be severely destructive.

Jesus taught love, peace, patience, and kindness. He valued love so much that it became the theme of His last speech to His disciples before He died. It is the way that non-believers can see that God is real, when we truly have love for one another. No wonder that Satan works overtime to see that Christians are busy with spats and quarrels. That way they won't fulfill their purpose in the world today.

How seriously do you take this warning from Paul? As a leader, what is your response to a divisive person?

THE NATURE OF A SERVANT
Read Matthew 20:25-28.   *May 23*

Jesus' whole orientation to life was submission. He was the servant-leader who chose to demonstrate His leadership by serving in the role of a servant. He wasn't a leader first and a servant second, but rather a servant whom people chose to follow. This is a profound distinction.

Some people want leadership so badly that they usurp power and authority. Then they try to appear humble by choosing certain actions that give the impression of being a lowly servant.

Jesus, on the other hand, chose the place of a servant first; it's at the core of His being. He wasn't acting when He behaved like a servant; that is completely who He was.

At the heart of true authority is suffering. There is mutual submission, a humility, the willingness to obey no matter what the cost. The leader's freedom to rule lies hidden in his willingness to submit in entire obedience.

Jesus knew this truth. He understood that serving others might appear to be the antithesis to leadership. Yet, He also was aware of the fact that God gave Him authority precisely because He did not usurp it.

Anyone who attempts to wrench away power and control from another person in order to establish his leadership is sadly misled. This leads only to an unholy dictatorship based in selfish arrogance and pride. No group or individual is meant to usurp authority for themselves. It was at the base of Satan's rebellion.

God's approach is totally that of submissiveness, humility, serving others, lowly places. Having the face buried in the dirt on the ground may seem uncomfortable, but it is the safest place to be when power and authority for leadership are placed into your hands.

Without this balance, the role of a leader is dangerous indeed. Power is frighteningly tempting to take up and wield. Furthermore, its misuse can ruin us.

We are not to lord it over each other, vying for position, honor, and notice. Choosing to stand in the background, to serve in quiet and unnoticed ways, and to humbly count others as more important than ourselves—all these are critical to being the kind of leaders God wants us to be. As a matter of fact, this servanthood stands at the core of it all.

IMEMY

IMEMY. Though it sounds like a foreign word, it is simply one I coined to describe what I believe to be the prevailing philosophy in our present-day, American society. This philosophy has become so pervasive that it deserves a name. It is really a kind of cult, brainwashing all of us to some extent and programming us to think in certain ways.

This cult is gaining great popularity. Hundreds of thousands of converts are participating. If you consider idol worship to be anything that sets itself up to be of primary importance other than God Himself, then idol worship is definitely involved. This cult has taken over our advertising, most of the media, the Mall of America, a great deal of our time and entertainment, our philosophical base, our country, and even our religious perspective.

In case you haven't deciphered it, IMEMY stands for what is at the center of our universe. I...ME...MY. It is selfishness and individualism at its height and extreme.

Think about it. There was a time in the not-so-distant past when the word "community" actually was a high value. People were willing to give up things for the good of the whole. Now, however, the IMEMY cult has imposed its way of thinking into our personal lifestyles, into our national consciousness, and even into our churches.

The message of the IMEMY cult surrounds us. It's in music and jingles. "You deserve this," one cries out. "Do what makes you happy," says another. A perfume is advertised as "a willingness to commit" and "the essence of being." Another product says, "Sure it's more expensive, but I'm worth it." An architectural firm advertises, "You've never settled for second best. Neither have we." One product states, "There's no denying it. Climbing the corporate ladder can be a long, arduous struggle for power. But isn't it nice to know that waiting in the parking lot at the end of every day is the ultimate power trip." A facial salon boasts, "Think of yourself as our only client." (Oh, sure. They wouldn't be in business very long!)

There are popular sayings like "Do your own thing" and "Make your own way" or "If you don't stand up for yourself, nobody else is going to." (Whatever happened to "God is my defense"?)

We hate to wait in line. We think we deserve whatever we want and that we deserve it right now. We're used to fast foods and drive thrus, to getting instant everything and having it all "at your service," and we get peeved when its not. We want to snap our fingers and have things done for us. If it doesn't happen, we get angry.

And you? Have you succumbed to this cult? Think about it.

IMEMY: RIGHTS

Read Philippians 2:5-8.   *May 25*

Since society has so easily accepted this thinking that feeds our selfish desires, it is not surprising that our economy also revolves around it. After all, in order to get our dollar, the merchants have really catered to our egocentric perspective. "What the customer says is right" and "the customer is number one" are the types of service-oriented commitments from merchants to consumers.

Some of this may be reasonable (after all, it's our buck). However, it only serves to exacerbate and enhance our selfishness. It has made us feel that we deserve to be provided for, taken care of, pampered, and served.

"I'm always right."

"How dare you contradict me?"

"I want it, and I want it now!"

"I demand service! It's my right!"

We Americans can sound like spoiled children who feel we have a right to anything we want. In the process, we care less about the rights of others or giving up something for the sake of the community. Remember those citizenship grades we used to get in school? Whatever happened to those anyway? Now we tend to expect benefits from the government rather than participate as problem-solvers. In place of being citizens, we seem to be turning into a nation of clients.

A further outcome of this egocentric philosophy is that if we feel we deserve something, then we don't appreciate it. We lose a sense of gratitude. Instead of being thankful for what God has provided, we are in danger of becoming dissatisfied and demanding.

Still another result of such selfishness is the inability to stand strong under pain and hard times. It becomes easy to say, "Well, I'm the leader here, and I don't have to put up with this. I have my rights, after all. I think I'll resign and go some place nice." If this is not God's plan, I can just about hear Jesus exclaiming, "Excuuuse Me! Who's in charge here?"

Jesus came to earth in total humility. He gave up Himself, to the farthest extent possible. He relinquished His rights. Even though He deserved it, He didn't demand to be served. He was the epitome of humility and servanthood.

I....

IMEMY AND THE CHURCH
Read Philippians 2:12-18.   *May 26*

We cannot have such a strong philosophy prevailing in our society without having the possibility that it will affect the church. Has the IMEMY (I...me...my) cult negatively impacted the church today?

180

If we think we deserve good things, for example, we may believe that we deserve salvation. However, we don't deserve salvation at all; we deserve death. We don't chose God, really; He chooses us. We're not doing God a favor by coming to Him; He did us a huge favor by sending His Son to die for us.

People may go to church and say, "I'm not getting anything there." But what are we giving? Staying home from church because we think we might be bored is a reasonable thought if we see church as a consumer-oriented entity that should satisfy our needs. However, it may be important for us to attend not just for ourselves, but because God wants to use us to touch another person's life. That is what the concept of community is all about.

Worship, also, is not just to help us feel good, but it is for God. It is meant to change us, not just to give us gospel goose bumps. Or perhaps the philosophy seeps through in prayer. Some act as if we should pray, and God will supply what we want. But Scripture explains that He will supply all our needs, and these may be far different from our wants. God is sometimes considered to be a blessing box that dispenses things to meet our whims.

Furthermore, there is a trend toward making Christianity what we want it to be, even in our belief system. We want our own form of eclectic religion, whatever makes us comfortable. When truth is reduced to what we want to make it, we are on dangerous ground.

The purpose of the church is not just to make us feel good but to be salt and light in a tremendously dark society. We are to fulfill the Great Commission.

We are not out to simply give people what they want so they will like us and stay. If this means tickling ears or offering constant fun and games, hype and entertainment, then we are back to our egocentric mentality.

The church is not meant to be expended upon ourselves for our own selfish, personal enjoyment and satisfaction. It is meant to provide the joint effort of reaching our world with the revolutionary message of a humble Savior who gave up everything so that we might live. What great news for our society today!

GOOD NEWS

Read Romans 5:6-21. *May 27*

"Negative. Try to find a more positive word." That's what my grammar and writing check program on my word processor had written throughout the page.

So I dutifully reread my writing. No, I couldn't say that any differently. ...Well, that one had to stay also. ...And this "negative word" had to remain because otherwise there was no meaning to the sentence. ...And, well, look here! That word is in a Scripture quotation. ...And that one, too.

Oh, now let me rethink this "negative word" suggestion from my grammar program. Should everything be written positively?

Is it possible to have "good news" without an understanding of the concept of "bad news"? Can we comprehend "right" without "wrong"? It is possible to truly appreciate "forgiveness" without knowing "sin"?

In our society today, there is an increasingly strong emphasis on stating everything in positive terms. Now generally that's probably all right. I don't believe in harangues, either. If something can be stated positively instead of negatively, people are more apt to receive it and more willing to make a change.

However, in the midst of this, we need to remember that it's appropriate to use words such as *no, death, pain, sickness, suffering,* and *sin.* After all, every one of them exists in this world. Satan has seen to that! And since they are here, we can relate with gladness, release, love and worship to a God who has added the words *yes, resurrection, healing, joy,* and *forgiveness.*

The good news of Scripture is that Jesus came to forgive us from sin. If we don't acknowledge the depths of deprivation to which sin takes us, we cannot experience the heights of release to which the good news of forgiveness leads us. Let us not minimize His grace by minimizing the depths of degradation that Jesus came to relieve through the shedding of His blood. Only when we see how truly black, awful and negative sin actually is, can we appreciate the real light, joy, and freedom of salvation. What a wonder the good news actually is!

3-D SIN

Read John 3:16.   *May 28*

It happened to me one night when I was driving by our community's gigantic discount store on the way home from work. Perhaps it was the flashing lights and seasonal decorations that triggered it. I'm not sure, really. The store just seemed so garish, touting its sales and wares.

Maybe it was the news from the car radio: Another domestic disturbance ending in a murder/suicide.... Abortion rights activists at the Capitol.... Homosexuals pushing for new legislation in another state.... A young convenience store clerk who was shot for no reason after a successful robbery.... Government officials accused of graft...

Anyway, all of a sudden, sin turned into capital letters. It became three-dimensional and grew. It got fluffed up. I always knew it was there. I was certainly aware of how terrible it was, and it grieved me rather regularly. But suddenly it took on a bigger force and another side. What was once flattened out rose up and slapped me in the face.

This 3-D SIN seemed to reach around the world, pervade all strata of society and every nation on earth. No one was exempt from its inexorable influence and demands. Every single person

183

was touched by it in some way. It was gripping, pervasive, massive, and horrible. Black and darkness howled as the heavy skies turned into night.

So much for our lives; we attempt to cover up or disregard the darkness of sin. Try to put some lights on those billboards advertising booze and greed. Make it cute. Add a touch of humor. Have it move; give it life.

Throw a party. Eat, drink and be merry, for tomorrow we... Aaahh, we...die.... Tomorrow we die.

Is there nothing else, then? This is it? These shallow attempts to pull off the dark blanket of sin that overwhelms us...is there nothing more?

"For God so loved the world that He gave His one and only Son..."

Oh, finally! A breath of fresh air, a real light. "...that whoever believes in Him shall not perish, but have eternal life" (verse 16).

BROKEN CISTERNS

Read Jeremiah 2:13.   *May 29*

God gave a powerful indictment to His people through Jeremiah. "My people have committed two sins: They have forsaken me, the spring of living water, and have dug their own cisterns, broken cisterns that cannot hold water" (verse 13).

Two sins. Two strikes. Not just one wrong choice, but two.

The foremost sin is that of forsaking God. "Forsaking" is a strong word. To forsake someone means we reject, turn away from, and leave that person. I wonder how God feels about being forsaken. God must find it especially difficult to be left by His own people, the ones He has loved so well.

Forsaking God is also costly to us. We are walking away from the "spring of living water." This is disastrous. We miss life. We get thirsty. Eventually we will die unless we find water.

This need naturally leads us into the next sin. We go off in search of water, looking in places other than the spring. We think that probably we can find it someplace else, and then later when it rains, we can renew that supply. To gather the raindrops, however, we need to make cisterns.

These can be made out of many materials and dug out in various places. Cisterns represent whatever we think will bring us life and happiness: a house, achievement, success, education, the perfect family, good looks and clothes, fame, wealth, accomplishing certain goals, power and control, position and title.

The problem is that these cisterns are things of our own invention, and they are never adequate. They may collect water for a little while, but only when it happens to rain. The water will get stagnant and brackish. Finally, the water seeps out of the breaks in the cistern.

How sad. What a contrast to the life-giving spring that is always pouring forth. We can't do without the real artesian well which is God Himself, spouting up inside of us. Whatever is stopping up that spring in our lives has to go. We desperately need the Water of Life on a regular basis.

"Lord, show me what cisterns are in my life. I yearn for You alone!"

STIFF UPPER LIP

Read I John 1:5-10.   *May 30*

The British are widely known for their "stiff upper lip," meaning that they value courage and not complaining. Lord Uxbridge seems the epitome of this. Having lost his leg when he had been hit by a cannonball at the Battle of Waterloo, he is said to have remarked to the Duke of Wellington, "By God, sir, I've lost my leg" — and then to have buried it with full military honors.

Recently, however, there is talk that the typical British stoicism is vanishing. People seem to be complaining more, and

185

personal injury lawsuits are increasing in England. Instead of accepting what has happened, there seems to be a growing tendency to blame someone else and try to find a "culprit."

This trend of externalizing responsibility has long been a trait of American culture and in other countries as well. None of us likes to carry the weight of thinking that something is our own fault. It feels too good to lay blame.

Many also seem to need a scapegoat in order to deal with tragedies. Today a fire in a school in India tragically killed 90 school children. They have already arrested the principal for negligence.

One often hears teachers bemoaning the fact that 30 years ago, if a teacher told a parent that Johnny was not doing well, the father would "support the system," as it were. Now the instructors are likely to hear, "You must be doing something wrong. Why aren't you a better teacher?"

There comes a point when we must accept responsibility for our own action and choices. The concept of sin is impossible to understand without this as a base.

The old adage, "The devil made me do it," can easily become an inappropriate excuse. But when it comes to sin, though Satan might tempt, he can't make us do anything. We have to own the problem. We make the choice.

As leaders we have to be responsible for internalizing our mistakes, errors, and sins. We can't always be pointing the finger and shifting the blame. And when it comes to our own sinful nature, it is ours. All ours.

THE WAY OUT

Read John 14:6. *May 31*

When we were in college, a young couple in our church determined to lead the college age group. They were wonderful.

I hope I knew enough to tell them so. They challenged us in the Lord, but they let us have fun. They fed us—real home-cooked food at that—and allowed us to hang out in their home.

One fall we had a party there, and the guys gathered huge boxes which we took down into the basement. I remember the hours of distraction from homework that we enjoyed making a gigantic, complicated maze out of those boxes. Once they got into those twists and turns, some actually couldn't get back out without assistance.

That's what happens when sin has a hold on us. It traps us. We get lost in the maze, and we can't find our way. There are so many people ensnared just like this. They are crawling around in the dark—lost, frustrated, and alone.

Jesus said, "I am the way and the truth and the life. No one comes to the Father except through me" (verse 6). In our postmodern world where people accept most anything, even opposite ideas, it becomes an increasing challenge to help people understand that there is only one true way.

It is just like Satan to influence societal thinking so that it won't be able to see things straight! The enemy creates diversions, distractions, darkness. He makes sure that people bang their heads against the wall because they can't see any other opening.

I once saw a giant maze in a farmer's cornfield. These are tough to maneuver because the corn is so tall that it is almost impossible to get one's bearings. You can't see a thing, except for corn stalks all around. The maze walker takes one hopeful turn and winds up in a dead end.

This is the way it is in life for people who do not yet know Jesus. They won't get out, either, until they discover the real way. He is the way, the truth and the life. There is no other. What good news to share!

JUNE

FREE

Read Galatians 4:21-31. *June 1*

A dream that finally comes into being as a result of God's promise is truly wonderful. We know God performed the work, and so there is great joy in seeing that He has executed what He had promised.

As we wait on the Lord to accomplish His desires, spiritual forces are at work. What ultimately transpires is pure, special, unusual. God is able to use it in stronger and more profound ways. Actually, throughout the *Bible*, we discover a trend that the best and most important dreams all have to die first so God Himself can be the One who brings them to life.

We see Samuel, the special prophet used by God, who was born to Hannah after a very long wait. We note Abraham and Sarah who were used to birth a nation—and not just any nation, but an uncommon one used by God for His special purposes. We observe John the Baptist who was the result of a waiting period with unique circumstances for Elizabeth and Zechariah. Of course, John the Baptist had a distinctive task in spiritually preparing peoples' hearts for the coming Messiah. And the timing of Elizabeth's pregnancy to coincide with that of the virgin Mary's—what a blessing!

Then there was the waiting period of Moses who was first reduced to feeling incapable before he was raised up to leadership. He was given no little task, either. There's Joseph whose dream was on hold for years while he waited in prison, but then he found himself reestablished overnight, being used mightily to save thousands of lives during the famine.

Spiritual things need to be birthed in the Spirit. Those who are not of the Spirit hold this all in derision, as mentioned in today's verses, but it is still the way to do it. It will always be true that what is spiritual will be persecuted by what is not. Get used to it. But also be strong enough to tarry and do it God's way.

Today are you waiting for spiritual offspring and outcomes? Be patient! The deepest spiritual things of all are birthed with time and waiting on God.

BEGETTING

Read John 3:1-15.   *June 2*

Everything in nature begets its own kind. A tadpole cannot give birth to an elephant. A racoon is not going to beget an eagle nor an apple tree produce an ear of corn. These are silly thoughts.

In trying to explain the spiritual birthing process to Nicodemus, Jesus makes an important observation. "Flesh gives birth to flesh," He says, "and Spirit gives birth to Spirit" (verse 6).

It really can't be any other way if you stop to think about it. People who are working in the flesh are bound to produce fleshly outcomes. They might be able to measure their success by worldly standards and receive trophies from men. There may be many accolades and affirmations coming their way from others, and the person can even become famous. Nonetheless, the result will still be flesh.

If we minister in the flesh we get spectacle, entertainment, diversion. The person is like a showman and takes over the center ring instead of God. The flesh is selfish, demanding attention. It seeks its own glory rather than the glory of God. People who minister in a fleshly way have the smell of sweat about them. They reek of it! It is like a rancid perfume.

There are mentors who teach these things. They point out to

their mentorees how to put on a successful "show." They teach the clever little ins and outs for getting in here, for making money there, for having people like you, for getting asked back. Their schemes are logical, appealing to the flesh-core in others. But the cleverness of man does not bring the Spirit. It is impossible to beget the Spirit out of the flesh.

Once someone called the church where my husband was on pastoral staff and said that he guaranteed to bring revival to the church. "Run in the opposite direction," I said, "because no one has God in a box." There is not a single person who can guarantee what God is going to do. That is arrogance. What he would probably bring is flesh and hype, a whipped up little program, but not the Spirit.

When the Holy Spirit is moving, something different happens. He draws people's attention to Jesus, not to anyone or anything else. There is deference and kindness, gentleness and peace. When the Spirit is in charge, what will be produced is more things in the Spirit.

Our programs won't produce it. Raising our voices and talking big won't make it happen. Demanding or cajoling, controlling or whining aren't effective. You want Spirit? You pray, seek God, soak in His presence. Because when His Spirit is on you, then you will produce of the Spirit.

SYSTEMS

Read Galatians 3:1-3. *June 3*

Systematic approaches appeal to me naturally. I'm the sort of person who loves order and organization. I also believe that God likes these things because the world that He created is so orderly. The regular movement of the sun, the seasons, the waves of the sea, planting and harvest, the structural realities of cells and amoeba, the interaction of plants and animals—all these speak of a God who likes organization.

God, however, is also full of surprises. He produces anomalies, wind and storms, fire. In Acts 2 on the day of Pentecost, the Holy Spirit came in with the sound of a mighty, rushing wind, and tongues as of fire appeared on each person's head. The Spirit won't let Himself be controlled. If someone attempts to do that, He'll just leave. He demands and retains freedom.

When the Lord does fresh things for His church, the Spirit is allowed to move. He is given space, and the church is changed and renewed. However, my study of revival history indicates that sooner or later, man wants to get his hands on the situation and control it. He starts to shape it, organize it, put in some structure.

As we have seen, structure is not automatically wrong. The problem arises when the system takes over and forces certain things to happen, when the Spirit wants something else. The organization can take up our attention, demanding time to be run and providing us with problems to solve. Soon our minds are off the things of the Spirit and onto the task of running the system.

Living in the flow of the Spirit takes faith, a total reliance on God. Even the Galatians in today's reading were moving back into the structure of the law, rather than trusting God by faith. So often we start off in the Spirit, but we end in the flesh. It happens barely without our realizing it. The Spirit is moving and flowing, but soon our man-made systems and methods sneak in and the Spirit has no room to flow where He wants. Instead, He hits walls, crashes into our rules, bashes headlong into a system, and is strangled off by control. God help us. Having begun in the Spirit, will we end in the flesh?

192

METHODS

One of the delights of my life has been the visits I have had to Argentina. I have visited churches running 15,000 and 13,000 and even 25,000 people. The pastor of the largest church said something interesting when I talked with him—one of those side comments that haunts a person, you know the kind I mean.

"I keep getting people who visit here," said Pastor Guillermo Prein, "who desire to know what I do to get this kind of growth. They want the methods and the system handed to them. They want the paper and the program. But there is no shortcut to meeting God."

I pondered this for some time. In the United States we tend to go for method. We read, we buy materials, we try out what someone else has done successfully. We might as well, we say. Why reinvent the wheel?

However, we may be circumventing the very thing God wants from us most: to seek His face. There is no substitute for this. God wants us to turn to Him for everything. We have to pray. We must spend time in His presence. These are what our churches need most, and no methods or systems, ideas or programs will ever satisfy.

Guillermo Prein ended with another comment, "It's not just an easy method. It cost me my whole life, you know."

My voice caught in my throat. What does one say to that? How can he reduce that to paper and give it to someone else? What system or program is inherent in sacrifice? Prein was right. There is no shortcut. And God help us if we think there is.

LESSONS FROM THE TITANIC: EXPERIENCE

Read Psalm 46. June 5

Experience is generally considered a boon to any person in leadership, and usually it is. Experience can teach us not to panic in a crisis. Options and alternatives rise more quickly to our minds. The decision-making process becomes smoother because we have navigated similar paths before. It is easier to stay calm and think clearly, to ask the right questions and be decisive.

Such was the case of the captain of the famous *Titanic*. E.J. Smith was a highly experienced seaman of over 40 years. He had been the chief officer for numerous voyages, including the maiden voyage of the *Titanic*'s large sister ship, the *Olympic*. In fact, after the maiden voyage of the *Titanic*, E.J. Smith planned to retire.

The captain's vast experience allowed the passengers of the large ship to feel secure and safe under his able leadership. Some would not go on a voyage unless E.J. Smith was at the helm of the ship.

However, in the case of the *Titanic,* Smith's experience may have actually worked against him. He had become complacent. He stayed too calm, didn't react strongly enough to the danger, and wouldn't decide there was a problem until it was too late. After all, his previous experiences had been "uneventful," according to his own words. Disaster had never threatened before. Therefore, when he should have been giving clear order, he held back, almost in disbelief that this could be happening.

The size of the Titanic and the sense of its massive structure added to the feeling of security. Safety measures were in place with water-tight compartments and doors in the ship's lower levels. This ship couldn't sink, or so it was thought. Man had faith in the progress and technology that had been developed.

As leaders with much experience, we could learn from the story of the *Titanic*. Although it is not wise to over-react, it is equally dangerous—perhaps more so—not to react at all when it

194

is merited. Even though many cry wolf, wolves still exist. When one is creeping near the sheep, it is time to act. Dangerous and life-threatening situations can occur for both people and organizations. Stay prepared. Be alert. Don't be taken by surprise.

But there's another lesson here. In the end, our security cannot be in another person, nor in the seeming stability of an organization or nation, nor even in ourselves. Our own wisdom, knowledge, and background may not be enough for what will come into our paths, even this very day. Our only security is in God.

LESSONS FROM THE TITANIC: WARNINGS
Read Ezekiel 33:1-11.   *June 6*

Since most people thought the *Titanic* couldn't sink, life-boats were installed more for public relations and a general sense of safety than for anything else. They could hold less than one-third of the passengers. Even after the massive ship hit the iceberg, most passengers had no idea that anything was really wrong. Many did not heed the verbal warning, thinking it was only a mere formality of safety. The band played in the lounge, and people continued to sleep or to sit around and chat.

Why are human beings often so oblivious to warnings? How can we not heed the messages of danger that come our way?

Most of us don't want to admit that something is very wrong. We think life will go on as it already has. Only when the crisis stares us in the face do we start to believe and understand. Many of the first-class *Titanic* passengers did not accept the severity of the problem until they saw the water rising through their own central stair well towards the top of the huge ship.

The responsibility of a leader is to weigh the validity of warnings. One does not want to speculate so that people are incited to fear and panic. However, there was not enough concern developed among those on the *Titanic* after the ship was mortally wounded by the iceberg. Even the first lifeboats left the ship only partially filled. People didn't want to be bothered with what they considered to be a little, unnecessary, safety precaution.

Therefore, as leaders, we must understand when to raise concern so people will be moved to appropriate action. We need to ring out clear warnings with directions on what to do. We can be used by the Lord to "save the ship" over which He has given us leadership responsibilities.

God has likewise asked us to warn people today. As Christians, we know that others will die if they do not heed the warnings and accept Christ as their Savior. If we do not even tell a person, Ezekiel says that then we will be held "accountable for his blood."

This may make us squirm and feel uncomfortable. So be it, then. Let's speak up and raise our voices, shake off our stupor and see the seriousness of it all.

The Lord wants to have the alarm sounded loud and clear. "Our offenses and sins weigh us down, and we are wasting away because of them. How then can we live?" (Ezekiel 33:10). "Turn! Turn from your evil ways!" the Lord says with urgency. Oh, leader, pick up that trumpet of yours and sound the alarm!

A FLOOD IN THE CANYON

Read Genesis 6:5-22.   *June 7*

We had covered the Christian Artists Seminar in Estes Park, Colorado, for the Christian newspaper of which my husband was a founder and owner. It was a very busy time. Interviews, concerts, photography, and writing had filled our days, so at the spur of the moment, we decided to head northeast for several days of unplanned but badly needed R and R.

When we got to the Black Hills, we discovered on the news that there had been a terrible flash flood in Big Thompson Canyon next to Estes Park. In fact, when we returned to Denver a few days later, we also learned that we were on the missing persons list. Some of our friends had expected us back and when we didn't show up, they assumed that a calamity may have befallen us in that canyon flood.

On the day of the flood the weather had been fine, and there was no advance warning that anything was going to be amiss. That's why so many people who were camping in the canyon—along with hundreds of homeowners who had never seen a flash flood in that region—couldn't actually believe that there was any danger. Although most were warned, many did not move out of the canyon or even go to higher ground. How could a whole canyon fill up with rushing water in a matter of minutes anyway? They were soon to find out.

Homes and roads were washed away as the huge wall of water came tumbling down through the canyon. Bus loads of people and cars were caught in the flood. Literally scores of people died suddenly in that terrible onslaught.

Yesterday we discussed the danger of not heeding warnings. Part of what lulls us to sleep is forgetting that God is capable of judgment. Now I'm not at all indicating that the canyon incident was linked to God's judgment, however, a flood was once a result of His wrath.

We are told in Genesis 6 that "the earth was corrupt in God's sight and was full of violence (verse 11). God noted "how great man's wickedness on the earth had become and that every inclination of the thoughts of his heart was only evil all the time" (verse 8).

One has only to watch television and videos for a short period before he sees the ease with which pre-marital sex, adultery, homosexuality, murder, robbery, and extortion are breezed across the screen, often accompanied by levity. If children watch TV for very long, they have seen hundreds of violent and sinful acts. No wonder crimes among younger children are increasing.

Although I am happy every time I see a rainbow that God promised not to wipe us out because of a flood again, I wonder. Would I be chosen, like Noah? Would you?

People still laugh when we build our arks today. However, flash floods occur. God will not hold back His wrath and judgement forever. What will our response—and that of our generation—be? We need to get up to higher ground.

THE GAP

Read Ezekiel 22:30-31 and I Samuel 12:19-25.   *June 8*

God said through Isaiah that "He was appalled that there was no one to intervene" (Isaiah 59:16). God noted injustice and sin and then tried to find someone who would warn, who would pray, who would be a part of seeing that things changed. How sad that He could find nobody.

The same problem occurred in Ezekiel's day. Again, God said through the prophet, "I've looked for a man among them who would build up the wall and stand before me in the gap on behalf of the land so I would not have to destroy it, but I found none. So I will pour out my wrath on them and consume them with my fiery anger..." (Ezekiel 22:30-31a).

It is indeed possible for God to pour out His judgment or wrath. This very generation probably deserves it for its sin and violence. Would God be able to say today that He looked for a person who would intervene, who would stand in the gap...but He couldn't find a single one?

One of our main tasks as Christians today should be to pray and intercede. We are to try to build up walls that presently have holes in them, repair the breaches that the enemy has made. Satan is out to make holes in people's lives, to steal, kill and destroy. He

198

will attempt to lead them into compromise and sin, riddling them with discouragement so they will give up the fight. Who will pray?

As we intercede, it is as if we step into that hole in the wall and hold up the wall's weight so it won't collapse. We can help mend wounded lives and broken people. We can encourage and exhort them, praying on their behalf.

Samuel was a great example of an intercessor. In I Samuel 12:19-25, the people were aware of their sin and asked Samuel to intercede for them. Samuel said he would teach them the right way, and he encouraged them to fear God and serve Him with all their hearts. Through this, he was building up the broken down places of their lives. He pointed out in verse 25, however, that the decision was still in their hands.

Samuel also promised to pray for them. "As for me," he said, "far be it from me that I should sin against the Lord by failing to pray for you" (I Samuel 12:23). Samuel said something profound here. He saw prayerlessness as a sin—not just against the people whom he would neglect if he did not pray for them, but rather a sin against God.

The Lord looks around even today for people to pray, to intercede, to stand in the gap between God and men. Will He look around and find you?

TORRENTS

Read Psalm 18:1-6.   *June 9*

The torrents of rain fell so rapidly that a lake quickly formed in our backyard, stretching out into the road beside our house and reaching into our neighbor's yard across the street. Although we were on a side of the hill, the area flattened slightly here. Water had streamed down the hill past other drains stopped up by debris from the numerous construction sites in this new housing development. Furthermore, the storm sewers just weren't large enough to handle such a deluge.

My husband and I looked down at the sight from our upstairs bedroom window and watched the water rise by the minute. "I didn't know we had purchased lakefront property!" I laughed. We were nervous, though.

Right then a car drove down the hill. It proceeded to inch into the water. "Doesn't she realize there's a low spot in the street there?" I asked Ray. "Surely she won't..."

But she already had. The car was now floating in the lake that was once our backyard, and the driver was unnerved to say the least. She rolled down the window and started screaming hysterically as her car floated helplessly in the water, moving toward a fence and knocking it down.

She floated for quite a while until she finally came to rest on a neighbor's front yard. Then she somehow got the flooded car started again and spun her tires into their brand new sod, driving off across several yards.

By this time, my husband had dashed down the steps and was directing traffic with a flashlight in the 10 p.m. darkness and rain, guiding other drivers up the hill so no one else would make the same mistake.

This had come in the midst of many other stressors. Within just five months the following had occurred: 1) this same lake scenario had occurred twice, 2) my husband had needed two angioplasty surgeries on his heart, 3) I had gotten stuck in an elevator in a parking garage for several hours with six strangers (including two children) in 90 degree temperatures, 4) my father had passed away, and 5) I had fallen on ice and sprained my knee, putting me on crutches for part of the winter. Then I fell all the way down my stairs at home while I was trying to maneuver on the crutches.

Life has a way of sending stress in torrents. I said to someone that I felt like a rag doll which someone had picked up and shook and shook and shook. However, in the midst of crisis and pain, when all else seems to be adrift, we can reach out and find God. He is our rock, our solid object to hold on to, the stability of our times. He will never be otherwise.

STRENGTH

Read Psalm 29:10-11.   *June 10*

"The Lord sits enthroned over the flood; the Lord is enthroned as King forever. The Lord gives strength to his people; the Lord blesses his people with peace," states David in this psalm.

Although the waters of trouble may rise in our lives, threatening to overwhelm us in their flood, God rules over these times. It can seem like everything is totally out of control. We may be buffeted and feel like we are being swept away. However, God is King forever, enthroned securely. He is most certainly in control of everything.

Every believer needs to come to grips with the absolute security of this truth—especially leaders. Otherwise, we will not be able to lead in stable and calm ways in the midst of a crisis. At such a time, we should be drawing upon our own established security in God, because He is indeed sovereign and "enthroned above the flood." Instead, we may lose our heads and go into panic before the people. This is not God's plan for leaders.

David understood this truth very clearly. He articulated it so well in today's psalm. He knew that even though all the world around him might appear to be falling apart and collapsing, God is still the King. Having pledged our absolute and unshakable fealty to Him, we will not run away now. We will trust Him.

"But I am weak," we might say. "God is God. He may be able to sit enthroned above it all, but I can't. It's just too hard. I'm going to give up—walk out—leave this horrible mess behind. I just can't take it any more."

However, David knew that God was not a distanced or distracted King. The Lord continually sees the needs of His people. He knows that we are weak, and in answer to this reality, He gives us strength.

When we don't think we can hold on any longer, we should look up and receive whatever we need from the hand of our King. We must not try to get it somewhere else. It is only from His hand that we will find it.

Furthermore, when our emotions are in a turmoil during a crisis and we are worried and burdened, the Lord will also provide peace. What an assurance. He will settle our troubled souls.

Read God's promise in Isaiah 43:1-2 and receive both strength and peace today.

HOW DO WE KEEP GOING?

Read Isaiah 40:25-31.   *June 11*

Although at times we may feel abandoned, as if God doesn't see or care what happens to us any more, we can be sure that this is not actually the case. Our Lord is the almighty God. He is the Creator of everything, not some small, disinterested entity. He doesn't sleep in heaven and disregard us. He never grows tired or weary. We can't even begin to perceive what He understands. It is impossible to fathom what He knows.

When situations are difficult, it is important for us to look to Him and not to the difficulties of the situation itself. If we do the latter, we will be overwhelmed every time. However, when we keep our eyes on God, we find He has absolutely everything we need.

Are you tired and weary? Even youths get that way, God says through the prophet Isaiah. Even those we would consider to be strong and motivated will stumble and fall. So what if we have been at this for a long time? What about those of us who are tired of the journey, for whom leadership no longer holds the youthful zeal of challenge or the zest of newness? How do we keep going?

The only answer is to look to God Himself. So many leaders have realized this truth and made it their own. Isaiah 40:31 says, "But those who hope in the Lord will renew their strength." What a promise! "The Lord is my strength and my song," said Moses in Exodus 15:2. "It is God who arms me with strength and makes my ways perfect," said David in II Samuel 22:33. "The Lord is my strength and my shield," David also said in Psalm 28:7.

"The joy of the Lord is your strength," said Nehemiah in Nehemiah 8:10. The sons of Korah wrote in Psalm 46:1, "God is our refuge and strength, an ever-present help in trouble." And then Paul said in his letter to the Philippians, verse 4:13, "I can do everything through him who gives me strength." Peter, too, stated in I Peter 4:11, "If anyone serves, he should do it with the strength God provides."

It seems that today, the flood of evil into our world is wearing down and wearying the saints. Stress is our modern-day enemy, and Satan delights in seeing it negatively affect us. Everywhere I go, Christians are exhausted, tired, weary, and burdened. If we stay that way and don't learn to find rest, refreshing, and strength in God, we will crash.

Certainly it is time to rise up and discover anew that God Himself is our strength, our shield, our refuge, our song, our help, the very source of everything we need! They can be found only in God and in Him alone. Won't you run to Him today?

SOAR, WALK RUN

Read Isaiah 40:31.   *June 12*

The strength God provides for us is at any level of activity that is being required of us. There are times in our lives when we feel we are flying high. At other times, we are running the race, wanting to win the prize and sprinting toward the finish line. At still other times, we are plodding, walking the muddy path with little feeling of exhilaration, It is difficult enough to place one foot in front of the other.

No matter where you are right now in your life, God has strength for you. Right now are you flying? Running? Walking?

If you are flying, think about the eagle. Eagles can soar very high, thousands of feet above the earth and the rocky mountain cliffs. When the *ruach* or desert thermal storm is raging, the eagles catch the wind and fly over the storm, 25,000-30,000 feet.

We, too, have times of catching the winds of the Holy Spirit and soaring high. It may be a dizzying encounter that God takes us on, swooping us away and almost out of control to the heights. But, oh, the perspective! It is said that eagles can see for 50 miles. Sometimes leaders need to be eagles. We must receive vision, insight, perspective, the larger view of things. At such a time, let us trust God to strengthen us to fly high, to come underneath us and buoy us up on eagles' wings to that place where we can see again.

If we are running right now, remember the race, the prize, the finish line (Romans 15:4-5). God can keep us running, maintain our motivation, and remind us that our running will not be in vain. Our goal is heaven, and there we will see the fruit of our labors. We are not to run and get weary because we are busy running in wrong directions, using up our strength in aimless and wasted sprints. Rather, we are to stay on the path, train and discipline ourselves, fixing our eyes on the prize.

Now if we are walking, it is tempting to faint. How easy it is to give up in the day-to-day plodding. It seems we are not getting very far. The movement is slow, ponderous, painstaking. Why do we bother anyway? Life seems like such a grind. We are trying to maintain pace or just keep going, but it is hot and wearisome. How hard it is to continue walking, but it is this everyday path that God gives us encouragement for as well.

At various times, we all soar, run, and walk. Each has its place and its purpose, its timing and its help. God Himself is there through it all, ready to provide whatever is needed to endure.

DUTY

Read Luke 17:7-10.   *June 13*

Duty: Another of those somewhat old-fashioned terms. People today tend to do what they want to do. It doesn't matter whether they have a duty or not.

In today's verses, Jesus addresses His disciples with a parable, and at the end of it He says, "So you also, when you have done everything you were told to do should say, 'We are unworthy servants; we have only done our duty.'"

Sometimes we are proud to have accomplished certain tasks for God. It is tempting to act almost as if God is lucky to have us. But the Lord says something else, "No, you're my servant, and you're only doing what you're supposed to be doing."

The parable is particularly interesting to ponder. Here is a servant who is working hard throughout the day, just doing his job. He plows or tends sheep (or writes reports and goes to meetings) and then comes in at the end of the day. He's tired and ready to unwind. But even though he's been working all day, the master is not going to tell him to sit down and then serve him his meal. It's the other way around. The servant still has more to do. He fixes his master's dinner and serves him first. Then he can eat himself. He doesn't even deserve a thank you for this, according to the parable; it's simply his duty.

Likewise, after a long day of work, we may feel that God owes us something. It's time for us to sit down and let Him minister to us. Instead, we must continue on in our duties a little longer. It may take faith to move into giving out still more. Worship and prayer are hard work. But as we turn our eyes to our Master and serve Him, even in the midst of our weariness, we are only giving Him what is due Him. Then we may sit down and eat ourselves.

We need to bestir ourselves to do our duty to our Lord. Regularly He must come first, whether we feel like it or not. It's our duty to get up and go to church rather than crashing on the couch. It is our assignment to serve Him and give Him our all. He will enable us to carry out our duty—always.

FOOLISH THINGS
Read I Corinthians 1:18-31.   *June 14*

In order to encourage others to have confidence in them, leaders tend to bury their fears, weaknesses, and needs. Sometimes leaders hide these lacks even from themselves. If they face up to what they're really feeling, they're afraid their self-assurance would wane, and they would lose their edge. Leaders, therefore, have a propensity to appear wise, knowledgeable, and capable for whatever may come.

God, however, made the salvation message exceedingly simple. The story of the cross seems foolish to many, and they cannot bend their semblance of "wisdom" to accept it. When it is embraced, however, the cross is exceedingly profound and much wiser than it first appears. It shames the wisdom of the world.

God has deigned to call people who will bend the knee and accept what many would consider foolishness. They have to reveal themselves as weak and needy in order to meet God. They must admit to sin and their great need for mercy. They have to become lowly and come by the narrow way.

In their arrogance and pride, many cannot bring themselves to do this. They think they need to keep up the show, stay strong on the outside, never admit to weakness of any kind. Afraid that their whole being may collapse if they were ever to do this, they stay hard. Breaking, bowing, bending low, these are too difficult.

Sadly, without these things people will never find God. The more foolish we admit we are, the more we finally come to understand God's wisdom. The weaker we become, the more we experience God's strength. The easier it is for us to finally admit to our lowliness, the clearer His greatness becomes. The more we see our sin, the more in focus the cross appears. As we step out in the emptiness of our need, God is there, and our faith finds the Solid Rock. So do you have needs? Come now; admit it!

THE MIND OF CHRIST
Read I Corinthians 2:1-16.   *June 15*

The more mankind seeks to flaunt his own wisdom, eloquence, and supreme capability, the less he really has. Paul came to understand this truth and despite his past learning, he knew that nothing really significant could be accomplished in himself alone. Oh, perhaps by man's standards he could do something wonderful, but not by God's standards. That was something else entirely.

Paul discovered that what man treasured, God didn't treasure at all. Man's precious gold is God's asphalt. It will line heaven's streets where it is simply walked upon. The wisdom of man is provided in books and on the Internet, but God created the world in the first place and knows more about it than we will ever be able to discover. Whereas man flaunts his wisdom, God hides His. He keeps the deepest insights concealed.

So often as Christian leaders, we face situations which demand wisdom and discernment. If we seek to have insight from our own understanding alone, we will be significantly limited. If we can draw only upon the wisdom of the world to determine our course of action, we will have slim resources indeed.

Paul knew that he needed to step out in faith at all those times when he didn't know what to do or say. After admitting to his own weakness, need, and limitation, he was free to look to God who could provide him with everything he needed—and more besides.

The Spirit will meet us at our point of need. Since God's Spirit knows the mind of God, He can show us even that. He can lead us into the depths and take us to the secret places, delivering to us the wisdom necessary for any situation whatsoever. The Spirit effectually connects us to the mind of Christ. Just think of it!

BRACE UP!

Read Deuteronomy 31:7-8. *June 16*

In other times and cultures, it seems there was more of a premium placed upon courage. This trait was highly esteemed, and stories of courageous deeds and acts of fearless strength were shared and touted.

The British would encourage by making statements like, "Brace up now, lad!" Society appreciated manly strength and courage, the ability to keep one's head and act decisively. Both men and women were expected to show a certain level-headedness and unflinching bravery in the face of trouble.

Today, the opposite is almost encouraged here in our American culture. If the going gets tough, friends encourage us to leave. "You don't have to put up with that," they say. "Just leave and forget it, if that's the way they're going to be. You can always find another job....or another wife....or another church...."

The problems with this approach are manifold. First of all, it is best for us personally to resolve issues before we leave. Otherwise, we do not grow or become stronger. We take our pain and problems with us from place to place and limit ourselves. God intends for us to go on from strength to strength (Psalm 84:6-7), but this cannot happen if we wimp out on the strengthening process.

Another problem is that the people do not move forward either. In today's verses, Moses encouraged Joshua in his leadership task. There was no hint at giving up when the going got tough. In fact, it was just the opposite. Moses told him to be strong and very courageous. He clearly wanted to see bravery and fearlessness emanate from Joshua. If Joshua had not acted this way, would there even have been another leader to arise and take the people to the promised land? Would they have moved ahead to the place God wanted them to be? Perhaps not. We cannot just quit and leave people in the lurch, expecting another leader to come along who will carry out the task assigned to us. Perhaps another one will not show up at all.

Leaders who are not strong and courageous give up much territory to the enemy. Rather than stay and fight through in the midst of spiritual warfare, they let Satan and his wicked ways have sway. They run and leave the people in the hands of evil men and in the controlling influence of demonic forces. The leader may be safe then, but the people are left in their struggles.

So brace up! Don't be afraid. Be strong and courageous, and don't even think of giving up now.

BY FORCE

Read Genesis 16
and 21:1-21 if you have time.   June 17

When we can't wait, or worse, can't bear to see a vision buried, the results are usually disastrous.

Sarai discovered this when she decided to take matters into her own hands and give her maidservant, Hagar, to Abram as a wife. After she conceived, Hagar despised her mistress (16:4), and as Sarai chafed under this attitude, she in turn blamed Abram saying, "You are responsible for the wrong I am suffering" (16:5).

Oh, what knotty webs of manipulation, intrigue, and uncomfortable relationships we weave as we attempt to raise up God's vision by ourselves. This is always ruinous because our minds cannot wholly conceive of God's plan. If we try to help God out, we usually succeed only to get in the way. We botch things up and throw an element into the works that was not intended.

We should not be surprised when this causes trouble for us later. Ishmael mocks (Genesis 21:8-13) when Isaac is finally born. Although the true vision has finally been raised up, Isaac is not respected or appreciated by Ishmael.

Furthermore, Ishmael himself is a sort of aberration. He becomes a "wild donkey of a man" (16:12), an archer inhabiting the desert. His mother and he are angry about being rejected when the real vision finally comes to pass. He is frustrated, living in hostility toward all his brothers. "His hand will be against everyone, and everyone's hand against him" (16:12), and even today there are troubles with this great nation which he produced. The ramifications of trying to raise up the vision before God's time and outside of God's way can indeed be detrimental.

The motives for getting prematurely involved are varied, but often they can be traced back to ego. We have talked about the dream when we should have kept quiet. Now others are expecting to see results. We can become myopic, feeling that we absolutely need to see it happen. As we try to force the issue into existence, we may become dangerously controlling and manipulative. Jealousies, strife, disunity, and imbalance can all result, and we may miss what else God has for us during this time.

So come now: Hands off!

BEING SURE

Read Hebrews 11:1-2.
(Read all of Hebrews 11 if you have the time)   *June 18*

Faith is a wonderful concept to discuss, and a difficult concept to live out. "Being sure of what we hope for" (verse 1) almost sounds like an oxymoron. If we can't see something, how, precisely, are we to be certain of it? We live in a world where skepticism is prevalent, and faith hardly seems reasonable or even psychologically healthy.

Nonetheless, faith is exactly what God desires of us. The list in the "Faith Hall of Fame" (as Hebrews 11 is sometimes called) is an incredible one. Consider what these people accomplished.

We have been looking more in detail at Sarah and Abraham throughout this recent study, and Hebrews 11:11 indicates a secret regarding the faith of this man of God. We are told that Abraham "considered him faithful who had made the promise." Here is an important key. We do not need to have faith in the impossible or the unseen itself. No, we are to have faith directly in the great and mighty God of the universe.

Verse 12 states that from just one man, Abraham, came descendants "as numerous as the stars in the sky and as countless as the sand on the seashore." This verse also inserts a somewhat humorous reminder that this prolific male was also "as good as dead"!

If Abraham had needed to have faith in his aging body, you

can forget it. If he had expectations of Sarah's barren womb, what a ridiculous idea! However, Abraham is told to trust in a God who is there—a God who can do anything.

I remember the time when my husband had a brain tumor which was inoperable. He was in great pain, losing his peripheral vision and unable to work. We faced a seemingly impossible situation; however, we also served a God who was capable of anything. He's the One in whom we can have faith, and that mighty God chose to heal my husband of that brain tumor. God worked a miracle.

Many things that are birthed in the Spirit require faith. In essence, they all do. As that dream is growing, we need to believe in a God who is able to do the impossible.

AND OTHERS

Read Hebrews 11:35b-40.   *June 19*

Right in the midst of this long list citing those witnesses of God's wondrous deeds, we have a shift that has always touched me. I call it the "And Others Switch."

In verse 35, the scriptures begin a list of those who suffered and were not miraculously released. Some were tortured, martyred, or persecuted. The *Bible* tells us that "these were all commended for their faith, yet none of them received what had been promised" (verse 39).

The fact that these men and women were not wonderfully protected from suffering cannot be ascribed to a lack of faith. The scriptures are quite clear about that. These people trusted God.

In fact, it takes far more faith to trust in a God who does not come through for us. But why doesn't He, especially when He has done it for others? Why won't He, when He is able to do so? We don't really know the full answer to these sorts of questions, and all we can do is trust in God. We have to display sheer faith, even when we don't understand or see the results we desire.

Hebrews 11:40 tells us that "God had planned something better for us so that only together with us would they be made perfect." I believe that what others have paid the price for, we reap the benefits of in the spiritual realm. They themselves may not see the results of their suffering in this world, but they will see it some day in heaven. People will be there who are saved because someone stood up for what was right years before, or prayed and labored in a difficult land or gave his life to bring the wonderful Word of salvation. Someday, together with us, they will see what has been produced as a result of their faith.

As leaders, we may be the ones who are called to fall into the "and others" category. We may have hard times and see few visible effects of our faithfulness. At such a time, it is tempting to give up. "What difference would it make if I just give it up?" we reason. "There seem to be no good outcomes and such a great price to pay for nothing." However, we are asked to continue in faith, believing that God will ultimately bring out fruit that will remain into eternity. Are you willing to be among the "and others"? What amazing faith! How challenging.

PAINS

Read Isaiah 66:7-9.   *June 20*

Babies and visions have some things in common. Consider this: They take longer than a day to develop. Both need time to grow, take shape, and be formed in increasingly intricate detail. It is also significant that both grow in secret.

That is why fasting and prayer are so important to the growth of a vision. I recall one time when the Lord was birthing a vision in my own life. He led me to fast for thirty days within a forty-five day period. It was an unusual fasting time, but God did so much during that time. I learned. I came to understand more of what God wanted. Although it was difficult in many ways, it was a wonderful experience.

Shortly after this time, however, there were many challenges as this vision came into being. Actually, it was quite painful, another similarity between babies and visions. Isaiah 66:7 indicates that it is impossible to birth something without labor and pain. "Who has ever heard of such a thing?" (verse 8). No, there is a cost when God uses us to help bring about spiritual dreams.

The good news, however, is that once the dream has grown and the labor pain has been endured, God will certainly birth the vision. Isaiah 66:9 asks the rhetorical question, "'Do I bring to the moment of birth and not give delivery?' says your God."

No, the Lord will bring forth what He wants to see happen. The dream certainly will be birthed and become a reality. Though we don't see it all now, by faith we can accept that God is already acting on behalf of the vision.

That is why Joseph went from sitting in a prison cell one night to being second in command to Pharaoh—all in one day. We may think that nothing at all is happening to bring about what God has spoken to our hearts. In fact, if we were Joseph, our logic would probably be to work our way up through the Egyptian ranks, doing well at each stage, and then being promoted to the next rank. But this will take so long, we reason, with no hope of even getting to the next step. We might as well give up.

However, quitting too soon short-circuits God's plans. More is happening than you know, and the dream is already alive. No matter how long the process seems to take and what little progress appears to be made, have no doubt: He will definitely bring us to delivery.

THE STATE BIRD

Read Psalm 141:8-10.   *June 21*

The big joke in Minnesota is that the mosquito is the state bird. You laugh? Then you've never been bitten by one. These insects are really a nuisance. Try going fishing and you get so busy swatting those pesky insects that you can hardly concentrate.

Satan acts just like a mosquito. He bites whenever he can, and he goes for the blood. The result is a welt that itches and demands to be scratched. Satan would love to get our minds off of fishing for men. When we're swatting at him or scratching his bites, we miss our real occupation. What an ingenious tactic!

As leaders, we have to stay focused on the task God has given us to do. In fact, this could well be one of the chief functions for any leader. If he gets side-tracked from the goals and purposes of God, the whole group will generally amble off with him. How effective. It explains why Satan sees this tactic as such an efficient stratagem.

God can provide us with eyes to see through this diversionary tactic of the enemy. Usually, it comes in the form of a "crisis" which appears to require immediate attention.

We begin, facing in the direction God desires, but then we hear something over to the side and turn our heads to see what it is. We can't quite tell what's going on so we run over to examine the situation more closely. A skirmish is occurring that needs to be handled right away or it'll get worse, we reason. We'll take care of it and then get back on the correct path. However, if these emergency side shows are simply maintained by the enemy, he can effectually prevent us from ever heading back in the right direction.

As leaders, we need to stay carefully focused and heading on the path God originally showed us. We need to avoid the commotion and, if anything, send out a small contingent to check it out and report back while we continue forward with the rest of the troops as originally ordered.

I don't care how big that mosquito is, even if it's as big as a bird. Don't swat that thing! Better yet, use the protection available so it won't even bother you—in fact, it will avoid you. Then just keep fishing....

STARS

Read Philippians 2:14-16. *June 22*

Walking is perfect activity for a summer evening when the lights of the city start flickering on, a soft breeze is blowing, and the moon begins its ascent into a twilight sky. I love to watch as the most brilliant stars burst forth and take prominence. They practically call out to be noticed as they sparkle with both beauty and mystery.

As Christians, we also are meant to be "like stars in the universe" (verse 15). While we hold forth the Word of God, we can't help but sparkle and radiate light and life. The world around us is a "crooked and depraved generation" (verse 15), so in contrast, we stand out. It was always meant to be so. We were not designed to fade into the scenery.

Within this context, Paul gives us a command. "Do everything without complaining or arguing" (verse 14). This is clean cut and clear. It's also an uncomfortable order. I would have accepted it more easily if it had been like this, "Cut down on your complaining and arguing, and don't get involved in these two activities quite so often if you can manage it."

However, Paul actually has the nerve to write a perfectly straightforward command that allows for no leeway, no give or take. How is it possible to do absolutely everything without complaining or arguing? He can't possibly mean not to complain about anything at all, can he? Are we never, ever to argue about something? Much as I dislike it, the exhortation is unequivocable.

Paul provides the reason why we are to act in this manner. We should behave this way, he says, so that we can become "blameless and pure, children of God without fault in a crooked and depraved generation" (verse 15). It is so unusual not to complain that this causes us to shine forth. Not arguing makes us stand out in stark contrast with a world that is basically contentious. The crooked generation we live in is so used to being self-centered, that complaining and arguing are seen as the norm. However, this is twisted and perverse. Not joining in with these activities brings about such virtue that we stand out, shining like stars in the summer sky at twilight. Let your light shine!

HUGGING A PRICKLY PORCUPINE

Read Luke 22:41-44.   *June 23*

We discovered the porcupine ambling non-chalantly down the wooden walkway that ran the length of the resort building. Apparently, the pristine setting by the bay allowed deer and other wildlife to feel quite comfortable. The porcupine was headed for a well-covered trash container which was made of wood to blend with the surroundings. However, this ruse in no way fooled the porcupine who desired a well-spread, gourmet feast. It was rather late, so he was as surprised as we were by the encounter. We quietly stared at each other and backed away. The quills made us naturally wary, and he wasn't quite certain what we intended either.

The lovely summer night lured me out to our private balcony, even though it was midnight. It was a perfect time to consider the lessons that God wanted to teach that day. This evening, it was porcupines.

I was quite certain, after eying this creature up close, that I could forego the experience of ever caressing the animal. It was not a cuddly sort of pet.

Recently I had come face to face with a set of prickly circumstances. They were not fun. They were sticky, painful, and uncomfortable. If I could choose, they would be gone instantly, and I would never have to deal with them again, touch them, or be hurt by them. The difficult situation had made me uneasy; it had disturbed my tranquility and peace of mind, even while at this resort.

What bothered me most was that there seemed to be no logical resolution. I had considered the dilemma from various angles, and not one creative solution had presented itself. Apparently, all I could do was live through it and accept it. To me, it felt like God was handing me a prickly porcupine and forcing me to hold it. Not only that, He was asking me to hug it!

Various times throughout my life I have considered this analogy. Everyone faces situations that are painful. God has allowed them—for reasons beyond our understanding. We can't change the circumstances; we can only trust Him through it.

Hugging porcupines hurts. It draws blood. But Jesus hugged the Cross to Himself, even though He didn't want to do so. "If it be possible, let this cup pass from me" (Matt. 26:39). His blood meant so much. How glad I am He was willing to suffer pain.

"Lord, help me to be willing to hug prickly porcupines that You want me to embrace. Ouch! Well, a little blood is OK. Look what a lot of it did...with my Savior! Thanks, God."

CREATIVITY AND THE ARTS
Read Genesis 1:1-3a.   *June 24*

"In the beginning God created the heavens and the earth. Now the earth was formless and empty, darkness was over the surface of the deep, and the Spirit of God was hovering over the waters. And God said, 'Let there be light,' and there was light......" (Genesis 1:1-3a).

How interesting that the *Bible*, the storybook which beats all story books hands down, starts with a story about creation. Without the act of creation, the earth would be formless and empty. It would be dark. God spent time developing a glorious world.

Annie Dillard's *Pilgrim at Tinker Creek* provides the reader with amazing stories of a world that is full of creatures and plants with nearly unfathomable, amazing details. Bamboo can grow three feet in 24 hours (*Dillard Reader* 370) and a single grass plant, winter rye, sets forth 378 miles of roots in a mere four months (371). But during that same time period, that little plant creates 14 billion hairs and these tiny filament strands placed end to end would total 6,000 miles in just a single square inch of soil (371). Amazing! How did the Lord come up with that one?

God made all of this. He thought it all up, designed it. He enjoyed it, too. "He saw that it was good." (Genesis 1:3, 10, 12, 18, 21, 25, 31). In fact, from the number of times it mentions this, perhaps we could infer that He enthusiastically enjoyed this process of creation. He liked His workmanship. He stood back and examined the progress every now and then and nodded with appreciation.

In truth it is really quite impossible not to appreciate God's diversity and beauty. There's that long neck of a giraffe, the zebra's stripes and the leopard's spots, that big elephant with the huge ears, salmon runs and grizzly bears, llamas and kangaroos, butterflies and humming birds, whales and tadpoles, the tides of the ocean and the splendor of the snow-capped mountain peaks. He paints us a sunset and surprises us with sunshine and breezes and rain and stars and fluffy clouds in blue skies.

All this comes with the Spirit of the God we serve, described in Genesis 1:2 in the midst of the creative act: a hovering Spirit ....a brooding Spirit...a creative Spirit....a Spirit who designs and develops and sculpts and forms, who makes watercolors of rainbows and sculpts human beings from clay. All these designs are created out of emptiness, formlessness, void. The world would be a dark place indeed without His creativity.

Work cited: Dillard, Annie. "Pilgrim at Tinker Creek," *The Annie Dillard Reader*. New York: Harper Collins Publisher, 1994.

THE SPIRIT BROODS

Read Genesis 1:1-3a.   *June 25*

At this time in our world it seems like things are out of control: formless and void. And the Holy Spirit is brooding over the surface of the waters, seeking to create.

I wonder. Are Christians right now able to adopt this wonderful trait of their Creator God? Sometimes it seems that our churches are not places of much creativity or artistic production. Are we, made in his image, able to recover what we seem to have forgotten? Where are the Christians who can speak eloquently, paint, act, draw, tell stories, write, make stained glass, sing poetry, weave cloth, design jewelry and communion sets, sculpt?

We are at a stage when I believe we could see a resurgence of the arts. Postmoderns are certainly open to this. They are creative, and they are inclined to pay attention to film, story, and art. What I worry about is whether or not the church will be represented significantly in this resurgence. If we are not, it will be a tragedy indeed. Without the meaningful input of the church, a burgeoning art scene could take us even farther away from God. It is a period when Satan, if he continues to try and hold sway in the arts, could have a great impact in the conceptualization of these postmodern times.

Through the power of the arts, the age could be "named." Right now the term postmodern only refers to "after (post) modern." This huge cultural shift does not even have its own identity yet. It is an amazing time for the church to enter this dialogue. We have a window of opportunity where we can help to develop and shape what this change turns into. What we shouldn't do is to hold back until we notice that it has gotten formulated into something we dislike. Then we will preach against it! But the time is now. The Spirit is brooding over the waters.

May the Lord help us to see the importance of our role as Christians at this critical stage. It is imperative that we talk and listen, give ideas and lend voice to Christian perspectives. Since the arts are such a strong medium for accomplishing this, we dare not be absent from this important and powerful vehicle of our times.

A POSTMODERN RENAISSANCE
Read Genesis 1:1-2.   *June 26*

With the historical shift into the Renaissance, the kicking off point of the Modern period, the church was in the middle of the dialogue. It certainly had artists who could make statements to the people of that age through Christian art. Go to Florence and visit the Uffizi Museum, walk around the streets, visit the Duomo and other chapels, and it soon becomes apparent that Christian artists were more than minimally in the midst of the thinking of that time. Out of the Renaissance comes Michelangelo and his sculptures of *The David* and the *Pieta* as well as the paintings in the Sistine Chapel. There was Leonardo DaVinci's *Last Supper*, Botticelli's *Adoration of the Magi*, and Donatello's sculptures of Habbakuk, Jeremiah, and the penitent Magdalene.

The number of people who still stand in line to see these masterpieces is proof that they are still drawn by truly beautiful art. But where are our Christian artists? There must be more than taking a picture and putting a scripture verse on it.

Actually, the Renaissance didn't see the initial budding of

221

church art. Look at the beautiful art in The Cloisters, the Romanesque and Gothic collection of church art that is a special arm of the New York Metropolitan Museum of Art. Even during the Medieval times, beautiful art forms proclaimed a God who exists, and they proclaimed it loudly.

Our churches often tend to be art-less. Recently I was given a photograph by one of my mentorees who had done an internship in a large church in Uganda. The picture took my breath away. Here was the stage of the church with the worship team on it and the first rows of people in that huge sanctuary. The entire front of the stage was a beautiful painted mural. It was a stunning country scene, and it extended the entire width and height of that huge stage. "That is repainted into a different scene every four months or so," Nathan said. "Can you believe that?" No, actually, I couldn't. It must have taken hours to paint. But they had embraced a true artist and were being richly blessed!

Will we allow artistic renewal in the church and in the workplace during this postmodern shift? Will we relate with it personally? Will we embrace it, fund it, encourage it, produce it?

THE CELTIC CHURCH OVERFLOW
Read Genesis 1:27.   *June 27*

Trinity College, Dublin, houses the Book of Kells, an illuminated Celtic church manuscript that is replete with beautiful pages signifying the four authors of the gospels as well as fanciful creatures and humans who appear to be literally interacting with the scriptures—intertwined and knotted into the Word. The Celtic monks spent hours making the Word beautiful and appealing through their artistic creativity. The colors are vibrant, no page is alike, variety in form and color abound.

Dublin also houses the National Museum, and one can see the beautiful croziers, book covers, crosses, and bells with their boxes.

222

Of exceptional quality is the lovely Ardagh Chalice, a communion cup with metalworking filigree even on the bottom of the chalice for people to enjoy when the cup is tipped up for drinking.

The Celtic church was composed of charismatics who moved in the gifts of the Spirit on a regular basis, including the prophetic, healing, words of knowledge, words of wisdom, miracles. It seems their fullness in Christ couldn't help but overflow into artistic expression.

Stand in the churchyard at Monasterboice, Ireland, and see the artistic stonework where the monks chipped out pictures of Bible stories on high crosses, several between 18 feet and 22 feet tall! On the underarms are hewn intricate Celtic knots and every inch is full of design which tugs at the heart as well as the eye. The pastors would bring their congregation round these imposing crosses and teach about the various Bible stories illustrated there.

But where are our Christian artists who are so full of God that they, too, have to create? Hand them some parchment, and they'd draw to God's glory. Give them a rock, and they'd hew out the Bible. Supply them with gold; they'd design an intricate communion chalice.

The interest in creating is inherent in God, and since He made us in His image, it is inherent in us. If we have shut off this flow into the world, we are missing many opportunities. Our "high crosses" need to stand tall in our culture and make an impact regarding our message.

STORYTELLING

Read Matthew 13:34-35.   *June 28*

Our postmodern world is full of story consumption. It is amazing to consider the amount of stories that the average person takes in during a week. There are videos, TV, magazines, movies, books, the news, drama, stories from family and friends and those told around the water cooler at work. What percentage of those are Christian? Jesus spent his life telling stories. He made his points in parables, not just once in a while but consistently.

Think of the cultures that always have been brought to better choices and better lives because of storytelling. In pre-literate societies, this was–and continues to be–the major form of communication. As many claim we are in a post-literate society, the need for storytelling skill is again becoming apparent. It is also a part of postmodernist worldview where people don't want things explained, they want to experience it.

So many stories in our postmodern world tend to be insipid and meaningless. If we look to the stories of television, the soap operas of the day, the situational comedies of the evening, and even the new trend toward true-life drama as-it-happens, these are all searches for story. But what do they tell us? Their messages tend to be that life is full of senseless situations, frustrating relationships, hurting people, vulgarity and selfishness. This is a far cry from the heroic storytelling by the bards that once moved ancient people to great deeds. With the stories of TV, it is not surprising that our world is actually becoming more like what is being portrayed there.

So where are the Christians with the stories? We tend to shake our heads and tsk-tsk at the things we see, but what have we offered to replace it? Jesus gave out stories that were well thought out, stories that made people ponder and consider their lives. He made them hungry for more.

Scripture reminds us that we overcome Satan by the power of Christ's blood and the word of our testimony. When the churches started to skirt testimonies, something was lost. If people don't know how to tell their stories well, let's not drop the mode. Let's do some training. We desperately need more Christian stories out there!

PARABLES

Read Matthew 13:36-52.   *June 29*

Jesus used piles of parables, metaphor and simile. His thick file of three-point sermons? Well, it just didn't exist. What does exist are memorable stories of pearls, sheep, workers, rich people, lilies and birds. Even the Bible, that wonderful Word that God designed, is not an instructional manual as much as it is a storybook. How can we forget Jonah and the whale, Abraham and Isaac at the altar, Noah and the ark, Esther before the king, Daniel in the lions'den, David and Goliath, Peter walking on the water, and Paul and his horse? We can't...and that is just the point. It is why these stories have been told for thousands of years.

Stories are well-nigh unforgettable. We will remember a good story long after we remember the intellectual point of a sermon. The stories can bring back a teaching rapidly and allow us immediate application because of a meaningful image that is invoked. It is important, however, that there be a depth of meaning imbedded in the story. A story with no point is a sigh of boredom in our day. There are too many of those out there.

Postmoderns enjoy good stories; it's how they like to learn and think. Perhaps this has always been in the heart of man until reason, logic, and three points took over and stuffed it down in the modern times. In the backlash against modernism, desire for excellent story is again rising.

This has many implications for how we teach homiletics. It is just as critical to explain how to gather a heavy file of illustrations as it is how to organize a sermon. It is important to teach the subtle skills of excellent storytelling.....how to find images and meaning and metaphor in the world around us.....how to give descriptions and bring the listener into the story.

With the postmodern trait of detesting judgmentalism, one way of still speaking truth is through storytelling. People listen to

225

a story, put themselves in the place of a character, identify with that person's problems and even sins, and find out what to do next. When they themselves are making the connection, there is not a sense of being judged...but the process brings truth and change.

Story does not give "easy answers"—another thing which postmoderns do not trust. Stories make people ponder and think, and I believe that's what Jesus liked about them, too. He did not usually say things very clearly. He made people dig for the truth. This method fits perfectly with our times. Leaders should be superb storytellers.

COMEDY AND TRAGEDY: THE DRAMA OF LIFE
Read Mark 5:1-13. *June 30*

Comedy is a significant portion of good storytelling as well. In telling a story, people can laugh at themselves and their world. They can relax and often God uses this to "heal" the inner person, their fears and tension. After a good laugh, people are often ready to hear something deeper and the message sinks in farther. Whereas a totally serious message may end up with some on the defensive, some laughter can bring a softened state where further deep work can be accomplished and accepted by the individual. This is a gifting and a sort of artistic expression.

Jesus had a way of bringing humorous twists into his life; it was really quite dramatic. For example, I think that it is amusing when Jesus sent the legion of demons into swine. Now that was surely a dramatic scene...with 2,000 pigs rushing into the lake and drowning, oinking all the way. How their carcasses piled up, and what a stench!

Comedy and tragedy are part of dramatic story as well. English drama started in the church during the medieval times in the form of morality and miracle plays. In these first dramas, clergy actually did the acting. They felt it was critical for people to know and understand the *Bible,* and so they acted out the stories. These turned into having others take part in the characterization and soon large productions were developed. Ultimately, this was taken out of the church into the streets with biblical themes still prevalent. However, without the impact of the church, the secular scenarios and language became increasingly prevalent.

Drama in the church has since tended to be related with church holidays. Sometimes a skit enters in and recently there has been a trend toward teen involvement in "human videos"—presentations which in many ways take on the form of the medieval miracle and morality plays. What is generally missing, however, is significant drama which is exceedingly well done and subtle enough to interest the postmodern soul.

If a pastor decides what he is preaching on at the last moment and calls some gifted actors to "throw together a skit" to go with it, the quality level of such a production may well be lacking. Our sophisticated audiences are wanting to see excellent acting and realistic scripts, and these do not come easily. What is desperately needed is pre-planning and careful working together in advance so that high quality drama can become a part of the church message again.

As leaders we need to support excellent drama. We also must find ways to be dramatic ourselves. Let's throw away the fear and put a little drama into our lives.

JULY

THE PSALMIST

Read Psalm 96 .   *July 1*

Music and poetry. From time before time we have combined the beauty of words with the lilt of music. However, in our church culture today I fear we are losing the meaning of words in the trend toward a sort of vain repetition. The appreciation of good meter, rhyme, alliteration, even the basics of spelling and grammar, are falling away. The length of a musical note does not necessarily match the length of a word, and choppiness results. This is poor artistic expression. So where are our poets? Poets and musicians should be functioning together. We need Christian lyricists as well as Christian musicians.

The love for words and the joy of working on proper word selection and an excellent turn of phrase are other traits that are badly needed right now in Christian circles. In a course, "Faith and Modern Literature," taught recently at North Central University, students asked some hard questions. Where are the Pentecostal authors who are writing excellent fiction that the world will pick up and read? How come a good deal of the writing sold in Christian bookstores is rather "fluffy," almost superficial? Why aren't there more of the kind of high caliber style and story among Christian books like we have read in class?

It is time that we step into the marketplace of our postmodern world with novels and short stories that will present a Christian world view in a way that others will hear. Non-Christians are curious. However, so much of our Christian literature is written for a church audience. It uses Christian clichés and phrases and does not easily allow a non-Christian reader into the critical process of identification.

Indeed, writing takes hard work. It entails rewriting, researching, careful word selection, and depth. Therefore, when we see talent budding in certain individuals, we should encourage them to get training and feedback. They ought to travel, meet people and see the world so they have personal, real-life material, and they should read a lot so they know what great literature is like. They need to write and write some more. They require people who will honestly critique their work and also encourage them. They need a deep calling from the Lord and the support of the Christian community.

What budding new psalmists have you seen lately? Are you fanning the flame of their talent?

ON THE EDGE?
Read Isaiah 45:18-19.   *July 2*

Recently I had lunch with a high school student. She attends an arts magnet school in her area. I was deeply moved as I realized that not only had there not been encouragement for her artistic expression in her church, but they had actually negated her calling. She did not feel accepted in the church, and she wondered what this meant for her future. People had spoken some rather harsh words that had wounded her, and I could feel the pain. Although the people were well-meaning and probably only had opportunity for a somewhat narrow experience and expression themselves, it nonetheless was difficult for a young woman to know what to do.

How often this has occurred with our budding, "creative" types is perhaps impossible to count. However, as these tiptoe along the edge of our church worlds and perhaps even walk out

230

of the church yard, something significant is occurring. Not only are they losing a great deal, but also, so are we.

There is a famous book by the Jewish author Chaim Potok called *My Name is Asher Lev*. Giving the story of a young, Hassidic Jewish boy with great artistic talent, the book pulls at the heart, reminding us that conservatism is perhaps almost naturally at tension with a truly creative bent. Is there room for them within our midst? Perhaps if we could find ways to embrace and channel their creativity, a wonderful blending and partnership would occur. It has been so long divided, so far removed, that we hardly know how to do it any more. We feel odd, unable, unsure, tense. So do they. It is easier to separate. Or is it?

Perhaps there has never been a greater need to find ways to make it happen—to see that they all become a part of the fold—these artists and poets and storytellers and comedians, dramatists and novelists and sculptors and weavers, potters and graphic artists and photographers and all of them walking around out there on the church sidelines, wondering what to do with themselves and their talents, feeling out of place. When they are finally assimilated, our churches will flourish. Expression of love to God will flow. People will be drawn in.

Work Cited: Potok, Chaim. *My Name Is Asher Lev*. New York: Fawcett: Ballantine Books, 1978.

GOD'S ARTISTIC WONDER

Read Revelation 21:15-27.   *July 3*

Keeping the artist close to the church is a marvelous concept. Recently two young women in our theatre department asked to see me. They are been praying often and regularly for several years, seeking God for His timing and opportunities in the release of their giftings. They did not want to step forth before that time, but now doors were opening, and they were seeking counsel about their readiness for these ministry opportunities. How beautiful it is to see submitted, humble young people who are bathing their creative talents in prayer and do not want personal fame or gain but instead the praise of their Creator God. I was moved by their desire for a covering. Is there a place for them in our churches?

As we enfold those with artistic giftings, I believe that we will see marvelous partnerships develop. It will be a blessing at this exact time in history. What could some of these look like?

This last week I met another artist at a conference where I was speaking. She was an art teacher and a wildlife artist. Her church had asked her to paint five murals for their church walls. She somewhat shyly told me a story of what had happened to her recently.

It had been a beautiful day and she wanted to be outside, but she was supposed to be doing these murals. She sighed and headed down the stairs into her basement studio that morning and soon got lost in her painting. Seven hours passed, and she had hardly even noticed. She explained that after many years of painting she never gets paint on herself anymore. As she finished the face of Jesus on one of those murals, she noted the time with surprise and looked down at her hand. Her left one..and then her right one. Both were covered with red paint. She was shocked. God spoke to her, and I think I'll let you make of it what you will.

But here is the point. Anointed artists of all kinds exist. They can be a blessing to us, sacrificially giving of themselves to express the fullness of Christ within them...and within us.

At a time when we tend to have white walls all over our churches, perhaps we need to pray for the Lord to raise up creative artists to fill those walls with expressions of the Creator. God's city is certainly not going to be bare!

FIREFLIES AND SPARKLERS

Read Colossians 1:9-14.   *July 4*

Fireflies always remind me of my childhood and our big back yard with the brick grill sitting under the maple tree. Somehow fireflies have attached themselves to the memory of sparklers, my little brother, cookouts, and the fourth of July. After lingering around the picnic table, we would run around with the sparklers held high in our hands, chasing each other and trying to catch fireflies at the same time. When we were sufficiently exhausted, sticky with sweat but happy, we would pile into the house for cold tapioca pudding studded with fresh raspberries freshly picked from our garden. It was magnificent.

Driving through the region of my childhood home in my later years, this rush of memories crowded in as I observed hundreds of fireflies blinking on and off in the cornfields. I smiled to myself and began to think. Many of my high school friends who had shown so much promise were doing very little. Some had started off strong but were crumpling in mid-life. They were like the sparklers, flaring and ablaze for a time, but later they turned into a burnt-out stick with toppling carbon.

Memories of other people I had known throughout my life came flooding in—people who had been aflame for the Lord, sending forth beautiful sparks of light, but now apparently not even serving Him.

God places great value on endurance, steadiness, and persistence. He doesn't expect us to become burnt-out sparklers or to be fireflies that blink on and off. His analogy calls us to be lights and not ones hidden under a bushel basket, either. He takes great delight in quiet, unwavering service that is consistent, the kind that keeps going and growing. Why? "So that you may have great endurance and patience" (verse 11).

For leaders, these are especially important qualities. If we blink off and on like the fireflies, people can't figure out where we

233

are. They dart around after us, just like we did as children trying to catch the fireflies. Then they become tired and exhausted.

People need steady light from their leaders. Flash and pizzazz can only be maintained for a while. It looks great for a time, producing a reaction of amazement and awe, but in the long-run, people deserve more than a dead stick that can't even be relit.

Sparklers, anyone? ....No?

THE BALLOON RIDE

Read Zechariah 2:13.   *July 5*

The gigantic hot air balloon we were in lifted off the earth and started rising smoothly into the sky. Other brightly painted balloons were taking off around the same time, and those of us lucky enough to be in the baskets of one of them, could see the magnificently painted designs of the various balloons and wondered what our own looked like to everyone else.

As we climbed higher, we could look down at the desert beneath us. We could see animals scurrying below us, and we watched breathlessly as the sun began its descent on the horizon. There were a few people in our big basket but no one said a word. The moment was not meant to be ruined by words; pointing was enough. Wide eyes and amazed glances said it all.

"Be still before the Lord, all mankind, because he has roused himself from His holy dwelling" (verse 13). There are times when we were meant to keep our mouths shut. Zip up our lips like lightning. Be still in words. Be still in spirit. Be at peace. If we do not, we miss what we were meant to observe. We lose the moment in incessant verbiage. When God rouses Himself from His dwelling and deigns to come down to earth, we need to be quiet.

God does this when He paints a sunset. He arcs a rainbow in the sky and shimmers the water with the sunshine of His glory.

234

He whispers in the wings of the hummingbird. The earth is full of His glory. Let us be silent before Him and breathe in of His Spirit all around us.

Likewise in a church service when God comes to visit us, these are times to be quiet as a congregation. We must be willing to sit in His presence and be still. At such wonderful moments, the profound silence opens up vistas to us.

That is what I remember most from the balloon ride. The silence was so deep. Up there so high, there were no sounds. I breathed it in. I praised the God who made heaven and earth. I watched as the vistas opened up far below me, and I saw the world afresh, from a new vantage point. Be still, oh my soul. God has roused Himself from His dwelling place!

THE GOOD SHEPHERD

Read John 10:11-18.   *July 6*

Down in Argentina where I am finishing this devotional guide, there is a beautiful Spanish chorus which is "Jesús, tú eres mi buen pastor; tú conoces mi camino..." The translation is "Oh, Jesus, you are my good shepherd; you know my path." In Spanish the word for pastor and shepherd are exactly the same word.

The Bible in various places tells us that pastors are to be shepherds and indicates that there are good ones and bad ones. I have noticed while staying here that the pastors are very caring. They have gone to great lengths to see many new converts (new sheep in their fold), and there are churches as large as 25,000 with 44 services a week. But at the same time they care fiercely that all those get discipled and cared for. They have organized in such a way that they are able to keep track of the people and know what is happening in their lives. They want each person to be "known by name."

One of the very busiest pastors with a huge church here

prayed for our visiting team and then hung around, going back to be sure that each one was receiving from the Lord and being ministered to. He prayed a second or third time for some. Another extremely busy world-wide evangelist spent three and a half hours with us instead of the scheduled one, taking time to talk and minister to the group I had brought. He cared. Yet another evangelist prayed, and there were healings. It was his day off, but he spent four hours. God came, and He just waited with us in His presence.

Each time I found myself heaving a sigh of relief. The pastor/shepherd was not running off. They were busy people; they could have. But each pastor wanted to be sure his sheep were fed...and in abundance at that. Each one wanted to be sure we were well taken care of. Many times I sensed the Lord's presence so strongly and squinted to see the form of the pastor, realizing I could be ministered to as the group leader and did not have to be up and "with it." The pastor was there. He fed us and quenched our thirst by leading us into the sheep fold of God's grace. He let us lay down and rest in our spirits. Then he protected us while we rested, making sure that what God wanted to do was not interrupted.

There's nothing like a pastor, a true shepherd, who cares deeply for his flock, even a visiting one.

Work Cited: Zamoano, Coalo. "Mi Buen Pastor," *Enciende Una Luz*. Performed by Marcos Witt. CanZion, 1998.

YOU HAVE NOT BROUGHT BACK THE STRAYS
Read Ezekiel 34:1-12
(and the rest of the chapter is you have time).   *July 7*

The task of pastors-shepherds is to tend the sheep, rather than simply to take care of themselves. Pastors must care for the flock, and this includes bringing back the strays and searching for the lost sheep.

In the history of revivals there is one movement that involved Titus Coan on the Big Island of Hawaii. So many people came to know the Lord under this man's ministry, nearing 6,000 in just two years from 1836-1838.

Although stationed in Hilo where many people moved to be near his discipleship and care, Coan went through all the villages visiting his converts. Every person's name was kept in a notebook. He read off a roll call in each place, and if someone was not there, he noted if they were sick and visited them or whether they had moved or were traveling. He even followed up with the sailors to see when they would be back in port and how they were doing. He exhorted and encouraged, searching after any in his large flock who were backslidden. He observed their growth carefully and encouraged the most sincere to come back with him to Hilo where leaders were trained.

When my husband and I were in the Highlands of Scotland, we saw more sheep than we could possibly imagine. They are certainly dumb animals. They stood in the road and often needed nudging to be moved. Sometimes they looked up at us with these funny, dreamy expressions. They just rambled around. I had to laugh, because I could understand more clearly why Jesus said we were sheep.

These characteristics are what make sheep need a shepherd. When the day gets overcast, sheep just wander away and scatter. The shepherd needs to call them back. The sheep come to recognize the voice of their shepherd and follow him wherever he takes them. If necessary, that shepherd hooks the crook of his staff to pull the sheep out of a tough spot. It's wonderful when a pastor's counsel gets us out of a predicament. Sometimes the shepherd uses his staff to guide or nudge and send the sheep in the correct direction. It makes one grateful for the true shepherds.

THE LAST DAYS ORCHESTRA

Read Psalm 98.   *July 8*

I believe that we are in the last days before Jesus will return to this earth for the second time and that God wants to have a last concert song. Is His orchestra ready? Here is what I see.

Jesus is standing in front of a conductor's podium with his baton. He is ready to conduct his major symphony orchestra. He taps on the podium and waits for everyone's attention. He raises His hand. Orchestra members should be picking up their instruments now, snapping to attention. He is ready to conduct the last song, yet He has hardly anyone's attention.

Instead, the orchestra is in total disarray. The violin section is having a hard time. One person is still taking the instrument out of the case, and a number of instruments are still in their locked up cases. Of the instruments that are out and ready, many are not in tune. Some people are trying to tune on the spot. Others have tuned separately, but they are not in tune with each other. They are not in unity, so there will be no harmony from that section.

The conductor has planned a certain song and tune, and he expects his song to be played. For those who are finally ready with their instruments, many do not have the right song. It is not the correct music planned for them in that section, or they are on last month's instead of this month's program. Some have the right music, but they are not on the correct page. In fact, in the same section, many are on different pages.

I can see the conductor's frustration. He looks around. What kind of an orchestra is this? I'm the conductor. It's not yours to decide what song to play. Come ready and trained with your instruments out and tuned. What is wrong with my symphony?

Right now God is saying to the church that the only way you can know what song to play is to come to the tent of meeting. It's in His presence that you know how to tune, which music to play,

238

and how He wants it interpreted.   Every instrument plays differently from another. The violin, saxophone, certain drums, each has a different part to play. He will pass out the music. He will let each one know what his job is. We must spend time in His presence because that's the practice run.

The conductor has stepped up to the podium. He is tapping the baton on the podium to get our attention. He raises his arms. Snap. Instruments up. We're ready.....aren't we?

WHY IS IT THAT...?

Read Matthew 9:14-15.   *July 9*

The disciples of John the Baptist surely had realized that the Messiah was here. They had helped John prepare the way for Jesus. But here they seem a bit testy. Unfortunately we do not have a tape recording to see what the tone was for their question: "How is it that we and the Pharisees fast, but your disciples do not fast?" (verse 14). However, it seems likely within the context that it was a little haughty.

How could Jesus respond? He was here to do a whole new and fresh work. The old traditions were fulfilled in the very presence of the living God.

So Jesus answered, "How can the guests of the bridegroom mourn while he is with them? The time will come when the bridegroom will be taken from them; then they will fast" (verse 15).

We are blessed to be on the other side of this statement. We understand that Jesus was referring to Himself as the bridegroom and saying that His presence meant that it was a time of rejoicing and celebration. However, it is unlikely that the disciples had the same understanding we do of who the bridegroom was.

I can picture them, talking among themselves. What does He mean? What kind of an answer is that? We ask Him about fasting and He changes the topic and talks about a bridegroom.

Jesus confuses the issue even more when He next talks about patches on clothes, and following that he moves to wineskins. (Note the next several days of devotionals.) What kind of an answer is this anyway? But Jesus has ways of making people think. He says things that are wrapped up in parables so that people will have to dig deeper into the truths of God.

So here they were. Sitting in the presence of the long-awaited Messiah. It was a wondrous and joyous time. Think of it. The bridegroom was around. Those eyes of love should be flashing from the bride. Her heart should be bursting with the marvels of it all. Instead, here was the bride saying to her beloved bridegroom, "Why aren't you sad? Why aren't you fasting? I fast."

When God is doing a new thing, we must not miss it! We need to be in step with the Lord.

NO PATCH JOBS
Read Matthew 9:14-16 and Luke 5:36.   *July 10*

God isn't fond of patch jobs. The problem with patches, according to the verses in Matthew, is that they don't always hold. If an unshrunk piece of cloth is used to mend a garment that has been through many washings, then that patch will tear away when it, too, shrinks.

Our lives tend to shrink. What was once exciting becomes old and commonplace. We get bored (and boring). The fullness of a special experience gets lost in our everyday existence, and we forget what God has done for us in the past. I can understand how easy it was for the Israelites repeatedly to forget like this.

When something new comes along, it looks intriguing enough to add it to our lives. We find the idea fascinating and think that it will give us a fresh look. It does work for a time. However, after one wash, it will have shriveled also and pulled away from our lives.

Many times we have a hole, a wound, a need. We keep trying things that might help. But even though these are new and exciting for a time, not only does the patch not stay, but the original problem becomes worse, tearing and ripping.

Jesus wanted people to get to the heart of the issue. He desired radical changes and a massive shake-up. That is why He told this parable to John's disciples when they came to see Him about fasting. They wanted to keep their seasoned, traditional ways, and it appears that they did not understand all the changes that were occurring with Jesus' disciples. They were hesitant about giving up their old practices, feeling secure with them. Even though these old ways had shrunk in meaning and significance, they were still comfortable.

In the verses from Luke, another important point is made. The new cloth for the patch job was being torn from a new garment. What a waste of a nice, new piece of clothing! Jesus was offering an all-new garment, but apparently John's disciples wanted to take just a segment of what He was offering them and patch it onto the old.

Jesus was challenging John's disciples to a completely new approach. Forget the patches. Throw in everything and relate to Jesus because in Him are wholeness and joy.

Even in our leadership, God will call us out to whole new things. Patches are not the order of the day. A small change here or there in an old program is not what's needed, but rather a whole new approach. Are you willing?

A WHOLE NEW SET OF CLOTHES

Read Matthew 9:14-16 and Luke 5:36.   *July 11*

God doesn't do patch jobs. When we have needs and problems in our lives, holes and wounds, He doesn't just want to fix us part way. He never does things partially. In the parables about the patched clothes, Jesus is making a strong point.

Often we want God to fix something, but we want it done on our terms. We will give Him what needs to be fixed, but we want to keep everything else the same. The hurting part is so uncomfortable that we are willing to have it changed. However, the other parts may not be so uncomfortable yet and we would prefer to have it left alone.

God has other plans, however. He would like to give us a whole new set of clothes instead of just doing a patch job.

I was preaching this message once in Chile when a woman to my left began weeping profusely. I knew that God was doing something special in her life, but I was not sure what it was. After the alter service was over, she came up to me and explained.

About three months earlier she had dreamed something unusual. In the dream she was awakened by Christ, and He bid her get out of bed and follow Him. He took her to a large warehouse. He opened the gigantic doors and told her to go in. Inside there were all kinds of clothes. "You can choose anything you wish," Jesus had said to her. "Take as much as you would like."

In the dream the woman began looking for her size. To her surprise, everything in the entire warehouse was in her size. In fact, everything fit her so perfectly that it was as if a tailor had designed it just for her. Besides this, all the clothing was exactly in her style and colors. She liked every outfit.

"I could not understand what the dream meant until you talked tonight," she said. "Then I suddenly realized that I had been trying to do patch jobs, while God has a whole new wardrobe for me."

Won't you let God have everything and do a whole new work in you? Why bother with patch jobs when you can have a completely fresh wardrobe change?

NEW WINESKINS

Read Matthew 9:17.   *July 12*

Jesus went on with another parallel in this lesson about newness. He talked about wineskins. After use, they get crusty, hardened, lose their flexibility, and finally break with age.

If new wine is poured into an old wineskin, a problem develops. The new wine is still fermenting, bubbling and on the move. It's getting excited in that old wineskin, and something finally has to give. With no flexibility or resiliency, the wineskin finally cracks and leaks. Unfortunately, the new wine spills out and is lost.

Now seems to be a time for new wine. Many people are waiting for it, hoping that something new will happen, full of expectation about what God might do.

However, it is tempting to think that when the new wine comes, it will do the work of creating a new wineskin. This is not so. The new wineskin is not created by the new wine being poured into it. Remember, old wineskins break and become useless when used for new wine. Then that good wine is lost. These are two negative and disastrous results. There's no win/win situation here—only lose/lose.

Therefore, while we are wanting new wine to make us into a new wineskin, we are at an impasse. People are waiting for the Lord to do something, while God is expecting them to take action. The answer? We have to become new wineskins first of all. Then God can pour in the new wine.

It is really quite difficult to do this. For example, I think about the programs I have founded and of how attached I feel to them sometimes. Another person whom I once supervised now oversees some of these old programs, and I have to smile at my internal reaction when he comes to talk with me about them. He describes how it is time for something new, and what idea his team has created. I have to swallow hard, smile, and remember that there are new people and new things happening. It's time to let it go.

If this reaction is found in relation to programs, think of how difficult it is to change our very selves. We feel so comfortable with the status quo sometimes. But God is waiting for us to become new....first. Let's do it! I choose to be an all new wineskin, Lord.

WHAT IS NORMAL?
Read Acts 5:12-16. *July 13*

My three month sabbatical in Argentina was an eye opener. It made me ponder the American church. "It's normal to see miracles here," the missionary was saying. "I once met a 53-year-old man up in Minnesota who had been in church his whole life and had never seen even one miracle. That is not normal. What is happening here is normal."

He was right. I saw it right away. In Argentina there were constant testimonies to God's healing, to His miraculous provision, and to souls being saved. I heard it everywhere in every kind of church. That is normal.

One of our students even received a healing while my university team was visiting. As a child, she had feet that turned in and had to have an operation. She was running track now, but she still had many problems with her feet. An evangelist prayed for her, and her feet were healed.

When the church began as recorded in the book of Acts, they

saw many miracles, signs and wonders. It wasn't unusual. It was normal. These were some of the ways that God used to spread the gospel. People saw God's power in action, were amazed, and got saved.

Jesus also said that miracles would be normal when He spoke to his disciples just before ascending into heaven. Mark 16:20 says that after Jesus left them the following events occurred: "Then the disciples went out and preached everywhere, and the Lord worked with them and confirmed his word by the signs that accompanied it."

When we have a great desire to see God's word preached so that souls can be saved, then I believe we will see signs accompanying it. The signs, the miracles and wonders, all are used by God to put a seal of approval upon the words spoken. They confirm the word, indicating that the words are accurate and true. When people see signs, they believe in the greatness of God.

In Mark 16:17 Jesus said, "These signs will accompany those who believe..." When we believe, the expected thing is to have signs follow us. We are not supposed to follow the signs, but the signs will follow us. Let's get back to what is normal. The Lord especially wants to use His leaders.

CLOTHED IN POWER
Read Luke 24:45-49 and Acts 1:7-8.   *July 14*

Before He ascended into heaven, Jesus gave some clear directions to His disciples. He asked them to spread the gospel everywhere, starting in their home towns and then region and finally into all the world. However, He asked them to wait until they were "clothed with power from on high" (Luke 24:49). When we are clothed, we know it. It is not a mystery to us. This promise would entail something they could recognize.

It must have been difficult for the disciples to wait so long because they did not know exactly what it would be like when "the Holy Spirit comes upon us." I can picture this waiting period. After all, Peter was so patient! Not. I can picture him talking to John. Perhaps it went something like this. "Hey, John, what do you think this power thing will be like? I mean, I feel powerful, don't you? I am so excited. Jesus was the Messiah! I'm ready. Let's just go out there and tell them about it. They'll listen."

Then John persuades Peter to wait a while longer. And this goes on for day after day. Pray and wait. Pray and wait. For what? They didn't really know what would happen.

When the Holy Spirit did come, the experience was unforgettable. The sound of a rushing, mighty wind filled the place. It wasn't just a nice spring breeze that blew a white organza curtain back a little at the window. There was strength and power in this experience! They even had tongues as of fire above their heads. I don't think these were one inch high little lighter flames. They were like a baptism of fire, a huge flame, with the fire burning so hard that tongues of flame were licking out and sparking from the fire.

The initial, physical evidence was that they spoke in tongues. But there were other evidences as well that they had been baptized in the Holy Spirit. They were clothed with power as Jesus had predicted. The disciples poured out from that waiting period into the streets and found that they had been given power to speak in tongues that others could understand, power to preach the gospel, power to do miracles. After Peter preached that day, about 3,000 people accepted Christ as their Savior. Peter was much more successful than he would have been had he gone out earlier, without the power of God.

If we don't have this power, then we should wait for it. After Peter preached, he told those who believed (Acts 2:38-39): "Repent and be baptized.....And you will receive the gift of the Holy Spirit. The promise is for you and your children and for all who are far off—for all whom the Lord our God will call." That's us.

THROUGH THE STAINED GLASS BARRIER

Read Matthew 28:18-20 and Mark 16:19-20. July 15

Jesus told His disciples to go into the all the world. This means they were supposed to get out of their places and leave. Mark 16:19 states that after Jesus ascended into heaven, "Then the disciples went out and preached everywhere."

Last I knew, "Go out" is the exact opposite of "Come in." However, today's churches are filled with a come-in mentality. We have programs so people will come in. We perform music and provide services so they'll come in. But we are not supposed to be satisfied with the come-ins. There are millions of people who will never darken the doors of a church. What will happen to them if we do not go out?

The church is not supposed to appeal only to those who will fit our cultural mind-set and way of thinking. We are meant to share the good news with everybody.

What about the homeless? What about the poor? What about the transvestites and the prostitutes? Jesus said, "Go out."

In Argentina the church goes readily into the world. The students from the Bible college where I am staying right now evangelize everywhere. One group has gone into a main plaza to preach the gospel. They are seeing many come to the Lord and have already started a number of discipleship cell groups, even though their budding congregation is only a few weeks old.

I had a language barrier so all I could do was watch, but here were these students who cared so much, standing up and preaching...and a homeless man got saved, and an older poor couple, along with a boy who was shooting up drugs just before the service started, and a rich man nicely dressed and very distinguished, as well as four children. Also saved that day was a prostitute who stood off to the side, not sure if she could come close, but who ended up finding God as one of our young women shared Jesus with her.

Now that's going out. And I believe that Jesus would be happy. I believe He would be pleased that these students are pastoring their converts, including the development of several cell for the cross-dressers. Jesus always reached out.

The church needs to stop being limited to "Come in" and develop a new, aggressive "Go out" mentality.

THE POWER OF GOD WAS PRESENT
Read Luke 5:17-20 and Acts 10:37-38.   *July 16*

Tucked away in Luke is an interesting verse that reveals a secret to Jesus' life and ministry. Luke 5:17 states that the power of the Lord was present for him to heal the sick.

The presence of the Lord is so critical to all of us. When His presence is in a place, then things happen. He is the one who heals, who perform miracles, who changes peoples' lives. Without God, nothing much can really happen.

Acts 10:38 shows us the same theme. Peter explained that Jesus was anointed with the Holy Spirit and power and how he went about doing good and healing all who were under the power of the devil. This happened "because God was with him."

When God is present, it is important that we linger in his presence. We need to go after it, seek it, do anything we can to get into it and stay in it.

In the Luke verses the colleagues of a sick man were determined to get their friend into the midst of this presence. They couldn't get in through the door so they went to a lot of trouble. They climbed up on the roof of the house where Jesus was. That must have been challenging all by itself. How exactly did they get up there, and how did they manage to pull up their friend on his sick bed?

Then they started digging a hole in the roof. That took gall! It wasn't their house. What would the owner think about that? I wonder what everybody inside thought about it, too. As the men dug through the tiles, the roofing material had to have been falling into the room below. Can you imagine the reactions of the people there?

It was no small hole, either. It was big enough to lower down a whole mat with a sick man on it. They let down their friend right in front of Jesus. He saw their faith and forgave the man of his sins.

As leaders it is imperative for us to spend time in the presence of God, no matter what it takes. We need it for ourselves, and we need it for our colleagues and friends. When God is present, we can be healed, changed, and strengthened. We must be willing to climb a roof and tear up the tiles if need be, to want His presence at any cost.

KEEPING PACE

Read Micah 6:8 and Psalm 69:15.   *July 17*

Micah says that God requires three things of us: to act justly, to love mercy, and to walk humbly with our God. These sound simple, but they're not that easily lived out. We have to step beyond ourselves to care for others. We need to keep our eyes on God.

Walking humbly with our Lord means that we are in pace with Him. Where He goes, we go. When He stops to set something straight, we follow Him. When He goes to the poor and needy, we do too. When He takes time to stop and talk to the broken-hearted, we tag along. Many of the places He goes are humble places. So be it. Nobody is outside of God's love and grace. He wants to pour out His mercy upon people and to see that justice reigns.

When we are walking humbly with our God, then we are being sure that we care about the things He does and go to the places He wants us to visit. I just watched a student walk out of the school with loaves of bread in a basket and steaming hot tea. He's going where the needy are, just like Jesus would.

Psalm 69:15 indicates that we are happy when we have learned to acclaim God and to walk in the light of His presence. He is light, and if we get outside of that light, then we can't see. When we don't walk in the presence of God, everything inevitably seems dark and confusing.

Many times God gives us a dream about our lives, but we get so excited that we run out ahead. When we get confused out there in front, we start whimpering. We can't understand what's going on, and everything seems like a mess. The same thing happens when we lag behind. We lose track of where He is and start groping. We can't afford to do that as leaders!

When we keep pace with God, however, then He will shed light on our paths. We will see clearly. We will not trip because the light will show what is in the path. In this place, right next to His side, we see what He is doing and what He cares about. His heart becomes our heart.

One other good picture comes out of this. Scriptures such as Psalm 73:23 shows that God holds our hand. When we are next to Him, He is able to grab it. How comforting to know that He has my hand in His. If I were trying to hold on to Him, my hand might slip away and I would trip and fall. But when He holds onto us, then His big, sturdy hand wraps around ours and there's no way we can slip out of the grasp.

As a leader out there in the midst of risk, I like the security of being right there by His side and letting Him hold on to me.

ACCREDITED

Our university is accredited with an educational accrediting agency. I have served on several of this agency's committees and also as a consultant-evaluator and chair of accrediting teams whose job it is to evaluate other educational institutions. All of this is an interesting and complicated process.

The institution that wants accreditation must write a self-study report, show that they meet some minimum general criteria, and prove an overall state of institutional health on some key indicators. The team that visits the school looks at pretty much everything. It all has to be open. After the team's report, there are many checks and balances, so that it is clear to everybody at the end that the institution has been fairly evaluated.

In Acts 2:22 Peter addresses a crowd and begins to persuade them about Jesus. Right in the middle of the conversation, to make a strong point, he says, "Men of Israel, listen to this...." He then goes on to explain: "Jesus of Nazareth was a man accredited by God to you...." Amazing. God is the highest accrediting agency of all! God Himself placed His stamp of approval upon Jesus. He looked at every aspect of His life, dug into everything, and made an evaluation. What was the outcome? God accredited Him and offered this sign of approval to the people.

The verse goes on to explain that Jesus was accredited "by miracles, wonders and signs which God did among you through Him as you yourselves know." The people themselves had a marvelous opportunity to see these signs, wonders, and miracles. They weren't done hidden away someplace. They were out in the open for others to observe.

We need more people to go through the accreditation process. It may take some self-study. We may have some work to do to strengthen various areas. But in the end we should be ready to open our lives to others and to God. I believe that as people would do this, we could see more signs and wonders among us, God's stamp of approval.

WE CAN'T HELP IT

Read Acts 4:18-20.
(Read Acts 3 and 4:1-18 for context).   *July 19*

A crippled beggar gets healed. He had wanted money. Tired of begging, but having no other option, the beggar couldn't even look at people anymore. "Look at us," Peter had said to him. He looked up at Peter and John, expecting to get some cash. Instead he got the surprise of his life; the unimaginable happened. He was pulled to his feet by Peter, and at that very moment his feet and legs were changed. He could walk. He could even run and jump, this man who had been crippled from birth. No wonder everyone was amazed.

Now what does the jealous Sanhedrin do with that? So many people saw it; they had known the man. There was no way of explaining such a miracle away. Peter and John stood around, talking about Jesus to the crowds that gathered, and about 5,000 believed. So the Sanhedrin threw Peter and John in prison that night and then dragged them into their meeting the next morning.

Peter said, "If we are being called to account today for an act of kindness done to a cripple and are asked how he was healed, then know this..." (verses 9-10), and he proceeded to preach Jesus. It wasn't gentle, either. Peter accused them of crucifying their Savior.

Folks do not know what to do with courage, and the Sanhedrin was no exception. There stood the man who had been healed. What could they say? So they sent out Peter and John and held a little strategy session. Then they called for the two disciples again and told them to be quiet and never again to speak or teach of Jesus.

Of course, this intimidated Peter and John and they said, "OK, we understand. We'll keep our mouths shut."

Well, no. that wasn't it exactly. Actually it was the opposite. "Judge for yourselves whether it is better in God's sight to obey you rather than God," they said, and then gave a line I love. "For we cannot help speaking about what we have seen and heard" (verses 19-20).

I like this so much because I can just see Peter and John raising their arms and shrugging their shoulders. Almost like, "Well, you know, we just can't help it."

I can picture the Sanhedrin, too. "What do you mean, you can't help it? Just do it."

"No, no, not really. You don't understand. We have to talk about Jesus. We just can't help it! It automatically comes out."

When we're so full of Jesus, we won't be able to help it either.

TRAINING

Read II Samuel 22:35 and 23:8-17.   *July 20*

All of us as leaders need some mighty men surrounding us. It is wonderful to watch God train them. At first they might not even be able to bend a regular bow, but little by little God trains them so they can bend a bow of bronze. Their fingers and their arms get so used to the work, that they can do amazing things.

These are the sorts of people who become like David's mighty men. They are downright crazy guys.

Who would ever think of taunting the whole Philistine army and then, while all your buddies run away, you just decide to stay there, alone. Before your friends even realize how crazy you are and come back, the job has been done. All they have to do is reap the spoils.

That was Eleazar. He was so determined that his hand froze to his sword. I have a supposed replica of Excalibur (King

253

Arthur's sword) on the wall in my office. It is gigantic and very heavy, and it is all I can do to hold it with one hand. Eleazar was determined not to let go of his sword until he had completed the job. I wonder how they got his fingers unwrapped from around the hilt?

Then there was Josheb-Basshebeth (Josh, for short). I wonder what it would take to kill 800 people in one encounter with a spear. Think of the strength to jab a person to death. That was at least 800 strong throws. And then he had to tear the spear out and do it again immediately. Josh must have been incredibly well trained and strong to do such a thing. It says he was chief of the three mighty men.

Finally we have Shammah who also must have been a pretty wild guy. As the Philistines gathered at a field of lentils, the Israelites fled, all but Shammah that is. He stood his ground in the middle of the lentil field, basically insistent that he was going to keep his territory and not give it up to the enemy. He fought from the center of that field all by himself, and the Lord honored him by bringing him a great victory that day.

We need to have people who are strong, trained, courageous. They must be able to imagine the impossible and take their stand. God will come through on their behalf.

They also loved their leader, enough to break through enemy lines to get David some water he wanted. He didn't drink it because he couldn't believe they would risk their lives for him, simply to fulfill a passing whim. But that's mighty men for you.

ANOINTING

Read Psalm 23:5.   *July 21*

Throughout the Scriptures God's servants were anointed. This is a special moment, to receive the symbol of God's oil being poured out upon us.

Yes, and poured out it was. The anointing oil dripped off the hair, off the beard. It wasn't a small smear, it was a great outpouring. It ruined clothes, but who cares, because to be clothed in the anointing, well, that's even more significant.

In Exodus 30 we are given the recipe for the anointing oil. It contained many special, fragrant ingredients and could not be used for any other purposes than those ordained by God. The special formula was not to be made up and sold or used by anyone else. Anointing a priest was a sacred occasion.

We talk about the anointing of God today, but could it be possible that we refer to it too lightly or perhaps even inaccurately? We say that sermons are anointed or that music is anointed. Actually, people are anointed.

As a leader, I want anointed people around me. I want those by my side who have the unction of the Holy Spirit. I am blessed when they come straight from God's presence, from dousing themselves in the oil of God. Because they have spent time with Him, they have the perfume of prayer and of a great attitude. They exude the fruit of the Spirit, and the aroma is beautiful. The anointing is just dripping from them.

We have to remember that once the anointing is flowing, we must let it flow. It is meant to drip from us and move into a steady stream. Others can come to it and be touched. God uses us as a vessel for the anointing to flow through, a fresh river of healing, of love, of grace and forgiveness.

What we mustn't do is to stop it. Neither can we grasp the oil in our hands. We can't keep it for ourselves. It's impossible to hold the anointing. It is meant to flow on, and it is not ours to keep. Won't you pass it on?

THE TENT OF MEETING

Read Exodus 33:7-18.   *July 22*

The Israelites had a unique task while wandering in their wilderness. They had to follow a pillar. During the day the presence of God manifested as a pillar of cloud and the nation followed, wherever it would go. At night it became a pillar of fire so the nation could see. It must have provided extensive light for so many people to be able to follow along.

Moses loved the presence of God so much. Sometimes the pillar would let them camp a while, and perhaps the people would start to feel settled. But when the pillar picked up and moved out, they had to get themselves ready to go. It didn't matter what hour of the day or night it was. If during the day, the mothers would be looking for their children. Everybody was tearing down their homes, packing up their tents and their belongings, locating their animals. If the move was at night, perhaps in the midst of a groggy sleep, I can just imagine the comments then. Who wants to be tramping around the wilderness through the dark in the middle of the night?

It is critical that as leaders we observe the presence of God. When He is off and on the move, we ought to be also. We cannot lag behind because we have gotten used to things as they are. Difficult as it is, we need to get everybody up and moving. We have to love the presence of the Lord more than anything and be ready to take any complaints from the people. Who wants to lose sight of God?

Moses would always set up a Tent of Meeting when they camped. Interestingly enough, anyone who desired to inquire of the Lord could go there. However, it appears that it was not overused. Sad. The people would stand at the doors of their own tents and watch as Moses and his young aid Joshua went into the Tent of Meeting. Then the pillar of the cloud of God's presence would descend upon the tent. It must have been quite a sight.

Moses spent time with God, and his young mentoree, Joshua, would hang out there even longer. He loved God's presence too, and it is not surprising who should be the next leader of the nation.

And what about you? Are you that in love with God's presence? Will you follow Him anywhere?

FACE TO FACE

Read Psalm 103:6 and Exodus 33:11.   *July 23*

Moses had a special position. He was considered a friend of God's. Psalm 103:6 reveals something interesting. This verse says that God "made His ways known to Moses, his deeds to the people of Israel."

When folks want to have God do things for them, then He shows Himself through His deeds. Israel saw many amazing works of the Lord. He parted the Red Sea, turned back the Egyptian army, provided them with fresh food everyday in the desert, and brought water out of the rock. Israel came to know the mighty deeds of their great God.

Moses, however, was shown something else. To him was revealed the ways of God. He came to understand not just what God would give them. He did not simply seek God's hands but rather His face. He met with God face to face (Exodus 33:11) and saw not only what He was doing but why He was doing it. He came to understand how the Lord thought and the way He did things.

I have a good friend and one night as we were talking over dinner, I began to relate our friendship to what God wants with us. I never go to her with a great, long list of wants. It wouldn't be right to ask her to do a lot of things for me. Now she will often, but that's not the main purpose of our relationship. I'd rather know her, how she thinks, what her perspective is.

This is exactly the kind of relationship God wants with us. We shouldn't go to Him merely with the expectation of His performing a whole list of deeds on our behalf. Rather, we should be open to talking with Him, sharing, letting God know our hearts, and listening to Him.

As friends I can be open to what He is bothered about and might like to share with me. Often this turns into a prayer burden as I go into intercession and pray about those things the Lord has shown me. I'd like to be His friend. What about you?

THE BRIDEGROOM

Read Matthew 25:1-13.   *July 24*

The marriage arrangement among the Jews of Jesus' time would be made between the fathers. If the groom was from another town, they would set a general time for the wedding and then give some space for the bride to get ready. She would be leaving her family, perhaps never to return since she would be getting married and then live in the groom's town. The bride's family wanted to have a great send-off.

The groom, after he started out, may send a messenger ahead to indicate he was on the way. But travel in those days was precarious, just as it is today. Bad weather, highway robbery, closed roads, a washed out bridge, any number of things could happen. So in this case the bridegroom was delayed in his arrival.

This is where we enter this story. It had, in fact, gotten near midnight. It's pretty difficult to have a nice send-off party at that time. The banquet meat was burning to a crisp on the spit. As a matter of fact, nothing was hot any more. The bride might even be crying, "He's forgotten me. He won't come and get me after all. He's changed his mind, and everything is ruined."

This is exactly how Jesus said things would be right before He returns. It would get late. The world would be gripped by Satan's darkness. Most would be asleep, not understanding what was happening spiritually, and this would include many Christians.

The bridesmaids had been invited to the wedding banquet, but five, or half of them, were unprepared. They got drowsy and were not ready when the bridegroom (referring to Jesus) arrived at the scene. They were off doing something else, rather than attending to their duties.

When they finally woke up to what had happened and arrived at the wedding banquet, the door was shut. They had to knock and ask for entrance. When the bridegroom opened the door, however, he said something which is gripping. "I tell you the truth. I don't know you."

How sad. All the virgins were invited to the banquet, but half did not make it in. Could this possibly mean that half of the church will not be ready when Jesus returns? It is sobering to consider.

In spite of our busyness, we can never neglect our spiritual preparation. We have to be ready for His return at any time.

DOUSED IN THE SPIRIT
Read Luke 12:35-36 and Matthew 25:1-13.   *July 25*

The ten virgins who were waiting for the bridegroom were going to light his way to the bride's house. The lamps they carried were different from the ones used inside houses. Those were small clay vessels with a handle that could be held by one finger. For illumination, the wick would be placed in the oil in the clay lamp and then lit. These cast a small light which was big enough to help find the way within an enclosed structure.

When people went outside, however, it was a different matter. Those little house lamps would do nothing much in all that darkness. With no streetlights outside, the town and countryside would be very dark, just like the world. Out there a greater light was necessary so they made big torches. These would start with a long stick, rather like a broom handle. Then they would take strips of old rags and nail them to the top of the stick. They would wrap these around on top and tie them into a big bundle. Then they would douse them in oil.

The amount of oil that it would take to soak up those rags was incredible. This explains why some of the bridesmaids ran out of oil. They had brought quite a bit in large jars. But they literally had to resoak those rags every fifteen minutes to keep their torches going. Soon, it is understandable, they ran out of oil when it got to be so late.

This is why the other bridesmaids could not share their own oil. They weren't just being stingy. They were close to running out as well. Their hesitation wasn't in sharing a small amount in a little lamp. Rather they were concerned about sharing a lot of oil for another dousing out of their rapidly depleting jars.

Here is what we have to realize. In these last days before Jesus returns, we all have to make certain that we have a great supply of oil. The anointing, the Holy Spirit, these are our dousings. When we pray, seek His face, spend time in His presence, read His Word, these are when we soak up oil. And we have to keep doing it every fifteen minutes so to speak, over and over again.

When it comes to the end, we can't borrow someone else's oil. We had to have maintained our own supply. One leader can't look to another, and no one else can rely on us. We're on our own. Lest while we're out hunting down some more oil, the door gets shut..... Sobering.

SLEEPY

Read I Thess. 5:1-11, Luke 12:35-48 and Matthew 25:1-13. (Read as many references as you have time for.)   *July 26*

We are told in various places in Scripture that when Jesus returns, the church will be sleepy. This malaise will be rampant and so many will be sleepy that the church may not even realize its state in enough time to shake off its slumber.

I believe that Jesus is coming back a second time, and I think our time is short. Sometimes I feel like the church needs to be shaken as we would a sleeping child. Wake up! There's an emergency here! Stay alert. We need to be picked up by our shoulders with some strong hands and jerked into reality.

Jesus warned us about how it would be in the last days. It seems to be coming to pass right before our eyes. I'm not sure we are ready and alert like we are supposed to be.

What can we do? First of all, let's move into more prayer. We must pay attention to what He is saying to us. We need to know what He wants us to do right now. We should be dressed, set to accomplish anything that He desires of us, ready to serve Him. I believe that Jesus is wanting to bring in one last great harvest before His return, but what is our part in this worldwide mobilization? Are we prepared?

God is calling to many people right now. He is asking them to give Him space, to clear the decks and stay by the door so they can open it. He wants people who are ready to perform their assigned work and don't have any hindrances, who can step up at a moment's notice because they are traveling light without a lot of baggage to haul around.

Leaders on earth could get so tied up with their earthly cares, that they, of all people, could be most in danger of not being prepared for their spiritual jobs. Wake up! Stay alert.

BUSINESS

Read Acts 16:11-15 and 40.   *July 27*

There is a small church located today on the site where Lydia and Paul were supposed to have met, and one can wade in the river there. I did it one hot day of a Grecian summer, and the cool water felt great.

Philippi was a bustling, sophisticated marketplace, packed with the flurry of capital-city business enterprise and the columns of Roman law and wisdom. On the Sabbath Paul and his companions walked away from Philippi, looking for a quiet place to pray and worship in their own way. Outside the city limits they ran into some women by the river and, considering them of value, they stopped and shared the gospel with them.

Listening to this conversation was an interesting individual named Lydia. She was a dealer in purple cloth from the city of Thyatira. This would have made her quite affluent. Let me explain. Purple cloth was extremely valuable and was a sign of nobility and wealth, especially in Rome. The material was very expensive because it was dyed from a certain mollusk which is rare and can be found only in a few places in the Mediterranean. One of them is in the coastal area near Philippi. Each mollusk provides only one drop of dye, so you can imagine the amount of work it would have taken to harvest the creatures and squeeze out the dye, then color the cloth. That's what made the material so expensive and Lydia quite a business woman.

While Lydia listened, scripture tells us that her heart was opened to respond to Paul's message. Now what is special about this is that she was the first Gentile convert and a woman besides. Paul got to know her well and undoubtedly got introduced to many people through her. It would have been typical for her to be part of a trade guild, and this likely had regular business meetings in her home. It appears that this became a church cell group in Philippi, because Paul and Silas go back there after their prison sojourn and "met with the brothers and encouraged them."

Marketplace ministry is great. Already established business relationships allow for the spread of the good news in natural ways. I believe that is one reason Paul kept making tents. It provided him with living expenses, that's true, but it also gave him an inroad into the business community. We should be so savvy.

LIVING

Read Acts 16:6-12.   *July 28*

Some name it the Macedonian call. That's good, but I choose to label it *living*.

Through the generosity of a donor, my husband and I took a special tour with some students last summer called "In the Footsteps of St. Paul." We loved it. We saw Athens, Corinth, Philippi, Berea, Neapolis, Patmos, Rhodes, Thessalonica and Ephesus, to name but a few. A trip like that certainly brings the scriptures alive.

In the midst of it all, something kept nagging me. I guess I had always seen Paul as this mighty, almost superhuman apostle. Now when I preach, I try to bring each scripture story to life as it might have really happened, so I knew he was a man. But somehow tromping around in his world made him seem much more human and normal.

Suddenly I could picture him sort of wandering around, poking into spots if you will. These verses in Acts are evidence. He thought of going to this place or that, but the Holy Spirit would check him if it was wrong. So he poked toward another place. If he was somewhat blind to what God wanted, the Lord gave him a dream to make it perfectly clear.

This is the way I feel in life sometimes—just a bungling, stumbling individual, wandering around on adventure. Will I get to the right spot? Will I be in God's will? Somehow the question wasn't such a big thing to Paul. He just walked, and God directed His path.

Paul also was so normal and natural. He kept up his trade, making tents. No church professionalization for him. He didn't have to come up with gimmicks and gadgets to make ends meet. There were no Paul trinkets to sell. He just walked to the next place when he felt like it, wondering what would happen there. Would he be accepted, kicked out, thrown into prison, stoned? Would he be able to leave a church there?

That was the main point, of course. To talk about Jesus, that was everything. But he did it as part of his everyday world, as part of his living. He did it because he couldn't help himself. It wasn't relegated to a special time of evangelization, it was an everyday, lifelong occurrence. He just lived, and the church grew.

GOOD FOR NOTHING

Read Revelation 3:14-22.   *July 29*

Laodicea was an amazing town for its day, a very wealthy and sophisticated city. It had many banks, made a special kind of cloth, and produced a renowned eye salve. This is why the message goes straight to the heart of the city when the angel says, "You say, 'I am rich: I have acquired wealth and do not need a thing.' But you do not realize that you are wretched, pitiful, poor, blind and naked" (Rev. 3:17).

The message goes to the heart of their pride. Their special eye salve did not help their spiritual sight, and their beautiful cloth did not clothe them in righteousness. They might be wealthy by the world's standards, but they were poor spiritually, and that's where it counts. In actuality, they were a wretched group. Their strengths were their weaknesses.

Sometimes the things that we think are so great are really not good for us. They blind us to the true needs of our souls, and they leave us spiritually bankrupt.

Laodicea was also famous for its hot springs and spas. People would travel from all over to find healing in the hot springs. A friend of mine went to present-day Laodicea and explained that there are two waters that flow down a big rock face. One is cold and is renowned for being good to drink, helpful for your stomach and providing minerals useful to your health. The other stream is hot, and this is the one that people use for the healing baths.

This information gave me another perspective on this verse. I could never understand why the angel said, "I know your deeds that you are neither cold nor hot. I wish you were either one or the other!" That is because either one is useful and helpful. But the lukewarm stream, where the two come together, isn't good for anything. It doesn't taste good when you drink it, and it is too cold to soak in for one's health.

When it comes to our deeds, the angel is saying that they need to be good for something. We can't just mingle and muddle, we have to be certain that what we are doing is useful, that it is blessing people and helping them. If not, it's time to repent. God loves us enough to warn us.

WHAT DO WE GET USED TO?
Read Luke 8:26-39. *July 30*

Jesus simply steps out of a boat and has a startling event occur. A stark naked man comes running up to him, screaming. He throws himself down at Jesus' feet, shouting at the top of his lungs, "What do you want with me, Jesus, Son of the most high God?" That would take you back a step or two. "I beg you, don't torture me," he continues to yell (verse 28).

This poor man roamed about and lived in the tombs. No one could help him. They had tried keeping him under guard. That didn't help. If they chained him hand and foot, he still managed to pop the chains and run off into isolated places. There was no keeping him in a house any more, that's for certain, so maybe the lodgings he seemed to prefer in the graveyard was a good spot for him. This had been happening for quite some time, and oddly enough, the people had gotten used to him.

Jesus found out that this poor man was inhabited by a Legion of demons. I'm glad He didn't have to cast them all out one by one. Instead, Jesus drives them out into a herd of swine. The pigs promptly run down the steep embankment and drown themselves in the bay.

Now that must have been quite a sight. Oinking, grunting, mad pigs...running, if you will. And the bay must have been quite a sight. The whole herd drowned there, and I can just imagine the stench in the next few days with the waters full of dead, decaying pork—heaps of it.

Then there are the swineherders. How would they report this to their boss? Well, sorry, sir, but you see, it was just a normal, sunny day, and this man got out of a boat and talked to that wild guy who lives in the tombs, you know the one, and the next thing you know, your whole herd was just running like crazy into the bay. They just went and drowned themselves. Honestly, sir, there wasn't anything at all we could do."

When the townspeople and other country folk came to check out this phenomenon, they found their deranged man clothed and in his right mind. That's when they became afraid. They got so scared of Jesus that they asked Him to leave their region. Odd, isn't it? They got used to a wild, screaming, naked man living in their tombs, and they became frightened when they saw him sane.

That's the way people are with the church when God moves. They get so used to the warped nature of sin, that when people are healed, when miracles happen, when God sets things straight, they get scared. Interesting.

OUR HOME

Experiencing places where God is present on this earth always makes me so hungry for heaven that I can hardly bear it. I wish that I could just stay in His presence. When I am in the midst of revival-type meetings where He seems almost palpable, I yearn to drop off this earthly body and go and be with Him.

Argentina has seen so much revival, and I am here, immersed in it now for about three months. I know by experience that it will be hard to leave. I brought a team of students and ministers down with me for part of my stay, and they are having a difficult time with reentry.

One of the students said that she has returned home to the States but that it doesn't feel like home anymore. It seems so strange, she said. Perhaps that is why we are considered pilgrims and strangers in this world. We know it's not our final resting place. We long to shuck off this body, this tent that we dwell in temporarily. We want to get to our real home, the one God is making for us in heaven. Then we will finally feel at peace.

In the meantime, I believe that Jesus is going to come back very soon, and I choose to think that I am here for a purpose. Like it says in II Corinthians 5:9, "So we make it our goal to please him." That is what I desire to do. I want to prepare for Jesus' return and do whatever I can here on earth to see that God's Kingdom is advanced and extended. I want to make His name even more famous in this world and to see more people rightfully bow the knee to their King.

When this time on earth is ended, however, I will not be one wit sad. What a joy it will be to see my Savior face to face. What a wonder it will be to shuck off this earthly tent and to settle into the permanent home He is preparing just for me. No more tears, no more pain. And maybe, oh, I hope, those words will come, "Well done, thou good and faithful servant," because I am trying to live with eternity in view. Why bother with what will decay on this earth and cannot be taken into heaven? I want to see treasure stacked up there for eternity—the treasure of souls saved, of lives changed, of other people who are passionately in love with my Jesus!

AUGUST

SHAMGAR THE MAGNIFICENT

Read Judges 3:31.   *August 1*

Think about this simple verse in Judges 3:31: "After Ehud came Shamgar son of Anath, who struck down six hundred Philistines with an oxgoad. He too saved Israel."

Considered one of the six minor judges, Shamgar did not attract much comment in the Scriptures. However, Shamgar probably deserves a title something like "Shamgar the Magnificent." After all, anyone who personally and single-handedly kills 600 of the enemy has performed a major feat! It's better than Spider Man or Robin Hood.

A closer look at the verse places yet another spin on this story. Shamgar did not win the victory with a cannon, a black belt or a sword, but with a simple, everyday tool—an oxgoad.

Why such a strange implement? Probably no weapons were allowed in Israel at the time. After they conquered a nation, the Philistines had the habit of placing a ban on the forging of any weapons. This policy effectively protected their monopoly on all iron technology. All the blacksmiths were removed from Israel, thereby disarming the Israelites and leaving them militarily impotent.

The Israelites must have despaired. Without weapons, how could they ever overcome the Philistines? These were impossible odds. However, Shamgar casts off the prevailing defeatist attitude and finds courage.. He picks up an everyday oxgoad and manages to view it as a potential weapon. He sees a normal implement as spiritual artillery.

Undoubtedly, God desires more Shamgars. He looks for people who will stop wallowing in their inabilities—people who see what He has made available to them, no matter how rudimentary and unlikely it is. Even if there's only one person, that one alone can be effective.

Shamgar had the courage to step out, and God performed marvelous works through him. The Lord took this apparently foolish, isolated action and multiplied it until it far surpassed what Shamgar ever imagined possible.

The second sentence of this verse is powerful: "He too saved Israel." Think of it. The whole nation was saved because just one person picked up a plain implement that was sitting right next to him. And it was enough.

YOUR BASIC TRUTH

Read John 14:6.   *August 2*

Yes, I know that most advertising is inane. It's not surprising, really. An ad is meant to gain attention, if possible, and then move people to action. No one intends it to be deep, philosophical, or meaningful.

Imagine my surprise, then, when I found an ad that was NOT inane. I'm fairly certain the ad designer was unaware of what the message in the ad really was. However, lack of intent had nothing to do with the outcome.

I was driving to work as on any other day. It's a long commute, and I can "see without seeing" for miles sometimes. My car is trained and knows how to get there by itself, I think.

So I only noticed the billboard at the last minute. I couldn't believe it at first. I didn't think it could possibly say what I thought I saw. So I drove by it the next day carefully, watching for it along the route, not wanting to miss this opportunity for verification.

270

Sure enough, I had seen correctly. There was a giant package of cigarettes up on that billboard. Lots of white space. And four simple words in large red letters: "It's Your Basic Truth."

Of course, the message was unbelievable. It was also impossible. Truth can never be inherent in a pack of cigarettes. Think how far truth had been reduced!

What kind of a society could possibly accept such a message? Ours, of course. It says much about who we are in the United States of America. The truth is that this is incredibly sad. Our world needs to realize that we cannot allocate truth to anything material. We cannot even describe truth as an ideology. Truth is resident in a person: Jesus Christ. It's basic all right.

FEET FIRST

Read Joshua 3.   *August 3*

When I was a child, there was no experience that came close to jumping into the swimming pool feet first. That deep breath, that rush of excitement and fear combined, the plunge, followed by an upward sweeping motion...and then sunlight splashing all over the head again.

Throughout various life situations God asks us to plunge in, feet first. That is exactly what God requested of Joshua and the priests as they prepared to cross the Jordan.

As the people camped and waited on the other side of the Jordan, they had to have studied that river. It was large. How could they make it across, let alone manage to get their animals and goods to the other side? Joshua, too, must have had lots of questions. As the leader, how was he supposed to accomplish this task? I wonder if he worried about it.

No matter what he felt, though, Joshua remained strong and directed the people through each step of the process. They were to strike camp and move out whenever the priests carried forth

271

the ark. Joshua had realized the importance of waiting until God moved. A leader has to hold until he hears God's voice and direction. Then everyone can feel confident to follow.

Leading is extremely difficult, however, when God directs us into a desperate situation. What exactly would happen while crossing that river? The priests were to plunge in, feet first, and get their shoes wet. They were to go into the water and stand there. But then what? Would the priests just stand there...and the people just stand there...and the leader just ...well...run away?

Often, God calls us to steps of faith where we need to plunge in, even when we don't entirely understand the situation. That is a frightening time, but there's a thrill in it, too. We need to recall the excitement of throwing ourselves as children into the swimming pool—and then just go do it.

Certainly there's more at stake now. Of course, people could think you're demented. Yes, there's always the chance it won't work, and you'll be humiliated. But God is going with you, just as He did when the ark of the covenant was being carried across that river. Plunge in by faith. You, too, will reach dry ground once more (verse 17).

GONE AHEAD

Read Judges 4:14-16. *August 4*

What an impossible situation. The Israelites had been "cruelly oppressed" by King Jabin for twenty years (Judges 4:3). That was easy to do since Sisera, King Jabin's military commander, controlled a huge army with nine hundred iron chariots. Not only did the Israelites not have chariots, they did not even have weapons.

In Judges 5:8, Deborah sings a tune explaining that "not a shield or spear was seen among forty thousand in Israel." This was truly a demoralizing scene. No wonder the Israelites were not particularly thrilled about fighting such a mighty army with no local military outfitters handy.

Deborah was quite a remarkable individual, and she had a sense of what God wanted. As the two armies prepared to face off, Deborah said to Barak, the Israelite General, "Go! This is the day the Lord has given Sisera into your hands. Has not the Lord gone ahead of you?" (verse 14).

I should certainly hope so. I wouldn't want to face this situation without it. Scripture tells us, rather matter-of-factly, "So Barak went down to Mount Tabor, followed by ten thousand men" (verse 14).

It is marvelous when God goes before us. If we really believe He has done this, then there isn't anything to fear. God can clear the path ahead of us and pave the way. He can take care of any danger that might be lurking or any ambush that may have been set. He can confuse all enemies, demoralize them, or strike fear into their bones.

Why is it that we're not so concerned about God's advance leadership anymore? We are prone to move ahead all by ourselves and pray that God will be with us as we go. When we do this, however, the timing might be off. Everything may not yet be ready for us to advance.

We need to spend time seeking God and waiting for Him to prepare the way. When He has gone out before us, we can follow in confidence, trusting Him to do a mighty work. This was what Barak did as he went to meet that potent enemy army. And Scripture tell us that "at Barak's advance, the Lord routed Sisera and all his chariots and army by the sword, and Sisera abandoned his chariot and fled on foot....All the troops of Sisera fell by the sword; not a man was left" (verses 15-16).

When God goes before us, He prepares the way so that our victory will be complete. Let us spend more time in determining whether or not God has actually gone ahead...and not move out until then.

A WOMAN

Read Judges 4:1-10 (and the rest of chapter 4
as well as 5 if you have the time).   August 5

Deborah was an unusual woman, especially within the context of the Jewish society of her day. She was a very busy judge, and I have sometimes wondered how her husband Lappidoth felt about her camping out under a tree all day long with people swarming around her. The responsibility of settling disputes is a heavy one, with much weighing in the balance. It takes thought, wisdom, and careful listening. He couldn't have seen very much of her, but he must have been supportive.

Deborah clearly carried out the judge's duties with much competence, for the scripture tells us that she was "leading Israel at that time" (Judges 4:4). To lead, a person needs followers, and she had them.

Deborah was also a prophetess. The spiritual task of staying in touch with God is a weighty one. It, too, takes extra time and obligation. She carried this out with excellence, since Chapter 4 tells us that General Barak came immediately when summoned by her and took very seriously her admonition to engage in war. He believed that she had heard from God, even though he wasn't excited about this battle for reasons we have already described.

Actually, his reaction has always amused me. He said, "If you go with me, I will go; but if you don't go with me, I won't go" (4:8). Women simply didn't go to war in those days, but Barak wouldn't set out unless she came along. Apparently he trusted her, needed her wisdom, and perhaps wanted her to take the risk, too. More than anything, I think he wanted someone along who heard from God.

It is interesting that the enemy king, Sisera, was killed by yet another woman, Jael. She was spunky and drove a tent peg through the king's head while he took a nap in her tent. That had to take guts. What if he woke up while she was in the process of doing it?   Chapter 5 celebrates this feat, sharing Deborah's exuberant joy at this wonderful defeat. The people volunteered for this war and followed their leaders. The result was success since everyone, men and women, leaders and common people, all worked together for a common end. So be it.

OUR EYES ARE UPON YOU

Read II Chronicles 20:1-15 all the
way through first.   *August 6*

Whether their armies are literal or not, leaders in our contemporary world also feel alarmed and inundated with problems. It is so easy to look around for solutions. Or to seek for people who have successfully overcome similar circumstances in the past. Or to find a consultant who can give expert advice.

At the end of it all, however, who can give better advice than God Himself? The people of Judah realized that. They came together—whole families—from every town—all for the sole purpose of seeking God.

Today we desperately need the same readiness to inquire of the Lord. Like Jehoshaphat, we should resolve to discover His viewpoint for each situation.

What a time it must have been as they recounted their history, remembering what God had done for them in the past. Furthermore, they humbled themselves and admitted their own lack of power against such a coalition of enemies. Easy? Certainly not today! But how we need it.

Many times as a leader I have felt just like Jehoshaphat, and I have said in my heart, "We do not know what to do..." Notice the very last part of verse 12, however, the part that reads "...but our eyes are upon You."

We can look nowhere else for effective help. We waste time letting our eyes dart around toward other people and their solutions. In the end, we must stand in His presence and fix our eyes upon the Lord.

Then God moves again, just as He has in the past. The Spirit comes down and comforts. What a tender word He gave to Judah, "Do not be afraid or discouraged because of this vast army. For the battle is not yours, but God's" (verse 15).

In the end Jehoshaphat would have taken personal responsibility for a battle that was not even his. As he sought God, he realized that it was not his burden. It was God's. The Lord saw it as His battle. What a relief!

STAND AND FACE THEM

Study II Chronicles 20:15-20 today
before you read on.   *August 7*

It is one matter to be told not to be afraid or discouraged; it is another matter altogether to obey. Leaders naturally worry about the safety and well-being of those who rely upon them. During crises, this burden weighs heavily and fear is natural.

Furthermore, the word from God in this passage defies reason. Would YOU find it easy to embrace this one? "You will not have to fight this battle. Take up your positions; stand firm.... Go out to face them tomorrow" (verse 17).

Right. Just march on out there and stand facing them. Look at the enemy ranks. There won't be any fighting, and we'll be the victors. It's quite ludicrous..

There are times in our leadership crises when God's chosen action confounds logic. The people may not all agree or understand exactly what God is calling us to do. Sometimes we feel like running to hide and putting out the press sign, "No Comment."

Jehoshaphat's reaction, as recorded in verse 18, is profound. He took the lead by getting down on his face before God. Do you think he wondered how the people would respond to this? Would they stare at him and whisper among themselves that their leader had finally lost it? However, the people, amazingly enough, all followed suit. They, too, humbled themselves and worshiped God. The worship leaders even got loud and excited!

What did that night hold? When everything was quiet and still, did doubts try to return? Might Jehoshaphat have wondered if that prophetic word was actually from God?

We do not know what Jehoshaphat experienced during his night of waiting. However, we do know that he arose early the next morning to carry out the action God had commanded. And we also read that out of the faith in his own heart, he encouraged the people to trust in God and in the prophets.

How critical it is for leaders to lead!

RAISING UP A VISION

Read Isaiah 46:10-11.   *August 8*

God will birth a real vision in us and then, more often than not, put it to the test, all because we tend to make one gigantic mistake: We think that it is our sole responsibility now to raise up that vision. Nothing could be further from the truth.

If a vision is God-birthed, it is something that God intends to do anyway. Furthermore, it is His responsibility to do it...when He chooses to do it...just as He wants to do it...and by the methods He desires. All we need to do is rest in Him, wait, and do what He tells us.

It will always become evident when the time has come for us to act. The way is smooth, God has gone ahead of us, and fruit falls ripe from the tree and into our hands. We look at it in delight, aware that God has been at work and has accomplished this wonderful thing.

I'll never forget a graphic example of this which occurred one

277

summer. I had been praying for a few years about a particular program. Although it had started, the program did not seem to be at the place where I felt God wanted to take it. My heart was excited and burdened for it. I saw in my spirit that God desired more, but I didn't know exactly how to make that happen. I could have made some moves, but I waited and prayed instead.

That summer was powerful because one circumstance after another all summer long fell into place. In Boston, in Detroit, in Chicago, and in Washington, D.C., people had been prepared by God to take part in raising up the vision. Due to unusual events, I came into contact with them all, within weeks of each other, and by the end of the summer, the plans had unfolded and the expansion of the program was a reality.

If I had tried to do this on my own, it could not possibly have happened so quickly or as well. Everyone could see the hand of the Lord in it, so there was an awe at what God was doing. He received the glory. Furthermore, each person was willing, supportive, and creative in his assistance.

You know what I learned that summer? —Waiting!

GOD'S TIMING

Read Genesis 17:15-19 and 18:9-15 plus
Exodus 2:11-25 and 3:1-12. (Save the Exodus
verses for tomorrow if you desire.)   *August 9*

One of the most difficult lessons to learn is that our timetable is not necessarily the same as God's. In fact, I can't figure God out. I almost always think that He should act faster than He does. His slow moves are also graphically evident throughout scripture. God seems not to mind when people have to be patient and wait.

Take Abram and Sarai, for example. Twenty-five years earlier, God had promised Abraham that he would have many progeny. It was a true vision from the heart of God. But then they waited. And they waited. And they waited some more. It wasn't until Abram was 100 and Sarai 90 years old, certainly past child-rearing age, that the promise was finally fulfilled. What a great story. God's timing is unbelievable sometimes.

And then there's Moses who had a heart for the plight of the Jews, even to the point of killing an Egyptian slave-master. However, in between his dream to help his people and actually being used to carry this out, Moses spent forty years on the backside of the desert, doing nothing more exciting than hearing the sheep bleat.

Hannah had to wait for her special baby, Samuel, and Elizabeth had to wait for her baby who, as John the Baptist, would become the forerunner of the Messiah. Joseph received his dream at age 17, but spent most of the time after that in prison until everything finally came to pass thirteen years later.

If you've ever had to wait like this, you know just how difficult this can be. When God places a vision into our hearts, we get excited about it. We tend to embellish it, get wrapped up in it, and start reckoning on ways to bring it to pass. After all, it is what God wants to see accomplished.

However, just because we are sure of the direction and the ultimate result doesn't mean that it is ours to raise up at all. Certainly it is not our own strain and frustration that God desires. If these rear their heads, they merely lead to trouble. We get Ishmaels and dead Egyptians instead of what God has in mind.

Never...never...never...never...jump ahead of God. Great trouble can ensue. No matter how tempting it is to get into it before God raises up the vision, resist this urge. Let Him do the work!

ERECTING TOMBSTONES

Read yesterday's verses again.   *August 10*

With God's vision beating in our breasts and dancing before our eyes, we can feel so alive and excited. Remember Joseph's enthusiasm after he had his dream and then the mistake of straightaway sharing it with his brothers? As we wait on God for His timing, however, the vision can get dim and our desire for its realization becomes weak. God puts us in prisons where the idea we once had seems not only unlikely or improbable, but downright impossible.

What happens when a vision dies...when we have waited so long that our own reasonable conclusion is that the dream will never come to pass? One response is to force it, if we can. (We'll talk about that in the near future.) The other response it to let the vision die.

Anyone who has ever had to let a vision go will know the pain of this action. What a contrast it is. Once excitement and the thrill of new things were reigning strongly. We dared to dream, to consider how God could actually use us. We wrote this all out, added curlicues to the letters, and colored them in. We prayed and sought to know God's way.

Perhaps God would do it in this way...perhaps in that. Maybe the Lord would make it happen when....or no, maybe instead it would occur right afterwards. We see ourselves involved...in lights...or in that country...or behind that desk...or singing or preaching or leading. We see that title or position or fame. Of course, we will be humble. God will use us.

But as the years stretch behind us, it does not appear that it will come true at all. Sarai gave up on that special baby. She was past child-bearing years. It was impossible now. Anyone knows that.

Moses had once thought that his extensive understanding of the Egyptian culture might allow the opportunity to do something for his people. But now, there is only the smell of sheep and the cold of the pasture.

It's time to get realistic again. Perhaps the dream was not real after all. Probably we imagined it. Surely God can't use the likes of us now. If it's dead, then let's be honest and erect a tombstone. It's mourning time.

WHY GRAVEYARDS?

*Read Judges 7:1-8a (continue reading through verse 22
if you have the chance).*   *August 11*

God doesn't mind vision graveyards a bit. In fact, it's a very safe place for us to keep our dreams. As long as we are holding dreams in our own hands, we can taint them, manipulate them, play with them, get too involved. We can place our own effort into raising up the dream.

The problem here is that when the dream comes to life, it can appear that we did it. People can "oooh" and "aaah" over what we have accomplished. We may smile and say humble things, but inside we are proud. *Of course, we did it! Well, sure, God helped, but He clearly used us. It took a lot of hard work and some talent, too.* How easy it is to get unduly puffed up!

Furthermore, God doesn't receive the glory and honor that is due Him. Who actually did this thing? God! But we are positioned beside it with a smile on our faces. Our chests are puffed out, and we are standing tall with our chins in the air. Where is God now? Who can even see Him? What did He really do, anyway?

Fortunately, God has the tendency to get us out of the way. He removes us from this scene of pride and effort. Who wants to point to bones in the ground, after all? Who wishes to touch a grave?

God is very careful to remove the flesh of men so no one will mistake who actually accomplished the work. That's why God reduced the Israeli army from 32,000 to 10,000 and finally to only 300. Otherwise, everyone would say it was Gideon and his great army who won against the Midianites. But now, the miracle of God's mighty power is evident, and He receives the glory.

When God works in our lives, paring down, stripping off, taking away, then what is our reaction? Let's get rid of the flesh of man and bury it. We need to allow God to do what only He can do: raise up the vision. Is that original vision of yours dead yet? Quit trying to keep it alive. Let go.

DRAMATIC TIMING

Read Acts 1:7.   *August 12*

Many aspects of good drama delight me. One of my favorites is what has been called the "deus ex machina," a Latin phrase literally translated "god from a machine." The idea is that characters often get themselves into a real fix. They are unable to extricate themselves from this dilemma, and tragedy looms on the horizon. If no one intervenes, they will die, lose their true love, become penniless, or end up with a broken dream. However, in the drama something wonderful happens—almost like God himself swooping down upon us.

The deus ex machine "saves the day," and machinery in the form of some stage contraption pulls the person to safety. Just as the main character is about to fall into a well, for example, a giant bird might swoop down and fly away with her. Or when the hero is about to be shot, someone catapults off the roof and lands in front of the approaching arrow, only to be safe also because the arrow hits his belt buckle and is dashed to the ground. You know the kind of situation I am talking about.

In real life, the "deus ex machina" is the power of God Himself. He saves the day at the very last minute. As a matter of fact, I have mused on the fact that God has a real sense of dramatic timing.

In my life and the lives of other people I know, God seems to have a habit of waiting until the very last minute to do His work. I don't always appreciate this timing, I have to admit. He seems to cut it far too close. Something serious could happen, you know, when one waits until the very last second to intervene, like God so often does. For our peace of mind, it would be handy to know farther ahead.

However, God's timing is dramatic and flawless. He loves to build suspense, to let us hold our breath, to sit on the edge of our seats. Just when it seems that there's no time left and tragedy is surely looming, God Himself works it all out. He comes in and saves the day. Aren't you glad?

THE BROWN PAPER SACK

Read Psalm 116:12-19.   *August 13*

There is a very touching story I once heard told about Abraham Lincoln. As the President he was used to an extremely busy schedule, full of appointments, but this particular day had been an unusually long and exhausting one. Many people had come to him with expectations, needs, and problems of all sorts.

It was the last appointment of that unending day, and the President wanted to get it over with as quickly as possible. He didn't recognize the lady's name and wondered what she wanted.

As President Lincoln opened the door to his office, he saw an elderly lady sitting hunched over in the waiting room. She was rather poorly dressed and clutched a plain, brown paper sack. With some curiosity, he ushered her into his office and then to the big, leather chair in front of his desk. Then he went around to the other side and sat down, trying not to show his weariness.

"What can I do for you?" the President began, giving her the cue to begin her story and share her request.

"Oh, Mister Lincoln," the little lady said in a quavering voice. "I didn't come here FOR anything!"

Lincoln didn't understand and gently prompted, "Well, what do you want from me then?"

"Nothing," she replied in that wavering voice. "I got to thinking about how you see so many people all the time every day who want you to give them something. So I just wanted to give you something for a change. This is all I could think of, but I heard you like this kind."

She smiled shyly and handed the brown paper bag to Lincoln. When he opened the bag, it was full of chocolate chip cookies, his favorite. According to the story, Lincoln got tears in his eyes.

"Lord, I want to bring You something today. Want some cookies?"

THE LADDER AGAINST THE WALL

Read Luke 9:23-25.   *August 14*

A ladder often symbolizes success, achievement, and advancement. Whether symbolically or literally climbing, we seldom stop to think about the action. But when it comes to the ladder of life, perhaps we should make it a habit to meditate on the cost of the climb. We need to ask some hard questions, the answers to which we might not want to face.

What will it cost in friends and allies upon whom we have to step so we can move ahead? What will it have to do with our time and our lifestyles? What might we pay in loss of integrity, honesty, and spontaneity? How much money will we have to spend on ourselves instead of having the joy of giving it to others? How much of ourselves will we have to nullify so we won't face the risk of bursting out at the wrong time? How might our consciences be affected? How much thought and effort will we lose trying to manipulate people and circumstances?

284

If we think that Christians are immune to such temptations, we need to reconsider. We, too, can get intertwined with the world. It is easy to rationalize our purposes, intents, and motives. Even in ministry callings, it can be difficult to sort through our motives. Should we accept a larger church as a pastor or welcome a leadership role in the denomination? Choice leadership positions in the church may tempt the layperson. Or it may appear more valuable to get invited as a guest speaker for a state or national conference rather than to serve in humbler circumstances for a small group.

Christ kept the importance and value of each person in mind. He was ready to link Himself with those of modest repute as quickly as He was with those of position. He lived His life with eternity in view and God's values solidly in mind.

Wouldn't it be sad to climb the ladder of life painstakingly and then discover that the ladder was propped against the wrong wall?

THE BUNDLE OF STICKS

Read Psalm 68:19. *August 15*

There was once a little, elderly lady in Ukraine who was slowly making her way along the dusty road. She carried a large burden lashed onto her back. The heavy load of firewood bent her low, but the need kept her moving.

Down the road clattered a horse-drawn wagon, empty after the farmer had shoveled out his grain at the market that day. As he rode along, the farmer saw the tiny, stooped figure in the distance and determined to stop and help her out as soon as he rounded that curve. He knew the old lady by name, knew she was a widow and had no children, knew that life had not been kind. She kept to herself in her small cottage a few miles down the road.

285

As the horse pulled up next to this life-weary lady, she could scarcely believe her good fortune. Little had she expected anyone to be so thoughtful, to waste minutes on her behalf, to even notice her, let alone care enough to stop.

The farmer reached out his hand to help her onto the wagon seat next to him. However, she shook her head conclusively and shuffled to the back of the wagon. She sat on the rim and let her feet hang over the edge. The farmer shrugged and moved off down the road.

After a mile, he glanced back at his passenger and surprise spread across his face. Instead of unstrapping the bundle so it would rest on the wagon bed, the old lady was sitting there still bent under its burden. The load continued to weigh her down.

When I first heard this little story, it made me look at myself. I'm independent, you see. I am apt to think that I should solve my own problems. There are certain responsibilities that are mine to bear, after all, and I need to stay strong. That's usually my way of thinking.

However, this independent spirit can mean that we don't allow others to assist us. We may resist the very help that God has provided on our path. How often have we left our burdens on our backs when relief was inches below us?

THE BICYCLE REPAIR SHOP

Read Matthew 6:25-34.   *August 16*

John was in another world when he rode that new blue bike. It was his ticket to freedom and exploration. He could pedal fast; he could meander by the stream in the park. He could fly down hills; he could dodge raindrops. Always there was a new stunt to try, a new bend to go around, a new friend to meet at his favorite playground.

It was no surprise, then, that John kept trying to ride his bike even when the wheel spoke got bent. Children can readily believe that kisses heal wounds and that bicycles can somehow repair themselves. That was why he kept riding his bike, though the spoke became worse with each day of summer.

When the spoke finally snapped, he could no longer disregard the problem. John dragged his dad out to the garage as soon as he got home and pointed to the problem wheel. Dad could fix anything. All would be well.

However, his father just shook his head. "We'll have to take it over to Harry's tomorrow. Only a bicycle repair shop can handle this one," he said with alarming finality.

John was not happy, but he could think of no other option. So the next day he accompanied his father to the bicycle shop and came out with a frown. Harry had said that the bicycle needed to stay there until they could get the right part from the city.

John went home and didn't know what to do with himself. He paced, sat, called his friend on the phone, and finally crept out of the house and down the street to the shop. Harry tried to explain that he couldn't possibly have fixed the bike yet. Nonetheless, John wheeled the bicycle out of the shop---broken.

Hmmm. Do I do that with God? The craziness and uselessness of my impatience need to become more real to me.

"God, help me leave broken things with You and not take them back until You have time to fix them. ...Even things that are precious to me!"

SEEK HIS FACE

Read I Chronicles 16:7-11.   *August 17*

What a wonderful time to celebrate. The ark had been returned to Jerusalem, and the King had led it in with great joy. David was a King after God's own heart, and he delighted in the Lord's presence.

The orchestra was in place and the chief court musician had

287

his work cut out for him. What a lovely, new psalm of thanksgiving and praise they sang.

"...Let the hearts of those who seek the Lord rejoice. Look to the Lord and his strength; seek his face always" (verses 10 & 11).

David understood the need to seek God rather than someone or something else. He knew that God Himself and God alone could provide what he needed. Only the Lord was able to do so.

David also realized the importance of seeking the Lord's face. Think about looking at the face of someone—into his eyes. The eyes are the windows to the heart and the emotions inside. The whole face expresses those feelings. It is a very personal time. We also can see how he is looking on us, with tenderness or frustration or any other feeling. David wanted to seek God's face to gain intimate understanding and to build relationship with Him.

How tempting it is sometimes to look to God's hands---what He can give us. Oh, He likes to give good gifts to us. However, it is mean and small to look to His hands first. We should rather look at His face and to the joy of knowing Him.

We might even be tempted to look to God's feet---where He is taking us. However, the Lord is more than a guide down the paths of life.

God's arm is also powerful and strong to accomplish great deeds on our behalf, but God is more than that, too.

In Psalm 27:8, this song of David states, "My heart says of you, 'Seek his face!' Your face, Lord, I will seek." We need to keep hearts that yearn to see God's face and maintain the wonder of relationship. Then, we need actually to do it. "Your face, Lord, I will seek!"

YESSSS!!!

1 Samuel 3:5. (Read all of 1 Samuel 3
when you have a chance.)   *August 18*

...."And he ran to Eli and said, "Here I am; you called me."

I had left a message on Aimee's answering machine saying that I wanted to talk with her whenever it worked out. Now here she was within the hour standing eagerly before my desk.

"Would you like to go....?" I began.

"YESSSS!" she grinned eagerly.

"But I haven't even told you what I wanted yet," I laughed as I sat back in my chair. I looked into her eyes and saw such enthusiasm, such desire to learn, such openness that it took me aback.

"You'll do anything I ask, won't you?" I chuckled. It was simply a true statement based upon what I had observed in her actions and her countenance.

"Yes, anything!" she said simply.

Her attitude reminded me of Samuel when he had run to Eli three times, immediately answering each call in the middle of the night. Samuel had such an obedient and willing heart, an ever-listening ear. I hope I'm like this with God, I thought to myself. I need to think about this.

Several weeks earlier Aimee had said that she would love to go with me whenever I spoke and ministered. She wished to learn from me, she had explained. She wanted to see me in action in whatever I did. —Just let her watch. Now I was inviting her for the first event.

As I reflected later that evening, honesty forced its way into my heart. Many times recently, my attitude of immediate obedience to God had not matched that of Aimee's. I was tired. Once in a while I had also felt afraid, just like Samuel did when called upon to share God's message with Eli (I Samuel 3:15). God had been giving me some tough assignments, and I had responded with a certain amount of reserve.

"Lord, help me to listen for your voice and be eager to obey. Teach me to be more open to learning and stretching. I want to please you with a ready smile on my face as I say, 'YES! I'll do anything!'"

"EVANGELASTICALLY" (sic) SPEAKING

Read Ephesians 4:15.   *August 19*

Public speaking opportunities are generally in such abundance for leaders that after a while they become almost second nature. Being comfortable with this role, however, should never lead to carelessness about what we say.

I'll never forget one particular speaking engagement a number of years ago. Two of us were speaking and therefore had the opportunity to listen to each other. I knew the other speaker's topic well, but in the course of her speech she quoted some statistics and referred to research by "Smith and Smith," material with which I was unfamiliar.

We happened to be seated next to each other at lunch, so I asked her about it. "You referred to some data and research in your speech with which I am unfamiliar," I said. "Who are Smith and Smith? I'd like to read more about this."

She took a deep breath and sighed, then looked at me out of the corner of her eye with a sly grin on her face. "Oh," she laughed, "Smith and Smith are my neighbors. Whenever I want to make a point, I simply make up some data to support it and then cite my neighbors. It works! Nobody knows the difference!"

Well, I knew. And frankly, I could hardly believe it. We should not need to embellish our statistics, quotations, stories, or explanations with untruths.

Yesterday I was writing a survey in which I quoted some figures I had heard. "I wonder if this one figure is really accurate?" I speculated. So I picked up the phone and called to check it out. Sure enough, I had heard it from someone who had heard it from someone who had.... Well, you get the picture. The statistic I had heard was incorrect.

We do not need to stretch the truth to prove a point or to persuade others to think in a certain way. Using incorrect data such as increased attendance, production or sales figures is a sham. Once I "called" a person on this, and he said, "Oh, I was just speaking 'evangelastically' (sic)."

Let's spread the truth and not some semblance of it. Even if the truth is harsh, we are told to speak that truth in love to one another. The truth might not be pretty, but it is the hearer's responsibility to handle it anyway. We don't need to build up either ourselves or our institutions with false figures. As leaders, let's call ourselves to task on this one!

OBSERVATION SKILLS: CONSIDER THE LILIES
Read Matthew 6:25-34. *August 20*

Jesus was an astute observer of the world around Him. He pondered simple objects, analyzed human nature, and considered the characteristics and properties of various subjects. Daily life was full of high drama for Him.

This becomes apparent when studying the parables, one of the main methods of Jesus' teaching. A rundown of parable topics found in Matthew provides insight into His observation skills and His ways of thinking about life: the properties of salt and light, treasure on earth and in heaven, the life of lilies and birds, narrow and wide gates, a tree and its fruit, where houses are built, sowing and harvesting, weeds and seeds, cities, the properties of yeast, pearls and what people value, fishing, sheep and shepherds, servants, mercy, workers in the vineyard, landowners and tenants, weddings, lamp oil, and the use of money. Obviously, Jesus took note of the world around Him.

How easy it is for us to sail through life without looking at it or thinking about it. If we do, we will miss the lessons that God has for us—lessons available in our every day lives if we will just stop to see them.

Many times life seems boring and dull. Each day can drag with it over the horizon a feeling of sameness and monotony. However, Jesus looked at what some would consider mundane and found something new in it. He discovered God at work on the earth. As He carefully attended to the world around Him, He was able to dredge up profound teaching material.

The detail that God has provided awaits our scrutiny. When is the last time you looked into a flower, studied the leaves on a tree, or watched children at play? Have you really looked at your office staff, enjoyed a sunset, or thought about shoppers at the mall? Scenarios are all around us.

How important it is for us to wake up and really see what is happening every day. We need to observe God hidden away in the apparent monotony of our lives.

HARRIED LIVING: PART I

Read Luke 10:38-42.   *August 21*

Mary and Martha had unexpected company one day. Without cell phones and fax machines, prior communication from Jesus saying that He was coming to stay with them was almost impossible. So they must have been surprised when everyone showed up on their doorstep.

There all these travelers stood, hungry and dusty, hoping to stay the night and to get some supper. I said "all these travelers" because Jesus rarely traveled alone. His disciples were with Him, of course, and in other passages we note that some women were traveling along. It does not take much to imagine that there might have been some additional tag-alongs who wanted to be with Him and hear what He had to say.

Now picture Martha needing to make up beds of some sort for 13 to 20 or more people. Could you find enough sheets, blankets and sleeping bags at your house to put that many people on the floor, let alone into beds?

Furthermore, there were no fast-food restaurants, no pizza delivery, no grocery store, no frozen foods, no deli, no carry-out, no ready-made anything. All food would need to be made up from scratch for this sudden contingency of guests. No doubt my blood pressure would go up, and I'd feel harried and distracted in such circumstances.

So I can understand Martha. If I were in her shoes, I'd be a little torqued at my sister, just sitting there while I did all the work. OK, more than a little, I'd be downright put out about it!

I can picture myself trying to get her attention first. "Pssstt, Mary," I'd say, poking my head around the corner so as not to make a big scene. I'd scowl a little and flick my crooked finger. "Come here!"

Mary would nod in agreement, hold up a finger to indicate that she wanted a minute longer, and turn back to finish listening to Jesus' words. However, her minute could easily turn into a half hour as she again got taken up with His words.

"Maaary!" I'd whisper again with more insistence. "I need help!" The glaring look would be stronger this time. However by now, Mary was really into it and scene two would be like scene one. Another half hour and my frustration level would really be at its height.

That's the way I respond quite often. I wonder why I let myself get so frustrated?

HARRIED LIVING: PART II

Luke 10:38-42 continues.   *August 22*

All Martha could do now was explain the situation to Jesus. Surely He could get through to Mary and help her understand that Martha needed assistance. "Lord, don't you care that my sister has left me to do the work by myself? Tell her to help me!"

Aaahh, yes. It was the perfect leadership solution. Now that should take care of it.

Being so frenzied and also being the action-oriented, get-it-done-and-then-sit-down person that she was, Martha undoubtedly thought that something would finally happen. She had been puzzled that Jesus had not noticed her distress before. However, maybe He was just tired and absorbed in other concerns. Now that she had brought it to His attention, surely He would tell Mary to get busy.

Her surprise at His reaction started with the way He said her name. She thought He'd say, "Oh, sure, Martha. I guess I've been keeping Mary from helping out. Sorry about that. Mary, go ahead and help your sister. We'll talk later." That's what she expected. However, I picture her name coming from His lips with a sigh. "Martha, Martha." He drew out the syllables and said her name the second time with a drop of tone. It stopped her in her tracks, and she looked at Him.

He saw exactly how she was feeling. "You are worried and upset about many things." Martha knew that certainly was true! At least He understood where she was coming from.

"But...." BUT??? But what? "But only one thing is necessary..." Right---like beds and dinner...." One. Only one thing. What is that one thing out of the many?

"Mary has chosen what is better, and it will not be taken away from her."

I've always wondered what Martha did next. We are not told. Did she say something more? Did she explode? Did she pout?

Did she slink away to think and calm down? Did she also settle at Jesus' feet?

In the midst of our unbelievably busy schedules, we have to keep our priorities straight. We, too, absolutely must spend time sitting at Jesus' feet. It is the one critical choice amidst all the many possibilities. Even though a plethora of needs and cares assail us every day, sitting quietly with Jesus is the prime need for us all.

THE GOD OF SURPRISES

Read Luke 24:13-35. (Ex. 3:1-10, Daniel 3,
Acts 26:9-18, and Luke 13:10-13 are the
references for the other stories.)   *August 23*

On an ordinary day during an ordinary walk along an ordinary road leading to an ordinary village, Cleopas and his friend met a stranger. This man explained life in ways that seemed extraordinary and then revealed himself as the risen Christ which certainly was not a usual event. Their lives were revolutionized by the experience.

On a plain, regular day while tending his father-in-law's sheep on a boring stretch of desert, away from anything unusual, Moses happened upon a bush that was on fire but did not burn up. The voice that spoke to him from within the bush had news that would change his life and that of the entire nation.

On a boring day for three Jewish boys, they found themselves with a sudden decision to make about idol worship. The outcome brought down the wrath of the king and in turn took them to a fiery furnace that did not lead to death but rather to a highly unusual result. Everybody was shocked, including the King, who consequently "warmed up" to religion.

On yet another normal day a man named Paul was just doing his job, making a little religious business trip to Damascus. About noon he was knocked off his horse by a sovereign God who turned his life inside out and set him on an entirely different path for the rest of his days on earth.

Eighteen years of being crippled and the day started just like the 6,570 before. Jesus called her when she least expected it—while she was visiting the temple for the umpteenth time of her life. He simply touched her and day 6,571 was entirely different from those that had occurred before.

These ordinary days with amazing surprises occur throughout scriptures and even today. So why do we not expect life-changing events?

Perhaps, like Cleopas and his friend on the road, our eyes are closed to Jesus, and we need to be jolted awake to the wonder around us. He is a God of surprises. Perhaps today....or tomorrow.

OUCH!

Read Matthew 11:28-30.   *August 24*

In Jesus' day, two oxen might be yoked together to pull a wagon. However, the animals might not be matched in age and strength. Any time the weakest ox lagged in the pull, the nail-tip sharp goads located at the front of the wagon would poke its heels. Since this painful and bloody experience was one the animals wished to avoid, they were more apt to pull in the yoke together, causing a matched stride.

When Jesus spoke to Saul on the road to Damascus, He certainly used a graphic and meaningful symbol when He said, "Saul, Saul, why do you persecute me? It is hard for you to kick against the goads" (Acts 26:14).

What a perfect illustration of Saul's life this was. He sought to live for God by persecuting the Christians (Acts 26:9-15). However, he was not in stride with what God was doing at that time through the revelation of the Messiah. Saul headed off his own way, trailing behind what the Lord had in mind. He was out of step, independent, and weak. The result was painful!

As we consider the hurts in our own lives, we need to ponder this image of the goads. People irk us. Events rile us. We just don't want to do certain things. So much of our pain is of our own making, simply because we're stragglers or rebellious and disobedient. We want to stay upset with people or to have events work out according to our own liking. We are basically fighting with God, desiring to go our own way and to handle our lives independently. No wonder it hurts.

The Lord gives us a way out. If we pull in the yoke with Jesus and walk beside Him, our matched strides will bring good results. When we get in step with Him and with His plans for us, we discover that, after all, the yoke isn't so difficult to bear. It isn't as heavy as it first looked, and the pull is not so burdensome either.

When we lag behind, get out of step, and struggle in the yoke of our circumstances, ouch! Are you strapped into the yoke in everything, or has there been some pain from those goads of late?

JUMP!

Read Colossians 3:3-11.   *August 25*

Kim described her dream to me because it had been so vivid. Standing on top of a hill on a beautiful, sunlit day, she saw herself peering into a dark hole in the ground, a narrow hole that appeared to descend for a long distance. It was very black, and the bottom was impossible to see.

There was a presence beside her in the dream, and she knew it was God. He told her to do something she did not want to do. "Jump!" He said. "Jump into that hole."

Obviously, she hesitated. She could crash and die. It was a lovely windswept day, a day for joy and celebration. Why jump into a dark hole, especially when the result would be disastrous?

However, the Lord was insistent and urged gently but unrelentingly, "Jump!" Kim knew that it was a matter of obedience. Still teetering on the edge, she thought about how much she loved God and wanted to trust Him. "Stop questioning," she told herself. Yet she hesitated.

Then she did it. After jumping feet first into the hole, the fall turned into slow motion. It was so black and difficult and long that she thought it would never end. It seemed to go on for years.

At one point she saw an opening. A stream of light was flooding through a tunnel that was dug straight out sideways to the outside of the hill. Since Kim was falling slowly enough, she could stop the descent by catching a branch protruding helpfully near the outlet. From there she could swing her body into the tunnel and crawl out. She knew it was her choice.

As the moment of decision arrived, she determined to pass it up. She felt she should keep falling. It wasn't logical, though. Through the darkness shone another faint light and along the journey this new opening and others after it provided options for squirming out. Each one would take longer to crawl out on the horizontal, but they would work.

Why, she thought in her dream, was she choosing to fall when the outcome would be certain death? Her imagination was kindled as the fall lengthened. Soon—when?—she would be broken on the ragged crags at the bottom. What kind of a person would choose this?

But she did. "And finally, what do you think happened?" Kim asked me. I waited in suspense for the answer. "I dove into a pool of oil!" she said with wonder.

What an awesome place to find an anointing...at the end of a fall to death. What life instead!

MANY APPLAUSE, MANY SORROWS

Read I Corinthians 15:58.   *August 26*

The larger-than-life envelopes were hanging in the display window of the Billy Graham Center in Wheaton, Illinois. With a rare two hours between appointments, I was happily ambling through the museum, taking time to read the notations and think.

So I stood in front of the envelope window for a while and read each one. They were copies of mail sent to Dr. Billy Graham. It was a true wonder that most of them ever arrived.

Mr. Billy Graham	Mr. Bill Graham	Mr. Billy Graham
(Evangelist)	(American Pope)	Gospel Preacher
Who lives somewhere	Anaheim, CA	U.S.A.
in America, U.S.A.		

What I particularly enjoyed were the spellings of Minneapolis, Minnesota, my home town and Dr. Graham's actual address at the time:

Belly Grayam	Mr. Billy Graham
Mennihapuls, Meni Sol Diem	Many Apple's, Many Soldier

Mr. Billy Grahm
Many Applause, Many Sorrows

I was giggling, but the last one was sobering. "Many Applause, Many Sorrows." What a true picture of famous people and any one, really, who is sold out for God. Indeed, there are "many sorrows" and "many applause." The good and the bad go hand in hand. People in leadership are loved, but they are also disliked. Certain actions bring applause; other actions create frustration and resistance. Even the same "move" can bring both support and opposition.

I have sometimes felt as troubled over gifts and excellent

299

treatment as I have over the opposite approach. Do people mean it? What do they want? What will they expect later? In addition, the stress and challenges of leadership bring sorrows that can run very deep. It's almost more than one can bear sometimes.

Today's verse states, "Therefore, be steadfast, immovable, always abounding in the work of the Lord, knowing that your toil is not in vain in the Lord." What a promise. What a hope. We need to keep on going through both sorrows and applause for the sake of the work of the Lord.

THE CHEERING SECTION
Read John 2:23-25.   *August 27*

The children sat in the on-stage bleachers of the television puppet-and-clown-show, happily a part of the "peanut gallery." Stage hands with cue cards told them when to clap and when to cheer. They smiled at certain times, and it was all part of the fun, an element of the act.

Leaders can get caught up with audience interaction. It appears that we must be doing something right if people are cheering us. When folks like us, it feels really good.

However, the motives of an audience can be mixed. They may have a desire to be in the limelight.. They don't want to miss out on the good times. They will have fun telling others that they were on the show. Perhaps they'll even win a prize.

John 2: 23-25 says of Jesus, "Now while he was in Jerusalem at the Passover Feast, many people saw the miraculous signs he was doing and believed in his name. But Jesus would not entrust himself to them, for he knew all men. He did not need man's testimony about man, for he knew what was in man."

Jesus clearly understood the "cheering section" tendency in those who watched Him do His miracles. He knew what people were like. They clapped when everything went well, but they could also be very fickle when things fell apart. He understood that they loved popularity and being part of the in-group. He realized that as long as His accomplishments and choices pleased them, all would be well. However, people can become disenchanted very quickly.

How easy it is to entrust ourselves as leaders to the likes and dislikes of other people. Jesus did not fall into that trap. "He knew all men" and realized that unlimited trust could not be placed in any man, for even His closest friends could leave or betray Him.

"Lord, help me to entrust myself only to you and not to be swayed by the crowd in the bleachers."

THE ENTERTAINER

Read John 5:31-44.   *August 28*

The entertainer was working his audience, building emotion and manipulating responses. The spotlights followed him wherever he moved, and he was consciously using his whole body to emphasize his points.

I sat in the audience but felt as if I were not involved, like I was looking upon the scene from the outside. It was an odd sensation, but it allowed me to observe more clearly and to analyze the process.

Certainly the singer enjoyed the applause as he led the audience into a near frenzy. I suddenly felt sick to my stomach as I saw people raising their hands to him, almost as if in worship.

Praise can be dangerous to the person desiring it. Jesus said in John 5: 41, "I do not accept praise from men..."

The desire for praise can create numerous failings and sins. We can get jealous of anyone else taking center stage because that person might gain the praise we have worked so hard to attain. We may want to maintain control of every situation from fear that someone may embarrass us or that God might ask us to do something unpopular. It is tempting to stay in the safe zone where everything will remain comfortable, because we don't want to fail.

The need for praise can drive us to great extremes in order to maintain popularity. Those people whose praise we need have an inroad to power over our lives. How easy it is to become people-pleasers rather than God-pleasers. We don't want to risk our reputation or take the chance of being ridiculed. All of us want to be liked and accepted, but a yearning for approval can yield devastating results.

That's why Jesus didn't even start down this path. He completely refused to accept the praise of men.

"God, I admit that it feels good when people like and support me. Help it not to turn my head so that I look at them instead of at You."

THE WIDOW DUCK

Read I Peter 1:3-7.   *August 29*

Two ducks started across the road, but only one made it safely to the other side. My husband was rounding the corner into the church parking lot and saw the drake get hit by an on-coming car. The widow duck was poised on the side of the road, stunned and waiting for her mate to cross.

She stayed on the curb throughout the morning and the afternoon. The church staff became concerned and sad when she was still there the next day, just waiting. They talked about what to do for her but couldn't come up with a solution.

Finally by the third day she had moved up next to the church building where she huddled by the wall. It was pitiful to see her. By the next day, however, she had disappeared.

Pondering this phenomenon of nature, we considered the grief that people go through when they lose loved ones. Shock sets in, and time is needed for healing and reorientation.

In a smaller, and yet very real way, the same process occurs in leaders when dreams die or projects fail. There are sorrows attached to such an experience. When many hours have been given to designing or implementing a program or product, it can be a terrible shock to see it fall apart.

All leaders have experienced this at one time or another. Sometimes the new programs even take off with promise, only to suffer a sudden demise. Or we may turn over a program to other people's care, but they don't own it and nurture it. How difficult it is to watch something we care about collapse. We need to give ourselves some space when this happens and just stand on the curb for awhile.

Sometimes we hide our disappointments, hurt and grief. We don't face those emotions, but instead pretend everything is fine, on as though life were normal. However, grief has a way of manifesting itself when we least expect it. Emotions may awaken during a situation that does not merit that level of response. We wonder where our reactions come from and why we are so angry or out-of-sorts.

It's all right to feel shock. That's what Jesus' disciples did right after He died—before they understood. We should give ourselves the opportunity to wait before God with our disappointments and let Him touch our pain. We need to be in touch with what is genuinely happening to us and deal with it... to let the Lord help us understand.

LIVING SACRIFICES

Read Romans 12:1-8.   *August 30*

The young people were lining the altar area of the sanctuary, jammed in so tightly that many were standing up on the platform itself. Still the lines trailed far down the aisles. I was somewhat surprised. This was the culmination of a three-day urban ministries chapel emphasis at our NCU downtown campus where the speakers had shared harsh reality.

Urban pastors from many cities told stories of being robbed of literally everything, of ministering to unstable people with big knives, of being beaten up, and of having bullet holes in their car windows. They had also shared marvelous testimonies of God's provision, protection, and presence. The Lord was obviously using them to change their urban centers. They all had paid a huge price and given up a great deal, but God was doing a mighty work through them.

The altar call was not an easy one. There had been an invitation for all those to come forward who were definitely called and committed to urban work. We had also invited those who weren't positive about a call but were willing. The challenge was to throw everything at Jesus' feet.

A great joy and desire to worship arose among these young people as they abandoned their lives to God's plan. It reminded me of Romans 12: 1, "Therefore, I urge you, brothers, in view of God's mercy to offer your bodies as living sacrifices, holy and pleasing to God; this is your spiritual act of worship." The students who packed the space at the altar had decided to follow that admonition. They were selling out, agreeing to lay down their very lives, willing to live with sorrows and even to die.

Although martyrdom is obviously a great price, the person willing to face it goes to be with his God, and there is no more pain. Sometimes it seems almost harder to keep paying a price and walking through each day as a living sacrifice. However, we need to be willing to do so. Let us decide to deposit everything at the altar and to present our very selves to God. No, don't just pass over this.

STACCATO

Long days of living at a violin staccato pace can wear out even the heartiest of souls. The stress and pressure of life mount up and threaten our very equilibrium.

So often at these times, when I feel like I have not one little ounce more to give anybody, I find myself face to face with a crisis or an extremely needy person. Since I am the leader, I must respond. Reaching into my depleted resources and expecting to come up empty-handed, I am always amazed to find in my hand the very thing that is needed.

At such a time I find a wise word for the person who needs counsel or a kind act for a friend in need or even the answer for the crisis. Where did these come from anyway? Not from me. Of that, I am more than certain.

What a joy to work with God and know that we are functioning together. I may be out of resources, but He is not. He is always there to help us assist others, to direct us in our leadership tasks, to provide support and strength and wisdom and solutions. How it makes us rejoice. How clear it is that truly everything is from Him.

Matthew 11:28-30 shows us that when we come to God, we find everything that we need. When we're weary and burdened, stressed and under pressure...when we feel like we can't take one more step or do one more thing, and yet we must... come to Jesus! He Himself will give us rest and complete provision. Even though our storehouse of resources is depleted, His repository is always full. We can go for days without discovering this wonderful secret.

I do not believe we were meant to run on empty. If we consistently do more than God calls us to do, don't get enough sleep, don't learn to rest in Him and fellowship with Him regularly, then we've got other problems we need to take care of.

However, when all of this is in place, and we are still stressed and weary, pressed and unable to think or respond anymore, then we must trust in our God. No matter what our circumstances, He is most certainly there with all that is needed. Let's go to Him today.

SEPTEMBER

THE VIOLIN

Read Ephesians 2:6-10.   *September 1*

Years of violin lessons convinced me of one truth. It takes an accomplished musician to make a violin stir the soul. A virtuoso can take the listener away on wings to other worlds, while those with less skill produce the most ghastly squeaks and sawing sounds. I know. I produced a good many of those squealing notes during my growing-up years.

Young people often come to me, bemoaning their inadequacies and weaknesses. They feel doubtful that God can actually use them. Many fears assail, and they don't know if they will be able to stand up under pressure. How exactly are they supposed to carry out what God gives them to do?

Through the years I have noted one common thread in all such comments. Those voicing their inadequacies are always focusing upon themselves and concentrating on their own deficiencies. They have forgotten to add God into the picture. Now that's a hole!

It's like a violin without a player. The master of our souls is a violin virtuoso par excellence. He can pick up any kind of violin and make it sound positively lovely.

So where do we fit into this picture? Devoting ourselves to study and learning, being open to personal development and change—these qualities help us become better instruments. We can work toward becoming a Stradivarius with the best sound possible. In the end, however, the beauty of the tune is heard when the Master picks us up and skillfully plays the most

307

exquisite of songs.

We may feel unable to accomplish certain tasks, but then it is tremendous to see God use us in ways that we could never have imagined. God Himself can pick us up as His instrument, tune us for the upcoming situation, and then play whatever He needs upon the strings of our lives.

Let's be available and not be afraid. The Concert Master is present in the symphony of life.

THE RIVER

Read Ezekiel 47:1-12.   *September 2*

Rivers are powerful forces in nature. I have seen them raging and broiling, carrying off vast amounts of debris at flood stage. I have also known them at peace, dancing along on a sunlit day.

The river described in Ezekiel has some unusual properties. The life-giving water originates within the temple on the south side of the altar. It flows under the very threshold of the temple and accumulates, becoming deeper and deeper. First it measures ankle-deep, then knee-deep, next waist-deep. Finally it becomes deep enough to swim in and so wide that no one can cross it.

Such is the way of our lives with God. At the beginning, we get our feet wet as we come to know God. We are curious and wanting to learn more.

Before we know it we are knee-deep, having walked farther into the water as we get comfortable with its temperature and feel. God draws us in, teaching us deeper insights, showing us new truths, and suddenly we are up to the waist.

However, this is where many Christians stop. They like to keep their feet on the bottom. Ezekiel was asked, "Oh, Son of Man, do you see this?" Ezekiel might well have answered, "Of course, I see it. It's a huge river!" However, the question leads to further contemplation.

We need to look at God in a deeper, more profound way. See how immersed we can become in the living water? Although it might be frightening, I believe God is calling us to throw ourselves into the waves and swim out into the fast-flowing river.

It's difficult to give up control, to place our lives at the mercy of the water. We are no longer in charge out there. What will happen to us? Will we get carried away? Will God ask us to do what we do not wish? "The water will not overwhelm you," His Word promises. Will His Holy Spirit lead us to act in a way that will embarrass us? Well, even if He does, are we willing to swim out and let God have control? It truly is living water, and we will find life in Him as we abandon ourselves to His care.

Christianity is not intended to be a wade in a kiddie pool. Nor is it a dive into the deep end of a pool. It is a deep river....an ocean dive. How deep will we go?

PLANTED BY THE STREAM

Read Psalm 1. *September 3*

Verse 12 of Ezekiel 47 echoes the description of a tree planted by the stream found in Psalm 1. Both passages remind me of Colorado.

That's because in my memory treasure trove I especially enjoy recalling a certain carefree day. It was spent by a diamond-studded stream under a regal aspen tree on a perfectly sunwashed day in Rocky Mountain National Park. I had told my husband that this scene was my one desire for vacation. It didn't matter what else we did, as long as we spent one day by a mountain stream. He had supported my wish by bringing our favorite lawn chairs. Cross-stitch, book and picnic basket completed the supplies, and I was happy.

As the river gurgled down the streambed, I studied the many types of trees planted along the shore, their roots banked into the water. The squirrels ran across the branches, and the birds were making forays into the picnic goods, but I kept thinking about those trees.

They knew where to get refreshment. They had planted themselves right at the river's edge and then drank greedily from the life-giving supply of water. They were healthy, verdant, thriving in every way.

Even if a drought were to devastate the countryside, those trees were planted where they could get water. There would be no withering for their leaves. When it was time, fruit—in this case, nuts—would certainly appear. Come what may, these trees would prosper.

Why do we often find ourselves planted in barren places and then get tired of the dryness? Sometimes I feel so brittle and crispy. Just a little spark could set my tinder ablaze. I need water.

According to Psalm 1 we find true refreshment when we "delight in the law of the Lord and meditate on it day and night." God will supply us with what we need from His Word and His own Spirit will course into our lives.

"Lord, help me to plant myself right by You. Only You have the life-giving supply."

FIGS

Read Mark 11:12-14 and 20-21.   *September 4*

Why, I have always wondered, did Jesus curse that fig tree? The scriptures tell us that it was not the season for figs (verse 13). How could it be, then, that Jesus responded so severely when the tree didn't have any fruit? True, He was hungry, but it is still strange.

While pondering this, I recalled another scripture. Paul said to Timothy in II Timothy 4: 2, "Preach the Word; be prepared in season and out of season..." We are admonished to be prepared whether we feel like it or not. It does not matter if it is winter or summer in our lives. We need to be ready to speak and preach no matter what—to minister, to give, to be productive in spite of how we feel. When God needs us and calls upon us, we should be available immediately.

Perhaps the reason this fig tree existed at all was to provide food for Jesus on the one day when He was hungry. However, that fig tree had nothing to give; it was completely unprepared.

On their way out of Bethany the next day, Jesus and His disciples went by the same tree. Verses 20-21 of Mark indicate that the fig tree had already withered overnight. This passage also provides another clue about why Jesus had cursed the tree. We are told that the fig tree had "withered from the roots."

Now that is interesting. The roots were perhaps already withering the day before. The tree leaves simply had not followed yet; they still looked green. However, when the root system is bad, the decay of the whole plant is only a matter of time. With no nourishment coming into the tree, the leaves will not stay alive for long.

Examples probably come to mind of people you know or have heard about who appeared to be thriving in their public lives. However, later events revealed that their root systems were failing. Their lives followed suit with a crash.

Jesus may well have had insight into the root system of this tree, and that is why He cursed it. Perhaps He knew that all was not well in the dark and hidden places of the earth. Nobody could yet see there, but that is where the tree must have its life-force. We, too, need to be careful of our non-public selves. We must be rooted in God, receiving the life-giving water He provides only in the secret places.

MOVING MOUNTAINS

Read Mark 11:22-25.   *September 5*

The next verses in Mark seem to have an integral relationship to the fig tree lesson. Jesus begins talking about faith. He may be referring to the faith it took for Him to curse the fig tree and have it wither within one day, but let's look deeper.

Based on the thinking we engaged in yesterday, we could ask some new questions. How, exactly, do we produce fruit out of season? Surely this is too difficult. When life is cold and hard, how do we find what it takes to give out? The answer is faith in God.

It may seem impossible to serve God at certain times, but we must have faith. Circumstances in life may loom so large that there hardly seems room for God. These mountains are towering over us. How can we serve Him in the shadow of pervading pain, stress, lack of resources, and problems? It may appear like these mounds of difficulty will never be moved, never disappear. It takes faith.

As we trust in God, our mountains can be reduced so they no longer loom over us, embracing us in their ominous grip. God Himself will emerge stronger, and our root system will receive His nourishment. We can be fruitful, even during the harsh times.

The root system symbolizes those hidden places where faith is built. So how does this mechanism work? Prayer is our method (verse 24)! Our relationship with God is based on the hidden times we have with Him in prayer. As we pour out our hearts to Him, He nourishes us, provides for us, calms our souls, and speaks to our hearts about our problems. In prayer we get a sense of what He wants to do with those mountains in our lives. He reassures us. We are not afraid to ask, because He has promised to give. The next step is to believe that what He promised will become a reality.

If we walk away from our prayer times and lapse into doubt,

we will be right back in the mountain's shadow and in winter's cold grasp. However, as we have faith, fruit will appear out of season, and mountains will be removed. For nothing is impossible with God.

WHAT DO YOU HAVE?

Read II Kings 4:1-7.   *September 6*

The prophet's widow had a terrible dilemma. The creditors were clamoring, and there was no money to pay the bills. As a mother, her heart broke as she realized that she might also lose her two boys to slavery. There seemed to be no answer, no way out.

When Elisha heard about the problem, he asked her an intriguing question. "Tell me, what do you have in your house?" I can picture the widow's reaction to this query. What do I have? Nothing! If I had anything, I would have sold it already and paid off the debts. Why would you ask me such an irrelevant question?

So she answered, "Your servant has nothing there at all...." Then she said, almost as an after-thought, "....except a little oil." A little oil. That's not much. What good is a little oil? It hardly bears mentioning.

What about you, what do you have? Sometimes it appears that we need so much that the lack consumes us. What we have does not seem to match up in any way to what is needed. The shortfall is so obvious that we concentrate on the gap.

Doing this can really get us down. It can also keep us from looking at what we actually do have. That's what Elisha considered. "What do you have in your house then?"

---Just a little oil? Well, that's something. So he told her, "Go around and ask all your neighbors for empty jars. Don't ask for just a few. ....Pour oil into all the jars, and as each is filled, put it to one side."

Can you imagine the widow's reaction? Pour the oil into all

313

these jars? The widow undoubtedly had a right to question this directive. It wasn't logical. She only had a tiny bit of oil. How could she pour those few drops into all these jars and see every one of them filled?

How she went about resolving this conflict of logic would determine her next step. She did go out and search for the jars. Her faith in this process would undoubtedly determine how many she found. I wonder what she finally located? We are not given the exact answer to this question. However, we do know that when she ran out of jars, the oil stopped flowing. She had enough to sell and pay off her debts. I can only imagine that she wished for some more.

In leadership it is tempting, just like it was for the widow, to concentrate on our needs, our gaps, and our tremendous lack. But what do we actually have? And how much faith can we muster? How many jars will we finally get?

THE HOUSE NEXT DOOR

Read Isaiah 58:11.   *September 7*

My good friend Mona was heading off to the mission field, inundated with boxes, moving crates, and paperwork. Loose ends were dangling everywhere. We met weekly as usual, even in the midst of the crunch, not willing to give up one precious moment before the inevitable day of separation.

One of the most alarming unknowns was their housing situation. It looked as if they would be arriving in their new country with no place to live. Attempts to get this concern taken care of beforehand had failed repeatedly. They had no option but to depart and spend their first days searching for a house to rent. The immensity of the city and the lack of transportation didn't make the task any easier.

"Pray," my friend had said, looking at me somberly. "I mean really, really pray. This could be bad, but I'm trusting that God has a plan and will reveal it to us."

Her first letter brought good news. Within days, a perfect house had become available in the wake of a strange series of events. They were able to move right into their new quarters. Even the colors matched the few belongings they had taken along, and there was a lovely garden with fruit trees in back.

"There are guards all around, too," Mona wrote. "A government official lives next door. We are praying for an opportunity to share Jesus Christ with this family, and we met them just the other day. They're dear folks."

Soon I received word that this official was running for the presidency of this South American country. A few weeks later I learned that he had won the elections. Think about it—my friend was actually placed right next door to the new president! He would continue to live in his own residence, too, since there is no "White House." International and national public officials come and go constantly.

Is it an accident that in this huge city, my missionary friend ended up right there? I think not. There have been other contacts with this presidential family and the guards. God is at work in the world today. Never doubt it.

WHEN GOD ADDS

Read Joshua 10:5-11.   *September 8*

Joshua had reason to be concerned. He was marching against five kings who had formed an alliance. The Lord gave a clear command to Joshua at this time of crisis. He said, "Do not be afraid of them; I have given them into your hand. Not one of them will be able to withstand you" (verse 8).

What an encouraging promise! Joshua had his entire army including "all the best fighting men." Furthermore, he had God's own assurance that all would work out well.

Joshua's strategy included an all-night march from Gilgal so he could take the enemy by surprise. However, God added to this advantage. In verse 10 we are told that "the Lord threw them into confusion before Israel." Although a surprise attack can be disconcerting all by itself, God contributed to the enemy's disorientation by throwing them into confusion. It makes me smile to ponder how God might have carried this off. Exactly what sort of dynamics occurred in the camp?

After this great victory at Gibeon, Israel pursued the fleeing enemy along the road. Apparently this chase was quite effective since the enemy ranks were cut down for miles. However, here again the Lord added, hurling large hailstones from the sky. This strategy was so effective that "more of them died from the hailstones than were killed by the swords of the Israelites" (verse 11).

As leaders, we must often move out with our people. We are called upon to lead them into the fray, and God tells us not to be afraid. We strategize, like Joshua did with his plan of a surprise attack. However, God actually contributes to our tactics by sending confusion or whatever extra is needed. Then we have to draw our sword and finish the work. Still God can multiply those efforts by any means He chooses.

We should not lead as if we are alone. We should not act as though everything begins and ends with us. When God adds, victory is accomplished. Let's look to Him.

FEAR IN THE WOODS: PART I

For meditation: Exodus 4:10-14
(For context read Exodus 3 and 4:1-17)   *September 9*

Several weeks earlier I had asked Brent why he wasn't dating. It was fall of his senior year, and I had never known him to date during his entire four years at college.

"I guess I really don't think anybody would go out with me," he answered. That response surprised me. He was a fine young man who was deeply committed to God. He knew how to pray and felt a call to the mission field. Besides, he had a great sense of humor, was gentle and sensitive, and was a good communicator.

"Brent, I don't believe that! You really don't think anybody would go out with you?" I asked.

"No, I don't," he reiterated. "I'm not all that handsome, and I guess I've always felt kind of shy about dating. My friends seem so much better looking and smooth. They know how to act; I don't."

"Well, but you're sincere. Women prefer that," I said truthfully, "and besides, I think you'd better consider it because you're depriving some woman of knowing a wonderful man. I want a report back in several weeks."

I thought about this situation as I drove home that day. His fear appeared to be so unfounded to me, but then my fears, well, they might seem just as unfounded to someone else. In leadership, fear can be gripping. It can feel like you're a child lost in the woods...unless those woods are ones you know well.

We also tend to focus on our inadequacies rather than our strengths and those of the Lord. Consider Moses. In Exodus 3:11, he indicates his inability to do the task. "Who am I, that I should go to Pharaoh and bring the Israelites out of Egypt?"

In Exodus 4:10-11, Moses complains about his speech problem, looking at his weakness instead of considering God's ability. Finally in verse 13 he states his inmost thoughts. "Oh, Lord, please send someone else to do it."

We need to move out past our fears and sense of weaknesses. Brent needed to do it, and so did I in several areas of my life. What are you afraid of?

FEAR IN THE WOODS: PART II

Read Exodus 4:17.   *September 10*

A week after the discussion just described, Brent came and shared with me. "I really need prayer," he said. "I know what you told me is right, and I should start dating, but I'm scared."

I was happy to pray, but I felt unable to break through this fear and sense of inadequacy that gripped him so strongly. How could he find the assurance and security he needed? Quietly, I asked God for insight.

As I prayed with him, a picture came to my mind of a clearing in a wood. I couldn't understand why I was thinking about woods, so I tried to shake off this strange impression. I wondered what I had for dinner! However, the picture only became more detailed.

I envisioned a path, leading to a clearing in the woods. Tree branches arched with golden-leaves where sunbeams danced. A fallen log beckoned as a seat, and little, white gentian flowers were growing beside it.

It was so odd to me. Why would I see woods when I was praying for someone about dating? It didn't seem one bit logical. However, the picture had been full of so many details. Perhaps it was the Lord doing something unusual. Just because I couldn't figure it out didn't mean that it wasn't God.

So I took a leap of faith. "Brent," I said after our prayer. "I had a picture of something while we were praying. It doesn't make any sense to me. If it doesn't mean anything to you, just think that I'm crazy or something," I laughed.

I went ahead and described the woods, and as I did Brent started to cry. He was obviously moved, and the Spirit was touching him deeply in ways that my earlier prayer had not.

"Do you know what that is?" Brent said through his tears when I ended the description. I chuckled; I didn't have a clue.

"Well, that place exists. It's on our farm at home, and it's my favorite place in all the world. I go there often to pray, and it's where I feel safest and most secure. You described it perfectly, right down to the gentians."

I was relieved, not only because I wasn't crazy after all, but also because of what had obviously happened in Brent. He was beaming by now. "I think God is telling me that dating will be as safe and secure as I feel in my clearing in the woods," Brent said. "The fear is gone!"

Brent started dating, fell in love with his first choice, married this wonderful girl, and they now have precious children and are in the ministry. Just as Moses took up his staff and marched forth in faith to do what God asked, let us always be open to ministering God's way. We need to have faith that God will make sense of it all. He is truly a miracle-working God.

SOME ADVICE

Read Exodus 18:13-27.   *September 11*

Jethro, the priest of Midian and Moses' father-in-law, came out to the desert where Moses and the Israelites had camped. It was a pleasant visit, and Moses had an agreeable time sharing with his father-in-law all that had transpired in bringing the people out of Egypt. Jethro was delighted to hear this news and worshiped God with a burnt offering and other sacrifices. It was a good day.

Since Moses had taken off one day for these family commitments, the next day he went back to his work. Sometimes it takes an outsider to see what is really going on, and Jethro was not particularly pleased with what he saw. Moses was being inundated with people and problems. It was almost unbelievable!

Jethro confronted his son-in-law in a straight-forward manner. "What is this you are doing for the people? Why do you alone sit as judge, while all these people stand around you from

319

morning till night?"

Think about how this might possibly have sounded. While doing this, try emphasizing a few selected words: "What is THIS?" and "WHY do you ALONE sit...while ALL these people stand around YOU...?"

Moses went on to explain why it had to be this way. Perhaps he was even a little patronizing toward his father-in-law, something like this: "Look, Dad, they have all these problems, and they come to me to get advice and help. What other options do I have? Sure, I know I'm working from morning till night, but I'm doing God's work."

Jethro was from the outside, though, and could see the circumstances more clearly. He didn't accept this explanation. He simply replied, "What you are doing is not good. You and the people who come to you....will only wear yourselves out. The work is too heavy for you; you cannot handle it alone."

This is an important lesson, and some leaders should heed it. They are in great need of a Jethro in their lives, of someone who will be straight with them. "Pay attention now to me, and I will give you some advice...."

Then they need to have the attitude of Moses. He "listened to his father-in-law and did everything he said." Moses proceeded to teach and train others to take the load. He delegated, and the process actually worked.

So...do you, by any chance, have some listening to do?

A FEW COPIES

Read Proverbs 10:9.   *September 12*

One of my work-study staff was standing at my desk with his mouth agape. His reaction did not seem merited in relation to my comment, so I think I was more surprised than he was.

"Take this five dollar bill down to the cashiers for me, will you please?" I had just asked him. "Tell them it's for personal copies I made."

"What do you mean?" he had queried.

"I mean that I made a few copies on one of the departmental copy machines that are for my own personal use. The college shouldn't pay for that; I should."

That's when his jaw had dropped. "Wow! That's really nice of you," he responded.

"No, that's simply right of me," I replied. He nodded, incredulity still registering on his face, and headed off to his task.

The incident caused me to reflect on integrity. Without intending to do so, I had provided this young man with a small lesson on the subject. His amazement disturbed me, however. I contemplated how easy it is for any of us to rationalize, especially about the "little things." Such rationalization can become so commonplace that we barely notice there is anything wrong.

Lack of integrity is like a ravenous animal. A breach on small items or events makes it easier to barter our integrity on larger concerns. That's why I hope I can always be painstakingly honest, even on rather insignificant matters.

Once integrity is lost over a larger item and becomes public, the leader's credibility goes with it. It becomes difficult to trust that person for anything, with others wondering if this time is once again a dishonest sham.

"Lord, please help me. I am not above rationalizing. Keep me face to face with the truth, and help me to walk in it."

RENEWED MOTIVATION
Read Nehemiah 2:17-20; 4:10-15.   *September 13*

Self-motivation is difficult. As leaders, we are expected to motivate others, and most leaders have discovered ways of accomplishing this to the max. However, who motivates us?

This is especially problematic when we must repeatedly come back to the group with new doses of enthusiasm, simply to keep the project moving. It can be most discouraging to expend lots of motivational energy, only to find the activities slowing to a crawl. Our dream looms large, and we feel as though we should be moving ahead and continuing to build. The people catch our dream at first, start the work with fervency, but then make little progress.

This happened with Nehemiah in rebuilding the wall around Jerusalem. He had persuaded the people of the importance and the feasibility of the task. They had set to the work and gotten half way. At this stage, however, a variety of circumstances and challenges demotivated them.

How good it was that they had a leader like Nehemiah. He did not give up, but rather reached inside and discovered optimism. He undoubtedly remembered that God had called him to this leadership responsibility in the first place. What a burden of prayer and concern had launched this huge effort to rebuild the wall. The Lord had blessed Nehemiah with favor from King Artaxerxes, enabling him to pursue the task. God would see him through to the end.

As leaders, we are called upon to give out. It is hard because what we provide has to come repeatedly from within ourselves. We need to find ways of renewing our own internal supply. Sometimes, these are challenging secrets to discover, but our lack, our emptiness, our drained resources can all force us into the presence of God. Here we find renewal of everything that we need, first for ourselves and then to pour out on others.

THE DAY OF SMALL THINGS

Zerubbabel was responsible for significant work in the rebuilding of the temple. He was involved in building the altar (Ezra 3). He also brought out the capstone and laid the foundation of the temple.

Zechariah 4: 8-20 records that the building of the temple was halted for an exceedingly critical task. Zerubbabel came out with a plumb line.

Now measuring is tedious work. It is much more exciting to bring out the great capstone and to lay the cornerstone and the foundation. Everybody can see progress in this sort of work, but measuring? That's slow-moving. It appears to be such a small, insignificant task.

God's word, however, tells us not to despise the day of small things. What looks unimportant may well be absolutely critical. Many of the smallest actions are actually some of the most meaningful.

So it is with a plumb line. Without checking whether everything is straight up and down, it is possible to produce a building that tilts and will ultimately collapse because it is as unbalanced as the Leaning Tower of Pisa.

Zerubbabel knew enough to stop the work for a while and not keep motivating the workers to drive forward indiscriminately. He realized how important it was to check and see that the building was progressing with accuracy. It is always good to stop and think, to test a project against the desired results.

The wisdom of their leader in stopping for this "small thing" was not lost on the people. They rejoiced when they saw it. They knew their work would not be in vain because their leader was careful to do it right.

We, too, need to take time to evaluate the work. Does it meet God's standards? Is it according to His design and wishes? Is the work being carried out in the correct way in God's eyes? Is every little thing straight and true? Let's not despise the day of "small things."

OF MY OWN ACCORD

Read John 12:49-50.   *September 15*

Jesus made a stunning comment in these verses in John. He said that He didn't speak on His own accord but rather uttered just what God told Him. Think about that. Could such a description apply to you?

As I asked myself that question one day, it really made me think. I remembered how many words I babbled off in a single day. The average person speaks between 15,000 and 20,000 words each day, communicating a great deal about personal ideas and needs.

Consider what it would be like to speak absolutely nothing of our own accord. If we completely held our tongue unless we had something that God wanted us to say, I wonder how much we would actually talk. This thought was painfully challenging to me.

Jesus had words that brought life. They changed the hearts of men. They brought forth healing, and they set people free.

John 1: 14 states that "the Word became flesh and made His dwelling among us." By this we understand that Jesus Himself was the Word of God (see also John 1: 1-2). What God wanted to say to mankind was encapsulated in the Son of God who became flesh as the Son of Man. Even as a man, Jesus listened to the Father and spoke exactly what God wanted Him to say.

We are called out to become more like Jesus, and as such we too ought to have our utterance under the control of our Father. How challenging it is to consider saying only what God wants said, not one word more and not one word less. I believe that as we seek the Lord, He can place His words in our mouths — words that bring life and hope, peace and grace to the people who listen to us.

God wants our tongues under His control. Let's seek to put aside any talk that is not from Him and to fill our mouths with precisely what God wants said in every situation.

OPINIONS

Read John 7:14-18.   *September 16*

Meetings. They fill my days and sometimes spill over into my evenings. Most of them are both important and necessary, but sometimes I get exasperated over this one fact: There are a good many opinionated people in this world....and most of them show up in meetings!

Well, we laugh about that, but it's true. We see it in all of us at times — that opinionated person who rears his head and stubbornly practices his elocution in front of everyone else. We even watch ourselves doing it and simply keep on. After all, what we have to say is important...and correct!

Jesus' comment in this passage directs us to a different viewpoint. He states that what He taught was not His own. That must mean that He did not share His own private perspectives or His own opinions and personal ideas or even His own answers. Rather, He looked to the Father and taught what God showed Him.

Jesus went on to say that "he who speaks on his own does so to gain honor for himself." Ouch! We enjoy sharing what we think because we believe we've got real insight into a topic or the best answer to a question. Secretly, though, we rather hope people will observe this fact; basically, we're just looking for honor.

How this must reek in the nostrils of God. Actually, God

probably cares very little about our fleshly ideas and opinions. He would prefer that we bring these into subjection to Himself.

If we are not speaking on our own to gain honor for ourselves, then our whole approach will change. We will seek God and what He wants us to say. We will be most concerned about bringing honor to Him and will therefore be free to speak the Truth. The truth may not be popular or understood, but we need to be willing to pay that price. After all, the Truth can so positively impact someone's life.

My tendencies toward being opinionated turn my stomach. Think about what meetings would be like if all opinionated people were simply quiet and said only what God wanted said. What a meeting!

A SMALL SPARK

Read James 3:1-12.   *September 17*

We drove for miles past the charred remains of what had once been a majestic forest. One tiny spark from one untamed campfire had started the destruction. The stark, blackened stumps reminded us of cremation rites, and the cemetery-like scenes moved us.

James likened the tongue to a fire that could likewise bring destruction, both to ourselves and to others. "The tongue also is a fire, a world of evil among the parts of the body. It corrupts the whole person, sets the whole course of his life on fire, and is itself set on fire by hell" (verse 6).

In a work or church environment, we have all seen such an aftermath of somebody's tongue-spark. Rumors can rage through a group, licking away good reputations or eroding the groundwork of trust that has taken years to establish. Fears of the future can spread false stories of plans and motives which do not even exist.

326

At times the spark is actually started by the leader rather than the workers. Without anticipating outcomes, words can be dropped which start the destruction. Boasts and promises are made which cannot be fulfilled. How easy it is to "wax eloquent," but say little that is of God.

Over the years, I have come to admire another type of person entirely, the one who knows how to conserve words. In meetings, they let other people say what is actually on their own minds. They don't monopolize conversations but are apt to listen and think. They stay on the topic and make contributions that are meaningful.

As a matter of fact, when it is important that something be said, these people are not afraid to speak. At those times, their contributions make an impact and deliver insight and solutions. Others listen to them, and the course of decision-making is often changed at this point. Contrary to the tongue which brings a spark and starts a forest fire of destruction, this type of person uses words to bring healing and life.

NOTHING!

Read John 5:19-20, 30.   *September 18*

"The Son can do nothing by Himself." Nothing. Not one little thing. He didn't come up with His own ideas and go about implementing them on His own. Jesus said He couldn't do that.

In this passage in John, we see unveiled for us the wonderful relationship that Jesus had with His Father. They were so intimate that Jesus could see what His Father was doing and then do those very things as well. They were in synch, working together.

One of my favorite paintings, called "The Helping Hand" by Emil Renouf, is of an old man and a little girl rowing a boat. The Swedish man's wizened face is alert to the surroundings, and his strong hands, wrinkled and worn, are pulling on the oars. Sitting right next to him is an adorable youngster in Scandanavian dress. Her hands are also on top of the oars, and she is apparently following his motions. Although she probably thinks that she herself is rowing the boat, it is obvious that she does not have the strength. The old man is doing the real work.

In our own independence, we may feel that we are too grown up to need the assistance of someone else. We want to row our own boat in our own direction. Just trying to go it alone, however, only brings frustration, wastes energy, and leads to false starts and ineffectiveness.

Jesus was well aware of this. He looked to His Father to see what He was already doing. And we are told that "the Father loves the Son and shows Him all He does" (verse 20). Jesus was one with the Father and was effective because He did what He knew God was already doing.

Think about the number of wasted actions we have produced. Consider how much we have tried to accomplish, only to see it fail. We get so discouraged, wondering why God has not blessed our efforts.

However, we can't expect the Lord to place His seal of approval upon our self-initiated actions. Rather, we should observe God, waiting on Him and spending time in His presence. What does He want to do in the world today? When? How? As we seek Him, He will reveal to us what He is up to. As we get in step with Him, we find ease of work that is coupled with a wonderful effectiveness.

"God, help me remember that You're rowing the boat. I choose to place my hands on Yours. Forgive me for my independence and help me to say with Jesus, 'By myself, I can do nothing.'"

HIS WORK

Read John 4:31-34.
(For context read John 4:27-42)   *September 19*

Wouldn't it be wonderful if we knew God's will at all times? Jesus did; He was so aware of what God was doing. Finishing the work of His Father was critical to Jesus. In fact, it was so important that He said it was His food. Doing what the Father wanted Him to do rejuvenated Jesus, provided nourishment to His spirit and kept Him energized.

Some of us may be malnourished spiritually because we are too busy accomplishing our own desires rather than God's. We strain to execute something that was not ours to do in the first place. This effort takes energy away from us rather than renewing us.

Jesus, on the other hand, realized that doing God's work was actually like a feast for Him. He explained this to His disciples when they preferred that He not talk to a Samaritan woman but rather come away with them and eat. His choice of person with whom to strike up a conversation had surprised them. However, Jesus knew it was what God wanted. The Father's work for Him to carry through that day meant sharing the gospel message with a lady who would find life. Then she would share that life with the townspeople, and many of them would also believe.

God's work called for harvesting souls for eternity. Jesus was so sensitive to what God was doing that He didn't miss a single action or forget to speak a word He was supposed to say. The results were powerful!

As we see what God is doing, there is an ease, an anointing, to that work. The task feels as if it is oiled, easy to flow with, smooth and full. On the other hand, actions that are not of God are exhausting, like trying to move an old, squeaky wheel. The cogs are not matching, and it is heavy and rusty. We exert so much pressure, but little is accomplished.

I've seen this squeaky wheel sort of thing happen often, haven't you? We may try to get something going, but no one is interested in helping out. We work and plan, but people don't seem motivated. Dozens of phone calls and committee meetings later, we are still no closer to getting the task accomplished than we were months earlier.

Oh, friends, let us stop wasting ourselves on what does not matter. Let us look to God, see what He is doing, and move into His will and plan rather than our own. Then we will find sustenance—and results.

FRENZY

Read John 6:28-36.   *September 20*

How often do we work ourselves almost into a frenzy trying to accomplish something? When the task is particularly difficult and is accompanied by a timeframe, then it is even more challenging.

Once I had a strange task to get done. We had received a big grant, and I was needing to get some curriculum written for urban ministries. A set of lessons in one of the courses revolved around demographics—certainly not my area of expertise, nor of anyone else I knew, for that matter. My first inclination was to start calling around, but I decided to pray instead. "God, You know where there is a Christian demographer. I need to find this person. Help, please."

I had been praying for about a week when I noticed something on my calendar that I didn't understand. "Who is this person coming in at lunchtime?" I asked my administrative assistant.

"Oh, some guy into urban ministries. After talking with him, I think you will want to meet him, so I squeezed him into your schedule."

When the man arrived at noon, he had a friend in tow. "This is someone else who wanted to meet you," he said. "He has a strange but interesting avocation. He collects statistics regarding church demographics in the Twin Cities."

I just laughed. God had sent me the very person I needed, and in a timely fashion, too. I explained our project, and he was excited and willing to help.

If I had tried my original search approach, it probably would have taken me many hours of frenzied frustration, and it is quite likely that I would have been unsuccessful. As it was, God did the work while I trusted. When we believe in God and have faith, God will provide everything we need. Our work is to believe; His is to provide.

THE SPIRIT FIRST

Read Genesis 1:1-2 and Acts 1:4-5
and 2:1-8, 40-41.   *September 21*

Scripture shows us the importance of allowing God's Holy Spirit to move first. We should notice that in great moves of God, His Spirit went before. We get a window on this principle in both Genesis and Acts.

At the time of creation, Genesis declares that "the earth was formless and empty darkness was over the surface of the deep and the Spirit of God was hovering over the water." After this, God spoke the world into being, creating the light from the darkness with all of creation following.

There is a similar picture in Acts 1:4-5. Jesus commands the disciples not to leave Jerusalem but rather to wait for God's promised gift. He said they would be "baptized with the Holy Spirit."

This time of waiting must have been difficult for the disciples. I wonder how many times impetuous Peter talked about "getting on with it"? After all, they were excited that Jesus was alive. The disciples knew that they had good news to communicate and undoubtedly wanted to share the message with everyone.

I wonder what would have happened if they had not waited. Would very many people have been saved? I doubt it. And yet it must have been difficult just to sit around and wait and pray. They really didn't understand what they were looking for or what the Baptism in the Holy Spirit would be like. They didn't even know how long they would have to wait!

Nonetheless, they were faithful and waited for the Spirit to move. Then, after the Baptism in the Holy Spirit occurred, they went out as powerful witnesses. God had enabled them and given them boldness, fervor, and a sign in the form of speaking in tongues. Consequently, many people groups heard the gospel preached in their own languages, and thousands believed.

It is God's way to have His Spirit move first. As we get into the flow of what He is doing, mighty deeds are accomplished. God does not delight in our fleshly efforts and ways. When we try to carry forth work through our own methods, the results are generally unproductive. Personally we do not have the power to be effectual nor to raise up anything in the spiritual realm. That is God's work!

A GOD-DIRECTED SCHEDULE

Read Luke 8:49-56.   *September 22*

Schedules. How frustrating they can be. Over the years, I've learned a few safety nets.

1) Don't schedule too tightly. Leave enough time for each appointment and a small buffer zone before the next one.

2) Before going out of town for business, schedule extra time during the day of the return for catch-up time at the desk.

3) Schedule "crisis time" on the calendar every few days. In

leadership, there is always something unanticipated that occurs. This way there's time for a needed appointment or extra minutes to solve the problem at hand.

4) Reserve space in the schedule ahead of time for your priorities. Otherwise, the time gets eaten up by pointless time-wasters.

5) Be sure you take time for the people who work for you. If there is good communication and they feel valued, more will ultimately get accomplished.

I accidently stumbled onto my favorite schedule-controller. For years I had prayed each day during my commute to work. However, I started to pray more specifically about my day, going through my entire schedule with the Lord. I began asking that God would remove from my schedule anybody whom I did not need to see. If a person could be handled by someone else, I prayed that he or she would be or would just not show up or forget. This actually started happening a few times a week.

I then prayed that God would bring to me anybody I should see: someone I specifically could help or minister to spiritually or who would encourage me or give me an idea. How amazing it was that people wandered in right at the time when someone did not show up.

My schedule feels so much more God-directed. There is peace in it. It seems that I'm about My Father's business.

SHOT THROUGH

Read Proverbs 12: 16 and Isaiah 51: 7.   *September 23*

The first shock of leadership is realizing that not everyone is going to like us. Furthermore, it's not only our enemies who take pot shots at us. I remember my husband making a tongue-in-cheek comment when we were about three years into the ministry. "The one fact they neglected to explain to us in seminary," he said wryly, "was that a person can get shot by those inside the church, not just those outside." The real battles—and often the most painful ones—can occur within the church.

It makes sense, really, so I don't know why it was that surprising to us. People in the church are all growing, just as I am. We are still not perfect—not yet completely what we should be. It should not be particularly amazing if people get grumpy, unhappy, and complaining. It's just that leaders are apt to hear it all, and the load can become overwhelming.

The leaders are often the ones to get the blame. As a result, we tend to get more thick-skinned with time. That's probably healthy, as long as it doesn't mean that we put up walls, keeping people out entirely.

Once I read a simple statement explaining that after a while, a leader doesn't feel the shots anymore. That's because the person is already shot up and so the bullets just sail right on through the holes! They don't hit anything so they don't hurt anymore. I have thought of that particular image many times, and it is both amusing and helpful.

After a while the barbs that used to attach themselves to us just can't find flesh to hook on to anymore. What used to knock us out can no longer pack a wallop. The hit has lost its power, feeling more commonplace and less aggravating. It's easier to shrug off the problems and simply trust God.

Jesus was not excessively sensitive to personal attacks. He took assaults with a certain equilibrium, not allowing them to wound him to the point of self-analysis and ineffectiveness. We need to grow in these inevitable processes of leadership. We'll survive being shot through. Actually, all we lose is a little flesh.

OUR OWN DEFENSES

Read II Chronicles 14:2-6 and 16:7-12.   *September 24*

One of the temptations of leadership is to get hard. If we do not crucify our flesh and allow ourselves to be "shot through," then we will build up our defenses and try to ward off all attacks. In my mind's eye, these tempting defenses take various symbolic forms.

Sometimes, it is a wall that we build between ourselves and other people. We think that if we can just keep that wall there, nobody can hurt us. Sooner or later, even our friends on the other side of the wall sense our defensiveness and give up trying to reach us. Being stonewalled is never easy. The wall may take on the form of anger or a surly manner, as it did for Asa. It may be constituted of rigidity or stubbornness. But whatever the wall is composed of, it is a sad hindrance to our relationships.

Other times, we may feel as though we are putting on a whole suit of armor—and it's not the spiritual armor either. This armor is uncomfortable, and it squeaks when we walk. We peer out through the peep hole in the helmet so that we can see others, but they can't see us. This blocks them from really knowing us, resulting in a lack of accountability and authenticity.

Another unfortunate defense that tempts us comes in the form of a hardened heart. Maybe we'll let people see us, but we won't let them hurt the real person on the inside. We can communicate on basic levels, but not share our hearts. Any relationship is on the surface.

The problem with each of these types of defenses is that we create them ourselves. They are not spiritual in nature, and God is not in them at all. We are not taking Him as our defense, but rather selecting our own methods—looking to other people or to our own wisdom rather than to God. This was also Asa's problem.

Not only are these defenses ineffective, they are ultimately self-destructive. They hurt us, cutting us off from other people and promoting poor relationships.

One time, when the "shot through" approach to my flesh was particularly painful, I could feel myself hardening. I watched myself as I tried some of these defenses, and then I went to a friend. "My heart is turning into a rock," I said. "Keep calling me back to openness and honesty. Confront me. Keep talking to me."

Asa finally got rigid with both men and God. He started well, but his hardened heart led him to disaster. God help us not to follow suit.

UPSIDE DOWN

Read Philippians 2:3-4.   *September 25*

The world generally has a view of leadership that is like an equilateral triangle with the point at the top. One climbs from the masses to lead from above.

The other day I saw a new black Jaguar with a vanity license plate that read "MADE IT." This epitomizes the view of ascendancy—of striving for position, power, and prestigious goods. In this lifestyle, leaders must keep climbing until they reach the place where others will serve them, standing in awe of their power.

This should not be true of the Christian view of leadership. Paul said, "Do nothing out of selfish ambition or vain conceit, but in humility consider others better than yourselves." Well, that effectively flips the triangle over, doesn't it? In Jesus' way, the real leader willingly moves to the bottom of the pile and serves all those above him.

There's no room for conceit or ambition in this model. It demands true humility to live out this leadership style. Instead of expecting others to do things for us, we do things for them. We grab the rag and wash down the table. We go to the end of the line. We dust the desk and set up the chairs when no one sees, so

336

that there's no risk of people being impressed with our humility. We listen when we'd rather be doing something else. We do what is inconvenient for us to make life more convenient for others. Since they are better than we are, why shouldn't we? We ought to be looking to other people's interests and needs, not just our own.

Leaders get all the pressure and pain, often being misunderstood and shot through. And now they receive none of the perks and have to be the humble servant as well?

Why would anyone want this kind of lifestyle? That's the point!

INSIDE OUT

Read Philippians 2:5-7.   *September 26*

One of my childhood memories is of a party my parents held for more than twenty of their friends. It was a costume party with the theme, "Inside Out, Upside Down, and Backwards Too." The invitations had been designed with this in mind, and the guests came wearing their clothes to match the theme. My little brother and I peeked around the corner and watched, giggling, as everyone arrived.

While reading through today's verses in Philippians, I thought of that party theme. God's way, as it is described here, is indeed inside out, upside down, and backwards.

Isn't it amazing that Jesus' attitude was not to have to hold on to equality with God. He actually was God in His inward self, but He didn't continue to hold on to His entitlements. Instead, He let equality go and poured Himself out. He made Himself to be nothing. No one else forced Him to do this, but rather He chose it, making Himself into "a nobody" in peoples' eyes.

It is almost too much to grasp. How could He do this? What must this have been like? He was God in His very nature, but He turned His deity inside out and became a servant instead.

337

When something is worn inside out, we see the ragged side. Seams show; pockets stick out; threads hang. The garment may look great on the "right" side, but on the inside it looks unfinished and not so beautiful. Jesus chose to come as a human being with the unfinished, humble side of Himself hanging out for all to see.

Think what it means to live out this attitude of humility. Jesus chose to leave His equality with God and to come to earth. Suddenly He found Himself in human likeness with the ragged side out. No longer was He presenting His beautiful, all-together side but rather His side that would not be readily appreciated or understood or even accepted.

What an example of servant-leadership! Let's not be afraid to "hang out" our ragged sides.

THE FEEDING TROUGH

Read Luke 2:6-12.   *September 27*

I wonder what process led God to design such a plan. How could He possibly come up with this one? He must have wanted to demonstrate humility to the absolute maximum.

Perhaps God reasoned something like this: How can I persuade this crown of my creation, these human beings, of my great love for them? I want to show that I care for them in a way they will understand. I must become like them, go and be among them, and come in flesh like they have. I'll become a human being myself.

Having made this decision, God could have chosen to come as an adult or at least as a child in a rich person's home or a powerful person's court. That would surely have commanded some of the respect and value He deserved.

Instead, God chose to become a baby---a little, gurgling, hungry babe. He chose a young girl and a carpenter father. Next, God so designed the timing of the delivery that Jesus was brought into the world when there wasn't even a simple hotel room available. He ended up in a stable, of all places. We put God out in the barn!

Consider it. The great and powerful God of the universe comes to visit His creation in the flesh and gets laid in a feeding trough.

This plan is a moving example of God's desire to show us humility in the deepest degree. There's little else needed to indicate the lengths of God's love and how thoroughly Jesus emptied Himself, becoming as nothing.

Still, there actually was more. Finding Himself in appearance as a man (what a discovery!), He further humbled Himself to die....and in the most ignominious way, on a cross. What a God. What an example of humility in leadership. It is almost too much to comprehend, especially since it goes against our self-seeking and self-fulfilling personalities. We need to study these humble traits we see in our God. How dare we not follow suit?

BACKWARDS TOO

Read Philippians 2:8-11.   *September 28*

It just doesn't seem right. The great, almighty Son of God chose to humble Himself and become a man. Although this was incredible enough, He then adopted an even more arduous approach. He resolved to obey God and submit to death.

What a difficult choice. He ought to have been highly honored on the earth and instead He chose to die. Not only that, but He selected the most ignominious of deaths — death on a cross. There were thieves on each side, and Jesus hung among them.

This is totally backwards! People should have bowed to the Messiah when He came to earth. It was only right that they be grateful and show Him esteem. Surely, they would not only recognize Him but also listen to Him, obeying all that He taught.

Instead, exactly the opposite occurred.

However, God did not let the story end there. Jesus may have chosen humility and found lack of respect here on earth, but it is equally true that God set everything right again. He did not let this backwards state of events stay backwards forever. Jesus was exalted in heaven to the highest possible place. It is there that people will finally accord Him the honor that they should have given Him on earth.

We may not get everything we want or deserve in this world when it comes to leadership. Certainly, it is not our place to demand honor, manipulate for it, or even expect it. Instead, we should choose the backwards approach. We should be a servant-leader, being willing to give up everything.

It is only out of this choice that God finally can set everything right. If something needs to be turned around, it is very possible that the reversal won't be seen until we stand in God's presence. When that happens, the Lord Himself will receive the glory. What a wonderful Savior...and what a model of leadership!

THE PROOF OF PRIORITIES

Read Acts 6:2-4.   *September 29*

How can you tell what your priorities really are? Are they what you say they are or what you wish they were? Are they the activities which are most meaningful or enjoyable to you?

One day as I was thinking about priorities, a simple, clear test came to mind. My priorities were demonstrated in one way: how I actually spent my time.

As I appraised my days with that thought in mind, I didn't always like what I saw. Frankly, I wanted to rationalize away some of the time-eaters that I found. There were certain activities in my daily schedule that I needed to do. However, other than some sleep and a little food and water, everything else is actually negotiable. As the saying goes, we make time for whatever we want to accomplish. There is sobering truth in that. What we choose to spend our time on usually signifies our true priorities.

If our families are our priority, then we will spend time with them. We must not simply sit around the television together but rather talk, share, listen and laugh together—interact as individuals.

My husband and I meet regularly with our respective calendars, scheduling two to three months in advance the times we will be sure to spend together. We discuss our individual work schedules, and when the other will need to participate with us in work-related activities. Then we also schedule times together when there are absolutely no work responsibilities involved. We never give up those personal weekend days or those evenings to anyone else without permission from our spouse. Otherwise, with two exceedingly busy and diverse schedules, the days would slip by without meaningful exchange.

How does all this pertain to our relationship with God? It is critical not simply to do something with Him, but to spend time sharing and talking. We need to have that intimate time in meaningful relationship where the Lord alone is the focus of our attention.

Jesus took time with His Father. He would even spend whole nights in prayer. They really communicated, and Jesus received assurance and direction while they spent time together, just as today's Bible passage illustrates.

So what are your priorities? Are there any adjustments you need to make? If so, start the changes today.

MODELING OUR PRIORITIES

Read Luke 6:12-13. *September 30*

Once our priorities have been set in order and are being lived out in our schedules, they should be evident to the individuals around us. People notice a great deal, and they desperately need to see important priorities modeled by their leaders.

One dilemma, however, is that certain actions and commitments are in the public eye, while others are not. When those which are not discernible happen to be on top of our priority list, it is dangerous. It is not perilous for us, but it is for those who might make incorrect assumptions about our preferences and then follow this pattern in their own lives.

A few years ago, I made an assessment of what I modeled to students. One of my personal priorities is prayer, but I realized that they couldn't see me praying during those times I have set aside. They didn't hear me pray very often. They didn't know my challenges nor my victories in prayer. All this was hidden from them. I didn't want to show off, but neither did I want to hide the fact that prayer was important to me.

My solution? I began a prayer meeting once a week after work to model, teach and learn more about prayer. In addition, I decided to be at the all-night prayer meetings that the college sponsored. Even talking about my own personal prayer times when I preach, teach and counsel allows me to demonstrate my priority in this regard.

Certainly, some of my prayer life is personal and can never be shared. There are particular intimacies that should remain between me and God alone. This is true of almost any priority area. Not everything is for public consumption.

Leaders may hesitate to reveal certain types of personal commitments, concerned that others might think they are bragging or being too transparent. However, I have discovered that usually the opposite occurs. People are curious about how their leaders manage their lives. They want to learn from them. We must find ways to open up what is important to us so that others can observe it. Then we will model the priorities that actually steer our lives.

OCTOBER

MAGNIFY THE LORD

Read Psalm 34:3 and then the entire
Psalm if you have time.   *October 1*

The chorus we were singing in church carried a particularly meaningful observation: "When I look into His holiness, when I gaze into His loveliness, when all things that surround become shadows in the light of You...I worship You, I worship You..." (Perrin).

Probably the best action we can take when we feel laden down with burdens and cares is to join other believers in worship and praise. As we look to God, we remember afresh how wonderful He truly is. We recall His attributes, His holiness, His goodness and love, and He becomes altogether beautiful to us. This process is healthy for our own inner selves.

In the highlighted verse from today's reading, David says, "Glorify the Lord with me, and let us exalt His name together." This verse has also been sung as a chorus, "Magnify the Lord with me..."

The idea of magnifying God is powerful. When we pick up a magnifying glass, we do so because there is something that appears small to us, and we want to examine it more closely. As we hold the magnifying glass up to our eyes, the print or stamp or coin or other object of examination suddenly becomes large. We see the details so much more clearly.

At the same time, everything else around what we are magnifying becomes smaller and more hazy. Our concentration is on the object of magnification, and all else is but a shadow.

That is one of the best reasons why we need to worship and magnify God. As we praise Him, He becomes larger to us, as He rightly should. Those things that seemed so important only a few minutes before become more obscure and less important. They fall away from us and lose their stranglehold on our thinking.

Come, my friends, magnify the Lord with me. Let us exalt His name together. Do it now. Do it often. It places our leadership concerns into perspective.

Work cited: Perrin, Wayne and Cathy. "When I Look Into Your Holiness," *Holy Ground/Songs 4 Worship*. Integrity's Hosanna! Music, 1990.

LIFE IS VERY INTERESTING

Read Proverbs 26:20.   *October 2*

Listening to people and then finding the proper response is a real challenge in leadership. With so much to do, it is often difficult to concentrate and hear what the person is really saying. However, it is even more demanding at times to devise a correct response. A leader wants to be caring and to let the speaker know that he is valued, that his concerns are important.

Because of this, a real dilemma comes when the speaker is upset at another employee. It is my duty to be fair and impartial and to value all of the employees. How can a response be formulated which will let the person know he's been heard and understood and still keep me from getting into the middle of a squabble?

I find these situations to be particularly difficult when I know that what the person is saying actually is true! However, I know it's not wise to join in running down the other person. That never helps the situation and usually succeeds in exacerbating it.

So over the years I have found a response: LIFE IS VERY INTERESTING! Coupled with a smile and a shake of the head, it can say a lot. The person knows that the difficulty hasn't been

344

brushed aside, but there is no negative comment to be gossiped about either.

I usually proceed to generalize such problems or situations, trying to provide some answers and perspectives. At times, however, people simply need to accept each other and to enjoy the different ways of perceiving life that each of us brings. Tolerance, patience, and cultivating an appreciation of diverse methods and manners, all these can lead a person far on the road of understanding.

After using the quote, it is fun to have it spoken back to me in the midst of tense times. It usually brings a smile and some calm with it. One of my co-workers enjoyed the saying and the meaning behind it so much that she cross-stitched the words and framed them for my office.

Since then, others have commented on the wall hanging, and one student in particular loved it so much that I gave her the picture years later. The other day she sent word that she had moved, and her life was greatly churned up. "Tell Dr. T. that there's nothing on my walls yet—except that cross-stitch!" she told my administrative assistant. It's true: Life indeed is very interesting. Let's enjoy it more.

MY HEART AND MY FLESH CRY OUT

Read Psalm 84: 1-4, 10.   *October 3*

The writer of this psalm had experienced God. There is no doubt about that. How else could he know that only one day with God was worth more than a thousand days away from Him?

It is so very good to spend time with the Lord. His Spirit is so sweet, and we rejoice in being near Him. Once we have experienced this, we can hardly have enough. Our hearts yearn for Him, and we cry out. We must have Him!

Every college year I have organized a prayer group that meets in my office on a weekly basis. When we first come together at the end of a busy day, each person has so many cares and distractions. However, as we put these aside and begin to pray, something wonderful happens. There is a special unity that we sense with each other as we seek God together. His Spirit comes into the room, and we can feel His peace and love. His pleasure in having fellowship with us is evident. We are moved away from our earthly cares and brought into His very presence, into His courts.

One of my favorite moments comes at the end of our prayer time. None of us wishes to leave. We hardly want to face the normal world again because there is such a sweet union with the Lord. It's rather funny, really—we just sit there and smile at each other as though we're loony. But it's the presence of God which is lingering, and who wants to run out quickly from that?

The psalmist said, "My soul yearns, even faints, for the courts of the Lord; my heart and my flesh cries out for the living God." In the same way we need to desire God with our internal selves, pressing in hard after Him. There's nothing more wonderful, more fulfilling, or more meaningful than being in His presence. What more could we want?

SET ON THINGS ABOVE
Read Colossians 3:1-4.   *October 4*

How easy it is to get earth-bound! We can get so concerned with what is happening in our own lives that we forget the bigger picture. If we remain bound up in our problems, we will feel constricted to our dreary cubby hole of a world. God calls us out of our corner and asks us to direct our hearts and minds to heavenly things.

As Christian believers, we have been raised with Christ and therefore our hearts are not supposed to be attached to anything on this earth. Instead, we are to set our hearts on things above.

Christ is there, seated on the right hand of God. He is elevated and has authority. He cares about us and wants to relate to us. When we look up to Him, our petty circumstances seem not quite so important anymore.

That is one of the wonderful purposes of worship. As we attune our hearts to God, we move our desires and perspectives to be in touch with His. "Set your hearts on things above," Colossians 3:1 states.

Likewise, the next verses call us to "set our minds on things above, not on earthly things." We are to engage both our hearts and our minds so they are focused upon what is above...both our affections and thoughts...both our desires and our reflections...both our wills and our problem-solving..

God knows how easy it is to get caught up in our own earthly concerns, but we are asked to move out of these and align ourselves on a different level—with God, with Kingdom building, with heavenly matters. Just as we set a watch or a timer, or set a gauge or other calibration, let us focus our minds and hearts heavenward. Let's be released from what bogs us down and drags us into irrelevant minutia.

Set your hearts and your minds on Christ Jesus. Do it now.

HIDDEN WITH CHRIST

Read Colossians 3:1-4.   *October 5*

Our minds and hearts are to be set on things above, because that is where we are now, hidden away with Christ. Colossians 3:3 indicates that when we die to the flesh, we have life. And that life is in God and in Him alone. We can find life in no other. We can only be satisfied as we tuck ourselves away with Him.

As a leader, I have always been amazed how people can find me even in the most unlikely spots. Although a leader feels like escaping from time to time, it is almost impossible to find a place in which to "hide away." I have been tracked down in foreign places that have been quite off the beaten path. One day they even found me in a convent where I had retreated to pray for a couple of days, "holed up" in a cubicle without a phone! Another time they located me in a little vacation house in Chile...again without a phone. It's both humorous and sad.

However, we can always find a secluded place for our spirits, and that place is with the Lord. What does it really mean to be "hidden with Christ in God"? It reminds me of playing hide-and-seek as a child. How marvelous it was to have a new hiding place that no one had ever considered before. It was such fun to snuggle into that spot and enjoy the sounds of the disturbance outside as the hunt went on. How cozy it was! I knew that my friends and sibling would already have admitted to my victory.

In the same way, we will put aside the commotion and the draw of the outside world when we have died to our flesh. In the spiritual realm, we can crawl into the safest place of all. Think of it! We can find our hiding spot directly in God.

In this case, however, we are hidden *with* Christ. We have a friend in our hiding place, enjoying the moments with us. That's the best: to be hidden away but also to have the company of our very best friend to enjoy.

When the going gets rough, we really can hide away. When events bring fear, we can find a secret place in Him. We can tuck away precious items for the Lord's keeping and know they are safe there. What a delight it is to be hidden with Christ in God!

THE STARFISH

One breezy summer morning, a little boy and his father got up early to take a walk together along the beach. Few others were awake yet, so it was a good time to find the best shells that had washed up on the sand during the night.

This morning, however, dawned on an unusual sight. For reasons that they did not understand, the tide had washed up hundreds of starfish on to the sand. They dotted the beach everywhere.

As the two walked along, the boy began picking up starfish that appeared to be alive yet and flung them back into the ocean, one by one.

Finally, the father became frustrated. "Stop now," he said gently to the lad as he was bending down to pick up yet one more of the unfortunate creatures. "There are so many of them! What difference will it make?"

The boy thought for a moment as he stood holding a starfish in his hand. Then he flung it back into the water and said, "It'll make a difference for THAT one!"

When I first heard this story, it really touched me. Many times it looks as though a task is too great. There are so many people who need Jesus in our workplace, so we get discouraged and quit trying to share the gospel. We wonder what difference it will make anyway.

Jesus, on the other hand, never got overwhelmed by sheer numbers. They were individuals to him, and each one made a difference. His parables about the lost sheep and the lost coin show His heart in this matter. God goes to great lengths to reach just one person and to bring him or her new life.

Yes, there really are so many who need Jesus. But take heart and share the good news one more time. It could make the difference between life and death for THAT one.

349

THREE SUITS AND A PAIR OF SHOES

Read Matthew 6:25-34. *October 7*

Recently, I heard two unrelated stories that thrilled my heart. They speak of God's intimate care and provision for each of us.

One related to a missionary on furlough who was speaking in a service attended by a number of pastors. One of them had just purchased a brand new pair of rather expensive size 10 dress shoes and was wearing them for the first time that very day.

Picture the missionary's surprise when the pastor came up and asked what size shoes he wore. The missionary raised his eyebrows at the strange question, but proceeded to tell him that he wore a size 10. Imagine the shock of the missionary when the pastor bent down and started to unlace his new shoes. He took them from his feet, handing them to the missionary with a smile. "Here," he said. "I feel that I'm supposed to give you these."

Tears welled up in the missionary's eyes, and he lifted his shoe. The bottom had a large hole in it. The missionary explained that it was his only pair of dress shoes, and he had no money to buy new ones. The pastor smiled broadly and walked away in his stocking feet.

The other story was of a small town pastor who was at a similar gathering a few months later. He had told his wife that he would have to wear the same suit for all the days of the church conference; he was down to his last one and could afford nothing else.

On the first day of the meetings, a gentleman approached him. "I know I've never met you before," he said, "but I have a feeling you might need a suit. Is that true?" A similarly touching scene followed. Within several hours, the man had three new suits and some new dress shirts as well.

God is still in the business of meeting our needs. We should not get so anxious about providing for ourselves that we are kept from serving God in less than lucrative positions. We ought not to be overly cautious. God is still calling us to a life of faith, and it might feel risky. We may not see Him move, because we never give Him the opportunity to do so.

Not only are we to trust God for our own needs, but God may call us to give to somebody else. Are you willing to give away something precious...perhaps even something you actually need for yourself? Would you walk away in your stocking feet?

WHATEVER

Read Colossians 1:9-12.   *October 8*

Most of us who love to travel have come to appreciate the fact that every state and region has its own set of unique customs, phrases, and communication patterns. The Minnesotan world of Scandinavians is no exception. In fact, this environment has spawned so many enjoyable Norwegian and Swedish peculiarities that whole books have been written on the subject. They are enjoyable beyond question, especially the ones on Scandinavian humor.

One of my favorite sayings is the often-used regional response, "Whatever." It is usually accompanied by a slight shrug of the shoulder, a little head jerk, and one hand gesturing with the palm upturned. It is always spoken in a monotone, and it is a proper response in a multitude of circumstances.

For example, when asked if you want to go to a particular restaurant, it is polite to say, "Whatever." You do this even if you have a preference. It is fine to say what you think, but only after the "whatever" is spoken. This shows flexibility and often even true indifference. Certain things just don't matter. "Whenever" or "whoever" are also well-used.

Spiritually, though, God does not want us to confuse patience with indifference. Having patience demands a fortitude of inner character. Patience requires that we hold on to a spiritual promise with great endurance, allowing God to provide the strengthening power that is needed. We must be willing to wait until the promise is birthed in reality.

If our "whatever" response to God indicates that we are flexible and open to whatever He has for us, whenever He has it, then I believe that God is pleased. This shows a deference to His will and a trust in His design for our lives.

However, I believe that God is not pleased when true indifference sets in. Through the process of waiting for God to unfold His plan, it is often tempting to become shoulder shrugging, uncaring, "whatever" people. If we give in to this, then the indifference will affect our attitudes and our intercession. We become de-motivated and cannot be used by God. We have all seen leaders who have turned into this kind of "whatever" people, and they have become sadly ineffectual. Let's not give up caring, but instead hold on with patience.

MORNING BY MORNING

Read Isaiah 50:4-5.   *October 9*

How pleasant it is to wake up before the alarm goes off, to be drawn out of sleep by your spirit and your heart which are rushing off to meet God. He calls, and we wake up, listening.

As the third of the "Servant Songs" in Isaiah, this section of scripture relates to the Messiah. He, too, experienced His Father waking Him up morning after morning. He knew what it was like to have the inner man brought to alert by God and to be in an immediate attitude of listening for instruction (Isaiah 50: 46).

God does not desire self-taught or man-taught people as much as He desires God-instructed people. It is because Jesus listened to His Father's teachings that He could have "an instructed tongue to know the word that sustains the weary." What a treasure was this ability of our Lord's! He knew exactly what to say to listless and worn-out people to help them keep going. His tongue had been instructed in the morning about what He needed to share that very day.

In leadership, it is critical that we not become so tuned in to our own needs and weariness that we miss the needs and exhaustion of those who work for us. We must observe them and care for them and love them. It is one of our chief leadership tasks to serve them in this way. When we've heard from God, we'll have just the right life-giving word of encouragement to speak into their weary hearts.

It is possible in the morning, when God awakens us, to be rebellious (verse 5). Choosing not to listen, we can stop our ears and then run off in our own ways and our own thoughts for that day.

However, if we close our ears to God, we may miss the very things He has for us. We may draw back and not exhibit that humble servant's heart that He wants us to have. How sad for us...and also for others who need a sustaining word from their leader.

ROW THROUGH

Read Isaiah 43:1-2.   *October 10*

One of my most enjoyable experiences in nature was white water rafting on a river with number seven rapids. It was a challenge, that is for certain.

The first rapids took almost everybody in the eight-person raft by surprise. Our guide had warned us that it was important to keep rowing through, but we weren't entirely prepared for the force of the waves washing over us. Several people ended up in the river. Their helmets and life preservers kept them safe as they were swept over the rocks, ending up in a calmer part of the river where they again picked up the raft.

I had been determined to keep my foot in the strap, but that hadn't happened either. So I threw my body to the right where I thought the raft should be, even though I couldn't see it. Thankfully, I ended up in the middle of the raft instead of being scooped out into the thrashing waves.

Now we listened more carefully to our guide and asked more questions. He explained the importance of everybody continuing to row, letting us know that this procedure would keep the raft moving and stabilized through the rapidly churning waters.

At the next rapids, everybody braced and kept rowing. What a feeling of exhilaration as we came out on the other side, having powered our way through!

In a church. we sometimes face challenges that could knock people off the course and make them lose their footing. They could crash personally, or the whole thing could even flip over, just like a raft in strong and tricky rapids.

Satan loves to come against us with waves that could overwhelm us. However, as everyone in the body of believers works together and keeps doing his part, the church will be victorious. There is strength in a group giving all they have to accomplish a common purpose. God calls us to unity of spirit and task, and as leaders, we must exhort our team to do whatever is necessary. The accomplishment can be wonderful, for there is great joy in winning a victory together.

THE COMPLETED PICTURE

Read I Corinthians 2:7-10.   *October 11*

One of the enjoyable parts of creating a picture or design with yarns or threads is seeing the front side emerge into perfect beauty. The creator, however, knows the backside well. During the cross-stitch, petit point, embroidery, tapestry weaving, or even knitting, the back of the piece is important. In fact, a look at the back always shows knots, tied color connections, slipped and skipped stitches, running threads, starts and endings.

Even to the creator it is amazing to turn over the finished piece to the front. On the right side is a lovely, ordered work with grace, beauty, and purpose. From the backside, however, it is almost impossible to tell what the picture even is, let alone to believe that it is beautiful.

So it is with our lives. We actually tend to live on the back side. There seems to be no pattern to life sometimes. Knots and loose ends are only too evident. The threads of our days appear "cross-wired," and our existence does not make much sense.

Some day, though, all of this will become clear. In heaven, we will see the front and understand that the whole design was emerging all along, stitch by stitch. We will understand why we had to use blue, red or green threads at the times when we did, in the shades and hues required, for the number of stitches that we were told to complete. What seemed painstaking and meaningless will finally be understood with incredible awe and a sense of completeness.

Everyone's contribution, resulting in an immense picture developed over the centuries, will become apparent.

Even now as leaders, let us encourage others in this truth. Whenever God gives us a preview of the bigger picture—such as our team's part of the work—let us be faithful to share it with them. Leaders sometimes get such glimpses which they are not to keep to themselves. Every creator and fellow laborer needs to be able to check the front side occasionally and be heartened by that perspective.

STANDING ALONE

What happens when God calls you to stand alone? This is certainly not an easy task. It is tempting to look around for a few cohorts before taking that bold step. Nobody likes to be out there all by himself.

Before the time arrives for such a singular, authoritative action, God will prepare a leader for the responsibility. In verse 17 the Lord tells the prophet, "Get yourself ready!" Leaders should hear from the Lord ahead of time so they will know what to say when the exact moment arrives. There needs to be an inner preparation, the gathering of both strength and fortitude from the Spirit, and finally praying for insight that flows straight from God Himself.

After such a time of preparation, God suddenly will say, "Stand up!" The command can come in a minute, sometimes when we least expect it. To a leader, this can be a frightening moment. The command is likely to be given when no one else is standing. It is daring and puts the person out there in a precarious position. There can be no more hidden views or sharing in secret. It is time for a public declaration that everyone can hear.

Furthermore, God determines exactly what is to be declared. "Say to them what I command," God tells Jeremiah (verse 17). They may bully, complain, whine or become angry when that word is uttered. However, God says, "Do not be terrified by them." If a leader wimps out and backs up at such a time as this, the mob will rule the day. They will run right over him without even looking back.

God personally encourages and strengthens leaders for these difficult times. They become able to withstand anything and anyone in any position (verse 18). Although there may be a battle, they will not be overcome. God Himself will be there and rescue them. What a promise!

How important it is to be able to take on difficult assignments, to stand alone with boldness, speaking forth whatever God wants said. No matter what the consequences from such a stand, God will ultimately see us through.

THOUGH THE VISION TARRIES

Read Habakkuk 2:1-3 (along with Habakkuk 1
when you have the opportunity)   October 13

The prophet Habakkuk had two complaints that he shared with God. The first was about God not having answered his prayers for help. Society was rampant with violence, conflict, lawlessness and injustice, and it deeply stirred Habakkuk's soul.

So God answered the prophet, "Look at the nations and watch—and be utterly amazed. For I am going to do something in your days that you would not believe, even if you were told" (verse 5). Over the last years, we, too, have seen amazing events occur among the nations, things we can hardly believe and probably would not have thought possible if told about them ahead of time.

The Lord also told Habakkuk to "watch," a concept that is further elaborated upon in 2:1. Habakkuk said he would stand at his watch, a task that was critical. The watchmen could warn if the enemy was coming. Furthermore, they were the first to hear the news about the outcome of a distant war, as women and children anxiously awaited news about their loved ones. The watchmen looked for these messengers, in the same way that Habakkuk waited at his station on his watch to hear news from God Himself. God calls us out to watch in prayer, and usually there is no more important task for a leader. We absolutely must hear from God.

Habakkuk received an answer to his second complaint as he watched and prayed. "For the revelation awaits an appointed

357

time; it speaks of the end and will not prove false. Though it linger, wait for it; it will certainly come and will not delay."

Many times it is tempting to give up the vision that God has given us in prayer. It is delayed. Days and even years go by. It tarries so long that we think we must not have heard correctly. Perhaps we were making it all up or exaggerating.

Truly it is frustrating when God's timing is not "in synch" with what we think it should be. We are far too impatient, and we hate to wait. However, God sees the end from the beginning. Time is not so critical to Him, for He perceives it all and knows what is the "appointed time" for each event.

As leaders we need to be patient, lingering and watching for the vision He has given us, no matter how long it tarries. When it comes, it will not be too late. Often God acts so quickly at His "appointed time" that it makes a person's head spin. He can bring the vision to pass overnight when He chooses.

TIFFANY GLASS

Read Psalm 29.   *October 14*

We drove through several states to visit the Tiffany Glass Exhibit in Chicago, and it was worth it. There was such a comprehensive collection of the famous artist's works that the viewers could grasp the wide scope of his art in glass.

Young Louis Comfort Tiffany had started his artistic endeavors by painting. However, Tiffany was not satisfied with this medium, feeling that he could not communicate all that he desired through it. Perhaps it was the sparkling jewels of his father's famous jewelry store in New York City that helped him decide to experiment with glass. Whatever his motivation, his work is magnificent.

The stained glass I had seen before this time had been basically flat, pieced together rather than blending into a unified whole. Not Tiffany's! It was "alive" and three-dimensional. He placed glass on top of glass to bring out shape and color. Here and there he scattered glass chip jewels, brilliant chunks and lumps, and medallions of glass. His glass colors were vibrant and flowing, with beautiful hues. Tiffany played with lights, enamel, and mosaics. He even rippled glass that so much resembled the folds of Jesus' robe in Tiffany's "Entombment" chapel window that I had to examine it more closely and see if perhaps it might be cloth.

The differences between Tiffany's glass art and normal stained glass creations were almost startling. The single-colored, rather drab, pieced-together sections of the usual stained glass seemed insipid after this experience. Many times, stained glass creations are painted upon to produce a face or figure, but Tiffany developed his glass pictures almost entirely through the glass itself.

So it is after experiencing God. The Lord's presence is so dynamic, vibrant, alive, and flowing. As we come to appreciate the beauty and creativity of God, everything else looks dull in contrast. We were never meant to be satisfied with just knowing about God and memorizing some facts concerning Him. Rather, He draws us into experiencing Him. Suddenly, greatness, vitality, and incredible glory are before us, and we stand in awe. Let us never be content with less.

We need to experience God this way before we can share Him in His fullness with others. How else can we make Him real, unless He is real to us? We must view Him in His true beauty and get to know more of His various dimensions. We need to note the nuggets of truth and the jewels of wisdom that He provides. His light will shine through so we can enjoy His brilliance and splendor. How can we possibly get bored with a God who is as radiant and alive as He is?

GIANTS IN THE LAND

Read Numbers 13:28-30 and 14:1-10.
(For context read all of Numbers 13 and 14:1-38).   October 15

All leaders will face difficult and threatening situations. Fear pushes against us hard. Circumstances emerge that look impossible, and failure seems inevitable.

Usually, the results of pushing ahead are most favorable. It is like the land of Canaan, flowing with milk and honey and laden with fruit. The leaders of the twelve tribes who spied out the land had a choice. Would they value the land and trust God to win it for them or would they let fear overcome them? All but two chose the latter.

Numbers 13:28 starts with one terrible little word: But. The scouts had described the value of the land accurately up to this point. Then they said, "But the people who live there are powerful, and the cities are fortified and very large. We even saw descendants of Anek there." These were giants, and this perceived menace blinded them to the opportunities.

Only two leaders, Caleb and Joshua, saw it differently. The people were already murmuring and afraid after the bad reports. Caleb had to silence their grumbling (verse 30) before he could even be heard: "We should go up and take possession of the land, for we can certainly do it." No hesitation for this man! We *should* go up; we can *certainly* do it. In Numbers 14:8, Caleb and Joshua said, "If the Lord is pleased with us, he will lead us into that land, a land flowing with milk and honey, and will give it to us."

There's the bottom line. Serve God and please Him. God is the all-powerful one, and He can handle any giants. Not trusting Him to do so is rebellion (see Numbers 14:9).

Leaders are supposed to put aside fear and doubt. They are to rise up and trust God to accomplish the vision He has given. This takes exceptional action at times, but it is absolutely essential.

The reaction of the people to this stand of Caleb and Joshua

360

is fascinating. The mob wanted to stone them! In the end, however, it was the other ten tribal leaders—the ones who grumbled and spread a bad report—who were struck down and died (Numbers 14:36-38). It is safer to stand up for what is right before God. It is also the best choice for the people. If more leaders had done so, the forty years of wilderness wandering may not have occurred. A sobering thought, isn't it?

FACE DOWN AND TORN UP

Read Numbers 14:1-28.   *October 16*

Expanding on yesterday's devotional, we can gain even more insight into the task of leading a rebellious people.

Grumbling is difficult for leaders to handle. A bad report, rumors, and gossip spread in a mere evening like a flash flood. By night time, this mood had so permeated the Israeli camp that the people were crying and hysterical. Nerves were frayed. The people had worked themselves into such a frenzy that they were convinced they were going to die.

At such times, the past looks like cotton candy. It appears to be light, sweet, and joyous. All of its troubles have been erased from the mind, and memories are elevated to a level of happiness that never actually existed. People are willing to overthrow the present leadership and find new leaders who will whisk them back to their idyllic memories.

The reaction of Moses and Aaron to this scene is striking. They could have argued with the people, trying to bring about some shred of sense. Or they could have thrown up their hands in frustration and retreated to their tents to see what would happen. Instead, they fell face down before all of the people. What humility they showed. And as if that weren't enough to make the point, Joshua and Caleb tore their clothes.

What a sight! What a state in which to find the leaders. They had their faces buried in the ground. They were dusty and in rags. But the leaders knew the cost of rebellion. They realized that it was actually not rebellion against them that was being exhibited, but rather rebellion against God Himself (verse 9). They didn't want the people to pay the price for that. Indeed, God did become angry (verses 10-12).

Moses and Aaron wanted God's name to be glorified and were concerned for His reputation. Moses turned down the honor of being made into a new nation. Instead, they both interceded on behalf of the people. Out of their humility, Moses and Aaron prayed, reminding God of His attributes of love and forgiveness—insight which only comes from knowing God and spending time with Him.

What examples these leaders are to us. May the Lord help us to have such traits of humility and love for people and for God.

WE'LL DO IT NOW

Read Numbers 14:29-45.   *October 17*

Still more lessons can be learned from the story we have been examining. In Numbers 14:29, we note that God forgave the Israelites, but that there were consequences for their sin. Various times as a leader, I have had the responsibility to mete out retribution for an employee's or student's actions. I'd be a rich person if I had a dollar for every time I have heard people say, "Well, can't you just forgive me?" By this, they mean that if I forgave them, then there wouldn't be any negative consequences.

I smile kindly and say, "Of course, I forgive you. I believe you know that I care about you and hold nothing at all against you personally. However, I can't wipe out the consequences. That is another matter entirely. Consequences of our actions are not related to my forgiveness or lack of forgiveness, but rather to your previous action."

Sometimes, this takes a little further discussion for them to understand, but finally it dawns on them. Pregnancy can result from a sexual relationship. Restitution is necessary if someone has been robbed. Grades will be affected if a student has cheated or plagiarized. Someone may need to be fired or a student dismissed or otherwise disciplined for certain on-going, serious actions. All of this must happen, even though I truly forgave the individual.

So it was with the Israelites. God forgave them, but they still wandered in the wilderness and did not reach the promised land immediately. The only exceptions, of course, were Joshua and Caleb who deserved no punishment because their attitudes and actions were right.

When the people heard of the consequences, they "mourned bitterly" (verse 39). There's nothing like negative results to make us face our sin. Then at last the people wanted to back- track. They didn't want to face the difficult outcomes, so they decided to obey. However, it was too late. They had already acted, and the fruits of those actions were already visible. They had turned away from God (verse 43), and He would not be with them, even if they tried to undo their sin now.

In spite of this, the people were presumptuous and went without their leaders, but this could not succeed. Moses and the ark of God's presence stayed in the camp, and, indeed, the people were beaten down by their enemies.

As leaders, we must be strong at those times when we need to deliver news concerning consequences. We have to stay in God's presence, even though the people continue to disobey.

TASSELS

Read Numbers 15:37-41. *October 18*

How fascinating that in the next chapter of Numbers there is a discussion about commandments. In the last three devotionals, we noted that the people did not follow God.

First, they did not want to be with the Lord as He led them into the promised land. They did not have faith in Him, and they desired to go back to Egypt.

Then they did not stay with the ark of God's presence in the camp but instead tried to go off on their own to defeat the enemy. This was pure folly. When they should have stayed, they went, and when they should have gone, they held back.

It comes down to this: Nothing can be done without God, and anything can be accomplished with God! It's really a matter of obeying Him. If only we could remember just how important this is.

What God asks of us should be done exactly as He directs. We ought not to procrastinate or lag behind. Rather than immediately obeying, however, we are prone to wait and think about it. This amounts to disobedience, which we frequently rationalize.

The Lord knew that the people were prone to wander with their hearts and with their eyes. They forgot God and His ways when it was convenient to do so. However, God really wanted them to remember His commandments, and so He devised a plan.

I am impressed by His method of assisting them to recall what He desired. He told them to make tassels. These were to be tied to their clothes as a reminder of how important it is to obey God's commands. Tassels. Attached to their clothing. Swinging around. Swaying here and there. Getting in their way. Tassels everywhere! It would be hard to forget or rationalize something for long if these tassels were always around.

I have a friend who makes tassels. She is talented with yarns and creative with colors, and I have a few of her tassels in my office. A pair of them hangs from the lamp shade on my desk. Just in front of my face it hangs there. Remember: Obedience.

FOR THE REST OF YOUR LIFE

Read Acts 21:10-14.   *October 19*

I was in the midst of one of those terrible stages that inevitably comes in any job or ministry. Life was miserable. Challenges were on every side, and I didn't feel like dealing with them any more. I was out of solutions. I was tired of the people. Simply put, I had had it!

The memory is still clear to me, and gripping. It was the middle of the day, and I was sitting at my desk in the office after a particularly difficult scene.

"Lord, I want to leave this place," I had said. "I'm sick and tired of it all. Obviously, there's nothing more I can do here. I've tried everything I know, and nothing has worked. Every single thing has failed to bring change. Well, OK, not *quite* everything, but almost."

I continued to feel sorry for myself before the Lord. I told Him that I was sure it was time for me to leave and go somewhere else. Surely God could bring in another leader who could be more successful than I. Undoubtedly, it was time for some new blood and some fresh ideas in this place.

Then the still, small voice of the Lord spoke to my heart with a simple question. "If I asked you to stay here for the rest of your life, would you do it?"

I got up from my desk, locked my office door, and the hot tears started to drip down my face. I knew it was a serious question. It was meant to be heard and sincerely answered. No flippant response I didn't mean would be allowed.

It took half an hour of prayer and agony. Suffice it to say, that I finally said "yes." Thankfully, God didn't make me stay in that place for the rest of my life. However, I had to be willing to do so. I needed to lay down my life deliberately in that place if He called me to do it. Paul said, "I am ready not only to be bound, but also to die in Jerusalem for the name of the Lord Jesus" (Acts 21: 13).

365

The determination to be obedient and to sacrifice without limits is not an easy one. It is ripping and awful. But there are times when He says, "Will you do this?" And there is no doubt that He means us.

CAMPAIGN MANAGER

Read Mark 10:35-45.   *October 20*

God is campaign manager to no man. He is not out to promote particular people who desire to be thrust into the limelight. In fact, a person's desire for attention, glory and power could well disqualify him from service in the spiritual realm.

The opposite is true in most human circles. In politics, for example, those who feel that they can do a good job are expected to step forward as candidates. Not only must they decide that they are equal to the task, but they must be able to persuade others that they are competent as well. Their best traits are selected for presentation in the campaign brochures. Pictures of their family and community service projects are put into print. Experience is listed, along with a litany of beliefs and promises. They are trying to persuade us that they're the ones for the job.

This human approach to spiritual leadership can slip into our lives all too easily. We may desire to attain certain things or wish for promotion. When elections for positions in church leadership are held, it is interesting to observe how much politicking or vying for attention can go on. It's subtle, but unmistakable.

This was the problem for James and John. They were certainly maneuvering when they asked, "Teacher, we want you to do for us whatever we ask." They had to have plotted this ahead of time, reasoning that if they could get Him to say "Yes," then He would have to follow through on His promise. They took their desire for promotion and power right into their thinking about the heavenly kingdom.

God does not smile on such maneuvering, nor does He help promote people who feel they are competent for a position. Instead God looks to the little guy. He finds David out in the field, the youngest, least likely fellow with the smell of sheep on him. God searches for the servant who simply trusts.

TENDERNESS UNDER HEAT AND PRESSURE

Read Isaiah 43:1-2.   *October 21*

On my desk is displayed a precious item that I found in Wales. Its value is more in what it represents than in the object itself.

I can still remember discovering it. We had stayed in the home of a very talented Christian family. The father made clocks that he tooled beautifully in leather. In his workshop was an array of items that he made, along with other crafts from artisans he had met at craft fairs around Wales. One such object was the eye-catcher for me. I could hardly believe what I was seeing.

There was a perfectly formed, white, seeded dandelion, encapsulated in a solid plexiglass casing. It was a stunning paperweight!

How did the artisan do this? How could something as fragile and tender as a dandelion puff withstand the heat and pressure of being enveloped in plexiglass and still retain its form perfectly?

Our host explained that his friend had discovered an unique process to do this. I was so amazed and delighted that I purchased the little treasure for my desk. You see, it spoke to me deeply.

Life brings its pressures. Sometimes I feel so tender and fragile as the challenges of life engulf me. I'm afraid I will not stand, that perhaps I cannot bear up under it all.

This fear is particularly strong when the heat and pressure have been constant for a long period of time. I can stand it just fine for a while. However, as the process continues, I begin to sense my strength waning and my inner self wilting. I am afraid that I will be burnt or crushed beyond recognition by the adversities of life, especially the stresses of the job.

When the going gets rough, however, there on my desk sits a perfect example of hope. It reminds me every day that when we go through the fire, we will not be burned. God is there. And in the midst of the fire, He is perfecting us and making us into something of incredible beauty. Tenderness under heat and pressure.

THE GUIDE

Read Psalm 48:14.   *October 22*

"For this God is our God forever and ever; He will be our guide even to the end."

At times, it is easy to take lightly the roles of God. I believe that we should consider carefully the various descriptors related to God in scripture. He has unveiled to us, throughout His Word, the various aspects of His job description. We are meant to apply this information to our lives and to allow Him to function in the roles that He desires to take.

One of these applications is God's chosen role as guide. I have visited with and counseled many people who either have not understood this role or who have not allowed God to carry it out in their lives.

Some are fearful of what lies ahead. They are good-hearted, desiring to do God's will but not sure about what it entails. Concerned that they will make a mistake and take a wrong path for their lives, they are nervous and uptight, especially in times of decision-making.

However, God wants to be our guide. What does a guide do? He may go ahead and scout out the trail. Then he comes back and lets us know the best choice. When we're standing at a crossroads, he'll direct us to the correct path. He makes a way, clears the track, and moves us around obstacles. His duty is to take us from the beginning and to lead us safely to our destination. A guide would not be doing his job well if he were to lose any members of his group.

God's Word promises that He Himself will lead us to the very end. What a comforting thought! He is not the kind of guide who might leave us part way through the journey. Imagine what it would be like to be on a trek with a guide in the north woods and to wake up in your sleeping bag the next morning...only to discover that your scout left you sometime during the night. You don't really know where you are, carry no compass, and have no clue how to get back. That would certainly be frightening.

Some people are so apprehensive about their future that they act as though they have exactly this sort of leader. Not true. God is the guide, and He is a good one, too. He won't abandon us, He'll do His job, and He'll do it exceedingly well. We will definitely arrive safely at our destination. If God is your guide, then trust Him to lead you.

GRUMBLING

Read Exodus 16:2-3 and 17:1-3. (If you have
time read Exodus 16:1-11 and 17:1-7)   *October 23*

Grumbling just simply gets old. Leaders become tired of hearing it. People grumble about the most unbelievable things like the new paint color or the brand of computer purchased. The smallest situations can create the greatest explosions imaginable. You can change some things to appease the grumblers, but someone else will grumble because you changed it. If it weren't so frustrating, it could be funny. I have to admit, I resort to humor and shaking my head more often these days. However, though I don't get as upset, the murmuring and complaining can still get to me.

I'm sure that's how Moses and Aaron felt. The people grumbled all the time. See Exodus 16:2-3, 7, 9, 11 and 17:2-4 and 7. In these two chapters alone, the people complained about food and then they grumbled about water. They blamed their leaders, so Moses and Aaron had to take the brunt of it all. These two men had simply been obedient to God and what He had told them to do. They weren't personally responsible to feed this motley gang of Israelites.

Moses' frustration spilled over when he cried out to God, "What am I to do with these people? They are almost ready to stone me." Moses was at his wit's end. Before this exasperated comment, he had tried everything he knew to do.

When it came to the food situation, Moses had tried to reason with the people. "Who are we, that you should grumble against us?" Moses had pointed out that God Himself had heard the people complaining to Him. "You are not grumbling against us, but against the Lord."

Moses and Aaron knew that they were merely God's agents. The Lord was the one in charge here. It was His leadership that the people were unhappy about, and therefore they had better be careful.

As leaders, we need to remember not to take complaints too personally. It is simply our duty to obey Him in our leadership tasks and then let Him do what He pleases.

God did care for the Israelites. He showed His provision and glory by giving them meat and bread. The leaders brought the people before God (16:9) and turned their eyes to Him.

Too soon, however, the people were at it again, this time grumbling about water. It doesn't take people long to forget what God has done. Again the Lord performed a miracle: water from a rock. Who ever heard of such a thing?

God can bring about the impossible. Remember, He is among

us, and He will help us as leaders. We just need to maintain faith in the face of all that grumbling, murmuring, and complaining.

THE CANNON FACING THE CHURCH DOOR
Read Matthew 16:18.   *October 24*

I had never visited this church nor had I been in this particular town. Desiring to surprise an old friend and former employee who was now pastoring, I had pulled off the interstate and somehow managed to locate the church. He was sure to be surprised, and we could spend an hour of fun, reminiscing and catching up on news.

As I placed my hand on the handle of the front church door, I was startled by an unbelievable, ground-shaking noise. My body jerked involuntarily, and I twisted my head rapidly in the direction of the sound.

There, on the block across from the church, was the town's courthouse. On the corner of the courthouse lawn was a cannon, and that cannon was directly facing the front door of the church. You guessed it. At the very moment that I had placed my hand on that door handle, the city officials had chosen to fire the cannon. It had boomed loudly, leaving my ears ringing and the adrenalin rushing through my body.

Although he had never heard the cannon being shot off during his time in that town, my friend shared that it had always been positioned facing the front door of the church. Interesting. Why didn't they make it face the courthouse or point it across the front lawn or cause it to look toward the gas station? Why was it always pointed at the front door of the church? Furthermore, why would it actually be set off just at the moment when a person was trying to enter the door?

This anecdote symbolizes what Satan attempts to do with the church. Satan is not pleased when a church is seeing souls saved.

He is not happy when a church is on fire for the things of the Lord. He never wants one more person to enter the Kingdom of God. Stop them before they can even enter the doors! Scare them off if possible.

The *Bible* has good news about this, however. The gates of hell will not prevail against the church. Satan cannot overcome it. Though a cannon may be pointed and even fired at it, the church will stand.

SUDDENLY

Read Mark 13:32-37. *October 25*

We were driving across Canada for our vacation, and it was a perfect day. Although it was warm, the air was so fresh and lovely outside that we turned off the air conditioning in the car and rolled down the windows. The sun and my relaxed state soon eased me into a deep sleep as my husband drove.

Suddenly, I was jolted awake, sputtering. Something had literally thudded on the teeth of my half-open mouth. I bolted upright with a jerk, as I tried to wake up and gather my wits. What had happened?

Then I saw it. The object that had caused the thud in my mouth was laying on the floor at my feet. It was a huge bumble bee! As my adrenalin rush slowed down and I began to comprehend the situation, my husband started to chuckle. Soon we were both guffawing helplessly, re-enacting the scene: the thud, the jerk, the sputter, the startled expression. It was hilarious.

The memory is still pretty funny. But the lesson behind it is not. It reminds me of what will happen when the church is raptured. Jesus told His disciples that the owner of the house can come back at any time, and the servants should be ready. Jesus warned them, "If he comes suddenly, do not let him find you sleeping."

Just as I was napping on that drive in Canada, Jesus can take the church away in an instant while we are sleeping. If we were dozing while the church was raptured, we could wake up with a jolt, like the bee thud, only to find that the event had already occurred.

This can be particularly dangerous for leaders. We are used to being in charge. People don't move into something big until we give the approval. We're responsible for the time line. We may think that nothing mammoth will happen until we are made aware of it.

However, God doesn't have to check with us. In fact, Jesus said to His disciples, "What I say to you, I say to everyone: 'Watch!'"

We'd better listen to this word of warning. We can't afford to be jerked awake too late on this one!

THE OYSTER

Read Matthew 13:45-46.   *October 26*

I felt like dirt. It wasn't a permanent self-esteem issue. It was the way the day went. It was the situation. It was where I was at for the moment. Nonetheless, it was the way I felt.

As I was on my knees praying that night, I thought of something that helped me. The idea of an oyster came to my mind. I could picture this creature getting a piece of grit or sand from its ocean environment and then chafing from it for a time. That irritant stays inside the oyster shell right along with the soft animal, rubbing it and bothering it.

So, that wise oyster acts, secreting a film that begins to envelope the piece of grit. Soon the impediment is covered, smooth and slick to the touch. No longer an irritant to the tiny oyster, it has actually been transformed into an object of great beauty.

I like to watch pearl divers hold their breath and dive deep for the treasures. They work very hard, but the gems are most precious to discover. Jesus talked about this in Matthew 13, referring to a merchant seeking fine pearls and willing to sell everything so he can purchase one that is particularly exquisite. Pearls have always been especially meaningful to me. It is my birth stone, and I remember receiving a pearl ring for a very special occasion when I was a teen. I treasure the whole strand that showed up on my wedding day from my husband.

I smiled at God's way of touching my own life with this special symbolism. Although dirt-and-grit days come, God somehow touches these and turns them into pearls. How does He do that? He takes our mistakes and covers them up. He helps us to learn, grow, and develop into something beautiful. He transforms our weaknesses and our very lives. How marvelous it is to serve a God like that. We are never relegated to dirt but have life-changing power available to us.

A MATTER OF LIFE AND DEATH
Read Matthew 10:37-39 and John 12:23-25.   *October 27*

I once heard a famous model, who will go unnamed, make a wild statement. She said, "When you die, you lose a very important part of your life." Well, yes, you do. In fact, you lose it all—that's the point of death.

The challenge of the Christian life is that Jesus asks us to lay down every part of our lives—every important part right along side every small part. Nothing is to be held back from Him, not even our closest relationships. We must be willing to obey God, no matter what the cost. We should hold on to nothing.

This is easier to think about than to do. It hurts to lay down everything. There are some areas of our lives that are enjoyable, meaningful, and important to us. We think that life comes from them and that if these were to be taken away, we could not make it.

This is why Jesus likens this challenge to taking up our cross and following Him. If we do this, it will feel like we are losing our very lives. However, there is a paradox at work here so that anyone who lays down his life for Christ will actually find it again. In contrast, if someone tries to hold on to his life, he will in fact lose it.

Death is not a pretty sight, but God wants it all. He wants our flesh in a coffin. We are to go into the dark, be laid into the deep, and get covered up with dirt. This is not just a literal rendition, it's a spiritual matter. When we give up our lives for God, they become like seeds falling into the ground. Dying to ourselves can be so dark, lonely, and meaningless. After the experience, however, we find that God has been at work, and much fruit has been produced. In fact, if we give up our very lives to God in this world, we will find ourselves again—with eternal life thrown in.

THE COFFIN

Read I Corinthians 8:9-13.   *October 28*

Experiencing the death of our flesh seems to drag on with such painstaking slowness. We want to hold on to the last vestiges of life. No one wants to die, so we grasp for what we think is still necessary. We assent in our minds to dying out to ourselves, but we act differently.

The *Bible* tells us, however, that "if you live according to the sinful nature, you will die" (verse 13). Therefore it is an important matter to take care of this flesh.

How do we know if someone is dead? Non-medically of course, if you kick him and he reacts, he's not dead! I laughed when I thought of this parallel. If people upset me (kick me), and I jerk in response or scream, then I'm not yet dead. The flesh is

375

still responding. I see it in myself, don't you?

I could picture myself in a coffin, still twitching. I recall praying about this matter and telling the Lord how much I would like to have it all be over. Couldn't I just die and be done with it? The process of dying out to self was taking such a long time!

However, we cannot commit spiritual suicide. We are unable to take the knife to ourselves and finish it off. This is a deep and profound work that can be accomplished only through the Spirit. Verse 14 states, "But if by the Spirit you put to death the misdeeds of the body, you will live, because those who are led by the Spirit of God are sons of God."

Thankfully He helps us if we are willing. By His Spirit, we learn how to die out to our flesh. We are moved to give up our very lives and let them fall into the ground. We are covered over. It must be complete.

I feel sorry for people who die only partially. They have given some areas to God, but they keep hold of some others. Half dead people in coffins are not a pretty sight. Are you dead or not?

SEEDS IN LITTLE CUPS

Read Romans 8:17-25.   *October 29*

After we have died, God tells us that we will find life. There are several problems with this process though. Not only is it terribly difficult to die, it is also costly and frightening. Although resurrection life is promised, this can only be accepted by sheer faith. To begin with, we experience only the pain, the suffering and the nothingness. There is little positive to the experience except the promise.

Think about seeds. They stay in that cold, hard ground for a long time. Darkness is everywhere, they can see nothing, and there is no activity. Not only can the seeds not sense any growth initially, but when it finally does come, the new life can't be observed from above the ground, either.

I remember an interesting lesson I learned from some of my elementary classmates when we planted seeds in little cups. We watered, set the cups in the sun, and watched. Days passed by, and finally some of my classmates could bear it no longer. They dug up the seeds to see what was happening. Of course, the sprouts were too tender to be dug up and examined constantly, so life never did arise from their little cups of earth.

No, we must wait. We must really die—all the way—perhaps for what seems like an eternity. However, sooner or later, the seed will germinate and sprout. Resurrection life will come, even if it doesn't come entirely till heaven, and there, too, we will see all the fruit that was produced from that one little seed.

This is the only way to life. There are no shortcuts whatsoever. Die out to sin, repent, turn, give up every single thing to God till there's nothing left that's yours. Hold nothing back. Jesus is there to save you, the Holy Spirit is there to help you, and some day, you will see God amidst eternal life.

THE LADY AND THE TEDDY BEAR

Read Exodus 33:10-14. *October 30*

Obviously, she needed a friend. The elderly lady probably had few people with whom she could converse on a regular basis.

I was on a business trip for a week, ensconced in a nice hotel on Capitol Hill in Washington, D.C., so it was the last place I expected to find such a scene. After all, it wasn't Johnny's Cafe in Smalltown, U.S.A. where this little incident wouldn't have been as surprising, perhaps.

I had entered the hotel restaurant that morning, and there she was, sitting with her teddy bear beside her. It was a large bear, and she had dressed it in as eccentric a manner as she was dressed. That included the jewelry.

The hostess seated me at a table next to hers so I heard the ongoing exchange between her and the waitress. She was complaining about everything. However, the wise waitress finally realized that the lady needed someone to talk with and just stood there and did that for a while. It was a very kind action, I thought.

—Just as kind as it is for God to listen to us. He is ready to pay attention to us any time we desire. God never half-listens. Symbolically, one might say that He sets down the newspaper or turns off the television. He faces us and looks into our eyes. We have His full attention.

Jesus is our friend in the true sense of the word. Always there for us, He is wonderful company at any time we desire it. He's a much better friend than a teddy bear. When we are feeling lonely or isolated, like all of us do at certain times, let's remember that it might be the perfect opportunity to get to know Him better. We can listen to Him, too.

BROKEN AND SHATTERED

Read Psalm 51:15-17.   *October 31*

A favorite crystal glass. Broken. Shattered. I stared at the scattered pieces with a sense of loss and helplessness. It would be impossible to put back together; there were just too many fragments. I couldn't even pick up the tiny pieces to throw them away. The mess had to be swept up.

How could God take delight in a sight like that? Especially when I knew that it was really my heart we were talking about. That broken glass was merely a symbol of how I felt inside, and God's love for brokenness is a mysterious idea indeed.

"The sacrifices of God are a broken spirit; a broken and contrite heart, O God, you will not despise."

So often we try to give God things that cost us nothing. We want a "sale," to pay a small price for something of value.

However, God knows that these exchanges are not genuine sacrifices. We cannot fool Him or appease Him with a fake or a replica of the genuine article. God wants the real gift; He desires a true sacrifice.

This is not an easy matter. Sacrifice that costs us highly is painful. We know when He wants us to do it. Giving something up—or being obedient—or paying the price, these can break our hearts. We are faced with the terrible decision of following God all the way or only when we feel like it. We are forced to decide between complete obedience or mere lip service. We have the choice of taking up our cross and giving up our very lives or trying to keep ourselves intact in an attempt to save ourselves.

Impossible! We cannot save ourselves. So we must be broken. We must pay the price, offer the real sacrifice, and allow ourselves to be shattered. Let us allow our spirits to be broken...and what do we find? God's Spirit floods in and shines out of the shattered places. Let our hearts be crushed as well...and what happens? The Lord moves in to touch the depths of our emotions, to reach to the bottom of our needs. Oh, the wonder of it! God does not despise a broken and contrite heart. How He delights in true sacrifice.

People who have been broken spiritually have such pleasant personalities and spirits. They are so beautiful; it's a paradox, really. God uses them in such profound ways. So let's not be afraid to break.

NOVEMBER

FRETTING

Read Psalm 37:1-17.   *November 1*

Fretting. Say the word aloud slowly and listen to how it sounds. There's a grumbling and growling tone to it. Fretting can be a pac-man, chewing away at us with fury.

It's just so easy to brood when an evil person's actions affect our lives. There are some louts who behave in beastly ways and somehow seem to get away with it. Wicked individuals may stomp on us and even on their friends without an ounce of pity. In fact, they almost look gleeful when others experience pain. Their evil ways cause them to be greedy, and they are never satisfied with their power, their goods, their position, their achievements, or their level of success.

Why is it that such ruthless human beings spread out in luxury? They appear to get everything they want, and furthermore, they pay no price for their wrongdoing. It is natural to become envious or angry. We may wish that we could somehow pull off what they do.

How easy it is to be afraid that their evil ways will overcome us. After all, they will stop at nothing, and at the leadership level, we have watched the power-crazed wreak havoc. They can be slick, manipulative and cunning.

However, the scriptures give us simple instructions for how to handle this situation. Don't fret. It's just that clear. Fretting "leads only to evil," David said. It can upset us so much that we can't see clearly anymore. Before we know it, we too can be involved in the same wrong methods (verse 8). We can get caught up in their games and their ways.

David reminds us that the evil individual will soon wither and die away. "A little while, and the wicked will be no more; though you look for them, they will not be found" (verse 9). It is far better to be righteous and possess only a little rather than to have corrupt wealth. Ultimately, the power of the wicked will be broken, and the righteous will inherit the land (verses 17 and 11). The wicked will disappear but the person of peace will have a future, for the salvation of the righteous comes from the Lord. In leadership, though the load of responsibility may tempt us to fret, God tells us clearly: Don't.

PERPETUAL DEVOTION

Read Matthew 19:16-22.   *November 2*

In Victor Hugo's famous novel *Les Miserables*, the main character faces many moral decisions. Choosing what is right is very costly to him. As a matter of fact, each successive choice becomes more demanding.

In one of these gripping scenes at the end of the book, Jean Valjean is pondering a dilemma. "The obedience of matter is limited by friction; is there no limit to the obedience of the soul?" he asks. "If perpetual motion is impossible, can perpetual devotion be demanded?" (1387).

In fact, God does expect perpetual devotion. It is so tempting to stop the process, however. "Well, I've relinquished this. I did what I should back there. That ought to be enough," we reason.

As Jean Valjean's thinking continued in this vein, he said, "The first step is nothing; it is the last that is difficult. ...Oh, first step of descent, how somber! Oh, second step, how black!"

This is what the rich young man discovered when he came to Jesus. He had kept the commandments, he claimed. Perhaps some of these had not been particularly easy for him.

Nonetheless, he had consistently chosen the moral high ground.

However, the rich young ruler still was not satisfied. Something was missing. So he asked Jesus to explain what more there was. This young man did not yet understand that God has a way of asking us for everything. His first requests are difficult to fulfill, but as we proceed, He asks for those areas that are even more near and dear to us. Where do we stop this process? How much is too much?

The rich young man found that the Lord could actually ask him for every single thing. There was no friction to slow down or halt the process of being wholly devoted. Boundaries to sacrifice did not exist. Limits to giving were impossible. God wanted it all.

We need to decide if we are willing to give up everything. You see, ultimately God will require it of us. He does not do this to be mean. He does it because He knows that we will not be happy and fulfilled until we give it all to Him. That is why the young man went away sad. If he had been willing to give every bit to Jesus, including his own life, he would have found the Kingdom of God. Think what he missed!

How devoted are you?

Work cited: Hugo, Victor. *Les Miserables.* New York: Signet Classic, 1987.

THE LIFE AND LABOURS OF...

Read I Corinthians 15:58.   *November 3*

"I'm reading an old biography on one of the Christian workers at the turn of the century," my friend told me. "It's one of those books you check out of the library, and it disintegrates when you take it outside because it hasn't seen sunshine for years," she chuckled. "It's called *The Life and Labours of...* Say!" she broke her thought. "Why is it that all those old biographies start with *The Life and Labours of....*?" We both laughed and continued our conversation.

383

Then later that same week, another friend said to me, "Our souls become downcast when we can't be productive." The two statements struck a chord in me.

I pondered how people one, two, even five hundred years ago used to view their lives. We're more into leisure time now than they used to be. Christmas letters tend to share news of vacations and travels rather than news of work. There are many travel books in the bookstores but few actually recount what people have accomplished. Even the biographies tend to focus upon personality rather than labours.

When the going gets rough, it is tempting to want to get away from it all. But Paul says in today's verse that we should "stand firm." He offers some clear advice. "Let nothing move you. Always give yourselves fully to the work of the Lord because you know that your labor in the Lord is not in vain."

At times it may seem like it, though. We can work hard and realize few results. It may appear that people are not growing or changing. How difficult it is to gauge the effectiveness of spiritual things! It's too bad that we don't have a Christian growth thermometer.

However, as we labor for God, it is true that our "labor in the Lord is not in vain." Slow and imperceptible as it might seem, God is still accomplishing many things through our labors. You can count on it. You'll even see it some day—but not in its entirety until heaven. How would someone write down your biography: The Life and Labors of.......?

AFTER HIS OWN HEART

Read I Samuel 13:13-14 and Acts 13:22.   *November 4*

After Samuel rebuked Saul, informing him that the Lord was seeking for a new leader, Saul should have engaged in some in-depth self-analysis. We will deal with that situation in the next several devotionals. At the center of this story, however, is the heart of God—a heart that is moved by the obedience of men.

Samuel said to Saul, "But now your kingdom will not endure; the Lord has sought out a man after his own heart and appointed him leader of his people, because you have not kept the Lord's command."

The essence of the problem was that Saul didn't obey. Acts 13:22 tells us that God considered David to be the opposite of this: "....a man after my own heart; he will do everything I want him to do." What a compliment this is to David! The Lord said that David would do anything God told him, and it was that attitude which moved the very heart of God.

Only yesterday the Lord tested me on this very lesson. I had a particular pastor on my mind for several days, feeling inclined to call him, though I didn't know why. I really didn't have anything to say. Finally I knew it simply boiled down to obedience.

When at last I reached him after the phone tag that is common these days, I hardly knew what to say. I explained that I had felt prompted to call him but wasn't even sure why. I apologized for sounding so silly, but explained that I just had to do it or be disobedient to the Spirit's prompting.

Imagine how relieved I was when he said that indeed the call was perfectly timed. He and his wife had just candidated in a church the day before, and they were earnestly seeking God's will on the matter. The opportunity for listening, sharing some perspectives, and praying was one I would not have wanted to miss. For his part, the call had reminded him of God's special care.

I wish that I could say I was always that obedient. Of David it was said, "He will do everything I want him to do." Think of it! No wonder David was a man after God's own heart. David was willing to sacrifice, pay any price, look foolish—anything—in order to obey. Let that be me, too, Lord.

BUT NOT QUITE

Read I Samuel 10:6-8 and 13:5-15.   *November 5*

When Samuel anointed Saul, the prophet told him to watch for signs that would verify his leadership calling. "Once these signs are fulfilled, " Samuel continued, "do whatever your hand finds to do, for God is with you."

So much confirmation, affirmation, and freedom of choice were given to Saul. However, there was also a single, clear directive. Saul was to go to Gilgal and wait there seven days until Samuel arrived to give him instructions. Furthermore, Samuel promised he would come to perform the sacrifices.

With such definitive orders, disobedience could not be due to a lack of clarity. Saul knew what he was supposed to do. He was hard pressed, however. Thousands of enemy soldiers and chariots arrived on the scene. The Israelites had virtually no weapons, no chariots, and comparatively few soldiers. As he waited day by day at Gilgal for Samuel to arrive, the troops became demoralized and the majority actually hid or ran away. Those who did stay with Saul were quaking with fear.

In some ways, one could understand Saul's problem. After all, who wants to sit around in the midst of crisis? Who desires to remain the leader of fearful and scattering troops? Who would relish the thought of facing a gigantic army when the odds were not even in favor of coming out alive, let alone for victory?

It's amazing, really, that Saul waited as long as he did—seven days. However, it was just short; it was not seven complete days. Saul almost did what God had commanded, but not quite.

Furthermore, it was not the king's role to serve as a priest or a prophet. He was not supposed to usurp that authority but rather was to rule within the clear-cut standards of checks and balances as shown in the law and the prophets.

God does not like obedience to be partial. Part-way is never good enough. We cannot rationalize away our "little" disobediences because each and every choice not to obey is critical. Even when we have been mainly obedient, we are not permitted to have our way at the last minute. We must wait for God as long as He chooses and do absolutely everything He says. We must never become power mongers in any way. These mistakes were enough to cause the removal of Saul from leadership. Hopefully, we're bright enough to learn from this!

THE BLEATING OF SHEEP

Read I Samuel 15:1-30. (If time is limited for a full chapter, consider the verses mentioned in the devotional. Then look over the entire context later.)　　　　　　　　　　*November 6*

Saul should have learned his lessons: Obey completely and have faith in God. There should have been no question, then, when Samuel gave him God's instructions to attack the Amalekites. "Do not spare them; put to death men and women, children and infants, cattle and sheep, camels and donkeys" (verse 3).

Why, then, do we get this "but" that starts verse 9? "But Saul and the army spared Agag and the best of the sheep and cattle, the fat calves and lambs—everything that was good. These they were unwilling to destroy completely, but everything that was despised and weak they totally destroyed."

Rationalization is all too subtle and far too easy. Saul decided to obey in areas that were not important to him. He destroyed what didn't matter and gave that to God as his act of obedience. He had so justified this line of reasoning that he said to Samuel, "The Lord bless you! I have carried out the Lord's instructions" (verse 13).

Samuel's next comment was particularly wry. "What then is this bleating of sheep in my ears? What is this lowing of cattle I hear?"

387

When caught in his rationalization, Saul did a most ungallant thing: He "passed the buck." His explanation for his own disobedience was that "the soldiers brought them from the Amalekites." But he was the leader, wasn't he? Surely he could have stopped it.

Next, he had a brainstorm that just might have rescued him out of this whole mess. He said the reason that the good animals had been spared was to sacrifice them to God. Oh, come on now. Try another one.

Samuel stopped him right there (verse 16). He spoke it straight. Saul had pounced on that plunder like a cat on a mouse. He wanted it, and he had disobeyed. When confronted with this truth, Saul did a brazen thing. He continued to argue! Samuel had to give further instruction about priorities, explaining that obedience is better than sacrifice and that rebellion and arrogance are serious offenses.

Finally admitting to his actions, Saul still excused himself by saying that he was afraid of the people and that was why he had sinned. He didn't want to accept the consequences, and he still desired to be honored before the people (verse 30).

Leaders must simply, purely, and completely obey God. There is no room for excuses, lies or deceit with the Lord. Let's not waffle in our leadership. Sheep bleat and cattle low, and that's the way it is.

THE SHEPHERD BOY

Read I Samuel 15:34-35 and 16:1-13.   *November 7*

What a tragedy to see a mighty leader fall. It is grievous and cuts to the core. This is especially true when you knew the person well, trusted him, saw his potential, and had great hope for his future. His vision crashes right along with him. The great promise he held, as well as the impact he was having, slip away.

Samuel mourned, and even the Lord grieved.

However, the human emotions that revolve around the fall of a person cannot be nurtured forever. There comes a time when God says, "How long will you mourn...? Fill your horn with oil and be on your way..." (16:1).

Saul was not indispensable. God looked and found someone who touched His heart. The oil of the anointing—God's own authority for the position—would change the lad He found.

How comforting these next verses are regarding the selection of a shepherd boy. Here was the oldest son of Jesse who was tall and handsome. People could flock around such a figure. However, it was not he whom God chose. Each of the seven oldest sons was summarily rejected as the future King.

The Lord does not look at what man sees. "Man looks at the outward appearance, but the Lord looks at the heart" (verse 7). When we select people for positions, we should remember this advice. It is not always the most striking or the most good-looking or the most charismatic person we interview who should be hired. A resumé does show everything. The person we want may have to be dragged in from the janitor's closet or the mailroom. David was summoned, all smelly and sweaty, from tending sheep. He was the youngest and the least likely, but God knew him well.

May the Lord assist us in perceiving what He sees when we make employee and leadership selections. God considers the heart as well as the potential. And when God chooses, He always enables. "So Samuel took the horn of oil and anointed him...and from that day on the Spirit of the Lord came upon David in power" (verse 13).

Let us not make critical employee decisions based upon our own understanding, but rather seek the Lord regarding every single one. God is the one who sees the heart and makes up for deficiencies.

DECEPTION

Saul and David both sinned, and each was faced with his sins by a prophet. However, the differences are striking in how each responded when confronted with his offenses.

Saul, as we have already discussed, rationalized away his sins in front of Samuel. David, on the other hand, responded to Nathan immediately with the clear truth, "I have sinned against the Lord."

David had added sin to sin, just like Saul. He had committed adultery and then arranged for the death of Uriah. However, deception had still not completely overpowered his heart. When faced with his sin, David did not excuse it. He did not waffle and play games with the issue.

David was a man after God's own heart. His understanding of his heavenly Father was still intact, and so he realized that he had deeply offended a holy God. Sin is against the Lord and cannot be explained away. Although sin affects human beings, more importantly it alters our relationship with God. David wanted that restored again.

Saul, on the other hand, had a difficult time facing his sin. His heart had been deceived. He could not even see that sin was sin any more. This is a most dangerous stage, and it doesn't happen overnight. It is based on a lack of understanding both of God and of ourselves. The comprehension of God's holiness and of our sinfulness progressively weakens. Rationalization and deceit build up a wall between man and God. Since it is a process over time, it has serious and long-lasting results.

Both David and Saul had to face the consequences of their sin. David's child by Bathsheba died, and David had many family calamities. However, he did not lose his relationship with God as Saul did (see I Samuel 16:14), nor did he lose his kingship. Leadership is defaulted when deceit is rampant. Deception takes time to undo, just as it took time to enter the heart in the first place. As leaders, we must watch over our hearts. The reality of sin must stay ever before us.

LITTLE BY LITTLE

Read Hebrews 3:7-15.   *November 9*

Deception can occur so gradually that it is barely noticeable. That is part of the danger. It's also why people have such difficulty coming to grips with deception and finally admitting that there is a problem.

We have probably all heard of the classic biology experiment of the frog and pan of water. When a frog is placed into a pan of boiling water, it immediately jumps out. However, something different happens when the frog is put into a pan of cold water. It stays there, even when the pan is held over a bunsen burner and the heat is turned up gradually. The frog adjusts little by little to the surrounding water temperature, and it will literally die from the heat rather than jump to safety.

What a sobering warning this is—and it can happen to any of us! In fact, we are in grave danger indeed if we think we are immune from this possibility. Every one of us lives and works in a society where the heat is being turned up gradually all around us. Little by little, society slides and slips away from the holiness of God. Bit by bit, we can become comfortable with sin. As it did to Saul, sin can appear to be both feasible and logical—even compelling!

We have to develop ways of measuring the rise of the temperature, of viewing the truth, of understanding the danger. Accountability, honesty and integrity should all assist us. However, we should never be tempted to think that we are out of danger—for that in itself is deception.

Peril constantly lurks, sometimes in areas we least expect

it—sometimes in places where we have won victories before and feel strong. It prowls about after great spiritual battles have been won. It sneaks in when we're tired and unobservant. It hovers when we feel sorry for ourselves and let up for a time. Feeling the heat lately?

THIS SIDE OF THE WORLD
Read II Timothy 3:1-13.   *November 10*

Christians will sometimes say, "We are different than the world." However, when asked how this concept is actually lived out, they are sometimes hard pressed to explain.

The concept often espoused is that somehow or other we need to stay a step or two away, on this side of the world. "This side," of course, means God's side instead of Satan's. It means, some say, that we are called out as Christians to be different and to maintain some distinctions from our unsaved friends. In this view, as long as we are a couple of steps away from everybody else in society, we must be safe. That's what it means to be "called out."

Or is it? I believe that there is a considerable hazard inherent in this thinking. The problem is that society is shifting morally. It is moving ever nearer to Satan's ways. Paul said that "evil men and impostors will go from bad to worse" (verse 13). Gradually, Satan has adjusted the thinking of America and brought it closer to accepting sin and the ways of darkness. The temperature has been turned up steadily, and we have not always realized it.

Now someone could argue that it is really quite good if Christians have stayed several steps from the world through all this. They will have remained on God's side, at least. But is this enough? Although we may be different if we keep two paces away from the world, as the line of society deviates, we will be moving away from God, too. We can still be compromising and shifting away from our Lord. Little by little. Bit by bit.

Where does Christianity stand today? Is God our standard, or are we satisfied with a few minor differences from the world? The answer to that question has serious implications.

DECEITS OF THE HEART

Read Jeremiah 17:9-10.   *November 11*

The Word of God sheds an interesting perspective concerning the heart. We may find it hard to believe, but the truth is that "the heart is deceitful above all things and beyond cure. Who can understand it?"

We'd like to believe this is too harsh a commentary on our inner being. After all, we tend to value the heart. We talk about "matters of the heart" and of having a "heartfelt emotion" or of loving someone with "all my heart." So how could we let something we value so much turn into such a mess?

The *Bible* says that our hearts are deceitful, even above all things. Not only does the heart let us down once in a while, it can very easily be tricked. This can happen all too quickly to anyone at all. Always a lurking danger, this proclivity can never be cured.

Our hearts are moved by many matters. We can be touched by a temptation and then become motivated toward acting upon it. We might have our own needs of the heart met by another person, when it is not appropriate for that particular individual to meet those needs. Before we know it, our hearts can get us into trouble. In scripture, deception is related to wealth (Mark 4:19), flattery (Romans 16:18), and empty words (Ephesians 5:6), just to name a few.

Deception is slick and clever, slithering in and making us feel so good, for a little while anyway. We can accommodate it for a time and decide to let it in, just for a day. The *Bible* says that we cannot know the heart. It can be so easily beguiled that we may

393

not even recognize what is happening. A little here, a little there, and the compromise has occurred. What is really darkness has come to look like light, and we are beguiled.

Scriptures tell us that Satan comes to us disguised as an angel of light. He deceives us into thinking that darkness is light and sometimes that light is darkness. Once our hearts are deceived, it is difficult to unravel. How dangerous!

"God, help me to keep a pure heart. Please continue searching my heart on an ongoing basis. Do whatever you need to do in my life to keep me open to the convicting work of the Holy Spirit. I need that desperately!"

WATCH THE HEART

Read Proverbs 4:23.   *November 12*

God's Word tells us, "Above all else, guard the heart, for it is the wellspring of life."

God Himself is as a fountain of water in our lives, and His entry springs from the heart. He should have all of the heart, then. Otherwise the source is stopped up. Perhaps this is why the first command (Deuteronomy 6:5) is to "love the Lord your God with all your heart...." Our hearts are not meant to be shared with any other. We are not to give part of it away to any person or cause other than God Himself. The Lord is to get it every bit of it.

God asks us to guard our hearts. We are to watch over them, even "above all else." If our hearts go wrong, we have real problems.

Perhaps that is why "the Lord is close to the brokenhearted" (Psalm 34:8) and "heals the brokenhearted" (Psalm 147:3). A broken heart is not nearly so dangerous as a deceived heart or a hardened heart or a divided heart.

The scriptures have many other admonitions about the heart: That it should be pure... That we should be kindhearted... That we ought to be upright in heart. To guard our hearts. we must spend time in God's presence. As we pray and seek His face, God shows us what our hearts are really like. He will shed light on the secret places and help us to be honest with ourselves and with Him. The Holy Spirit will convict us and lead us to repentance. This is one of our best guards.

We should always be open to this sort of examination. Romans 8:27 says that "he who searches the heart knows what the mind of the Spirit is because He intercedes for the saints according to the will of God." We need to let the Lord do His work and expose our inner core to His searchlight on a regular basis.

Additional safeguards can be good friends to whom we are accountable, who know us well and who will be honest with us. The Spirit also convicts, and the Word of God can speak clearly to us. We can use as much protection as possible when it comes to something as valuable as our hearts.

A HEART OF STONE

Read Ezekiel 11:18-19 and 18:31-32.   *November 13*

We are supposed to give our hearts totally over to God. When we look in other directions for comfort or help, when we set our hearts on other things, when we let our desire for satisfaction roam, then our hearts become divided. We may give a little to God, but we reserve some for ourselves. We are not wholehearted.

To do this is devastating. No one else should have our hearts other than God Himself. We are meant to entrust our hearts to no person other than Jesus. He alone will treasure it and keep it alive in Him.

I have seen many young people mix up love with giving their hearts away. You can love someone as God loves them and still keep your heart. Love like this is good. However, when your heart is given over to another person, it can be wounded. Only with God is it entirely safe. He never wounds us, and He knows how to preserve our hearts. However, He needs the whole thing in order to do this task completely.

God told Ezekiel that the people's hearts had been divided. Because of this, their sins had hurt them. To keep from being hurt, they had hardened their hearts. Sin ultimately had betrayed them, and their hearts had become like stone.

What a sad commentary! God says that He can take a hardened heart and make it new. He can change a stony heart into one of flesh—alive, soft, beating again—open to His love. Won't you let Him do that today if you need it?

I'll never forget a wonderful symbol of God's love to me. My leadership tasks had been particularly costly and burdensome for a few months. I took a trip to minister and preach in another state, but God ministered there in a special way to me as well. It was a wonderful and refreshing time in every respect. The trip home took me over the Rocky Mountains, and as I looked out of the plane window, I saw something amazing. I could hardly believe my eyes, but it was there: A perfect heart out of snow on top of one of the snow-capped mountain peaks. Tears welled up in my eyes as I remembered how much God loved me. He really does deserve the entirety of our hearts in return.

OFF BALANCE

Read II Samuel 1:17-19. (Read II Samuel 1:1-17
also for context if you have a chance.)   *November 14*

It was one of the most embarrassing moments of my life. There I was in a very fancy restaurant for a business meeting where we were entertaining out-of-town guests. Furthermore, I was the only woman at a table of five men—all sophisticated and brilliant. I was dressed up in heels and my best attire, trying to listen and contribute with a certain amount of clarity and astuteness.

The waitress was beginning to serve the salads when I saw it. My purse was down by my chair there at the end of the table. I had set it on top of my portfolio and tucked it away, but the purse strap trailed out into the aisle.

"That nice waitress is traipsing around with such a big tray of salads," I thought to myself, "and she could so easily hook her foot in my purse handle and go sailing." I bent down to slide the purse further under my chair to avoid a potential catastrophe for the poor girl. However, it turned out I became the "poor girl."

You see, the big chairs we were sitting in had arm rests, rather high ones at that. As I bent over, my armpit hit the arm rest, forcing me to lean over even further to reach the purse on the floor.

You guessed it. Everything went off-balance, and I ended up tipping over onto the floor right along with the chair. I told you it was embarrassing! Nice restaurant. Elegant place. Sophisticated business meeting.

My boss had turned around for just a moment to catch the attention of the waitress, so he missed the spill. When he turned back, I had quickly stood up at the end of the table, and he was trying to comprehend the scenario. It was pretty funny, really. I just started to laugh. How else does one recoup?! ...And my colleagues have never let me forget it, either, I can assure you.

However, there is a lesson in all this. When we get off-balance in our lives, we can fall. Consider this, and then evaluate your own life. It's serious, you know, because an unbalanced life can bring even more embarrassing results. Look at what it says in II Samuel about Saul. "How the mighty have fallen" (verse 19).

IN THE EYES OF THE LORD

Read I Kings 11:4-11.   *November 15*

Following God part of the way is not sufficient. God asks that we do it completely. In today's verses, Scripture tells us that Solomon "did not follow the Lord completely, as David his father had done." It's described as a matter of the heart again.

Solomon's heart had turned to other gods, and evil took over. Matthew 15:19 states that "out of the heart come evil thoughts, murder, adultery, sexual immorality, theft, false testimony, slander." It is apparent that when our hearts are turned away from the Lord, then the heart itself becomes a source of evil.

What is evil? It is anything different from the holiness of God Himself. Verse 6 states that "Solomon did evil in the eyes of the Lord." Evil needs to be viewed from God's vantage point, because what really matters is what He sees as evil. We may feel good about what we're doing; however, this is not really the point. Throughout the scriptures, there are numerous instances of man doing what was "right in his own eyes." This juxtaposition of viewpoints is a poignant one. The issue is not what we consider good, but rather what He perceives as right. The only way to determine the difference is to get to know God and His views.

Verse 9 tells us that God had appeared to Solomon twice. What an experience that would be for any of us. However, we cannot live only on experiences. We should not become casual with God, resting upon our past. Even seeing God twice was not enough to keep Solomon on the right track, nor was the great amount of wisdom that he was given. Solomon did not continue to grow in the Lord, to get to know Him, to stay attached in relationship with Him. As a result, Solomon lost track of God Himself and of how He viewed matters.

Listening a great deal to other people can get us into trouble. Now, of course, it's generally good to ask advice and receive counsel, but other people's viewpoints are not necessarily God's viewpoint. Solomon listened to his wives, and they didn't see things correctly. Worshiping other gods, they ultimately influenced Solomon's perspective.

If we see from our own viewpoint, our sense of perspective will certainly be off. This is serious, because perspective is needed or we can lose balance. We can fall because we're not seeing things correctly. Examine your own life from His perspective right now. Are you doing what's right in your own eyes or in God's?

ON HIS HAND

Read Isaiah 49:13-16.   *November 16*

The rest of the group was obviously not in the habit of going to church. They found out I was a committed Christian, and one remarked that he would have to clean up his language. Why does that always seem to be the first reaction? It's the condition of the heart that grieves me, more than what emanates from it.

One of the ladies in the group mentioned that several weeks earlier she had been in a situation where she was asked to bless the food. She laughed about being the person who was sought out for such a thing since she wasn't used to doing so.

"In fact," she said, "God was probably quite puzzled. He undoubtedly thought, 'Now who is that lady speaking to me? ...Eunice who?'"

Everybody laughed, but it made me think. God promises His people that He will never leave us or forsake us. In Psalm 139:17-18, God's thoughts toward David were said to be vast. David realized that if he "were to count them they would outnumber the grains of sand." So many tiny little grains of sand....and God thinks about us more than that!

Furthermore, in today's scripture verse, we are told that God will not forget us, that it would be as unnatural as a mother forgetting her baby if He did. But even if that were possible, God would never forget us. He has us inscribed on the palm of His hand. That's the place a teenager might write a phone number he doesn't want to forget. He'd be bound to see it there and not forget that he's supposed to call. God will remember, too. He knows us. He doesn't forget to think about us in numerous ways. How comforting this is today. In an increasingly impersonal world, we have an exceedingly personal God.

THE WAKE UP CALL

Read Matthew 25:1-13.   *November 17*

I hadn't gone to sleep until 2 a.m., busy finishing a project. The night before it had been around the same time. Don't feel sorry for me; I'm a night person. It's my best time to work and create, so I love it.

However, I wasn't happy at all when the phone in my hotel room rang exceptionally early that next morning. It was a wake up call that I hadn't ordered. It did the job all right; it woke me up. But I didn't need to get up that early, and I lay there, aching and sullen, not able to go back to sleep.

God sometimes gives wake up calls and probably finds the same results: tired, sleepy, unhappy people who don't want to be awakened right then. It's so tempting to go about in the lethargy of our ways, basically settled and coddled in comfort. However, whether we like it or not, God is in the business of trying to wake us up to the world around us. It needs to happen!

---The world is getting worse. Wake up!

---People are crying out in pain. Wake up!

---Spiritual darkness is pervading the land. Wake up!

---People are headed for hell. Wake up!

---Jesus is coming soon. Wake up!

---Sin is still sin. Wake up!

400

---Have you talked to God today? Wake up!

---God still hates immorality. Wake up!

---People are spiritually thirsty. Wake up!

---God wants people who will stand in the gap. Wake up!

---Satan is stalking around, seeking whom he may devour. Wake up!

---God desires intercessors. Wake up!

---The *Bible* still speaks truth to people today. Wake up!

---Do you have a supply of oil for your lamp? Wake up!

Get prepared. Shake off sleep. Forget the aches and pains. Fix your attitude. Repair your relationships. Jesus is coming again!

Lazy, sleepy leaders will let their followers lounge around. There are grave issues, and it's a serious time, so we'd better get a move on.

THE HAPPINESS OF MAN

Read Psalm 10:5-6.   *November 18*

Though happiness is doubtless desirable to all of us, it should never be our main goal. If it is, then it becomes elusive. Happiness should come as a by-product of days lived out for God. It ought to peek out and surprise us.

I recall an interesting conversation with an esteemed veteran missionary. There were many people at the table, but he had zeroed in on me. It seemed that he could sense the burden of my spirit, and I could feel his compassion toward me. Tired and stressed that day, I felt weary to the bone. Although I hadn't spoken about it, I knew he didn't need lots of explanation. The fact that he looked at me and gently conversed was enough to know that he cared.

We talked of many spiritual things, and then, toward the end of the meal, he looked me in the eye and asked me, "Are you happy?" I was surprised at the straightforwardness of the question.

"No," I replied, "I'm not happy. However, that's all right because it's not a main goal of mine."

He raised his eyebrow and smiled a little. Then he nodded slightly and looked down. When he faced me again, the smile remained, and he was silent for a time. Nothing needed to be discussed, really. We both knew that what I said was the bottom line.

We continued in our conversation, talking about many topics, but we were both moved because we had looked into the length and depth of each other's commitment.

If happiness is a personal goal, it can lead an individual astray. We were not placed on earth for self-fulfillment or a problem-free life. Psalm 10:6 talks about the man who says, "Nothing will shake me; I'll always be happy and never have trouble." This is impossible. Life doesn't work this way. Trouble will come, and happiness is a tenuous emotion. A person can think they've found it, only to have it vanish very quickly.

Our purpose in life extends beyond ourselves and the elusive search for happiness. We are here to please and serve God. Happiness may be a result of this, but it is never to be sought for itself.

MAKE GOD HAPPY

Read II Corinthians 5:9-10 and
Ephesians 5:8-10. *November 19*

The charge for the committee meeting was to design a plan that incorporated a fresh approach to ministry in the city. We had brainstormed and shared lots of ideas. Which ones should we select and why?

In the midst of this conversation, someone said, "It would

probably make God happy if we focused on evangelism."

"Well, then," I said, "let's make God happy. After all, shouldn't that be our priority?"

Everyone thought for a minute, and we all agreed that, of course, that was true. "Make God happy," someone mused. "What a concept!" We began to sort out our options with this gauge in hand, and the discussion was fascinating.

Ephesians 5:10 admonishes us to "find out what pleases the Lord." This is truly a discovery process. As we come to know Him, it ought to become increasingly clear exactly what it is that brings Him pleasure.

Too often, our first thoughts are for our own desire. We are tempted to make decisions based upon what we think will be best for us, what will make us happy. How easy it is to fall into the trap of measuring our choices by our own level of pleasure rather than God's. The danger is that what pleases us may not please God at all.

Paul's conviction that this was important is expressed in II Corinthians 5:9 when he says, "So we make it our goal to please Him, whether we are at home in the body or away from it." Our goal—what we work for all of the time—should be to make God glad, both here on earth and finally in heaven.

Paul reminds us that someday we will all appear before the judgment seat of Christ. Then we will receive what is due us "for the things done while in the body, whether good or bad." When that moment arrives, we are going to wish that everything we ever attempted to do here on earth had been done to please God. That would be good!

Do you make God happy? Is that your goal?

LAGNIAPPE

A lagniappe (lan-yap') is a little something extra. While you are at a party that is already most enjoyable, the host or hostess may unexpectedly add something else: a party favor, a little gift wrapped up at each dinner plate, or small prizes hung by ribbons on the Christmas tree. Lagniappes like that are such fun! You may find one in a mail order when you pop open the box, and there, snuggled in a corner, is a little something you did not expect. Or it might be a free sample placed in the bag along with your purchase. Perhaps you open a present with which you are thrilled, and as you pull it out and examine it, you find another little present has been tucked away inside.

God Himself likes the concept of lagniappes. He gives us a blessing, and then He pours out even more. The Lord habitually gives out in abundance, throwing in a little extra for good measure. He did this with so many people mentioned throughout scripture such as the widow at Zarephath, the blind man healed by Jesus, and the apostle Paul himself.

In each of these cases, God performed a wonderful deed. Then He turned right around and did something else that was even more splendid The widow must have been so excited to get supplied with food that never ran out. What a miracle. Then to top it off, her son—who had stopped breathing—was brought back to her alive (I Kings 17).

The blind man must have been ecstatic to receive his sight, at last enabling him to observe what he had never seen before in his entire lifetime. But then to find salvation and to know the Messiah, well, that couldn't be beat (John 9).

Paul must have been so amazed that God would save him, after he had so severely persecuted the church. Then the Lord went farther and made him a leader and an apostle. To think that God could use him that way after his kind of past.

God loves to heap on favors. He pours out so much on us that sometimes we barely even notice, taking it all for granted.

Let us be grateful for the many blessings God has given us. And then, let us be generous and throw in a little extra something in our dealings and ministry with other people. Lagniappes are wonderful.

FEELING BAD

Read Psalm 122:1.   *November 21*

The lady cutting my hair was intrigued by my profession and asked a lot of questions. Sometimes people change the topic when they find out what I do and won't pursue more information. This woman was different, however, and we had an interesting discussion about our spiritual journeys.

At one point she made a particularly poignant statement. "When I was young," she said, "I decided that the main purpose of church was to make you feel bad." What an interesting and sad viewpoint, but I can see how it can happen.

Of course, the opposite of this should not necessarily be true either. The purpose of church is not simply to make us feel good. We are not meant to get our ears tickled. The false prophets in the Old Testament issued prophesies that proclaimed what the leaders and the people wanted to hear. It might have made them feel great, but it was a false front.

Thankfully God did not institute the church so we would feel miserable all of the time either. His Spirit may well convict us, but He always shows us a way out. He corrects us, challenges us, changes us, and tells us what we need to do to get matters right.

Satan is the one who accuses and shames. He points a finger at us and makes us feel terrible about ourselves. We see no way out, and we build a wall of division between ourselves and God.

The Lord is in the business of tearing down walls and relating

405

to us. He's kind enough to show us where we need to change, even if it doesn't make us feel too good for a little while. He wants us to see how negative and destructive sin can be in our lives. This is primarily because He doesn't want us to get hurt by it.

If I had a friend who saw that I had cancer and furthermore could fix it, but he didn't tell me, I would not think that person was a very good friend.

God shows us our sin, and then takes the scalpel and carefully removes it.... specifically going after bad cells and leaving the good ones. Then God wraps His arms of love around us. Forgiving us, He ministers deeply into our lives and gives us hope. When this happens at church, it is so good!

THE SUIT OF ARMOR

Read Ephesians 4:20-25. *November 22*

Some people have a difficult time being open and vulnerable. They have been stung so many times that they have built an impenetrable fortress around themselves. With this protection they hope to maintain their inner beings in a certain amount of equilibrium. Putting on a false front, they hide their true selves behind a wall where no one can really find them.

Having defenses may feel safe to the leader, but they are a formidable barrier to truthful communication and problem-solving. Unfortunately, there are leaders who have withdrawn into defensiveness as a permanent part of their personalities.

Seeing this always reminds me of someone in a suit of armor. The person is protected and safe inside. Peering out from beneath the visor on his helmet, he can see others; however, people have a difficult time seeing him. His true feelings cannot be discerned, and real expressions and reactions cannot be observed.

Perhaps this armor-cover feels good for a while. However, sooner or later the armor becomes heavy and hot. It creaks and becomes rusty. It's hard to get comfortable inside; freedom is hampered and moving around becomes laborious. Worst of all, these people cannot be touched, hugged, or even receive a pat on the back.

I always feel sorry for those leaders who have lived so long in their armor that they hardly know what it is like to be without it. After a while, it is so frightening for them to come out that it becomes almost impossible. Walking into the open brings a vulnerability that many just can't handle.

Certainly it is understandable, with all the burdens and pain of leadership, to try to protect oneself from wounds. That is reasonable when events are life-threatening. However, to do this on a regular basis as a lifestyle is a tragedy that leaders should avoid at all costs. That armor is far too constricting! It is personally uncomfortable, and it hinders healthy relationships. Come on, friend. Why don't you take it off?

LAY DOWN YOUR LIFE FOR A FRIEND
Read John 15:9-17 and Romans 5:6-8.　　　　　*November 23*

I once knew a man who thought he had many friends. In one way, he did. Some people cared for him, and they would listen and try to help whenever they could. He talked a great deal, sharing his own viewpoints, concerns and ideas. He considered it important that people knew what he was thinking.

The difficulty, however, was that the sharing went only one-way. He knew how to let others befriend him, but he did not quite know how to reciprocate. He was willing to be vulnerable, mainly because he had come to value the additional understanding that others could contribute through their input. Furthermore, he needed the ministry and spiritual insight that others provided. It was sad that he found it so difficult to return friendship.

Seeing this truth would have been difficult for him. He asked about certain areas of a person's life and tried to show concern in crisis. However, the answers to his questions needed to be very short and within the area of communication he had chosen. He wasn't interested in anything too deep or complicated. When people shared their pain and the real dilemma of their struggles, it made him uncomfortable. The conversation soon moved to something else or back to himself and was dismissed with a platitude.

I felt sorry for him, really, since he didn't even realize what he was missing. People who tried to help him couldn't get very far since he was comfortable right where he was. It is difficult to be a friend with someone like this.

Actually, we are much like this ourselves in our relationship with Jesus. We expect Him to listen to us, but do we listen to Him? We enjoy having Him minister to us, but do we care about His burdens? We want Him to provide for us and to show He cares, and yet how often do we demonstrate this in return? How does Jesus manage to maintain such one-sided relationships?

Jesus Himself said that He was our friend, so much so that He even laid down His life for us. "While we were still sinners, Christ died for us" (Romans 5:8). He reached out to us in the midst of our selfishness, even when we didn't care or love Him. If He could do that for us, surely we can continue to befriend and keep ministering to people like the one described here. Isn't that part of what it means to "lay down your life for a friend"? It's a profoundly Christian action, even when it isn't reciprocated.

THE SQUIRREL OF HESITANCY

Read I Kings 18:21.   *November 24*

Driving through the isolated region was like a north woods safari. We had seen a porcupine, a raccoon, numerous deer

408

including a cavorting fawn, a red fox, and a huge turtle. However, it was the squirrel that taught me a lesson.

He had run onto the two-lane highway ahead of our car and then heard us coming. First, he darted to the left, then he started toward the right, and finally back to the left again. By this time, we were on top of him.

I held my breath. What would he choose to do? If the squirrel stayed still, the car might glide right over the top of him, and he would be safe; but if he moved now, it would unquestionably mean death.

There are certain times to move, and hesitation can mean that it is forever too late. Indecision can be deadly for a leader! While we waver, life keeps moving, and events can easily crush us. But it's difficult to decide sometimes. This way? No, it seems too dangerous. That way? Not a good idea either. We see possible negative consequences in all directions. What do we do? We dart here and there just like that squirrel.

This hesitancy can be a problem when it comes to our relationship with God. Elijah saw it in the people. "How long will you waver between two opinions? If the Lord is God, follow him; but if Baal is God, follow him." Will we go God's way or not?

Sometimes, God will show us a direction that is costly if we choose it. Perhaps the decision will be unpopular or likely to be misunderstood. Maybe it is risky and fraught with hazards, but when God shows us a path to take, we need to move out.

Unfortunately Satan's way often appears to be better, easier, safer, more logical. If we hover between the two choices, though, it could cost us our very lives. Stop wavering and commit!

SLOTHFULNESS

Since true leadership is usually the result of much hard work, few people would consider such trailblazers to be characterized by slothfulness. Leaders simply have to expend a lot of energy to keep a system running smoothly.

When we consider the things of God, however, this heightened level of work can create spiritual slothfulness. It is easy to get so busy that we actually don't have time for the Lord. There can be a sense of laziness in our relationship with God, especially when we are actively engaged in so many other activities and with so many other friends.

The trait of being slothful is evidenced by a delay or sluggishness. How often have you been slow in responding to the Lord? Do you ever feel that He is drawing you to spend time with Him, but you hold back, putting Him off for a while? Do you obey Him immediately or do you hesitate, waiting for Him to get insistent or wishing He would change His mind? If our employees treated us the way we sometimes treat God, we would be quite peeved.

God loves to have us *press in* to know Him. Why then, when it comes to spiritual things, are we so often disinclined to exert ourselves? It is hard work to pray and intercede. Spending time on our relationship with God means we have to move out of our spiritual inertia and draw close to the Lord. He loves to see us throw off our lassitude, exert ourselves, and exercise spiritually.

In leadership we are always so busy expending energy for regular work that we get tired. We collapse at the end of the day, and indolence sets in. But this is a great danger for us. Before we know it, we are actually demonstrating laziness in the most important area of our lives.

On a recent trip to Costa Rica I had an opportunity to head into the jungle and see sloths hanging from trees. They're interesting to watch. The torpor! However, we can't afford to languish like that. Let's not just "hang around" when it comes to spiritual things. God needs us to be spiritually energized leaders.

THE MERCEDES EMBLEM

Read Matthew 23:1-11 (and also
Matthew 6:1-8 if you'd like).   *November 26*

My husband was chuckling and trying to get my attention. "Look at that!" he tugged on my hand. I followed his outstretched arm past his pointing finger and squeezed my eyebrows together. Why would he want me to look at an beaten up, very plain, faded red car?

Then I spied it and joined in the laugh. A large Mercedes emblem was stuck to the grill of that ordinary car. We both understood the dissonance of that emblem, and the thought tagged along with me into the day.

Just as the emblem did not turn the old, red car into a quality one, so emblems in our lives will not make real changes. The religious leaders of Jesus' day tried this approach, attempting to demonstrate the quality of their religion by making a show of their giving, their praying, and their legalistic habits. They dressed in special ways and enjoyed the superiority of being recognized. However, it is never the external emblem that counts. That which really matters is what resides on the inside of a person.

Even today, leaders can fall into the same trap. I've observed it in others and know the tendency for myself. How tempting it is to spruce up what is on the outside. A person can easily counterfeit many things such as 1) accomplishments (I have known of two people who faked a complete professional profile including a Ph.D.), 2) adventure (Another person I knew kept talking about being a calming influence with gangs and assisting the police, but he made up all of the exciting stories), and 3)

411

wealth (Rent a limo and purchase one set of great duds). Furthermore, I've watched leaders fake calm, faith, their relationship with God, assurance and enthusiasm. The list could go on.

We need to be who we are, to be real, and to trust God to use us in spite of our inadequacies. He makes up the difference in whatever we lack, and it will be exactly what we need for that moment. We don't need to be a counterfeit—ever! Who are you really—without the emblems?

MISTAKES

Read Romans 8:28-34. *November 27*

Some people live in constant fear of making a mistake. Their anxiety keeps them from trying new tasks. It inhibits their risk-taking, stunts their growth, and limits their opportunities to learn. For many of us, making a mistake is a horrible thing. Perhaps, that's because of our perfectionist tendencies. We hate the thought of failing.

What is really so awful about mistakes, however? Everybody makes them. By admitting to this fact, we can be more real as leaders, become more approachable, learn from our errors, and work together on changes. Being willing to identify mistakes can open up an environment conducive to problem-solving, a valuable commodity at this time in history.

As leaders, we must be able to admit to our own weaknesses, shortcomings, errors, and sin. If we are unable to do this, it readily leads to a lack of patience and generosity with others, creating a critical spirit. Eventually, we have to deal with great inner tensions caused by our impossible expectations. But we need not hide behind a cloak of perfection in order to be a good leader.

Even when we can humble ourselves and admit to our

mistakes, another roadblock to openness looms before us. We may be afraid of failing—not only ourselves and others—but God as well. I remember feeling abject and despondent over a mistake I made, thinking that it affected the Lord and His reputation. However, the Spirit so kindly whispered to my heart, "Don't worry so much. Don't you know that the Lord is bigger than your mistakes?"

How freeing it is to remember this! Although we don't want to fail, it is likely to happen. We will do something wrong in the future; you can count on it. However, the God of the universe is there to love us and forgive us. He heaps grace upon us, picking us up, brushing us off, and setting us on our feet again. Then He takes the worst circumstances and somehow turns them around for good. How does He do that?

RISKY

Read Acts 23:11 and II Corinthians 11:23-25.   November 28

Paul always appeared to be walking the tightrope of risk. He was not afraid to move into uncharted territory, taking the gospel message to far-off places where people had not yet heard the good news. In the course of journeying miles to accomplish what God desired, Paul had to endure many hazards.

He was beaten, stoned, shipwrecked, and thrown into prison. There were attempts on Paul's life. In the city and in the country, on the rivers and on the sea, he was in danger from mobs, bandits, Jews and Gentiles. At different times he was starving, thirsty, cold, naked, and sleepless.

In the midst of all this, it would have been only reasonable for Paul to conclude that circumstances were far too difficult, way too dangerous, and exceedingly risky. Why walk on the edge constantly? No one would blame him for taking it easy and playing it safe for a while—well, if it weren't for those people who

413

would not have been saved if he hadn't continued. Perhaps they'd have something to say to him later at the judgement seat of God.

As perilous and uncertain as the situation was, scripture tells us that "the Lord stood near Paul and said, 'Take courage! As you have testified about me in Jerusalem, so you must also testify in Rome.'" God encouraged Paul to give up his security for the sake of the Kingdom of God.

One of the valuable traits of a good visionary is being able to take risks. Great feats can be accomplished when people have the courage to step out of their safety zones.

Are you willing to risk anything and everything for the sake of the Kingdom? Will you tolerate hardship so you can march into a danger zone and take that new territory for the Lord? Or are you inclined to shrink back and find an old, familiar path rather than proceed on the new way that God has provided?

We need bold, courageous leaders who will step forth and risk everything for the sake of the Lord. Are you one of these? Will you be?

UNCHARTED TERRITORY

Read Psalm 37:23-24.   *November 29*

How comforting it is to know that when God delights in our way, He will make our steps firm. We can walk along the precipice and discover where to plant our feet. As we tread on new terrain, God will establish our steps.

The leader so often finds himself in uncharted territory. He is the first to have to mark the way for others. This can be exhilarating, but there are also times when this can almost strike terror to the heart. What will we find? Do we have enough strength to cope with these unforeseen circumstances? There might not even be time to think or plan a course of action, when suddenly we need to deal with an impending danger. It might even mean the safety of the rest of the group, so responsibility weighs heavily.

The good news in today's verses, however, is that God will be with us, helping us to strike the path. Even if we should fall, we will not be hurled headlong, dashing ourselves against the rocks below. We will be safe.

I remember watching a little two-year-old girl as she walked and played with her father after a rain. Her blond pig- tails shone in the sun, swinging back and forth as she joyfully hopped over mud puddles. Her pixie nose crinkled in delight above a bright smile, and her blue eyes danced with glee. She was skirting around those puddles as though there wasn't anything to it at all.

Why? Because her tall father was holding her hand. He was strong and could help her deftly maneuver through the obstacle course. He swung her here and there, steadying her.

Psalm 37:24 says, "When he falls, he shall not be hurled headlong, because the Lord is the One who holds his hand" (NAS). If the girl had her small fingers wrapped around her daddy's, she might not have been able to hang on. However, her dad was the one who held on to her. His big, strong hand grasped hers tightly, and even when she stumbled in the slightest way, he merely swung her to safety. She really couldn't be pulled away from his grasp.

What a picture of protection: A God who holds our hand!

RUBBISH

Read Philippians 3:3-9.   *November 30*

The man perished prematurely in his prime in a tragic auto accident. His friends considered the death from a spiritual vantage point and found no answer. After all, he had been in charge of the entire effort to move into some uncharted Muslim territory with the gospel message. He was effective, great progress was being made, and Satan was angry. Now this. Why? Some questions are not easily answered this side of eternity.

I knew his son quite well. Many members of the family were in ministry, serving the Lord in various capacities. The family was not prepared for the suddenness of this tragedy, and it all took some time to sink in.

A few weeks after the funeral, the family was sorting out the man's office. It was a tough chore because of the memories that naturally come flooding in during times such as these. He had been a productive person, and so his office was packed. They had worked at the clean-up job for quite some time and were nearing the end at last. One of the family members arrived at the last file in the bottom drawer of the big desk.

"Look at this!" he exclaimed. "This is really odd. Here's a file marked 'RUBBISH.' Why didn't he just throw away his junk?" Everyone gathered around.

The file lay open, and the family members stared. Tucked inside were amazing contents. Here was each degree the brilliant man had received. Included was every award he had been given, and there were many. Also filed were numerous letters of commendation and appreciation. It was what most people would consider as the best accomplishments of their lives—all marked "RUBBISH."

This is also the heart of Paul's message. He, too, had given up everything to serve Christ. What man had considered important, Paul had counted as trash, dung, rubbish. These things were nothing to him when contrasted with knowing Jesus Christ. He couldn't earn anything of value in this world, because Jesus had given him everything that was important. Given, not earned.

DECEMBER

THE MISSION RESTAURANT

Read Hebrews 5:11-14
(and 6:1-12 if you would like).   *December 1*

For several decades it was a thriving congregation, but recently there had been signs of decline. One year the sanctuary finally stood empty with the church sign taken down. We didn't know the reason for the decline since we visited only once a year on vacation and couldn't follow the local turn of events.

The next year the "Mission Restaurant" had established itself in the former church building. It was always busy now, but we couldn't bring ourselves to try the food there for several years. I felt badly that the church had disappeared.

However, in the restaurant's third year we again noted the crowds and decided to give it a try. "Must be good food," we muttered. "And after all, we can't change it back to a church."

Well, the food was delicious, it's true. However, the decor moved me to sullenness. The pews of the old church were used as seats for the restaurant's tables. Too bad they couldn't have been as filled with people when it was a church, I mused. The stained glass windows still glowed with a beauty that was originally intended to lead people's thoughts toward God.

Perhaps the spiritual food served up in this place when it was a church had not been as tasty. Maybe the pastor(s) hadn't provided meat. Were the messages preached from the pulpit seasoned properly and was the church itself being salt to the community? Did people find God, repent, and get changed?

As we walked out of the restaurant at the end of the meal, my eye caught the old altar moved up against a wall. On it sat numerous gooey and tempting desserts, beautifully arranged. But altars are for sacrifices—for blood and guts—not a pretty sight. We need to stay true to the real mission!

DEEPER THAN PAINT
Read Matthew 23:27-28.   *December 2*

A person's integrity needs to reach deeper than paint. So do his righteousness...his spirituality...and his morality.

Almost anything can look better with several coats of fresh paint. But it won't stay that way long if the old chipped paint and dirt are not sanded off first. Likewise, God expects us to be cleaned up. He is not happy with a thin veneer covering us over and giving the appearance we are something that we are not.

This is the picture of true hypocrisy. Jesus was not pleased with the religious leaders who acted this way, and He described them in less than complimentary terms—as whitewashed tombs. He pointed out that although these tombs looked beautiful on the outside, we could find something else entirely on the inside. The interiors were putrid, holding dead men's bones and rotting flesh. Not a pretty sight...or odor!

Whitewash is an interesting substance. It is even shorter-lived than paint, and one has to keep whitewashing a thing to maintain its appearance. This effort would be much better applied toward cleaning up what's inside.

As leaders, it behooves us to do some regular deep clean-up jobs. We need to allow ourselves to be convicted. We should not be afraid to have tears of repentance. We also need to kneel at altars and offer ourselves afresh to God. Our rotting flesh must be removed and our infected wounds reopened. The chips and scars of our lives need to be sanded smooth. The dirt should be cleaned away, and our sins washed by the blood.

Indeed, this is much harder work than whitewashing. It takes time and attention in the presence of God to do such an in-depth cleaning job. But we must do it or we will appear one way to people, while inside we are something else entirely. This is pure tragedy and true hypocrisy. It is certain death.

No whitewashing now.... It's what's inside that counts.

THE DEAD BRANCH

Read John 15:1-8.   *December 3*

The big plant was dying. At least that's what it looked like to me. I had enjoyed that plant for years, twice having successfully moved it across the country. Then it had thrived for another decade here, and so the thought of losing it was sad.

As I studied the situation more closely, I found dead leaves scattered throughout the vine-type plant that twisted and turned around itself. Most of the plant, however, still appeared green and in good health. Carefully, I began to strip off the dead leaves and realized that they were mostly along one branch. As I tugged at that particular offshoot, it gave way. I pulled more and then still more, hauling out a long, winding stem that ended up accounting for nearly all of the dead leaves scattered throughout the plant. The very end of that branch had not even been attached to anything—not to the main vine and not rooted into the ground. It was not connected anywhere!

In John 15, Jesus warned about this. He said it was imperative that the branches stay attached to the vine. "Remain in me, and I will remain in you," He exhorted. "No branch can bear fruit by itself; it must remain in the vine. Neither can you bear fruit unless you remain in me" (verse 4).

Even if we start by being attached, it is not enough. We must remain there, maintaining the connection to Him. No matter how hard we try, grit out teeth, and exert ourselves, it is impossible to

419

produce fruit unless we do remain in Him. This means staying joined completely, not simply by a few sinews. Only in this way can we take in all the nourishment that we need to stay alive. The production of fruit will be a natural by-product of remaining in the vine, of staying attached to Jesus.

The Lord's warning is stern in verse 6. "If anyone does not remain in me, he is like a branch that is thrown away and withers; such branches are picked up, thrown into the fire and burned." That's what I did with that unattached branch in my plant; I just threw it out. Hopefully, God will never have to do that with us.

PRUNING

Read John 15:2.   *December 4*

I hate to prune; it just seems so illogical. Here we have a healthy plant that has blossomed and is doing well. It's big and has grown quite full. Prune it? What a waste of good foliage.

The branches, however, have extended away from the vine. It takes more time and effort for the plant to get the nutrients out to the extremities of its branches. This results in less life-blood going into the production of fruit, flowers, and leaves.

So get those scissors out and snip away. Give that plant a hair cut—even a butch. Cut it way back. It looks dreadful for a time, but it will grow again, becoming fuller, more beautiful, and far more productive.

God does this with us as well. In John 15:2, Jesus said that "He cuts off every branch in Me that bears no fruit, while every branch that does bear fruit He prunes so it will be even more fruitful." I should submit more easily to the pruning process and not fight it so much. After all, the results are worth it.

When we go through the pruning procedure, however, it is easy to become angry. "Why," we groan, "since we remained in the vine and produced fruit, do we still have to endure this awful shearing?" It's not like we were one of those dead branches! Why must good growth be cut off—that which we worked hard to produce in days gone by? We are intimately attached, so the pruning hurts, cutting away what is still alive and connected. Ouch! What a painful operation to endure. It is tempting to get upset with God for such treatment, wondering if it even pays to stay attached in the first place.

After pruning, the skimpiness of what remains is embarrassing. We are reduced to practically nothing, and our beauty has been shorn off. Why would God do such a thing?

Just remember, ultimately He has a bigger plan. More fruit, more beauty, more fullness and wholeness. So prune away, God. Hey, that hurt! Not THAT!

THE PERFUME COUNTER

Read Matthew 7:21-23.   *December 5*

The line was snaking its way up and down the aisles, and I had stood in it a long time. The French-speaking Caribbean island of Martinique was so famous for its perfumes, however, and the prices and selection were so good, I knew it would be worth the wait.

At last it was my turn to step up to the counter. Just then, another tourist came up from the side. She had not been standing in line, but she acted as though she was used to getting her way. My eyes must have widened with incredulity; she was trying to purchase perfume from the clerk as if it were her turn! I decided to wait and see what the clerk would do.

After asking to see a certain perfume, the woman watched impatiently as the clerk simply gazed at her, not saying a word. "What's the matter with her?" the line crasher said to me with derision. "Can't she speak English?"

Just then, the clerk took a deep breath and with a slow

staccato in perfectly enunciated English, she quipped her reply. "Of course, I can speak English, madame...but you're going to haaave to wait your turn!" Then she turned her attention to me and said, "May I help you?"

"Oui!" I smiled without missing a beat and proceeded to give her my request in French. The clerk smiled back broadly and moved into that language, while the lady gawked for a few moments. Then she pivoted on her heel and marched off with a "Humph!" It was most fitting, and the clerk and I exchanged knowing glances and shook our heads in disbelief.

When it comes to heaven, it will not be possible for someone simply to demand a place. Even if the individual was wealthy here on earth, accustomed to power and getting his own way, this will not be the ticket for entry. Haughtiness will not open the door for anyone, nor will there be instant service upon demand.

The only way to get into heaven will be through the blood of Jesus Christ. To gain this privilege, we must humble ourselves, repent, and recognize our need of His grace. Even doing deeds in God's name will not exempt us from this basic step of salvation. It will not matter what we've done or who we were on earth. If we have not accepted Him, Jesus will look at us and say, "I never knew you. Away from me, you evil-doers!"

Have you gotten in line and done it correctly—God's way? Have you humbled yourself before Him and asked for forgiveness? It's the only way.

FAVORITISM

Read Romans 12:16 and James 2:1-7.   *December 6*

Log your time and be honest now. Exactly how many hours (or would that be minutes?) do you spend each week with poor people?

I work in an inner city area where I can walk from my car to the office and see a number of indigent and needy persons, many with a bottle in a brown paper bag. It's a reality check, and it's not so easy to remain merely theoretical about spreading God's love. Needs cry out from the cement of the city.

James gives very clear instructions about showing favoritism. He says not to do it! It's quite simple, really, and can't be skirted around or rationalized away.

As busy leaders, we must prioritize our time. However, when someone of lesser "significance" is told to wait or is brushed aside in favor of a wealthier person or one with a title, what are we, in fact, doing? Paul said this indicated pride and conceit. James said it was insulting and made us into "judges with evil thoughts."

As Christians, we ought to take notice of and be kind to those around us every day—a janitor, a cook, a secretarial assistant, a security guard, a waitress, a store clerk, or anyone in a support position. Each is serving in quiet and humble ways, often for minimum wage. And God infinitely values each and every one.

One evening after our college graduation ceremony, this truth hit me forcibly. I was standing around in my doctoral robes because students had requested pictures with me or were introducing me to their parents. It was such a fun and festive occasion, and I was enjoying myself immensely.

At one point, my eyes trailed off to a now-quiet and distant part of the auditorium. There was the man who heads up our housekeeping department, dressed in jeans. He was bending over, picking up trash and putting it into a big plastic bag. It touched me, and the next day I looked him up.

"Max," I said, "after graduation last night, I saw you working so hard while the rest of us were celebrating. I just wanted you to know how much I appreciate what you do around here. We keep going because of people like you." Were those tears I saw welling up in his eyes?

I decided right there and then to be more expressive in my

thanks to all kinds of persons who serve us every single day. Each one deserves to be noticed and appreciated. Favoritism? Yes, I'm guilty of it at times. *"Forgive me, and change me, Lord."*

DIFFERENCES
Read Galatians 3:26-29 and Colossians 3:9-15.   *December 7*

When we shut ourselves off from a certain type of person, it is our own loss. God intended that we gain balance from each other and learn from those who vary from us. For this reason, we need to listen, observe, and treasure different perspectives.

It has always amazed me how I can be treated differently, depending on whom I am with. I have been discriminated against when I am with persons not deemed "proper" for a particular establishment or situation. It has made me realize that not everyone values differences but rather reacts with disdain or fear. What richness they miss!

It should not matter whether a person is prosperous or poor, young or old, male or female, educated or not, black, red, brown, white or yellow. We should be open to what all people can show us. For example, I have had some very poor and uneducated people teach me the marvels of simplicity, appreciation for the basics, and humility. A wealthy person has taught me the enjoyment of quality. I also discovered he had needs, too; it's just that they were hidden behind a dark grey suit, polished shoes, and a fashionable tie.

Women can teach us to communicate and to be honest with our feelings. They can model nurturing and sensitivity to others. Men can demonstrate how to move through problems, bear up under a load, and take responsibility. The elderly have wisdom and experience which are greatly needed, and the young remind us to be creative and full of zest for life.

Cultural differences can make us rich by expanding our own

understanding and the limited perspective that has developed from our own heritage. Viewpoints, time frame, values, and ways of life can all be so drastically different, and how enjoyable it is to listen and learn how another individual sees it all.

When we encounter people different than ourselves, we have a choice. We might avoid them, just not seeming to notice. Perhaps we do not esteem them or count them important. Or perhaps we feel uncomfortable and don't know how to act or what to do. Maybe we are afraid that we'll make a mistake and look foolish.

But how enjoyable it can be to try to move through all these feelings and purposefully establish relationships. After getting through the awkward stage, the joys can greatly exceed our highest hopes.

I have heard it said that people living in the inner city are culturally deprived. However, the richness of cultural diversity that thrives in the city center allows these people to be much more aware of the habits, philosophy, food, and celebrations of various groups. Perhaps it is really the suburbanites who are culturally deprived.

Let's ALL of us grow in this area and try to understand each other. After all, in Jesus we are all one.

PRESUMPTION

Read I Corinthians 9:19-23.   *December 8*

A cardiologist I know well had an interesting time during the first several weeks in the foreign country to which he was assigned. He had come to live there for six months, working with other professionals and learning their techniques.

Don is culturally astute and a keen observer. He is also humble and not pushy. Therefore, during the first days of his stay, he didn't say much. In meetings, he stood up against a wall or in the back of the group. Only when he was invited did he sit down at the meeting table. He waited in every instance to be included or asked to voice his opinion.

During this time, Don had a perfect opportunity to gather information. He watched how everyone related to each other. He noted everyone's tendency to speak quietly and in low tones. This was true, also, in their restaurants and other public places. A multitude of data filtered through his thinking during those first days: How they solved problems. What they valued. Their carefulness and attention to detail. Their recognition of high quality and their level of expertise. He came to admire them and appreciate them, both professionally and personally.

A few weeks into his time with them, the head of the department took him aside. "Thanks for behaving the way you have," the doctor said to Don. "You see, just before you another visitor was here who did not act this way. He was arrogant, bold, loud, and demanding. It seems he always had something to explain and acted like he knew everything. When he saw we did things differently, he automatically assumed we were wrong, rather than to take it as an opportunity for mutual learning. He was so presumptuous!"

After that, Don was invited to participate in numerous surgical procedures and became an accepted member of that professional team during his visit. His opinions and knowledge were often solicited.

Surely, we are meant to fit in first with a group so that we might earn the right to be heard. We must show others that we value their differences. If we are insensitive, arrogant, brash and rude, why should anyone ever hear us?

I remember a compliment my husband and I received once. We were sitting at a large banquet table with people we did not know. The couple next to us was from Europe, and we enjoyed the opportunity of getting to know them. Finally, the man stopped and looked at us squarely. "You're from Europe, too, aren't you?" he asked. We smiled and shook our heads. "Well, then, you lived there for a while." Again we said no. "I can't believe it," he said. You're different from others we've met here."

Later, as my husband and I discussed that incident, we promised to try to continue "fitting in" gently, just as Paul did. It's the means by which we may win some!

APPRECIATION

Read Romans 12:9-10.   *December 9*

She blossomed like a tender, white trillium opening its bloom to the sunlight that dapples the woods. Her growth was so beautiful! When I first met the girl, I wondered what would become of her. She was shy, frightened, confused and shriveled inside from the wounds of life, and I wasn't sure just what it would take to guide her to wholeness. It could only be a work of God and of people who would love her.

Gradually, various ones began to regard her life. Some looked closely and saw seeds of talent. Others saw a sweet spirit. Many noticed her life of prayer and love for God. Then a wonderful creativity with children began to emerge in her, and her heart for the city was large. She cared.

As these and many other wonderful characteristics were coming alive and being tentatively tested in her life, some took notice. They smiled, patted her on the back, and gave her words of encouragement. More traits of high quality unfolded. Now she is serving the Lord in a full-time pastoral position, working with troubled children and teens in a tough inner city setting.

To note what is excellent in people and to tell them we recognize it can bring such healing. Simple appreciation can do wonders. When we provide positive comments, it fortifies those good traits and helps bring them into fruition. A little esteem can encourage, strengthen, provide faith and cheer, and unfurl the best in anybody.

Leadership is not provided simply to correct and give orders. It is a position meant to speak life and hope into peoples' hearts by taking notice of who they are and what they are becoming. Leaders should take time to thank others for their service and to call attention to their positive character traits.

Verses 9-10 tell us to "honor one another above ourselves" and to love one another. Let us show more appreciation to others. It can change lives!

BRUISED REEDS

Read Matthew 12:15-21.   *December 10*

When people are bruised and broken by their past, like the young lady we mentioned yesterday, there is a tendency for others to spurn them. Dealing with those who have emotional instability, wounded spirits, and great needs is certainly not an easy task. In fact, the temptation is to abandon the chore because it's simply too difficult.

"Why bother?" we might think. "That person will never come around anyway. There's too much they have to deal with, and wholeness seems too remote."

However, God never gives up on us. How glad I am of that. When we are broken, God does not despise us or send us away. He will not break off a broken and bruised reed out of frustration.

Rather, God pays attention to the places that are rent and binds them up. He seeks to heal and make us whole again. Ever so carefully He nourishes the tender shoot, watering it and keeping the weeds away until it grows to health and strength.

Another wonderful metaphor from these verses presents the idea that Jesus will not snuff out a smoldering wick. This reminds me of a story I once heard about a man lost on an island in a winter storm. Circumstances were such that his final hope was to use his one and only dry match to start a fire. Perhaps it would be seen by a villager from across the bay, and he would be rescued. Imagine with what care he struck the last match with those frozen fingers. Consider how careful he was to get the kindling he had prepared to catch fire. Think about how he held his breath as the first trails of smoke curled upward, the kindling finally catching fire. Picture how carefully he protected those first tentative flames. His very life was at stake!

Jesus considers our lives to be just that precious. He protects us, is cautious, and desires for all the world to see us catch fire for Him.

If our Lord is that painstaking, how much more careful should we be with the smoldering wicks in people around us. He desires for us as leaders to be tender and protective, caring and not harsh, loving and kind, and very careful with the lives of the people He has entrusted into our care. It is an exceptional responsibility, and we should have great caution that we don't arrogantly stomp on embers or inconsiderately break off a bruised reed.

THE '58 EDSEL

Read Psalm 40:5.   *December 11*

Many propitious events in life appear to be happenstance, but lots of those circumstances are simply too unusual to be attributed merely to chance. They are too perfect, too meaningful, and too well-timed.

I remember several that surprised me immensely. Once, I was out of town on a holiday. I had read till 2:30 a.m. the night before, which was late, even for a "night person" like me. However, I was into this book and relished the luxury of finishing it since I didn't have to be up early the next morning. The book *Saint Ben* was written by a friend of mine, John Fischer, and so I was particularly enjoying it.

The story revolved around a metaphor linking the life of the main character, Ben, to the fate of the '58 Edsel. The themes in the book spoke to me particularly since they pertained to various incidents that were occurring in my own life.

Therefore, imagine my surprise later that day when the story came alive. You see, I had never even seen a '58 Edsel, at least as far as I remember. Perhaps there had been one in a car museum someplace that I had visited, I don't know. The last spot I expected to see a '58 Edsel, though, was in real life right in the tiny village we were visiting.

My husband and I pulled into a gas station, and there it was. That automobile was actually being driven around and was in perfect working condition. I looked it all over carefully with a smile in my heart. I've never seen a '58 Edsel since!

Now what are the odds I would see that very car on the exact day I finished a book where it figured in such a prominent and meaningful way? Is that chance? Perhaps. I can't actually prove otherwise, I guess. But don't you think that God plans little surprises for us sometimes?

In today's verse David says, "Many, O Lord my God, are the wonders you have done. The things you planned for us no one can recount to you; were I to speak and tell of them, they would be too many to declare."

Someday we'll know for certain exactly how many "coincidences" were actually the hand of God. At that time, our eyes may be opened to far more than we ever noticed or considered possible.

Work cited: Fischer, John. *Saint Ben.* Minneapolis, MN: Bethany House Publishers, 1993.

CONTENTMENT

Read Philippians 4:11-13 and I Timothy 6:6.   *December 12*

Contentment comes easy for very few people. However, it seems to be a difficult attitude especially for leaders to develop. Perhaps it is because of our dreaming...or our inherent self-motivation...or our dissatisfaction with the status quo. Probably our yearning to see circumstances change and the desire to be a player in that process prohibit us from easily gaining this wonderful commodity we call contentment.

Commodity? Yes, I'd say so. There has to be an exchange in order to gain contentment. We have to give up our urge to control and manipulate events. We need to relinquish our dreams, our pounding perfectionism, and the short-fused demands. We must stop acting as if everything should go our own way. I have known of leaders who practically throw temper tantrums (adult ones, of course) if they do not get what they want.

This, of course, is all counterproductive to being contented. In the letter to the Philippians, Paul indicates that he has "learned to be content whatever the circumstances" (verse 11). This indicates that contentment is not a natural trait which simply flows from us. Instead, it is a learning process.

Paul had learned how to be content when he was well fed and had plenty of whatever he needed. But he didn't have to hold on to this. He could relinquish it all. Even when he did not get everything he desired, he still had learned to be content. God was with him, strengthening and helping him. It was enough for Paul.

If we do not come to the place where we can rest in Him and truly have peace and contentment in our lives, we will always be driven, dissatisfied, unhappy, and displeased. This is a sad commentary for any leader. Are you content? Right now, today?

THE RETURN

Read Genesis 28:10-22 and 35:1
(and 35:2-15 to get the full story).   *December 13*

In "Four Quartets," from a poem called "Little Gidding," T.S. Elliot penned some marvelous lines:

"We shall not cease from exploration
And the end of all our exploring
Will be to arrive where we started
And know the place for the first time" (145).

Jacob's dream took shape at Bethel. Here, God spoke and gave him many promises regarding his life. At this time, Jacob was not aware of the Lord's presence—of the fact that God was walking with him and guiding his life.

Jacob's reaction after his dream was to tell God that if He would be with him, allowing him to return home safely, then the Lord would be his God.

"Then"? What is this conditional acceptance of God as Lord? Jacob had an untried, impersonal relationship with God at this point and did not yet understand many things.

So he went out to explore life, just as the poem stated. Through these years, he ended up with wives and children. He also became wealthy because of God's unusual procreation of certain sheep and goats. During his exploration, Jacob wrestled with God and received his new name, Israel. He learned more about himself and about his God.

Finally, of all wonders, Israel was united in peace with his brother. This was certainly unusual, given the past hurts that this relationship entailed.

Through all the events of his life, Jacob had come to discover the reality of God. The Lord spoke to him now in different locations, even telling him (35:1) to go up to Bethel and settle there—the place where he had once experienced God's presence in such a dramatic way.

432

So Israel headed back to Bethel, the location where it all began, and a desire for holiness overcame him. Moving toward that place where he had first met God in such a special way, he prepared himself. This time he knew that God was there. The experience was so profound that "the terror of God fell upon the towns all around them so that no one pursued them."

Have you been exploring? Have you learned more about yourself and your God? If so, Bethel will look entirely different when you return! Why not go meet Him there?

Work cited: Eliot, T.S. *The Complete Poems and Plays 1909-1950.* "Little Gidding." New York: Harcourt, Brace and World, Inc., 1952.

MAY IT BE TO ME AS YOU HAVE SAID

Read Luke 1:26-38. *December 14*

Mary was an remarkable young woman. When the angel came to her, she would logically have had many concerns struggling for supremacy. She was engaged to be married; what would her fiancé think if she were to get pregnant? Would her parents understand? Society wasn't very forgiving on these accounts. What would it mean to her for the rest of her life? Would she always have a tainted reputation? Would her fiancé dump her and would no one else ever want to marry her?

Although the dynamics of how and what was going to happen must have been rather obtuse to her, even after the angel's explanation, she nonetheless willingly submitted herself to the Lord.

She made room for Jesus in her life right away, pushing down all of her own hopes and dreams. She set aside her personal plans for the future, including the man she loved. She welcomed Jesus right into her own life and let Him do with her whatever He chose.

So often we have our own agendas. Giving those up, when

God requires this of us, is not an easy task. To void the fullness of our own dreams and make ourselves empty and open to the tiny seed that God may plant in us.....this can be a frightening process.

Mary very simply said, "May it be to me as you have said." She didn't jump up and down and get excited. She didn't talk about it to everybody. She didn't cry over what she might lose. She didn't worry and fret. Rather, she let God have His way in her life, and she was at peace.

God is looking around for people today whom He can grow in, developing what He wishes. In the fullness of time, that will be delivered. Are you that kind of person?

LONG AWAITED

Read Luke 1:39-45.   *December 15*

Elizabeth had waited years for a baby. Special babies are often long awaited in the Bible stories. God had a particular timing for this baby she was carrying. As John the Baptist, he would be the forerunner of the Savior, announcing Him, getting ready the hearts of the people, preparing the way. John's lifework would be tied up with that of the Messiah. It seems that he sensed this very early on indeed.

When Mary comes to visit Elizabeth, she gives a simple greeting. John, even from his mother's womb, recognized the Savior to come. He danced, pounded, jumped, and gave a leap. *Whee! Hey, mom...guess who this is! Just guess!*

We would probably laugh together about this. "Hey, Mary, you just say *hi* and this baby is doing a loopty-loop!" But Elizabeth wasn't overwhelmed with humor, she was overtaken by the Spirit. Can you imagine how the Holy Spirit must have been oozing from Mary and the baby she was carrying? Elizabeth gets filled with the Spirit and proclaims some memorable words "in a loud voice." There are times when a person just can't help getting excited about what God is doing!

One of Elizabeth's revelations was about Mary: "Blessed is she who has believed that what the Lord has said to her will be accomplished." That seed she had made space for was developing. Mary had faith, and the long-awaited promise was being fulfilled. It would take some months, but soon the Messiah, the very Son of God, would be delivered into the world.

The fullness of time was about here. The Jewish nation had been waiting. Rome had built its roads, and civilizations had developed. God breathed into the life of a simple, young Jewish girl, and soon the most amazing event possible would occur. God was about to come in the form of a man. Hold your breath, everyone!

NO ROOM
Read Luke 2:7.   *December 16*

"....there was no room for them in the inn." It's a simple little statement in the scriptures, tacked right onto the end of the sentence explaining that God himself had been born and then placed in a feeding trough. There is no exposé and no complaint from Mary that is logged. I think I would have made enough of a mark in that vein to have merited recording if I had been the one who had been pregnant. It's bad enough not to have a hospital, but then to be alone in a strange town with no friends around and not even a bed? Yep, I definitely would have said enough that it would have gotten transcribed in there somewhere. However, Mary seems to have patiently and quietly endured...and brought the true Christmas into the world.

Christmas. The word holds Christ's own name. But many times we hardly have room for Him during the very holiday that was designed to celebrate His birth. I can understand how this could be with those who hardly know who He is. However, for

435

those of us who do, we need to be careful that the world's way of handling this holiday does not encroach on how we Christians should celebrate it.

One year I decided to fast Christmas...all the outward part of it, that is. I put up no decorations: no Christmas tree, no lights, no candles. I kept gift-giving to an easy minimum and wrapped the gifts simply. I didn't bake. I didn't participate much in the "programming" of the season.

Well, think about it. If we get so tied up in the "trappings" that we get consumed, aren't we squeezing Him out? Isn't that the same as relegating Him to a manger....because there is no room in the inn of our hearts? I don't want to be so busy that I can't show hospitality to the King of Kings and the Lord of Lords. That was a remarkably wonderful Christmas, and it has been a model and trend for me ever since. No room? Try fasting some things that don't count so you have room for the One who does.

BURDENED?

Read Matthew 11:27-30. *December 17*

The other day I woke up and the world might as well have been on my back. I was bothered by some situations, burdened for them, and the heaviness of it all was weighing me down like a massive rock.

At such times, it is not always easy to pull out from under the load. We know we should, and we may manage it for a time, but the weight can soon return, and we drag it through the day and even into bed at night. Sleep comes hard at such times, and we toss around the perplexities throughout the night.

Sometimes the load is personal. We are fearful for ourselves and our jobs, our reputations or our finances, our health or our fulfillment. It can be extremely difficult to sort out our motives, ambitions, and ego from the whole situation.

At other times, the weight is for our family—our relationship with our spouse or the rebellion of a child or our ability to provide or inability to "fix things."

In still other instances, the load is related to our leadership responsibilities. Our company or church is in financial straits. People may need to be laid off. Perhaps relationship problems are occurring, or there are power struggles.

What happens in such cases as these? What's next? Jesus clearly gives the answer in these verses. He simply says, "Come to Me." How often do we worry, fret, and stew rather than come to Jesus? How many times do we try to work it out, plan it through, and find solutions rather than come to Jesus? How can we be so slow to come? He promises to give us rest.

Rest certainly is there in Him, too! Quiet and peace as well. Whatever burdens there are with Him they become easy, and as we yoke ourselves together with Him and pull alongside, the burden is light.

The cost of following Jesus is high. He demands it all! But He is of such value that He is worth all of that and more. Once we throw in everything with Him, we find that He is right beside us. For though the cost of following Him is high, once we've paid it, the burden itself is easy. Won't you come?

LETTING GO

Read Colossians 3:8-14.   *December 18*

Forgiveness is nice theoretically but much more painful in reality. It is disturbing because we really do not want to give up our anger and frustration. When we have something against others who have hurt us, we can feel superior to them and almost enjoy wallowing in our self-pity.

Nonetheless, scripture tells us to forgive. It is mandated; it is not an option. We are to bear with each other and show compassion, patience, and gentleness.

I think of it as letting go. We let go of the past and its pain, choosing not to dwell in it. As I have struggled through this personally, I have been struck by how difficult this task truly is. It's hard to stop dwelling on something that has wounded us or has disappointed us deeply.

Actually, as I consider how Christ died for me in the midst of my own sin, it assists me in learning to be generous with others. I think of how ignorant I was of God and of how I have done so many things that wound Him, though I didn't even realize it at the time. Aren't people likewise growing and learning? If I want "space" given to me by God so I can change, surely I can extend that to others as well.

Additionally, I find that my expectations of others have often been the cause of the wound. I thought a person should be different or that she should treat me otherwise. Listen to those "shoulds." Perhaps we are causing much of our own pain by expecting more from people than they are able to give to us. In some ways, forgiveness isn't even the answer in these cases. Designing more realistic expectations is.

Sometimes we need to let go of anger we have toward God as well. Perhaps He didn't come through exactly when or how we expected. Our lack of understanding His choices may cause us to hold anger and bitterness, even against God. But perhaps we need to change our expectations of God as someone who does things our way. Instead we need to trust in the Sovereignty of a God who does all things well—whether we understand them or not.

We can even have expectations of ourselves that are too high. Therefore, we find it difficult to enjoy life and God. We have a need to be "just right," and if we're not, we fall into melancholy with a multitude of negative results. So why not let go, forgive, and put on love?

438

BOASTING

Braggarts are not particularly pleasant people. It seems they always have something to say about themselves and what they have done. Often the story has been embellished, and their place of importance has been exaggerated.

When the bragging is about an accomplishment that is projected for the future, however, it becomes even more sickening. This was the case of Ben-Hadad, king of Aram. In trying to intimidate Ahab, the king of Israel, Ben-Hadad not only said that he would take Ahab's goods and family, but he sought to humiliate King Ahab and stir up a scene. Ben-Hadad wanted to be on top, but he wanted everyone else to be aware of it too. If that meant putting down other people, small loss!

Ben-Hadad's bragging reached the point of claiming total annihilation for Ahab and his kingdom. However, Ahab did not quake with fear and give in to this boasting king. Rather, he put the entire episode into proportion with one great statement. "Tell him [Ben-Hadad]: One who puts on his armor should not boast like one who takes it off" (20:11).

Indeed, when we are beginning a job or initiating a new program, it is wisest to keep our mouths shut. Perhaps we have too much trust in our own abilities to accomplish anything we wish. Even is we have done well in the past, that doesn't mean that we can step into something new and pull it off better than anyone else who has gone before us. There are always surprising factors and challenging realities that we do not anticipate.

The premature brashness is both irritating and unnecessary to others. Wait and see. Time will tell. Try it first and see what it's really like, but don't brag before the time. Ben-Hadad discovered this the hard way.

As leaders, we need to remember that success isn't always as easy or simple as it looks from the other side. We have to learn about the God factor. Even if we fail, He can intervene, and then we need to brag on Him!

LENIENCY

Read I Kings 20:31-43.   *December 20*

Leniency is not always a godly trait. Ahab discovered this fact after it was too late. God again gave the Arameans into king Ahab's hand. However, he is lenient with the king of Aram, allowing him to go free merely on the basis of a treaty.

A prophet finds Ahab, asking him a question that requires Ahab to make a decision about a similar situation. It was staged in order to discover what was really in Ahab's heart.

By his answer, it is clear Ahab knew that the king of Aram should not have been set free. However, Ahab was compromising, probably wishing to win an ally and the good will of the enemy.

God was not pleased with what Ahab chose to do, and He said through the prophet, "You have set free a man I had determined should die. Therefore, it is your life for his life, your people for his people" (20:42).

It is serious when God asks us to take care of something that is the enemy in our lives, and we procrastinate and let it go. We rationalize that we'll get back to it. Or we like the results of keeping it around. When God calls upon us to completely rid ourselves of sin or a compromising situation, we must do it. If we don't, that sin will become our own death.

Unfortunately, even after being confronted, Ahab still would not change. He could have repented of what he had done when he allowed Ben-Hadad to get off Scot-free. Surely it was serious to allow this enemy free reign. However, instead of being willing to admit his error, Ahab became sullen and angry.

This nasty temperament holds when he can't get his own way

in the future, such as with Naboth's vineyard. Finally, though, when confronted again for his wrongdoing with Naboth, Ahab humbles himself and repents. As a result, God relents and postpones the negative ramifications.

Being lenient when it comes to sin and compromises in our lives is never satisfactory. We must follow God all the way.

VISTAS

Read Micah 4:1-2. *December 21*

My roots in Colorado produce memories of great vistas seen from mountain peaks. The views found from crag-lookouts in Rocky Mountain National Park are enough to steal both your breath and your balance. Straggly rivers meandering in deep valleys and crushed ice lakes sparkling their mountain melodies in the sunlight—these are never-to-be-forgotten sights.

Above the timberline, the rocky surface defies growth, but even here the world is alive against all odds. Tiny tundra flowers with stunning colors and intricate designs jab their way into the same sunshine that makes the rivers and lakes do their sparkle-dance.

We, too, need to enjoy all levels in our leadership holdings. Get down and study the tundra flower or we will miss an exquisite sight. There is extreme beauty in small places that other people might simply step on. So it is in our world. Don't miss it!

However, if we are only looking to the small places and worried only with the details, our myopia will produce blinders that hinder our sight.

Since they are unable to see the whole picture, myopic leaders are not as effective as they could be. They can't explain to those in the tundra-flower world why the air is so cold and the surface is so rocky. They are unable to assist with perspective, purpose, and vision.

We need to get high enough so we can see. ...Climb if we have to so we can report back to the others. Study the view and enjoy the perspective. How necessary it is to get the vista-view grasped in our minds. We can put all the pieces together better.
See—there's the road. It'll be winding down past those waterfalls but not before that steep section. Say, I guess it's that river that flows into those gorgeous waterfalls ultimately. Oh, and there are switchbacks in the road. That'll be important. It will only seem like we're not making progress, but we are. And that stunning lake, why it probably can't even be seen once we get past that one point there. However, it will still be sparkling, and I'll need to explain it. Oh, the view!

Have you seen any vistas in your leadership lately? If not, why is that? Could it be that you are myopic right now? Because if you are, you will miss a great deal of what God wants to reveal about your work. God calls you to His mountain for the view of a lifetime! Go on up and meet Him there. "He will teach us His ways so that we may walk in His paths" (verse 2).

BOXES

Read Matthew 23:13-28 (continue
to the end of the chapter if you have time).   *December 22*

"How do I get a balance between my spiritual life and my studies and social life?" the young man asked me.

"Well, I don't want to answer that because I don't believe it's the right question," I stated. I went on to explain that our spirituality ought to infuse and inform every single area of our lives and not be in a little "balanced" section by itself.

How easy it is to create boxes. We tend to segment our lives, giving a section to our work, a portion to our family, and this part to God. But the Lord invades the individual's entire life and breaks down these segments, making them into a whole that is full and complete.

I have known some people who like to have everything in their lives all nice and tidy. They have an answer for everything, and their rigidity permeates everything. Each part of their lives is boxed up and in control. When something comes in which threatens that system, they become insecure, frustrated and even more rigid.

God, however, desires to be in control, pervasive, and all-encompassing. His plan allows for events to occur in our lives which break down the walls, shattering our expectations and shifting everything around a bit.

This happened to the Pharisees and Sadducees. They knew what God would do when He sent the Messiah...or so they thought. They lived safe little lives with everything in its place so they would be ready when the Messiah showed up. And then they missed Him...mainly because they were too rigid.

God called this box religiosity, and Jesus pushed down the walls. He showed up in the form of a gurgling baby. He healed a man on the sabbath, took it upon Himself to forgive people's sins, came into Jerusalem on a donkey, and died on a cross. He's still into box breaking today, too. He crashes through our walls and shines light into the corners.

We are often like wind-up toys, stuck in a corner but still attempting to go forward. We face the corner, see nothing, but keep moving, trying to go somewhere. God rescues us from this dilemma and simply turns us around in another direction. Then He may even use us to bash down a barrier, make a dent, surge through a hole. Say, there's a lot of places we can go, aren't there? It's no longer a corner; it's a whole new world!

WORD

Read John 1:1.   *December 23*

"I was getting ready to pay our restaurant tab, and that lady barched (sic) right in front of me! It was very interesting." My husband had been tripped up by his own words, as all of us do from time to time. Then he tried to cover it up with an additional sentence without changing his expression. He pretended that nothing was wrong, and I can't blame him because I love to "razz" him mercilessly.

However, the slip-up had not been lost on me, and I grinned. "Barched!" I said with emphasis. "A lovely new word! A combination of barged and marched, I dare say?" He cast up a shoulder and gave me a sideways glance and a smirk. We laughed.

My classes in languages, especially Latin, provided me with a great interest in words and the joy of using them accurately. As an undergraduate English major, I was intrigued by the history of our language and its ever-changing facets. Perhaps that's why I still enjoy coining new words and combining old ones.

How marvelous that God should call Himself the Word. He places great value on the spoken and written word, for whatever He says is truth—alive, meaningful, poignant, applicable. The *Bible* has so much that we have not yet understood, so many gold veins that we have yet to discover and mine. God's Word is so rich and so full of life!

Human communication is limited. However, this seems to be particularly true when it comes to describing spiritual things. So many times I feel something or understand it at a level which is too deep to express. I struggle, trying hard to choose the correct words. However, I am limited, not so much by my personal vocabulary, but rather by the fact that man has been able to contrive only a rather limited spiritual vocabulary. We strive to describe a concept or experience that we have comprehended in

444

the Spirit, only to find language far too incomplete and imprecise to describe it well. Even coining new words and devising new phrases and titles do not suffice.

Perhaps this is why Jesus was sent by God. He became the Word in human flesh so we could understand. Then Jesus Himself explained the most difficult concepts, such as the Kingdom of God, forgiveness, love, and the end of the age. As a master storyteller, He was a lover of parables, images, similes, and metaphors. As leaders, we always need to learn how to communicate better. Let's gain a lesson from the Word Himself. Tell a story next time!

ALL THE WAY
Read Romans 5:8 and Matthew 22:37-40.   *December 24*

"Well, if he would just greet me once in a while, I would be a little friendlier."

"I'll come half way if she comes half way. Forgiveness is a two-way street."

"Let's have a little compromise here, a little give and take."

Leaders are often too sophisticated, too proud, or too contained to make the first move. Or, if we do, we are tempted to be reserved in our overtures, especially when the other person is at fault. Human nature hates to be humiliated or looked upon as "easy." We work hard to keep our ego intact.

God, on the other hand, flows with fullness and freedom rather than reserve. When He decided to save the human race, for example, He didn't just come part way, expecting us to take care of the rest. He knew we could not do so. He came all the way down to earth and showed us the far reaches of His love and the extremities of His grace.

I have always been amazed at the striking differences between man and God in this regard. Human beings tend to talk in terms of meeting part way, finding balance, compromising, and sharing blame. We will love if we are loved in return, give if we are properly thanked, and be patient and forgiving if the other person is thoroughly contrite. In marriages and friendships, as well as in work relationships, our half-way concept is continually evident. Just watch for a few days, and you'll see what I mean.

God crashed through our half-way point and kept going. He loved with no stopping point and forgave before we even knew to ask. He came all the way to meet us just where we are. God's truth comes, not through a partial salvation but through a complete work of transformation and rebirth in our lives. God never does things part way!

Isn't it time we followed suit? Marriages would be better if each partner determined to go all the way. They'd find each other in there somewhere rather than standing near their half way gap trying to touch fingernails.

It's the same problem with God because we are so afraid to love Him with all our heart and soul and mind and strength. He came all the way, and we should go all the way, too. He chose us first, marched right down here and stood on our side. Now He beckons us to march right over to Him and lay everything down also. In this—not in half-way, balanced, compromising living—we find the truth. And the truth sets us free!

THE CHRISTMAS OF LIGHTS

Read John 3:19-21.   *December 25*

Lights everywhere. On the trees. In the windows. On the street posts. But the world is still dark. Many don't even realize that the season of lights is here to symbolize the true light that has come into the world: Jesus. How tragic it is to live through a season in which the lights literally increase in the physical realm, without at the same time letting the light spiritually increase in

446

our own hearts.

Our celebrations and preparations should not squeeze us into more darkness. If we find ourselves getting more frustrated, increasingly exasperated, with more anger flaring, this is just indicative of more darkness. We have let Satan, the god of the dark, lead us a little further into the murkiness.

This Christmas, let's take the time to let the light come in. Find some time to relax. Take some deep breaths and remind ourselves of what the day is really about. Smile. Sing "Happy Birthday" to Jesus. Remind ourselves that nothing is worth getting more uptight. What makes us uneasy and upset now will fade within the week.

Whatever may have a tendency to bother us, let's take it into the light of the Savior. Let the season bring more light into our lives....exposing any darkness, revealing the truth. When Jesus enters the world, He is like a beam from a flashlight. Look what you can see! Indeed, Jesus is the light.

ESCAPE

Read Hebrews 2:1-4.   *December 26*

We have all watched escape artists get out of handcuffs, ropes, chains, and locked-up places from which it appeared impossible to get free. With such thoughts in mind, there was a time when the word "escape" had great spiritual power and meaning. Preachers used to talk about escaping from hell and the bondage of sin by accepting the great offer of salvation provided for us in Jesus Christ.

Even to a Christian, I imagine that the word "escape" would not convey these images today. No, our society sees escape in a much different way.

True, life is still hard. Sin still brings destruction and pain from which people want to be released. Hell still exists, and

447

salvation through Jesus Christ is still available. However, rather than accept salvation, people today are trying to escape through other means.

Products are named with the idea of escape in mind. Advertising flaunts it, declaring to people that they deserve to escape. The travel business calls us away to an idyllic place, and the entertainment industry woos us. Everywhere there beckons escape, and people answer the call to the tune of thousands of dollars.

Why escape? Because it covers up the pain of sin, assuages the conscience, anesthetizes the mind, and gives the illusion of joy...but only for a little while. People, even Christians, are giving themselves permission to escape much more often than is healthy. Their every day lives are still difficult when they return, and God remains the only answer.

The pain of sin is designed to be felt so that we will turn away from it and look to God. The only way to escape from a meaningless life without the Lord is to come to Him, repent and accept Christ as Savior. Otherwise, "How shall we escape if we ignore such a great salvation?"

PEDESTALS

Read John 4:23-24.   *December 27*

The flesh and blood that hold the human spirit simply create a form to which we can relate. People smile at us, hug us, speak to us, and likewise shun us, frown, and say unkind words.

As a result of the ability to observe the reaction of human beings, it seems easier to form relationships with them than it does with God. After all, God is Spirit. And although He came in the flesh when Jesus Christ walked this earth, all we can do now is read about that. Usually He does not speak audibly to us or give us a hug we can literally feel.

448

This fact may explain some of our difficulty in relating to God. Often we can sense His presence as the Holy Spirit moves in a worship service or other special time. However, we generally have to take His presence by faith and imagine how He might be looking at us. The Scriptures speak to us, but sometimes it would be nice to have a real discussion with the Lord Himself where we could literally hear, see, and touch Him.

Nonetheless, Jesus challenges us to worship the Father in Spirit and in truth. This is an action we need to learn! We have to become more aware of our own spirits and learn to respond to God's spirit.

This is probably why it is so tempting to place human beings on pedestals. We can see these people with our eyes, and the reactions of some of them become very important to us. This can happen so subtly that we do not even realize how we have elevated them. They can turn into idols rather easily. Their responses to us become far too significant, and likewise, God's response becomes not nearly as important as it should.

I remember once being very hurt by someone I knew. He was not a particularly sensitive person, and he would do things which diminished me. Certainly, I did not feel very much valued or appreciated. As I sorted out my thoughts and feelings, I had to question why his opinion was so significant to me. Why did it matter what he thought about me or how he treated me? My mistake was that I had elevated him to a place that wasn't his.

We must worship God, and never—not even in a subtle fashion—place anyone else on a pedestal. They'll crash every time, because only God belongs there.

THE COST

The cost of being a disciple of Jesus Christ is high and all-encompassing. There is not a single thing we are to hold on to, nothing we are supposed to retain for ourselves. When we decide to follow Jesus, it has to be total because He makes a complete exchange. "Anyone who does not give up everything he has cannot be my disciple" (verse 33).

Why would God require this of us? Actually, He wants us to let go of everything else so we can hold on tightly to Him.

Family, for example, is wonderful, but it can stand in the way of listening to God and being obedient to Him. Our parents, spouse, children or siblings can all suggest we shouldn't go where God wants us to go or give up what He is requiring.

Sometimes it is more difficult to watch someone we care about paying a price and suffering than it is to do it ourselves. We try to keep them from pain, but this can hinder them from serving God, and we can likewise be hindered by those who love us.

We are not to hold on to our goods, house, clothes, or anything else. After all, people are supposed to use things and enjoy them. But when people are used instead of material items, this is sad. Sometimes, it is easy to get so concerned about certain articles that they become more important than people. I've seen someone get angry and ruin another person's reputation or self-esteem simply because that individual accidentally ruined an inanimate object. Something is backwards in this!

Our money is meant to be used to serve and minister to others, not to hoard. Our careers are to bring us joy rather than to become something that masters us.

When we choose Jesus, the choice means we give up absolutely everything to Him. If we hold on to anything, God will ultimately point that out, tapping us on the shoulder and asking if we will release it to Him. If this is difficult and painful for us, if we are kicking and whining, then we should realize that this thing means far too much to us. Perhaps it is really an idol which is standing between us and God.

Indeed, it is worth anything and everything to gain Christ. Hold on to all else loosely!

LIGHTS! CAMERA! ACTION!

Read Psalm 56:13.   *December 29*

Are you desirous of being in God's spotlight or in man's spotlight? The distinction is profound, and the choice produces directly opposing results.

You see, I just got up in the dark and stumbled over the cat. She screeched, and I felt badly for her, but it's just like what happens when we do not walk in God's light. We can't see where we're going, and we stumble around, stepping on things we shouldn't. Like a bumper car, we bounce off the walls till we find the right door. We grope for the light switch and turn on the fan instead. Darkness is not conducive to much, really—except to hide.

Some people live their years trying to locate the light. If they think that it can be found in man's spotlight, they are sorrowfully mistaken. Man's light is not true light at all. It blinds the eyes so that darkness results. It makes a person play to the cameras and brings out acting rather than genuine living. Man's spotlight can be switched off at any moment because it's at the whim of the fickle crowd. Action in the spotlight can look like strobe movements, awkward and jerky.

However, God's spotlight does the opposite. It's true light brings out flaws and the real creases and lines; no cover-up allowed. It's painful, but real. It allows for authentic response and draws out truthful action. Since God is in charge of this spotlight, it is always turned on. We can see clearly and keep from stumbling, so that we may "walk before God in the light of life" (verse 13).

Which spotlight would you rather be in? Because many people want greater-than-life leaders who appear perfect, they sometimes push leaders into the wrong spotlight. Little wonder that so many grapple with questions of authenticity, truth, image, and integrity! Is it safe to be real? Ego shrinks from the searchlight of God. We cower in fear of what it might require of us. We will see our sin in God's spotlight and need to repent.

However, God's spotlight is "the light of life." Without it, something inside us dies as we play to the camera. It would be a pity to live out our days in man's spotlight instead of God's. And we have to choose; we can't live in both. Light and darkness cannot dwell together.

ONLY ONE

Read Luke 17:11-19.   *December 30*

The ten men whom Jesus met in his travels along the Samaritan and Galilean border were definitely all in need. Leprosy kept them both sick and ostracized from society. Death was inevitable as the disease progressed in excruciating and horrifying form.

The group called out to Jesus from a distance, hoping for Him to make them well. Showing themselves to the priests—as Jesus instructed them—was necessary before they would be able to re-enter society. As they started off on this task in faith, they were cleansed.

One would expect a real excitement from all ten of them, as well as overwhelming gratitude. Why, then, did only one of the ten come back to thank Jesus?

The man who did return knew that God had accomplished a wonderful miracle. He praised the Lord in a loud voice, looking to the One who had done this work. Throwing himself at Jesus' feet, he thanked Him. What a wonderful thing God had accomplished on his behalf!

Some in that day would have said that the Samaritan might be least likely to show spiritual sensitivity and proper gratitude. However, the man who came back was a Samaritan, and Jesus Himself notes, "Was no one found to return and give praise to God except this foreigner?" (verse 18)

No, it's true. Sometimes real gratitude, appreciation, worship and praise come from quarters where it is least expected. Perhaps it is the most needy person, the shyest, the poorest, the least polished—who ultimately displays the most open heart toward the Lord. In the end, God chooses just such a one and says, "Rise and go; your faith has made you well" (verse 19).

Let us minister to and care for all people, no matter what. God cares for each and every one, and we are not to be a respecter of persons.

Then let us be careful to be thankful for what God has done for us. How often does God answer our prayers, and we actually take it for granted, even forgetting to return and give thanks? We all need to be more grateful, both to God and to men. Have you thanked Him properly for what He has done during this last year? Are you the one out of ten or do you belong to the other nine?

NEW

Read Revelation 21:1-5. *December 31*

America, perhaps more than any other country, is into "new." We like new clothes, new cars, new buildings, new homes, the latest gimmick, the most up-to-date technology. When New Year's arrives, we just look for more new.

This time it's new selves. I'll reform, we think. We make new year's resolutions and decide this year will be different from the others. We'll tackle it successfully this time. We can do it. But within three weeks our zeal weakens, and by three months we can barely remember what we resolved.

Now with God it's different. When He says He'll make something new, He means it. He changes our lives. He heals our memories and the hurts of the past. He sets us free.

When my husband and I visited the island of Patmos this last summer, I saw the cave where they believe John had his vision. Think of what it must have been like to "see" the book of Revelation. Recorded in chapter 21 is a picture of God sitting on His throne and saying, "Behold I make all things new."

Think of it: not just a few new things, but all things. Every smackin' thing! New. All of the earth will be made new. The heavens will be made new. A new Jerusalem will appear as beautiful as a bride adorned for her husband. God Himself will dwell with us. There will be no more tears, no more pain, and no more death.

It makes our own New Year's resolutions seem measly and insignificant. How amazing to see the level of newness that God has conceived. Let's consider new spiritual resolutions....more beautiful, creative, and fresh than ever.